PRAISE FOR JONATHAN CLEMENTS

"The medium's most sought-after translator."
The Sunday Times

"Impressive, exhaustive, labyrinthine, and obsessive — *The Anime
Encyclopedia* is an astonishing piece of work."
Neil Gaiman

PRAISE FOR SCHOOLGIRL MILKY CRISIS

"Insightful and bitingly funny — you don't have to be an anime fan to
enjoy this brilliant book."
Kimberly Guerre, Founding Editor, Newtype USA

"The secret history of the global anime industry, written by the man who
was there from the beginning."
Hugh David, ADV Films

"Jonathan Clements knows his stuff and tells it like it is. His insight into
the manga and anime industry is unique, humorous and incredibly
accurate."
Jerome Mazandarani, Manga Entertainment Ltd.

"Some of the most hilarious and strange stories about the industry that its
employees dream of being able to tell while keeping their jobs!"
Andrew Partridge, Beez Entertainment

"Clements always has the inside scoops, industry truths and straight talk.
Even when the powers-that-be don't want to listen."
Tony Allen, MVM Entertainment

SCHOOLGIRL MILKY CRISIS

ADVENTURES IN THE ANIME AND MANGA TRADE

SCHOOLGIRL MILKY CRISIS
ADVENTURES IN THE ANIME AND MANGA TRADE

9781848560833

Published by
Titan Books
A division of
Titan Publishing Group Ltd
144 Southwark St
London
SE1 0UP

First edition February 2009
10 9 8 7 6 5 4 3 2 1

DEDICATION
For
Helen and Steve

Visit our websites:
www.titanbooks.com
www.schoolgirlmilkycrisis.com

Did you enjoy this book? We love to hear from our readers. Please e-mail us at:
readerfeedback@titanemail.com or write to Reader Feedback at the above address.

A CIP catalogue record for this title is available from the British Library.

Printed in the USA.

SCHOOLGIRL MILKY CRISIS

ADVENTURES IN THE
ANIME AND MANGA TRADE

JONATHAN CLEMENTS

With Illustrations by Steve Kyte

TITAN BOOKS

CONTENTS

Introduction

I t was the best of shows. It was the worst of shows. Whenever I had to cover my tracks, I simply called it *Schoolgirl Milky Crisis*.

When it all started, I was still a student of Japanese, catapulted from the classroom to the recording studio. I've translated the scripts and directed voice actors; I've stood in front of a microphone and boasted I would rule the world. I've seen this business from almost every angle you can think of, and I've chronicled the myriad concerns of the people in it, from the creator with a pencil who has the initial silly idea, to the mailman who dodges a rabid dog to hand you a parcel.

Outside the anime and manga world, I've watched animators turn my words into moving images. I've written for radio and TV and hammered on the doors of the film industry. I've lectured at universities and presented a TV show; I've written books and comics. I've even been the author who discovered that what was once mine now belonged to four squabbling producers. And at the end of it all, this wealth of experience qualifies me for… nothing.

Nothing, perhaps, except the chance to take potshots at Japanese cartoons and comics and related fields, to spread scurrilous gossip and tell tall tales. And my friends in the business didn't seem to mind, as long as they had plausible deniability. Which meant that sometimes, even though the real name of a work was obvious to everyone, I needed to call it something else.

So I picked three random words out of nowhere: *Schoolgirl Milky Crisis*. At first, it was one of many fake titles, along with such creations as *Warriors of the Test Card*, *Geek Gets Girls* and *Devil Devil Beast Beast*. But there was something about *Schoolgirl Milky Crisis* that captured readers' imaginations, and the non-existent show began to crop up regularly in my columns on the UK SCI FI channel's website, in *Newtype USA*, and later in the *Judge Dredd Megazine*, *NEO*, and *SFX Total Anime*.

As time passed, colleagues approached me with woeful grievances and axes to grind. They would press documents into my hands naming names and stirring trouble. All they asked was that if I talked about *this* terrible show or *that* awful production experience, I should make sure everyone knew it was *Schoolgirl Milky Crisis*.

The material for this book has been drawn from nineteen years of my published work. There are serious newspaper articles, seminar speeches, frivolous web journalism, and bitchy gossip from the specialist anime press. There is hard, useful information here, even in stories about gloves full of custard and snowball fights with martial artists. As part of the selection process, my editors and I have focused on material that educates and informs, even if also discussing the ethics of sending celebrity guests to bondage clubs.

In the meantime, remember that *Schoolgirl Milky Crisis* can work for you. If you ever need to confuse the fan who thinks he's seen everything, if you ever want to search for the perfect Japanese cartoon that can never be found, you know what to do. Just ask for *Schoolgirl Milky Crisis*.

— Jonathan Clements

BEHIND
THE SCENES

DON'T YOU KNOW WHO THIS IS?

Star Spotting at Toei's Movie Village

I wander a traditional Japan of backstreets and stone lanterns, with wooden buildings and paper walls. I think I took a wrong turn somewhere by the blacksmith's, and need to retrace my steps if I want to get back to the pleasure quarter. As I head back towards the Yoshiwara, I bump into a samurai leading two associates across a stone bridge. We bow at each other curtly and he rustles onwards with a scowl. The lower-ranking lieutenant behind him rolls his eyes at me playfully, pointing at his sullen associate as if to say, "Bad Agent Day."

Toei's Kyoto studios, a series of nondescript warehouse buildings in a long line by the railroad tracks, is closed to the public, but literally anyone can walk in off the street to wander the neighboring Movie Village backlot. Comprising several blocks of period housing, the Movie Village stretches from a Victorian-era town square complete with trams and coffee house, to a sector of samurai-era Tokyo that includes an attractive replica of Nihonbashi bridge, a pleasure quarter, merchant housing, a courthouse, and a prison. Wait for a gap in the milling school children and tourists, and the opportunity presents itself for a snapshot of the Japan of two centuries ago — a situation helped greatly by the many samurai, artisans, and geisha wandering the lot in full costume.

The Movie Village isn't so much a theme park as a working studio. Sure, there's a museum to the Power Rangers and their greatest enemies, some of the houses have been turned into snap joints where you can have your photo taken in samurai get-up, and there's a ninja booth where you can throw shuriken at targets to win prizes, but all the minor attractions play second fiddle to the Movie Village's true function, as a giant location set for samurai dramas.

Attend the Movie Village on any given day, and you can easily find that the courtroom area has been cordoned off to shoot a finale for next season's *Toyama no Kinsan*. Don't bank on always seeing the robotic sea monster that pops out of the SFX lake, since there remains an eternal possibility that it will have been turned off for the day so that someone can film a dockside sequence for *Ooka Echizen*. On the day I'm there, they are recording the latest episode of *Mito Komon*, a series that has been running intermittently since 1969. Boasting thirty-one seasons and a 1981 anime spin-off, *Mito Komon* is the apocryphal tale of Tokugawa Mitsukuni, uncle of the Shogun Tsunayoshi, who wanders seventeenth-century Japan in disguise, observing criminals as they prey on the innocent. At the right moment towards the end of each forty-five-minute episode, Mito's retainers will stop proceedings and brandish the Shogun's seal. They point at the unassuming old man and bellow: "Don't you know who this is!?" and Mito throws off his disguise.

A runner with a loudspeaker tries with increasing panic to control a group of bewildered kids from San Francisco, who still think this is your average run-of-the-mill theme park, and don't understand why they can't cheer every time the samurai on the other side of the square fight each other.

There is a rustle among the Japanese crowd and a series of excited "Ooohs!" as a man in peach-colored robes and a white goatee rides onto the set on a small silver scooter ready for his next scene. It is Kotaro Satomi, the latest of several actors to play Mito Komon, who has been with the series for so long that he also played one of Mito's young companions during the 1970s and 1980s. He stares in bewilderment at the San Francisco school kids, who stare in bewilderment back. As the seconds tick by, it becomes obvious that if someone were to brandish the Shogun's seal at this moment and ask the 64,000 yen question, these kids wouldn't have the faintest idea who he was.

"This man is very famous," explains their tour guide desperately. "He's a very famous actor who plays a very famous person in a very famous series." He says this all with the characteristic vagueness of many Japanese tour guides, who have long since given up trying to get foreign tourists to remember people's actual names.

The Americans nod excitedly and immediate start demanding to have their pictures taken with Satomi. Perhaps realizing that this is celebrity snapshots for the sake of it, and that none of them know who he really is, Satomi agrees with a weary smile. But he has the magnanimous charisma of a true professional, and the tourists go away happy, ready to tell all their friends that they met "someone really famous" while they were in Japan, and that he was "really nice", whoever he was.

The peak rating for *Mito Komon* is 43.7 percent — a night in 1979 when almost half of all the TV sets in Japan were tuned to the show. Satomi knows that there are already plenty of people in Japan who know *exactly* who he is. San Francisco's chance will have to wait.

(*Newtype USA*, July 2003)

WINGING IT
Directing an Anime Dub

I was the youngest person in the room. Behind me was a mixing desk big enough to handle a movie, microphones on stands, and a TV screen spooling through a Japanese cartoon. In front of me were actors I'd been seeing in movies since I was six years old. There were guys from *Batman*, *Aliens* and even *Star Wars*. They didn't know it, but I was the translator responsible for the English script they were holding, a title we shall refer to, in avoidance of legal action, as *Schoolgirl Milky Crisis*.

"Er…" I said, carefully.

A couple of them looked up.

"Yes, er… Hello," I added, stammering in Hugh Grant mode. "My name is Jonathan, and…"

"Black coffee, two sugars please darling," said an actress near the front.

"…and I'm your *director*," I finished through clenched teeth.

The actors weren't convinced. The reason I looked like I had barely graduated was that I hadn't. My graduation ceremony was that afternoon, and I was skipping it to be there. The choice was wear a silly hat and stand in line for a piece of paper I already owned, or push actors around.

I picked the option that paid. But before long, I was wishing I hadn't.

There's a fundamental difference between recording Japanese and English dialogue. When the original is done in Japan, the animation is highly unlikely to be complete. Instead, the actors face something that the Japanese call a Leica reel, and we call animatics — a moving set of storyboards that passes in front of them at the right speed. This gives the actors a little leeway in improvising, and they can make their own grunts and groans and effort noises. Whatever the actors say or do, the animators will draw stuff to match.

A lot of the Japanese animation scripts I've seen have blank spots simply marked with the phrase "ad lib". The Japanese love it when that happens, because they can do whatever they want. Many Japanese voice-actors are typecast in a particular kind of role — hot-headed hero, timid love interest, cackling Rose Queen — so they normally have an excellent idea of what they should be saying. Many anime are also road-tested with a series of radio or CD dramas, so that by the time an actor walks into the studio to lay down the tracks for the cartoon, he or she has already got a good grasp of his or her character through playing them several times in advance.

None of this is guaranteed in the Western anime business. Whereas most anime are fixed up around whatever was recorded with the animatics, when the time comes to do the dub, you're going to be stuck with whatever visuals are there. Get the picture? The animators have made their images to match *the original sound*. Now you, your translator, and your English voice actors are going to have to come up with sound that matches *those pictures*.

And those scenes marked "ad lib"? You have to decide either to translate the writer's open-ended intention or whatever it was the Japanese actors came up with on the day. In attempting to be faithful to the original, you already have to choose between two mutually exclusive possibilities! And whichever you decide, somewhere on an Internet forum is someone who is going to hate you for it.

That day, however, it was the actors who hated me. I had foolishly assumed they would have seen a subtitled version first. You might get that in your fancy anime distributors, but not at The Company That Shall

Remain Nameless. They were already paying the actors so little, they didn't *dare* ask them to spend an extra half-hour preparing.

They didn't know their roles, they hadn't read the story, and they certainly hadn't watched the tape. Which is fine if you are just reading out a script, but embarrassing if your director wants you to do anything else. By expecting them to know anything beyond the location of the toilets, I had unwittingly caught them out.

"Who wrote this script!?" yelled one of the actors in exasperation.

"I don't know," I lied. "What's the problem?"

"'Ad lib'!? Ad lib!? You want me to write my own dialogue as well! I'm not being paid enough for that!"

"Er… right," I said, belatedly realizing that they weren't as keen as their Japanese counterparts on making stuff up on the spot. This was my first translated script. It was also the last time I would ever let the words "ad lib" get through. From now on, I would simply translate whatever the Japanese had said on the day, and never tell the actors they were simply repeating a stranger's improvisation.

"Okay," I said, "stay there and I'll come in and write some dialogue based on what the Japanese are saying."

"Whatever, dude. I'll just wing it," he said.

Which made two of us.

(*Newtype USA*, April 2003)

JAPANESE WHISPERS
A Producer Scorned

Babylon 5 creator J. Michael Straczynski, who paid his TV dues by working long years in cartoons, tells horror stories about Korean animators handed a literal translation of a sci-fi script that instructed their astronauts to "strap themselves in". The film was delivered with the characters reaching the end of the countdown, suddenly changing into bondage gear, and tying each other up. Animation writer Alastair Swinnerton tells a similar tale, in which a chance pun in a French co-production led to a character who was supposed to be lifting weights being shown on film hefting a giant sardine. But this was the animation world: the producers looked at it, laughed, and decided to keep it in the final cut.

Straczynski's bondage astronauts, a tale told in his *Complete Book of Scriptwriting*, were caught before they could frighten viewers in the Midwest. Swinnerton's sardine-lifter was a victimless crime, but sometimes international co-productions have far less happy endings. Let me tell you about Ken Obie (not a real name), a famous creator from Wales (not his real country) who sold a series to a Japanese company.

Obie's big all over the world, but particularly so in Japan, where they've always wanted to work with him. There have been approaches in the past, but they never came to anything. This time, however, he had his chance. A Japanese production company, which we shall call Rosebud, told him they would love to do his next series, and so Obie signed the paperwork for something which, by popular reader demand, we shall agree to call *Schoolgirl Milky Crisis*.

There are always communication difficulties. There are unconfirmed rumors floating around the anime business that *Ranma*'s Rumiko Takahashi once had an entire crew fired because she didn't like their work, and that the late *Moomins* creator, Tove Jansson, threw a fit when she saw what Tokyo Movie Shinsha had done to her happy little hippo-things. There were quite a few liberties taken with *Lensman*, but creator Doc Smith was already too dead to care. Then there's the bondage astronauts, of course. But this time, the "misunderstanding" was nothing of the sort.

Rosebud had no intention of listening to a word Obie said. The world was already full of crappy anime series, and they just wanted to make another one. But they figured that they'd have an edge if they called it *Ken Obie's Schoolgirl Milky Crisis*, and they were right. The last thing they wanted was any input from Obie at all. But the old man gave it to them anyway. He gave them designs and wrote them a story (about schoolgirls who inherit a dairy farm which has been settled by undercover aliens). They thanked him, and threw them in the bin, because production was already underway and they couldn't care less.

Obie realized something was wrong when he saw the new character designs. Bronwen Zeta-Jung and Gwyneth Freud, the pretty heroines, were now "hot-headed Japanese schoolboy Ken Hoshi, and his adoring childhood friend Miyoko", accompanied by their comedy sidekick, Daisy the dancing cow.

So Obie grabbed Mr Tanaka, boss of Rosebud, and demanded an explanation.

"Hey…" said Tanaka. "It's gonna be fine. When you see the first episode, you'll see that everything we've done is for the best."

"Well, when *do* I see the first episode?" growled Obie. "Because unless you change everything back again, I'm gonna –"

So help me, Tanaka pressed a button. He pressed a button, and with a whirr and hum, a giant TV screen descended from the ceiling like something out of *Thunderbirds*, locked into place in front of him, and began running the first episode. It was as bad as Obie had imagined, and they *had already finished it*. In fact, as Tanaka smugly informed him, they were already in production on episode 17. What was Obie going to do about it, huh?

Obie did the only thing he could. He demanded that they take his name off. It was an empty threat to Rosebud, as they already had a TV deal. So they told him to shove it, and he went back to Wales. But he had the last laugh. Because when Rosebud delivered the show to the TV channel, the channel asked where Obie's name was, and when Rosebud said he wasn't involved, the channel backed out. It turns out that the TV channel wasn't interested either if Obie's name wasn't attached.

Which meant that Rosebud had spent over a million dollars on a show they couldn't sell, not unless they could somehow convince Obie to come back onboard. And they'd just flipped him the finger and told him they didn't need him. Obie had his development money, and no need to ever talk to them again, and Rosebud were stuck with over a dozen episodes of a show nobody wanted.

Who's laughing now?

(SCI FI channel (UK) website, March 2003)

YOUR ANIME IN THEIR HANDS

The Less Glamorous End of the Anime Industry

The show was about a dorky boy who lives with half a dozen gorgeous women — an idea of such stunning originality that the marketing people decided to have a launch party for it. Just in case the chance to see *Geek Gets Girls* wasn't attractive enough, they laid on some alcohol. It had the desired effect, particularly on the boozy journalist who cornered a suited Japanese producer, and was quizzing him about his culture.

"I LOVE YOU JAPANESE GUYS!" he bellowed. "I LOVE THAT THING YOU DO, WITH THE... WITH THE..."

He paused to belch loudly, and his victim smiled in pained politeness.

"THAT THING YOU DO, YOU KNOW?" continued the drunken hack. "WHERE YOU HIT EACH OTHER WITH STICKS."

Maybe, I wondered, it was time for me to come to the rescue. Except someone else needed my help more urgently. The potted plant behind me was trying to start up a conversation.

"My boy!" it hissed with a Londo Mollari accent. "You have to help me!"

Crouching behind the rubber plant was Vlad, a video distributor of indeterminate European origin. I had recently signed up to translate a number of titles for him, but this was the first time we had met socially. I should have taken it as a hint.

"Hide me," he whispered. "That girl over there... I left her in a hotel room in Cannes. I went out to get more champagne, and I never came back."

"And?" I asked, wondering why this was that big a problem.

"That girl she's talking to?" he said. "*She's* the girl I left with."

"Okay," I said. "I'll distract them, and you go for the door."

"No! No, my boy!" he said. "I can't! The girl at the door from the marketing peoples? She is the one I *went* with!"

I would soon discover that such relationship shrapnel was a common feature of Vlad's life. It was the way he did business. If he couldn't flirt with someone, he felt he wasn't doing his job properly. Everything was always done at the very last minute, and had to involve a girl somewhere.

Not that I ever had direct proof. I never got to slink around Cannes like a louche lounge lizard, eyeing up the locals and haggling over anime rights at the film-buyers' fair. Oh no, the closest I came to Vlad's international jet set lifestyle was at two o'clock in the morning, when he insisted on driving out to a freezing-cold airport. This was anime glamour at its most miserable.

"You stick with me, my boy, and life it will be great!" he chuckled as his BMW burned rubber towards the freight terminal. He was picking up a copy of *Schoolgirl Milky Crisis*, his latest anime acquisition. It was arriving on a late-night flight from Lufthansa, and we needed to meet it at the airport, for reasons Vlad never properly explained.

The two sleepy-eyed girls at the courier counter were surprised to see anyone at all. Vlad took it as a come-on.

"Hello babies!" he yelled enthusiastically. "I'm here for the *film*, yes? It has arrived?"

They blinked, perhaps hoping that he would disappear.

"I am," he said suavely, leaning across the counter, "a *film producer*, you see. A *film producer*, honey! How about that?"

"That's nice," said one of the girls after a while.

"You like the jacket?" said Vlad, modeling his anorak for them. "You see it has the Japanese writing? This is my company name, yes. If you like it, *you* can have one. What are you, an XXL?"

The girls busied themselves looking for his package, thereby hoping to get rid of him.

"Here's my card," he added, slapping down three on the counter. "One for each of you, and one for a friend, okay babies?"

By now, I was lurking as far away from Vlad as humanly possible, but we were the only other people there. It was so obvious that I was With Him.

One girl plonked the *Schoolgirl Milky Crisis* master-tape on the counter in front of him with a scowl, proffering a docket for him to sign.

"Thanks babies," he said, grabbing the tape and heading for the door. "And the mobile number's on the back."

Back in his BMW, he threw the tape at me and drove us out of there with a squeal of tires.

"They want me," he said. "It's the whole Hollywood thing. You'll see."

At that moment, Hollywood had never felt further away.

"Okay, my boy," he said, keeping his eyes on the road. "You got eight hours to translate that puppy, and we subtitle it tonight. Oh, and can you try not to write a script that uses the letter 'Y'. It's fallen off my keyboard."

I opened my mouth to protest, but his mobile began to ring. It was the girls from the freight terminal, seeing if he was for real.

"Hell-oo, babies!" he yelled excitedly into his phone. "I knew you couldn't resist a movie mogul like me!"

He turned to me with a happy grin.

"I love my job!" he whispered.

(*Newtype USA*, December 2003)

FOLEY MOLEY

Hanging with the Sound Effects Guys

There was something distinctly odd about Goro. From the waist up, he was clad in the polo shirt-sleeves that are the unofficial uniform of Japanese animation, *casual-but-not-casual*. But he stood in the studio lobby wearing bizarre Hawaiian shorts, his bare feet and calves spattered with grayish mud. He also wore a manic grin, and carried, rather unsettlingly, a large mallet.

"Come on," he said, "we're doing the battle in the swamp."

The studio making *Schoolgirl Milky Crisis* was spread out over several buildings in a Tokyo suburb. I'd rung three doorbells just to find the particular "annex" where Goro worked, a garage by a townhouse, across the road from the third-floor apartment that was the official business address. Goro was in the garage itself, the walls covered with egg boxes to deaden the sound, the door obscured behind curtains of heavy polythene. Goro's colleague Toji was watching TV while standing in a low bath ankle-deep in mud. A washing line hung above his head, from which was suspended a solitary lime-green rubber glove, which, I would later discover, was filled with week-old custard.

We watched in silence as he went for the next take, sloshing his feet in time with the silent movements of the anime girl on screen. She waded through mud, but Toji supplied the sound, every trip and slide and scrape, until the red Recording light went off. There was total quiet for a perfectly timed two-second lead-out, and then there was a crackle from the overhead speaker.

"OK!" burbled a happy voice in Japanese. "You must be tired." It was the default way of thanking a performer for a take well done, and Toji was off the hook.

The battle scene was next up for us, although the animators hadn't finished it. Instead, an animated storyboard, mystifyingly referred to by the Japanese as a Leica reel, rolled across the screen in front of us, complete with swinging swords, axes clashing on shields, spears burying themselves in yielding flesh.

Goro and I were sent out to a large refrigerator in the studio kitchen, containing a half-drunk bottle of Calpis, some day-old noodles, and a dozen cabbages.

"Just crisp enough," said Goro appreciatively, snatching the cabbages and passing them to me. When he saw me staring at him as if he'd gone mad, he grabbed a meat cleaver, placed a cabbage on the kitchen worktop, and stabbed down into it.

It made a satisfactory THAKK noise.

What? You thought they just got their sound effects from a CD? Sometimes, maybe, on the OAVs and the kiddie shows, but anime fans are too obsessive. They spot repeated sound effects. If you want quality original audio in your anime, you're going to have to do it the old-fashioned way, recording new sound effects one at a time. Goro and Toji, and people like them, pride themselves on their work — particularly when they get to play with guns. But the hand-to-hand combat can be just as much fun.

My initiation into the world of anime foley was almost complete. Next time, that could be me you hear smashing a cabbage with a mallet, or stabbing it with a kitchen knife. But they won't be my feet you hear trudging through a swamp — I left that to the professionals.

I thought I had got clean away, but they made me do at least one demonic SQUELCH. They said that everyone had to try the custard glove at least once.

(*Newtype USA*, July 2005)

SON OF...

An Old Director Attacks the Marketing Men

He potters over the stove like a kindly grandfather, wrapping a small towel around his hand before lifting the black iron kettle onto the hotplate. Droplets of cold water on its base immediately begin to fizzle and pop. The water inside, for our tea, will take longer.

He sits back at the table. A cigarette is already in his mouth, the blue flame of his lighter hovering in front of it, before he even looks at me, one eyebrow raised, asking if I mind him smoking. In his own kitchen.

"I don't know how long I've got," he says. "Another year. Another ten, maybe." He laughs dryly, half to himself.

"Nobody lives forever."

He takes a long, happy drag of his cigarette, pausing momentarily as if he'd seen the irony.

"I don't want to go *simple*," he says, using an English word. "They say I could die at a drawing board! Frankly, that's what I'd like. I don't want to be in a home. I don't want to be in a hospital. What did that Otomo boy call it? The *Roujin Z* bed! Ha! Maybe one of those!

"It's what They'll do when I'm gone that annoys me."

I ask him what he means. Who are They? The union organizers at the studio, perhaps? The government stepping in to tax his estate?

"The suits!" he laughs. "The suits at the studio."

He looks back out to the garden, and then at the carved wooden door behind me, as if checking for eavesdroppers. Then he speaks in a bellowing voice, as clearly as possible, as if hoping a spy will hear him.

"They're not animators, you know. They don't know the smell of acrylic paint. They've never stayed up until two in the morning inbetweening! Nobody comes up through the ranks any more. These kids with corner offices study *Marketing*." An English word again. "They study *Sales*." In English.

"I make animated films. I think up stories and I tell them to people. They say I'm pretty good at it."

He puffs merrily on his cigarette for a while, looking back to the gently steaming kettle.

"They think they're selling soap powder!"

I laugh, but he raises an admonitory finger.

"It's true! I've seen the books they study. It's all about soap powder and soft drinks. Establishing *Brands*. Diversifying! Saying something's *New* because new means good, did you know that?

"They say to me, 'Sensei,' they say, 'that *Schoolgirl Milky Crisis* you did. That was a nice film. That did *numbers numbers numbers*. We sold that to America. We sold that to France. Do that again!'

"And I ask them, I say, 'What? Do what again? I made a movie. I told a story from the heart.' And they say, 'Do that again. Make *Milky Crisis 2*. Make *Return of Milky Crisis*. Do something different, but the same!'

"And if I don't cooperate, they'll lean on my family instead! They think if someone with my surname is in charge, it'll be the same *Brand*!" He giggles. "The same *Brand*!"

He sighs and stretches his feet by the stove.

"When did it get to be so difficult to make good movies?" he asks. But he isn't talking to me.

(*Newtype USA*, February 2006)

MUSIC, MAESTRO
Why Composers Love Anime

Ryu has a little townhouse in Nerima, close enough to the studios that his producers don't bother with bike messengers. Instead, if there's a package that needs delivering, someone can run it over in person.

He answers the door in the world's worst sweater — a pastel monstrosity full of blue and pink shapes. It looks like something one might wear to please a half-blind great aunt with a knitting obsession and no other ideas for a Christmas present. It's doubly surprising because the last time I saw him, at a prestigious London recording venue, he'd been decked out in a $2000 Versace suit. But today he's working from home, and there aren't any British musicians to impress.

Inside, the house is surprisingly cold. It's November in Tokyo, and I can see my breath in the air. Is the central heating even on? No wonder he's wearing woolens. It's an expensive place to live, but his job pays for it. Ryu is the boss of his own company, and as the company head, he authorized the purchase of this "studio facility".

I don't get to see upstairs. Instead, I'm ushered straight into the studio area — occupying much of the lower floor of the two-storey house, kitted with polystyrene sound dampers and massive mixing desks.

"That's an Audiofile," he says proudly, pointing to the huge, dusty bank of dials and faders, which he scandalously uses as a place to put my coffee.

"Twenty years ago," he sighs, "it was a big deal. Nowadays, it's an antique."

Now, he uses ProTools to mix and match his compositions — much of the work required to produce finished music is held on an off-the-shelf Macintosh hard drive.

Ryu was classically trained, although his keyboards are fully digital. If he needs an analogue instrument now, he'll hire it for the day and sample the sound.

"I never wanted to work in movies," he says. "Producers don't know about music, and then try to tell me what they want when they don't know. And they'd fiddle with what I did. They'd come back and say, 'Oh, sorry, this bit of music we asked for, it needs to be three seconds shorter'... Three seconds! And I would say, 'WHAT!? WHAT ARE YOU DOING TO MY MUSIC!?'"

He laughs again, hearing himself ranting like a prima donna. But there is a glint in his eye. He looks at me, as if daring me to say he's wrong.

"But anime," he said. "These boys came to me with an anime job. They said, 'It needs to sound like this. It needs to be two minutes and seventeen seconds.'"

He smiles in bliss.

"Two minutes and seventeen seconds. Exactly. I went away and wrote it, and then I handed it to them, and that was that. Isn't that wonderful? Because anime is all planned in advance, you see. They have storyboards for every scene, down to the nearest second. They already knew before they started exactly how long it had to be."

He pats the old Audiofile machine with a grin.

"They didn't change a single note."

(*Newtype USA*, December 2006)

LIVING COLOR
The Tribulations of an Anime Colorist

Reiko is cleaning out her office. She's not leaving the company, but production after production has caused anime material to build up in her little cubicle, and suddenly she has a free hour to spring-clean. The ubiquitous polystyrene noodle bowls have piled up somewhere beneath the detritus of forgotten 'crunch' times — twenty-four-hour Big Pushes where Reiko worked, ate and slept at her desk. Old newspapers are there, too, covered with test daubs of many colors… or rather, reds… reds and more reds.

"Did you know," says Reiko, "Chinese has more than a dozen words for red? We've got them all in Japanese, too, from the characters. But we never need them. We've got your *akai*, for normal red. And we've got your *kurenai*, for scarlet. And then there's *shushoku*, for vermilion…"

She stops and thinks for a moment.

"How many times in your life," she muses, "do you really need to say *vermilion*?"

Reiko is a colorist. She's the woman who used to sit hunched over animation cels with a palette of every red you care to name, and a bunch of in-between colors that nobody has thought of.

"My daughter wanted me to name them all!" she says with a smile. "She picked this murky orangey-grey-red we had for the shadow of the lapel on a prisoner's jumpsuit, and she said, 'Okay, mom, what's this one?' I could have given her a Pantone number. I could have said I didn't know.

But I just lost it and made one up, and I said, 'That's *zong*, okay, honey? That's the color *zong*.'"

Reiko needs so many colors because red is never just red. It's red in sunlight, red in shadow. Red at night just before a car drives past. Red of lipstick. Red of fire type one. Red of fire type two… red of fire type two in shadow on a sunny day…

"Night scenes are the worst," she says. "We say to the directors, nothing looks good at night! Everything is just duller, greyer! Oh that's great in a black and white manga. You do that in color anime, and what do you get? Me staying up until three in the morning trying to find the right kind of *murk*!"

But Reiko doesn't use actual paint any more. She started coloring in computers ten years ago, and these days everything is digital.

"You think that makes life easier?" she says in mock annoyance. "It doesn't! Now the director doesn't have twenty shades to choose from! Instead he has sixteen million! You get a perfectionist, and it's all 'Reiko! Can we have a little more orange, a little more grey, just a pixel more green?' It can still take forever. But at least it's cleaner."

Reiko stops herself from throwing out the paints. The last of the old-school palettes are still dotted around her office. Little half-squeezed tubes of acrylic, and the dry crusts of forgotten art jobs. She saves them for her daughter to play with.

"I know what she'll do," she says. "She'll get all messy in the kitchen trying to mix up some *zong*."

(*Newtype USA*, March 2007)

CALL WAITING
When Doctor Who Came to the Supermarket

You can't hide from Doctor Who. He has a time machine. He has a sonic screwdriver. He can reach into any phone network and, with a bit of jiggery-pokery, track you down. There was no place on Earth that I would be safe, even if I were hiding out in an Eastern European supermarket. And when I say that, I mean a supermarket *in* Eastern

Europe, not just a grocery that sells beetroot.

I rarely have my cell phone switched on — I'm a twentieth century kid, and I prefer not to have meaningless conversations about when my train will arrive, or how late I'm going to be. But for some reason it was switched on that day, when the call came through from BBC Cardiff, where the *Doctor Who* TV show is made.

"What the hell," said the voice at the other end of the line, who we shall call Mr Russell, "are you doing *there*?"

I stammered that I was in the process of buying some milk. And maybe some mince. But he meant what was I doing out of the TV loop, hundreds of miles away from the cocktails and schmooze of the television world. Not that he cared much for the answer; I'd had my twenty-five seconds of obligatory touchy-feely catch-up. He got down to business.

"There's this big floaty aircraft carrier thing called *Valiant*," he began, "and it's under attack from zillions of darty alien things called the Toclafane."

"Okay," I said guardedly. "Am I supposed to save the world?" A woman in the frozen food section of the supermarket shot me a curious look.

"No!" he said. "No, the Doctor will save the world, of course. But first we have to destroy Japan."

"You want me to destroy Japan?" I asked, perhaps a little too loudly. People with shopping carts began edging away from me.

"I've sent you an email," he said. "It's a distress signal from the Tokyo Base. They're under attack by the Toclafane and they are sending out an SOS to the *Valiant*."

Suddenly, I realized what he wanted. The same thing as everyone else who ever called.

"What I would like," he continued, "is if you could translate it all into Japanese for me. In the next hour, because we're shooting the episode this week. Oh, and by the way, I'm going on vacation in ten minutes, so you'll have to deliver it to my boss. She's expecting your call. Uh… at least I hope she is."

Luckily, I have been here before. I knew there wasn't time to establish the precise nature of the message — the gender and rank of the sender, the precise translation required for the term "Tokyo Base", the Japanese translation of "Toclafane". As ever, I'd have to wing it, second-guessing the dozen answers a translator would really like to know, dashing through a suitable set of lines, and hoping that they would be read out in the right order, by a native speaker, in the right place.

"You can hear it for yourself when the episode airs!" he said, naming a broadcast date, which would later turn out to be wrong. And with that he was gone.

I stumbled from the supermarket in a daze, my mind full of spaceships and invaders and Japanese distress signals. This happens more often than you'd think.

I forgot to buy any milk.

(*Newtype USA*, September 2007)

INTERVIEWS

AND PROFILES

FROM THE ASHES

An Interview with Keiji Nakazawa

"**I** haven't been successful at all," says Keiji Nakazawa, with customary Japanese self-deprecation. "Human beings are really stupid." His complaint is with governments who continue to support war — be it conventional, biological or nuclear — as a means of resolving disputes. As a boy who witnessed atomic destruction in person, he's made it his mission in life to stop it happening again.

"If people understand the dreadful nature of wars and nuclear weapons," he says, "I am happy as the creator. It's my sincere wish."

He was born in 1939, in Hiroshima. He was six years old when the atom bomb was dropped on the city, and somehow survived the appalling conditions of the aftermath. Information on radiation and its effects was classified and denied during the Allied Occupation. Those who had experienced Hiroshima and Nagasaki learned to keep their origins secret, for fear that other Japanese would discriminate against them.

Official recognition did not come until Nakazawa was a teenager. A Japanese fishing boat, the *Lucky Dragon V*, was hit by fallout from one of the post-war American bomb tests on Bikini Atoll. Initial Japanese anger focused on the exclusion zone around the test site, widely believed to be an attempt to interfere with Japanese tuna fishing rights. Then, one of the fishermen died as a result of his injuries. In paying compensation to his widow, the American government admitted that there were side effects from atomic weapons. The people of Hiroshima and Nagasaki were not malingerers or ambulance chasers, as they had previously been painted; many of them were genuinely still suffering the lingering after-effects of radiation, and would continue to do so for the rest of their lives. The idea of a radioactive monster eating at the heart of post-war Japan would inspire an icon of the local film industry — *Godzilla*. The Japanese government eventually answered the problem in the real world with new legislation, the Atomic Bomb Victim Medical Care Law of 1957, granting free hospital care to the victims — the *hibakusha*.

But in achieving recognition, the *hibakusha* also became subject to discrimination. "The situation hasn't really changed," notes Nakazawa on the sixtieth anniversary of the bombing. "Gradually people have started to understand *hibakusha*, and the way they see them has been altering... a *little*."

Trying to put his childhood behind him, Nakazawa moved to Tokyo and became a comics artist, publishing his first work in 1963. His early creations were boys' adventure stories, including *Spark One*, about intrigue and sabotage between rival racing teams, and the mind-boggling *Space Giraffe*. Although he is largely known outside Japan for his Hiroshima stories, back in Japan he has a much more varied output.

"I drew manga on many subjects," he says, "baseball, samurai dramas, racers, and so on. So I think I always would have found a career as an artist, in the entertainment world."

Just as in everyday life, Nakazawa kept talk of Hiroshima out of his manga.

That all changed in 1966, when he rushed back home for his mother's funeral. Although it is usual to find shards of bone in cremated human ashes, Nakazawa saw none at all, and described the discovery as a chilling revelation that "the radiation had even invaded her skeleton." Clutching her ashes on the train back to Tokyo, he realized he couldn't keep quiet any longer. Back in the city, he risked pariah status by openly discussing his experience of the bomb, with the first of his 'Black' series, *Beneath the Black Rain*.

Nakazawa began trying to sell more stories about Hiroshima, but ran into difficulties. Now it was the height of the Cold War, and shortly after student demonstrations over Japan's Security Treaty with the US. There was revolution in the air, and the images of riots and street protests would also inspire in another well-known manga, *Akira*, drawn by another arrival in Tokyo, Katsuhiro Otomo.

Large magazines had previously refused to publish Nakazawa's

Hiroshima tales, afraid of finding themselves on a mythical CIA blacklist. Now that Japan was an "unsinkable aircraft carrier" for America, Nakazawa feared that it might be subject to a nuclear attack, and resolved to continue retelling his life story, both of the Bomb and, more crucially, the prejudices and hardships of its aftermath.

In 1972, the boys' magazine *Shonen Jump* began running stories about the lives and careers of manga artists. Nakazawa used it as an excuse to sneak in *I Saw It*, an account of Hiroshima, which eventually formed the opening chapters of his ten-volume *Barefoot Gen* (*Hadashi no Gen*). Three decades on, he is keen to assign credit where credit is due, to the man who took a chance on him. "It was easily accepted," he says, "thanks to the fine editor, Mr Tadashi Nagano."

The resulting family saga was not completed until 1987. Later volumes detail the attempts of the survivors to stay alive in the ruins, surrounded by the mortally injured and the permanently disfigured, as starvation sets in and the war stumbles to a close. Told in a squat, cartoony style popular in comics of the 1970s, the horrors of the war seem all the more shocking when presented in a 'children's' format. Unlike most of the manga that run in *Shonen Jump* today, *Barefoot Gen* was genuinely educational, and served to teach an entire generation about the conflict.

"Seventy percent of the story in *Barefoot Gen* is completely autobiographical," says Nakazawa. "It is based on my own experiences in Hiroshima." And in the finale, it comes full circle. "The English translation of the tenth volume will be out in a few years," he says proudly. "The translation is underway already. Gen heads off to Tokyo and becomes an artist — that's how it ends."

A group of Americans, including Jared Cook and future *Manga! Manga!* author Frederik L. Schodt, acquired Japanese copies of *Barefoot Gen* in the 1970s, and began the 'Project Gen' charity to translate it for a Western audience. Thanks to their efforts, the comic became the first manga to be published in English, and soon made its way into many other foreign languages.

What distinguishes *Barefoot Gen* from its many imitators is Nakazawa's even-handed approach. Unlike many other Japanese writers looking back at the war, he is prepared to deal with Japan's military role objectively. He is unafraid of mentioning that Japan started the war, or that many of the common people were duped by a military-industrial complex into fighting a war they couldn't win. The Americans don't drop the Bomb on Hiroshima until 250 pages into the first volume of *Barefoot Gen*, giving Nakazawa plenty of time to present the event in its historical context, and to catalogue the motivations of both Japanese war-mongers and pacifists. Nakazawa seems able to do this because he has little interest in assigning blame for the war. He genuinely believes that it is the Bomb itself that is evil, and concentrates his anger on chronicling its terrifying after-effects, which are with the Japanese to this day.

"I think they understand the message," says Nakazawa. "In the places where US bases exist, such as Okinawa, the feeling against Americans still seems stronger." But elsewhere, he feels, he gets his ideas across.

The story was also adapted into live-action films (the first of which won Best Screenplay at the Czech Film Festival in 1977) and two animated versions. For a whole generation, Japanese animators had avoided discussion of the war, instead allegorizing it in space adventures or alien invasions. *Barefoot Gen* the anime rode a wave of change inspired by an exhibition in Tokyo about the life and famous diary of Anne Frank. An Anne Frank anime followed in 1979, establishing a new sub-genre within anime: war films about children, in which Japan's baby-boomers cast themselves as a blameless generation, forced to endure the consequences of their parents' martial past.

After the success of *Barefoot Gen* in 1983, other animated works appeared, many of them similarly autobiographical and child-centered. These ranged from Isao Takahata's masterpiece about the fire-bombing of Kobe, *Grave of the Fireflies* (1988), to less polished TV movies such as Toshio Hirata's *Rail of the Star* (1993), depicting a Japanese colonial family's desperate rush to reach American-occupied South Korea. Almost every major city in Japan seemed to gain a personalized film about the horrors of World War Two, but many of *Barefoot Gen's* imitators used youthful protagonists to present the Japanese as innocent victims. This played well at home, but also into the midst of the 'textbook controversy', a long-running debate over the selective information imparted about World War Two to Japanese school children.

Nakazawa is known as the manga chronicler of Hiroshima, and the large part of his work deals, directly or indirectly, with the Bomb. His lesser-known comics include *Beneath the Black Rain* (animated 1984). The original focused on a Bomb victim who is tried for murdering an American black marketeer. The anime concentrates on the plight of Hiroshima's women, with one character who avenges herself on Americans by giving them syphilis, another who uses her scarred body as a "living museum" to show the Bomb's effects, and a third who frets that she will have a disabled baby. Other stories help illustrate Nakazawa's over-arching theme, often overlooked in surveys of his achievements — the triumph of the human spirit in the face of adversity. Examples of this aspect of his work include *Fly On Dreamers* (animated 1994), about a group of war orphans who get to play against the Hiroshima Carp baseball team, and *The Summer with Kuro* (animated 1990), in which two Hiroshima children befriend a black cat. His most recent manga work is *Okonomi Ha-chan*, a tale of a Hiroshima bad boy who tries to reform his ways as a short-order cook, and finds love into the bargain.

When Nakazawa talks about *Okonomi Ha-chan*, he sounds as if he is trying to lay another element of his past to rest, as if the war has dominated enough of his work, and it is time to move on.

"In *Okonomi Ha-chan*," he says, "I depicted a person who makes an effort to live through life from a different angle to Gen. I wanted it to be a powerful piece that would conquer the influence of the Bomb in Hiroshima."

It was turned into a live-action film in 1999, with Nakazawa writing and directing, a change in career direction that he seems keen to pursue in his later years.

"I haven't drawn manga on Hiroshima recently, nor on anything else," he confesses. "These days I am more interested in tackling challenges in film. Next, I would like to direct a film that poses questions to the world."

For Nakazawa, working in a new medium only requires a small change in his working habits. He has a reputation for telling things as they are. As an artist, as a writer, and as a director, he has a simple rule for getting his message across.

"The road to understanding is not necessarily long," he says. "When you tell the truth, people always understand you. If you cannot make them understand, you are not telling the truth."

(*NEO #9*, 2005)

CASTLE OF CAGLIOSTRO

Script for my filmed introduction to the Optimum DVD release.

When Hayao Miyazaki left university, he went straight into a job at the Toei Animation studios. Fifteen years later, he was still there, and had worked his way up from the lowly rank of inbetweener to TV serial director. But at the age of thirty-eight, he was looking for something new. He had worked on hundreds of hours of animation, all at the breakneck pace and squeezed schedules of television cartoons. He'd also spent his early life adapting other people's work. His most notable successes during his long period in TV animation were chiefly of comprised cartoon versions of classic children's stories: *Anne of Green Gables*, *Heidi*, *Ali Baba and the Forty Thieves*, even an abortive adaptation of *Pippi Longstocking*.

By the late 1970s, it was time for him to move on. If he was going to remain fresh and enthused by the world of animation Miyazaki would need to make two leaps in his career. His ultimate destiny, the creation of his own stories and his own works of art, would come to fruition in the 1980s with an incredible outburst of original work: *Nausicaä of the Valley of Wind*, *My Neighbor Totoro* and *Porco Rosso*.

But to get there, he would first have to make a far more difficult and testing change in his working habits. He would have to make a film.

The demands of making an animated film are very different from television. You need to be a sprinter *and* a long-distance runner. Whereas harassed animators often have only a week to make twenty minutes of TV animation, *Castle of Cagliostro* had a production schedule that lasted for an impressive seven months. But making anime for the cinema audience also requires a far greater investment of effort. Miyazaki needed his staff to produce something of movie quality. He was heard to utter that seven months was not enough, and he wished he had another few weeks.

Castle of Cagliostro is a watershed in Miyazaki's work. Although he would labor into the 1980s on several TV productions, most notably *Sherlock Hound*, *Cagliostro* was in many ways his farewell to television. When we watch it, we see Miyazaki the TV director becoming Miyazaki the movie director.

For his first film, he also chose to adapt the work of another, in this case the comic artist Monkey Punch, whose *Lupin III* series first appeared in 1967. Lupin III is a gentleman thief, a harmless hustler with a heart of gold who steals from the rich and hangs on to the cash for himself.

He is also the subject of a recurring copyright dispute, since, as the name implies, he has a more illustrious ancestor. Monkey Punch's comic was itself inspired by the work of French author Maurice Leblanc, whose master thief Arsène Lupin enjoyed an impressive popularity at the turn of the twentieth century. Lupin III is supposedly the grandson of the original, a family resemblance with which the estate of Monsieur Leblanc was not entirely happy.

But Lupin is not the only character in the movie with a backstory. Zenigata, the unstoppable detective who pursues him around the world in every film, is himself the distant descendant of a famous samurai-era sleuth who has his own long-running live-action TV series in Japan. Cagliostro himself is the descendant of a famous counterfeiter from the renaissance. And Goemon Ishikawa, Lupin's samurai sidekick, is the thirteenth generation descendant of a seventeenth century thief from the Japanese theatre.

With hindsight, we can perhaps see why such complex relationships appeal to Miyazaki. In much of his own work, he tantalizes us with glimpses of a much bigger story; in *Spirited Away* and *Howl's Moving Castle* we often feel like bystanders witnessing fragments of a much bigger tale that has gone on before our arrival and will continue after we leave. In *Cagliostro*, this is actually true. We are witnessing the sequel to an earlier movie (in fact the previous year's *Mystery of Mamo*), and the *Lupin* chronicles would continue long afterwards, with both another TV series and many more movies and annual TV specials.

Cagliostro is also loaded with references to other films; look out for a Chaplinesque chase sequence inside a clock, and languorous Riviera settings, often shot with the rich colors of nicely-aged caper movies, particularly Hitchcock's *To Catch a Thief*, whose female lead, Grace Kelly, was an additional source of inspiration for Miyazaki. Maurice Leblanc's novel, *Countess Cagliostro*, might have similarities to this film, but Kelly, the beautiful American actress, famously married Prince Rainier, the ruler of a tiny European city-state. Art, to a certain extent, was already imitating life.

Other references lurk beneath the surface. Although we can't hear it in the English language version, the actors' voices were already familiar to a Japanese audience. Lupin himself might have a gangly, simian visual look, but he is played by the late Yasuo Yamada, who is better known as the Japanese voice of Clint Eastwood. This gives him a certain steely charm to a Japanese audience. Our damsel in distress is Clarice, played in the Japanese version by Sumi Shimamoto, who Miyazaki would later cast as his heroine Nausicaä, and in older roles in both *My Neighbor Totoro* (the bedridden mother) and *Princess Mononoke*.

When we watch *Castle of Cagliostro*, we see Miyazaki setting out at the beginning of a long journey. He would make some of the greatest animated films in the history of the medium, based on both his own work and that of others. He would win Japan's first animated feature Oscar, for *Spirited Away*. And ultimately, he would return to the idea that people don't need to be thieves to steal each other's hearts, choosing to make it a central motif of *Howl's Moving Castle*.

IMAGE IS EVERYTHING

Mamoru Oshii Discusses *Ghost in the Shell*

"**B**lade Runner," says Mamoru Oshii, "is something that we cannot surpass. The film is a vision, it has the visual power to make us believe its world exists — it wasn't the first film like that, but it was the first to define it for America, I think. The same goes for *2001: A Space Odyssey*. I believe these two films in many ways define the films to follow."

Mamoru Oshii slouches in a crumpled orange shirt, eternally weary. He doesn't cultivate the hang-dog expression, that's just the way he is. He's a mumbler, too. Bless him for doing the run of press interviews — he is far more generous with his time than other anime directors — but he often seems distracted. When he talks about his love of movies, his lifelong obsession with *Blade Runner*, or his deep respect for David Fincher's *Alien 3*, the words stumble as they leave his mouth. *Blrunnr. Aln3.* I know this because I am supposed to be translating his words for the production company, and it's taking twice as long as usual. I have to call in native-speaking assistance, and even then we struggle.

But he has a right to be tired. He's been working on *Ghost in the Shell 2* for three years. No last-minute dash for him this time, like on *Patlabor*. No film cancelled partway, like the one that inspired him to make a murder mystery set in an anime studio. No money-saving Polish location shoot, using Polish actors, speaking Polish, like on his live-action *Avalon*. Finally, thanks to the international success of the original *Ghost in the Shell*, he gets to do what he wants.

"I don't sit here and think about how to change the world," he says. "That's not a film director's job. Unless you're, you know, that fat guy." He means Michael Moore.

No agitation-propaganda, then, for Mamoru Oshii, although the stories he has chosen to adapt have often had political bite. *Patlabor 2* featured a Japan under martial law, as did his script for *Jin-roh: The Wolf Brigade*. And the original comic of *Ghost in the Shell* was right-wing in the extreme — the jury is still out on whether creator Masamune Shirow made it so satirically, or religiously. But Oshii feigns lack of interest.

He doesn't do story, he claims with Japanese self-effacement. He likes images. It's the cityscapes in *Blade Runner* that stayed with him, the grand vistas and the gritty mood. Like many Japanese cineastes who struggle in a world where almost *everything* has to be subtitled, he has learned a way of watching films that admires the scenery and pays less attention to the plot. As a film director, he expects the same from his own audience. The main character in his movie is the future itself, its melting-pot of foreign ideas, its bustling crowds and stunning images — one scene of a Chinatown carnival took a solid year to animate. There's a story in there too, somewhere, but it's not Oshii's main aim.

"If you don't have a big enough budget, you have to make a film interesting with story, action and so on," he shrugs. "But when I have time and money, I want to tell a story with visual images alone."
(*Judge Dredd Megazine* #242, 2006)

A NEW TYPE OF BOMB!

Katsuhiro Otomo, Creator of *Akira*

"**I** like working on any animation project," says Katsuhiro Otomo during a Japanese press junket for *Steam Boy*. "The art, the sketching, the backgrounds, I'll get involved in anything. The only thing I haven't been is a voice actor!"

Akira is almost single-handedly responsible for the early 1990s boom in anime in the English language, but its creator is not *of* the anime industry — his output has been tiny, even when one includes those films on which his role has been minimal. In August 2005, he celebrates 32 years as a professional writer, artist, and commercial designer. As well as science fiction in the style of his most famous work, he has written stories about New York jazz, Asian politics, King Arthur, Jesus Christ and Godzilla. His early work in particular is very difficult to get hold of — rumor has it that Otomo himself suppresses any work he created before 1979, preferring to be judged on his later achievements.

Otomo grew up on American counter-culture movies such as *Easy Rider*, *Bonnie and Clyde* and *Butch Cassidy and the Sundance Kid*. "All the movies were about leaving home," he says, "about people with boring lives who wanted to go somewhere else. Everybody wanted to hitchhike their way to Woodstock."

Most critics see little further than *Blade Runner* when looking for influences on *Akira*, but real life provided plenty of inspiration. When Otomo was in his teens, Japan hosted the Olympics, there were riots in the streets over a Security Treaty with the United States, and students-turned-terrorists died in a gunfight with police in the resort town of Karuizawa.

Otomo was nine years old when Japanese TV first screened *Astro Boy*, which famously begins with a car crash victim "brought back from the dead" by a scientist father.

He was also inspired by Mitsuteru Yokoyama's *Gigantor* (*Tetsujin 28*), the story of a secret World War Two robot-warrior project resurrected in the 1960s by a master criminal and opposed by the son of the original inventor. Little of *Tetsujin 28* remains in the final story of *Akira*, though sharp-eyed fans might notice a weapon that survives the *Third* World War, that the Colonel character is the son of one of the original Akira Project scientists, Akira's code number is "28", and that protagonist Kaneda's full name is Shotaro Kaneda, just like *Tetsujin 28*'s boy-hero Shotaro Kaneda.

Akira is also a retelling of Otomo's manga *Fireball*, an unfinished 1979 work that drew heavily on Alfred Bester's *The Demolished Man*, and depicted scientists fighting terrorists for control of an apocalyptic energy source. Although *Fireball* made his name, Otomo missed a deadline and did not complete the story — perhaps if he had, he might never have approached the same material with much better results later in his career.

In 1983, Otomo worked as an artist on the animated film *Harmagedon* (sic), where he and his colleagues grew disenchanted with the lack of creative opportunities in the Japanese studio system. After making his mark on the two anthology films *Neo-Tokyo* and *Robot Carnival*, he landed the chance to direct the animated movie version of his *Akira*, by then a bestseller in comic form.

Determined to combat executive interference, Otomo co-wrote, designed, and directed, giving free rein to many animators and running far over budget: "Even after *Akira* was in the can, I kept on getting into trouble over last-minute revisions. I'd keep wanting to check it just one more time."

Akira was a visual tour-de-force, including experiments in digital and analogue animation that were to stun audiences worldwide, but its creator remained unsatisfied. "It was the worst possible idea for me to make the film version of *Akira* before I'd finished the manga," he said at the time. "As I worked on the film, I came to like the idea of having two different but similar versions of the same story, but part of me still thinks that too much of the original was sacrificed."

A NEW CENTURY

Since then, Otomo has had his name on many projects, though has been significantly less involved than he was on *Akira*. He made the live-action *World Apartment Horror* on a shoestring, wrote but did not direct *Roujin-Z* (in many ways, a superior script to *Akira*), and then shared the *Memories* anthology piece with two others (typically, Otomo's segment ran over budget). As a producer on *Perfect Blue*, Otomo was able to secure excellent staff and funding, but left financial control in the hands of others. On *Spriggan*, he performed high-level duties, but rejected a suitable label. "All I said was that I hated the title supervising director."

Though hailed by most of his Western fans as a prophet of the future, Otomo began the twenty-first century looking to the past. He scripted *Metropolis*, a "double homage" to both the landmark manga by Osamu Tezuka and the Fritz Lang original that inspired it. He also wrote and directed *Steam Boy*, although some of his fans made vocal calls for him to stick to what they already knew him for. But he'd heard it all before, particularly with reference to *Domu*, his big break before *Akira*.

"Way back," he says, "when *Akira* was still being serialized, I'd get people who liked *Domu* saying to me, 'Why are you doing *this* kind of science fiction manga?' That's just the way that people are. And steampunk isn't so new any more, either, but I thought I'd have a go at it when I was making the *Cannon Fodder* section of *Memories*. I did it simply because I wanted to.

"I really became very keen on seeing more of that kind of world when I was working on the art for *Cannon Fodder*. Really, I just wanted to have a go at doing gears and steam-powered machinery. For artistic reference, we're paying close attention to Hayao Miyazaki's *Sherlock Hound*. Not an exact copy, but we want to recreate the same sense of Englishness."

Steam Boy's release came more than five years behind its original schedule. One of the delays was caused by the opportunities in computer coloring. It's now possible, but expensive, to go back and change subtle shading, a dangerous temptation to the perfectionist Otomo. "There always used to be a limit to the available color palette. Now, with the computer, we can use 16.7 million! That's a number high enough to be infinite to the human eye. So the old standards for color have been completely destroyed, and the director has to adjudicate. And of course, once something has been painted, now it can be changed. If it's not exactly what you envisaged, you can pick away until you get it right."

The cost of such experimentation, according to Otomo, has narrowed rather than expanded the focus of his stories; he was forced by producers to re-use the virtual environments he spent weeks designing, even though they were originally intended to have very little screentime. A virtual set or technique has thus become as much of a liability as a 'real' set or special effect in the film business; once paid for, it has to be used. "And right now, when you make something using computers, it still costs more than making a normal film. It's very difficult if you're always keeping your eyes on the 'payline'. Because you don't want to compromise the integrity of the images, you end up narrowing the focus of the story. You *bet* you have to make it entertaining. And you also need to make something that you can sell into foreign markets. If you can't do that, then the animators will be stuck in a vicious circle of falling budgets."

Although there are always rumors of offers from Hollywood, and occasional forays into US comics (he drew a short story for DC Comics' *Batman Black & White* series), Otomo remains an elusive figure. One of a handful of creatives who genuinely justify the claim that anime/manga is not "just kids' stuff", his is still the vision that most often introduces new fans into the medium. And unlike so many other anime directors, he still puts people ahead of the machines: "My interest in illustrating is a matter of seeing the people and things around me and not a matter of longing to see beautiful scenery. More than the picturesque, I love those places alive and sweltering with humanity."

(*NEO* #5, 2005)

DREAM TEAM

An Interview with Neil Gaiman

"**T**he Dream Hunters came from a bunch of things coming together at the same time," says Neil Gaiman of his job on the *Princess Mononoke* script, the Japanese publication of his *Sandman* series, and

Yoshitaka Amano's Tenth Anniversary *Sandman* poster. Three years after the 'last' *Sandman* story, these influences combined to tempt him back for one more story in his award-winning saga, this time with a distinctly Oriental angle on his Dream King.

It took Katsuhiro Otomo's *Domu* to swipe a literary award in Japan and change the establishment's perception of manga, and Gaiman achieved a very similar coup in the US at the thirteenth annual World Fantasy Convention, when a *Sandman* issue won the Howard Philips Lovecraft Award for Best Short Story. And following his win, the FantasyCon changed the rules in order to stop a comic ever getting nominated again, let alone, as Gaiman's friend Harlan Ellison put it so succinctly, get another opportunity to "kick serious artistic butt".

Since then, there have been further spin-offs and constant speculation about a film script in development. "I think that I am always better off not talking about *Sandman* movies," says Gaiman, "except to say that I'd love to see what Miyazaki would do to it…" And almost as if he were getting *Sandman* ready for an anime production, Gaiman set his latest story in medieval Japan.

KING OF NIGHT'S DREAMING

The *Sandman* tales cross all cultures — Morpheus rules the dreamworlds of all people, from ancient Greeks to modern-day goths. He is recognized by a Martian and even consorts with cats, where he fills their dreams with yummy images of hunting miniature humans. But despite being all things to all races, *Sandman* is primarily inspired by Indo-European myths. The Japanese god Susano appears briefly in *Season of Mists* for a tongue-in-cheek joke about efficiency (the Japanese gods have retained their power by adopting the forms of Hollywood icons), but only one story, 'Exiles' in the *Wake* collection, deals with explicitly Asian themes. So is Gaiman now trying to redress some politically-correct idea of balance?

"Not really," he replies. "I always fought against what I perceived as fans wanting to turn *Sandman* into a 'Myth of the Month Club' — which it would have been very easy for it to have become." As for the earlier Chinese-themed 'Exiles', it was in fact an homage to one of the earliest and most prolific Oriental linguists. "The Chinese story came from a love of Arthur Waley's Chinese translations," says Gaiman, referring to the man who first translated *Monkey*, *The Tale of Genji* and *Mulan* into English.

"*Dream Hunters* is set in Heian Period Japan, mostly because that gave me an *Onmyoji* (a Yin-Yang Diviner) as a villain," says the author. "And a fine and wonderful villain he was. It begins with a badger and a fox who begin to covet a little temple on the side of a mountain. It's not a very impressive temple, and there's only one Buddhist monk there. They decide that whoever can drive the monk out of the temple will have it.

"The first night, the monk is woken up by these huge horsemen who ride up to the temple and say, 'You have been appointed to be a monk at the Imperial court. If you don't arrive there within a month, the Emperor will cut off your head.' The monk agrees, but he needs to know why the Emperor has sent a badger. Because he noticed that all the horses had horse-tails apart from the one at the back, who had a badger's tail. The badger runs off. The second day, the monk almost gets seduced by the fox, but he susses the fox. On the third day, the badger comes back as a horde of demons, and he routs the demons, but the fox has fallen in love with him. When she discovers that he's being killed in his dreams, she goes to the Sandman to find a way to save him."

And how could you possibly have a Japanese dream-tale without the Baku — the infamous 'dream eater' seen in Rumiko Takahashi's *Beautiful Dreamer* and, in a more sinister incarnation, in *Vampire Princess Miyu*? "I ran into the Baku one night just before bed, in a book of mythical creatures," admits Gaiman, "and they were certainly one of the inspirations for the whole story — although I expected them to play a larger part in it than they did."

But the first *Sandman* story for three years is a little different, because it is illustrated throughout by Yoshitaka Amano. "I can't imagine having written it for anyone who wasn't Amano to draw," Gaiman says.

"AMANO DOESN'T DO COMICS"
Yoshitaka Amano is known to old-time fans as the original designer of *Vampire Hunter D* and *Battle of the Planets*, and to the younger ones as the

man behind many *Final Fantasy* games. But to a mainstream Japanese audience, he is better known as the illustrator of some of Japan's best science fiction and fantasy novels.

Born in Shizuoka in 1952, Amano's early talent got him work for the prestigious Tatsunoko Productions at the tender age of fifteen. He was still in his teens when he was designing for shows like *Cashaan Robot Hunter* and *Hutch the Honeybee*, and barely thirty when he tired of the company life and became a freelancer. "Even the tax authorities questioned my decision," he says. "But once your life is too stable, your creativity dies."

Amano became the illustrator for Michael Moorcock's *Elric of Melniboné* novels, as well as Japanese fantasy such as Kaoru Kurimoto's *Guin Saga*, Yoshiki Tanaka's *Arslan*, and *Chimera* by the suspiciously-pseudonymous Baku Yumemakura. He also collaborated with *Patlabor* director Mamoru Oshii on the film *Angel's Egg*, before finding fame with a whole new generation for his work on computer games such as *Front Mission*, *Gun Hazard*, and of course, *Final Fantasy*.

"It was only once that I published a comic book," says Amano. "I was happy with it, but at the same time, the experience taught me that I was not made for comics." Instead, when Vertigo editor Jenny Lee approached Amano about drawing a *Sandman* strip, he suggested something else.

"We had the idea to do it as a comic, but Amano said he doesn't do comics," explains Gaiman. "He's an illustrator." So the pair agreed to do an illustrated book, alternating paintings and text, and *Dream Hunters* was born.

"I did not draw upon Japanese sources for inspiration," says Amano. "I rather concentrated on the imagery from Gaiman's works. I am Japanese, but I don't know Japan very well, and I suspect that's a case for many Japanese today. In a sense, I came to rediscover Japan through the works of Neil Gaiman. I relied totally on his works for understanding certain aspects of Japanese culture and Japanese history. Getting acquainted with his works inspired me to undertake trips to Kyoto, the ancient capital of Japan, so that I could experience and relive the past of Japan myself. I enrolled in classes for making a kimono and porcelain works of my own at Kiyomizu in Kyoto. I went to see with my own eyes a shrine dedicated to, and inhabited by, foxes. They were all discoveries I have made of Japan after reading Mr Gaiman's works."

MYTH CONCEPTIONS

Although the Japanese are no strangers to multi-volume comic epics with the depth of novels, it took a long time for the *Sandman* tales to make their way into Japanese. Perhaps it was the requirements of color printing, which push up the expense of *Sandman* books for publisher and reader alike. More likely, it was the demands of translation. *Sandman's* references run so deep that it has already spawned a critical concordance — not the sort of thing you'd throw at the first translator to come along.

"As I wrote *Dream Hunters* I would send the text, a chapter at a time, to Amano and his people," explains Gaiman. "A translation was done for him to work from, although I believe it will be newly translated — for literary merit as well as functionality — when it comes out in Japan.

"They started publishing *Sandman* in Japan about a year ago, in beautifully-designed collections about half the size of a Western collection — so *Preludes & Nocturnes* took two books to tell. From what I understand, they are very popular there, although it's a new kind of reading for the Japanese, who are used to the much faster pace of manga."

Quite possibly, it was the availability of *Sandman* in Japanese that pushed Gaiman up the list of potential script rewriters for Hayao Miyazaki's *Princess Mononoke*. A good job too, since, as rumor has it, the studio was first tempted to hire Quentin Tarantino — hardly the Ghibli spirit (though readers are hereby invited to try *Reservoir Racoons Pompoko, Porco Fiction* and *V.V.'s Delivery Service* on for size in the things-that-might-have-been department). Instead, the gig went to Gaiman, and he immersed himself in books on Japanese folklore in preparation.

"I don't think there were any specific *Princess Mononoke* sources that were inspirational," he says. "It was more the experience of steeping myself in Japanese myth, which I did for the first three or four weeks after seeing *Mononoke* to try and understand as best I could who these people were, who these gods were. And it reminded me how much I'd loved Japanese myth and legend as a boy — particularly the tales of foxes who could transform themselves into beautiful girls. And it meant that, when I saw the Amano Tenth Anniversary poster, the realization that I had never written a Japanese *Sandman* story became almost palpable."

But *Princess Mononoke* did have a more important influence on *Dream Hunters* in terms of the resources Gaiman was able to call upon. "My secret source was Studio Ghibli — Miyazaki's people. I would run things past a guy named Steve Alpert. But every now and then, when the facts were against us, we'd go with the poetry. There's this one moment with a little dragon sculpture that the fox keeps as her treasure and drops into the sea. Originally, it was ivory and jade, but Steve Alpert said, 'It would never have been ivory and jade in that period. You have to pick another material.' So I made it gold or whatever. But Amano said, 'But I like ivory,' so I made it ivory again."

Dream Hunters was clearly an exciting task for Amano, but when asked to identify the best part, he is unable to decide. "I have many favorite moments," he says, "but if I go over them all that would be the whole story. If you were to ask me which was the most memorable in terms of story development, it's the scene in which the monk makes his appearance in the Dreaming for the first time. There's a series of sequences leading up to that scene, and I felt that scene alone would be material enough for one book. I will continue to draw on that experience for some time."

(*Manga Max* #12, 1999)

RISE OF THE ROBOTS
A Profile of Masamune Shirow

It's the next step in Japanese animation, a high-tech hybrid that mixes the motion-capture of real-world actors with digital backgrounds. Anime finally meets the world of computer animation head-on in *Appleseed*, a movie that exploits its origins to the full by digitally treating its stars to *look* as if they are manga characters. *Appleseed* isn't just a landmark in the history of Japanese animation, it's a celebration of its creator. In 1985, it was *Appleseed* that first brought Masamune Shirow to the attention of the world. Twenty years on, it's still doing it.

STAYING LOCAL

Sirow was born in November 1961, growing up in the progress-obsessed Japan that greeted the Tokyo Olympics. But he was nowhere near the capital — he grew up in Kobe, the port city in Japan's Kansai region. Kansai is radically different from the Kanto plain over which Tokyo sprawls. The two regions can be as competitive and antagonistic as England and Scotland; Japan's civil wars often divided on Kansai/Kanto lines, and by the end of the pre-modern era, Kansai was the Emperor's land, Kanto the Shogun's. It is often said, only partly in jest, that it is more likely for a Japanese person to marry a foreigner than it is for a Kansai boy and a Kanto girl to get together.

And Shirow was a typical Kansai boy, avoiding Tokyo like the plague. He stayed in Kansai for his education, studying oil painting at Osaka's Fine Arts University before returning to his native Kobe to become an art teacher. By that point, he had already published his first fanzine work, a chapter of *Black Magic* in *Atlas*, an anthology he set up with a school friend.

Black Magic was a loosely linked collection of stories set on ancient Venus, an advanced society split into warring North and South factions in an allegorical Cold War. It shows Shirow the fanboy in full flow, indulging his dual obsessions for pretty, athletic girls and painstaking recreations of high-tech hardware.

"I don't know why, but the heroes Japanese children first identify with in manga and animation all seem to be robots," Shirow told Frederik L.

OTHER UTOPIAS

Appleseed owes a debt to Aldous Huxley's *Brave New World*, a classic science fiction novel in which humans are given paradise and yet still yearn for something else, society is classified by letters, and everybody knows their place. Reflecting Shirow's interest in sociology and politics, it also seems influenced by the *Rise of the Meritocracy* by Michael Young. This satirical book, published in 1958 but set in 2033, posited a society where everyone genuinely did receive a position in society based on how smart they were. Young pointed out that in a society like that, if you were at the bottom of the heap, you would know that you didn't stand a chance of getting out, and that this could actually cause more discord...

Schodt. "This is true of characters like Doraemon or Arare [from *Dr Slump*], and many others. As a result, most people have implanted in their heads the idea that robots are all-powerful friends, or pals." But Shirow's robots weren't all good. The strongest and most coherent chapter in *Black Magic*, 'Booby Trap', featured two battle robots going rogue. Typically for Shirow, it's the female that's deadlier than the male, courtesy of her long 'hair' that is really a heat-sink for her inner core.

Read any manga creator's biography, and the next step is a cliché. This is the part where the bright young talent ups stakes for Tokyo. He gets a job as an assistant for a bigger name, learns his craft, and eventually publishes his first professional work in one of the big magazines. But Shirow didn't play along. He stayed in Kobe. He continued working as a teacher, fiddling with his manga work as a hobby. He hit it off with a small local publisher, Seishinsha, and published his first professional (i.e. paid) work in 1985. It was a comic called *Appleseed*.

Shirow was separated from the Tokyo world by distance and his continued use of his fanzine pseudonym — his real name, Masanori Ota, was a closely guarded secret for many years. He also stayed with Seishinsha, enjoying the friendship and camaraderie afforded by the small press. With a strong background in fanzines, they also let him do whatever he wanted. The *Black Magic* series rolled along, its ultimate destination the destruction of all civilization on Venus and the establishing of human society on Earth. But Shirow was already reworking his ideas into *Appleseed*, a tale that was not subject to the usual monthly or weekly serialization of most manga, but which sprung haphazardly onto the market in fully-formed volumes.

BRAVE NEW WORLD

Like *Black Magic*, *Appleseed* featured a computer ruling an entire society, at odds with a group of artificial humans, or bioroids. In *Black Magic*, our sometime-heroine was Duna Typhon, the daughter of the lead bioroid. In *Appleseed*, she becomes Deunan Knute, the daughter of the scientist who created the mega-city Olympus.

Some have confused Olympus with the many Neo-Tokyos that clutter modern anime, but it is actually supposed to be a city off the western coast of Europe, somewhere near the Azores. Olympus is an artificial paradise, containing a mix of snooty bioroids and tainted human beings. There's tension between the democrat faction, who think humans should have a say in how things are run, and the technocrats, who think that humans are an unwanted evolutionary throwback. But Olympus has enemies outside as well. The old superpowers, America and Russia, still exist — the people described in Olympus as "terrorists" are actually agents of these enemy nations. There's still another enemy, and that's the original programmers, some of whom have changed their minds. One in particular is Deunan's dad, Carl.

Many anime centre around a child whose father gives them the ultimate toy — a giant robot to play with. Carl Knute has given Deunan a whole lot more than that. He's created an entire society of cyborgs, some of whom share his own genetic material. But Carl is one of the conscientious objectors who've refused to become part of his new society. Olympus is populated by people who are almost like genetic step-sisters and step-brothers of Deunan, but by supporting the city, she isn't sure whether she's doing her father's bidding or rebelling against him.

The tough soldier-girl Deunan and her towering cyborg companion Briareos are found in the Badlands after a global war and taken to Olympus, where the city elders hope they will join the utopian society. Their liaison is Hitomi, a slight, dark-haired little thing who likes robots and starts snogging girls when she's drunk — Shirow once famously said that he didn't enjoy drawing naked men, the sole excuse for a number of lesbian scenes in his comics. *Appleseed* had girls, guns, and often outrageous political statements about what makes an ideal society — as with the later *Ghost in the Shell*, it was never all that clear whether Shirow was a right-wing philosopher, or a left-wing satirist who liked overstating the case for the opposition.

Whatever its creator's politics, *Appleseed* was a hit. It scooped the Seiun Award (Japan's Hugo) in 1986, and both it and *Black Magic* were rushed into production as anime. It also gained something that would be far more lucrative for Shirow, who at the time was still teaching art at night school. His hard-SF attitude was exactly the kind of thing that Studio Proteus's Toren Smith was looking for. Smith was in Japan hunting for titles to adapt for what he saw as an untapped niche — translated Japanese comics in America. Smith snapped up everything he could find by Shirow, ensuring that by the time *Akira* made Japanese comics famous, Studio Proteus was already sitting on the rights. When the manga boom of the 1990s kicked off, the works of Shirow were able to ride the coat tails of Katsuhiro Otomo to international success.

APPLESEED (1988)

Akira also changed the rules. At the time that *Appleseed* went into production as an anime, a sci-fi cartoon was a cheap, straight-to-video affair. After *Akira*, everything else paled into insignificance, and the first *Appleseed* anime, directed by Kazuyoshi Katayama was left behind. The only place it received a cinema outing was in the West, where distributors pushed it into cinemas in order to ensure extra press coverage.

Appleseed lifted just part of the manga storyline, the events leading up to a revolution in Olympus, after which Deunan would find herself even more unsure of which side she should be on. Moreover, Shirow had nothing to do with it. Shirow's manga are made for fun; this remains part of their appeal to this day. His foreign success had left him untouchable, his Kobe residence meant he mainly worked in complete isolation, without the stable of art assistants that Tokyo artists hire to speed up their work. As his later works, *Dominion*, *Ghost in the Shell* and *Orion*, continued to enjoy success, he was simply unable to keep up with the massive demand for his work. The publication of new Shirow manga, in most cases still from the immensely proud Seishinsha, became rare events in the manga community. By the end of the 1990s, he seemed to spend more time creating single images — CD covers, book illustrations, and portraits, than he did on his manga. He had stormed off the anime adaptation of *Black Magic* after his comments on production had not been welcomed. Shirow's involvement in other animated versions of his work would prove similarly problematic. The same fan status that had won him acclaim was simply not suited to a more corporate life.

His tinkering attitude, which kept him happily occupied missing deadlines and fiddling with digital illustration, was too risky a liability on the tight schedules of animation. Although his name continued to prove a bestseller, he was kept at arm's length from the anime adaptations, his name on the credits merely a contractual obligation, rather than an indicator of hands-on involvement. Ever the fanboy, he noted to one set of producers that he had learned something from playing *Doom* — that the future of animation lay in 3-D environments around which a character could be made to move.

"At the time," he confesses wryly, "my comments were *unusual*." It's polite Japanese for *unwelcome*.

APPLESEED (2004)

Half a decade on, the world changed again. Digital animation was not only well known, it was a fundamental part of all anime. With Shirow's *Ghost in the Shell* finding new fame in a TV spin-off, the time was ripe to remake *Appleseed*, this time with 3-D animation. In a radical step, producers did not choose someone with a background in computing, but director Shinji Aramaki, who had a long track record in conventional anime.

Their reasoning was based on the failure of the *Final Fantasy* movie, after audiences had rejected its attempt to get too close to reality. Instead, the new Aramaki *Appleseed* would use full motion-capture, but treat it with Toon-Shading software to give everything a cartoonish look. The result would be a hybrid of live-action and animation, incorporating the strong points of Shirow's wishes for digital backgrounds alongside live actors — Ai Kobayashi, who voices Deunan, also functions as her own body double.

Where the original *Appleseed* anime jumped straight into the middle of the action, adapting the second book of the manga series, the remake elected to go back to the beginning. Thus, where the 1988 Katayama

WHERE ARE WE AGAIN?

If Olympus is in the Atlantic, then where are the other cities in Shirow manga? With names like Bayside and Newport, they owe more to his native Kobe than to the Tokyo megalopolis of other creators. And yet, the Newport of *Dominion: Tank Police* was later said to be on an island in Tokyo Bay. The unnamed city in *Ghost in the Shell* appears to be Tokyo, but was relocated to Hong Kong for the *Ghost in the Shell* movie, since director Mamoru Oshii wanted the city to have a grotty, lived-in feel, with lots of confusing signs in Chinese instead of Japanese.

version kicks off with Deunan and Briareos on a police raid, the 2004 Aramaki version features a variant of the induction scene from volume one of the manga. It takes the time to introduce Deunan's hand-to-mouth existence in the Badlands, but when we first see her, she is on her own. It also accentuates a sub-plot only hinted at in the manga, that Deunan and Briareos had once been lovers, but that only tiny vestiges of their relationship have survived his mutilation and cyborg rehabilitation.

The Aramaki *Appleseed* has been a long time in coming, the result of successive manga drafts, an earlier animated version, and twenty years of Masamune Shirow's rise to fame as a pre-eminent creator. It would never have existed without its forerunners, *Black Magic* and *Ghost in the Shell*, nor, probably, would the original story have ever survived unscathed the unforgiving editors in Tokyo. *Appleseed* is a culmination of its creator's love of changes in technology, and of the sudden, world-altering interest in Japanese comics than sprang up in the 1990s, but also of strange real-world coincidences, like the geographical factors that kept Masamune Shirow out of the Tokyo system, down in his own Newport City, tinkering with computers for the hell of it.

(*NEO* #10, 2005)

VOICE ACTING

AND TRANSLATION

IN THE CLOSET

The Logistics of Voice Recording

I was shut in a closet the size of a phone booth, with just enough room for my legs. Or rather, there would have been, except for the microphone stand that loomed above me, its chunky business end swelled by a gauze spit-shield.

"This mic is designed for singing," mused the engineer, tapping it thoughtfully.

"Is that good?" I asked.

"Only if you're gonna give us a song," he admitted. "You're supposed to yell at it from six inches away with a band behind you. We're going to have to move it closer."

"How much closer?" I began, as he jabbed me in the eye with it.

This was the fourth anime DVD commentary I'd recorded in as many weeks, but the smallest studio I'd seen so far. In fact, there was so little space, the anime (which, because lawyers like it that way, we're going to call *Schoolgirl Milky Crisis*) was actually in a different room, playing on a domestic VCR I could only see out the window. So I couldn't hear the dialogue, and had to refer to my notes — although, with fifty percent of my field of view obscured by the microphone, that made things a little difficult. The whole thing was giving me voice-actor flashbacks. Because I was back in a cupboard.

The great thing about any recorded medium is that you can do stuff out of order. Shoot the end first. Do all the crowd scenes after lunch. If you've got a star, do him first and get him out of there before the groupies arrive (or the cops). On one project, our leading man fled the building just minutes before a whole group of fans arrived to mob him. The director decided to make the most of it, and made them play extras in a crowd scene. If you ever find a copy of *Strontium Dog: Fire From Heaven*, they play Religious Fanatics #13 through #26.

There are financial benefits, too, to recording things out of order. Actors in the UK, where I've done most of my work, have a fee payable per *session*. And since there are morning and afternoon sessions, you have to use your time wisely. Book someone to arrive at eleven and leave at two, and you've just eaten up his entire working day — you'll pay for two sessions unless you can do some arm twisting. Book the same guy, for the same amount of time, but have him arrive at nine and leave at twelve, and you've halved your cost. But for some producers, the way to go is cupboard acting.

If you schedule a full day's recording, and bring in six actors, that means you're paying for twelve sessions. You're also paying for the studio and engineer by the hour, and if the clock goes just a single minute past six, everyone except you starts getting overtime. Meanwhile, at any given moment, most of the actors are sitting in the lounge, doing the crossword and drinking your coffee.

One day, someone realized they could get the romantic leads to do all their scenes together, at once, and send them home. They could get their bad guy to make all his speeches in an hour, and then show him the door. Sure, they need a crowd for the big battle scene, but they only need them *all* for a few minutes. And then there's those handy multi-track recorders, that allow you to *make* a crowd with just three performers and a sharp stick.

This is cupboard acting, so called because you might as well have cast-members hidden in the closet, and because often there literally *will* be someone in a separate booth — reading out lines for the actor in the studio to react against. It can soon turn into the audio equivalent of acting in a special effects movie, where you spend three months running around a blue room emoting to a tennis ball on a stick, and have no idea how it's going to look when it's finished.

Some might say (rightly, I think) that performances can suffer as a result. As the voice of an anime bad-guy, I have delivered stirring speeches about my desire to conquer the world, to an empty room, while watching a dumb-show through the soundproof studio glass as two engineers try to convince the cleaning lady that, yes, they have paid for the studio till six, not five.

Sometime the following morning, the hero and his love-interest, along with their comedy sidekick and the token schoolgirl, would assemble in the same studio and hear my threats in playback. They will gasp and groan and yell at me that I'll never get away with it. But I already had, and so had the producer, who'd shaved thousands off his budget.

It wouldn't kill them to make the booths bigger, though. Or maybe I'm just fatter than I used to be.

(*Newtype USA*, May 2003)

GLAMORAMA
A Day in the Life of an Anime Voice Actress

Tomo sleeps in a single bedroom, close to the front door. There are a few stuffed toys ranged on the bed, and a ballerina poster on the wall. A pitifully small collection of books is on the shelf. When I look closer, it comprises school texts and an unopened Shakespeare.

Everything seems sanitized. Tomo is 24, but her room looks like it hasn't changed for ten years. And even then, it would have been a little bare. Where are the posters of the unthreatening boy bands? Where are the school-days art projects and the messy pile of romance manga? There aren't even any photographs of her family.

There's more of her out in the living room. Ranged across the mantelpiece, I know, there are ballet awards and gymnastics trophies stretching right through her teenage years. There are photographs of Tomo taking runner-up in dance competitions, and smiling with scrunchy-faced glee, giving a victory 'V' sign to the camera while wearing a silly sash for a long forgotten soap product.

It's an early start, but she's already dolled up. I arrive at her place looking like death warmed up, but Tomo's real face is already invisible beneath a wall of beige Shiseido. Her hair is fabulous. Her clothes are expensive. She looks great.

"My driver's bringing the car," she says. It sounds impressive, although

I've seen her driver before. He's more like her bodyguard.

Tokyo in rush hour is like everywhere else, except the roads seem miserably narrow. Even the expressway is a cramped two lanes. The car smells new. So does Tomo.

This Tomo is not the Tomo on your screen. That one has an insane exuberance, a breathless enthusiasm. It's an energy that's difficult to maintain every single minute. When nobody's watching, Tomo switches it off. She loses her ingénue status and her little-girl happiness. She gets paid for that.

Nerima is an anime nexus in Tokyo. It's where Toei Animation set up in the 1950s, which has made it the default address for dozens of other companies — one-room layout ateliers, recording studios, even paint shops. Tomo's job today has nothing to do with Toei, but it draws her inexorably towards the cluster of companies that sprang up around it — Anime Valley.

She looks forlornly at the set-up — a set designed to look like a girl's bedroom. It's messier than hers, full of product-placed items. An as-yet unreleased laptop sits open on the bed, next year's DVD player over by the wall. Even the plushie toys are studio franchises.

The crew comprises three pony-tailed film school dropouts who really wish they were making French art movies. But they're Japanese, and they need to make a living, and the smiles are pasted on as they set up for her shot.

She's wearing far too much make-up for an intimate pajama-party bedroom chat. She looks far too good, but if anyone notices except me, they're not saying anything. Because that would mean a half-hour to take it off and re-apply, and everybody here is on the clock.

Tomo perches on the bed and perkily addresses an imaginary visitor.

"Welcome," she says, "to my place." She gestures expansively at the fake room behind her. It's bigger than the one she actually sleeps in.

By midday, Tomo is driven a few hundred yards to another recording studio. She's there to lay down a radio track "as-live" — her regular one-hour program, to be broadcast and podcast in a week. The time allotted for the recording is one hour only, meaning it's a single take, and if there are any problems or accidents, they just have to keep going.

I'm stuck on the other side of the glass with The Driver, who I've taken to secretly calling Wide Load. He has nothing to say to anyone, including me. He just sits there reading his *Spa!* magazine while Tomo enthuses behind the glass partition about listeners' cats and fan art. Studio gophers occasionally whisk past, but this is Japan; they don't ask you if you want anything unless you make eye contact, and they're not going to make eye contact with a foreigner unless I jump up and down and set off a klaxon. At least we're in a private studio. Some actors have to record their lines at the new Anime Center, with a bunch of fans gawping through the window.

I'd really like some water from Wide Load's cooler, but he's made it very clear that it's for Tomo. Today, she's eating and drinking on the run. Wide Load has a big list of foodstuffs and beverages that will affect Tomo's voice. He's not being precious; they affect everyone's voice, but Tomo is the only person whose voice needs to be recorded and preserved for posterity today. And once you're in a studio recording anime, every cough or burp is going to waste about a minute of studio time, going back for a retake. Which, incidentally, costs roughly twenty bucks.

"Where are we going after this?" I ask Wide Load. I kind of hope it's to the anime studio, since this is why I'm here.

"Hotel," he grunts. And suddenly I wonder if Wide Load really thinks of me as more than a friend.

"Hotel," he says again. "For magazine interview."

Tomo is out of her radio show and we're all running for the car. She is excitable and happy, until Wide Load pointedly hands her some spring water.

"I shouldn't really waste my voice," she whispers. "Not with everything else happening today." Everything hopefully to include the anime performance I'm supposed to be watching her give.

But first we have to pick our way through *kimono*-ed wedding parties and *omiai* at an ostentatious Tokyo hotel. The interviewer from the magazine has a pink jacket and a Hello Kitty bag. She wants Tomo in the restaurant because the view and light are better. She also wants her to be photographed behind a giant fudge sundae with parasols and sparklers, which Wide Load steadfastly refuses to allow her to touch.

Tomo is pressed for her thoughts on pets, television shows and anime goodies while the forgotten sundae slowly melts into sludge in front of her. I realize that I am staring hungrily at it and tear myself away to find Wide Load. He is smoking a cigarette and reading his magazine.

"This is all very well," I say to Wide Load, "but I'm supposed to be covering her anime performance.... Are we getting to that any time soon?"

Wide Load looks at me like I'm mad, and looks pointedly at his watch. "Night Time," he says. "Night Time."

Tomo steps up to the mic, at last. Beyond the interviews, the occasional singing recording, the more regular miming gigs in shopping malls, the waving and the chatting on radio and video shows, there is something that feeds it all. She is a voice actress. This is what she does.

It's nine at night, the lights are on, but not everyone's home. No movie stars recline on the white leather couches, no advertising executives thumb through the *Oricon* magazines on the coffee table. They were here in office hours, when the studio time was more convenient but expensive. Now we're into the graveyard shift; you know, when they record the anime.

Tomo's script looks like nothing you'll see in Hollywood. The page is divided by a thick black line — words on one side, images and action on the other. Her dialogue for the next minute is almost nonsensical — a series of exclamation marks in square brackets, a few wiggly lines, and an "eh!?" or two.

The screen in front of her plays a "Leica reel", what Hollywood calls animatics, a timed storyboard of the way the anime will look when it's finished. Right now, as a character onscreen tries to ski through an Alpine village ahead of pursuing mutant teddy bears on snowboards, Tomo provides the noise. She twists and turns in front of the mic, emitting little grunts and groans and *eeks* to match the action.

I time her. She manages a minute and a half before she trips up and coughs. I look over to the director to see if he calls a cut, but his finger doesn't touch the talkback button. In the booth, Tomo keeps on going, her coughs and wheezes incorporated into her character's flight from peril, her breathlessness now a part of the show.

Twenty more seconds flit by, as the animatics show her racing past the finish line, evading her captors and grabbing the skids of a passing helicopter. She's done it. Her character made it, and so did she.

"You'll never catch me, McEvil!" she yells as her onscreen image fades into the distance. On the animatics, the lead bear shakes his fist in rage.

For the first time all day, I see Tomo's babysitter, Mr Wide Load, smile.

"Cut," says the director, and Tomo collapses in a heap of giggles. Her fellow actors pat her back approvingly and laugh. That's two minutes of action recorded "as live". That's a recording dragged back onto schedule where only two minutes ago we were half an hour behind. That's a fair chance that everyone will even make it to the last train home, for once.

Those of us without drivers, anyway. The stern Wide Load's made it clear he's not giving me a lift to my hotel. My day shadowing Tomo is almost over, and they're going to make me find my own way home.

"Thanks for coming along today," says Tomo, turning on fifteen percent of her available charm for a perky goodbye. "It's been fun to have you around."

Wide Load waits by the car, his arms folded.

"Maybe I'll see you soon," I suggest, haphazardly.

She looks back at Wide Load.

"I don't know," she says. "I'll ask my dad."

And with that, she's in the car as it drives away, waving perkily through the side window.

Wide Load raises a goodbye eyebrow for me. Maybe Tomo takes more after her mother.

The car turns a corner, and I am alone in Nerima. It starts to rain.

(*Newtype USA*, May-July 2006)

WAITING
The Fickle Nature of Fame

Anton was heading that way anyway, so he gave me a lift to the theater. He was just turning his car into the car park at the Royal

Shakespeare Company, when the security guard blocked the road.

"Sorry, sir," he said. "This area is restricted for staff only."

"But I *am* staff!" protested Anton. "I'm in *Troilus and Cressida* tonight!"

"And who are you playing?" asked the guard, with an eyebrow raised in disbelief.

Even in the midst of such antagonism, Anton knew just the right amount of pause to leave. Eventually, he spoke up with a sad smile.

"Troilus," he replied.

Just think — if that's what it's like in Shakespeare's birthplace, imagine what it's like if your name isn't even on the poster behind a security guard's slowly reddening face. Imagine what it's like if your sole claim to fame is as the gruff growling voice of a big-eyed cartoon hero's talking dog.

It took me a while to realize that the actors I knew had already made it. They had regular gigs in top-end theaters, with movie and TV show roles in between. I hadn't been there for their early years, when they were doing McJobs and struggling to pay the rent. I didn't get to see that kind of horror until I was working in anime. I see a lot of people in anime fandom proclaiming they want to be a voice actor. Here's my advice: don't.

Out in the mainstream, voice acting is often regarded as true drama's poor cousin — performing with half one's repertoire; a morning's anonymous labor to pick up some pin money. It can also be an honest day's wage for actors who have stepped back from the jet set, and now just need to be home in time to put the kids to bed. But in shows like *REC* and *Kappa Mikey*, in manga like *My Voice*, the voice actors are the heroes.

The cartoon world is one of the places where voice actors enjoy the greatest respect and status. But don't fall for convention glamour and resume spin. Perilously few people can afford to work full-time as anime voice actors. The work simply isn't steady enough. Most have other strings to their bow, even in Japan, where famous anime voices moonlight on the many, many dubs of American live-action shows — an alternate income stream that simply won't be available to you here.

If your heart is truly set on a career in acting, make sure that there is more to you than your love of *Schoolgirl Milky Crisis*. If you're *lucky*, you'll also be doing audio books, commercials, voice-overs and narrations. You'll be performing onstage, doing TV or theater. If you're really lucky, anime voice acting will be something you do once in a blue moon, like a Miyazaki movie, while you're counting the money you made off your TV series.

Don't aspire to be an anime voice actor. Aspire to be an actor, period. Even then, you still might end up waiting tables and working call centers until that big break comes along. Even then, you still might have to fight for your parking space.

(*Newtype USA*, November 2006)

DOG DAY AFTERNOON
Studio Report on *Strontium Dog: Down to Earth*

L ast time Johnny Alpha stood beside Judge Dredd was in *Judgement Day*, an epic comic series in *2000 AD*. The mutant bounty hunter traveled back in time to help Mega City One's toughest lawmaker save the world. As the stony-faced pair marched across the smoking ruins, Dredd said, "Who the hell's gonna mess with us?"

Their second meeting is somewhat less iconic. It's during a coffee break at the Moat Studios, in Stockwell, South London. On a Saturday.

"Have you got a PlayStation 2?" says Judge Dredd.

"Yes," replies Alpha indignantly.

"Have you got *Gran Turismo 3*?"

"Yes."

"Ah, but have you got an Xbox?"

"I'm getting one tomorrow."

"Well, I've got two, actually."

Toby Longworth, who plays Dredd in the Big Finish audio dramas, is teasing *Spaced* star Simon Pegg, who's here to play Alpha in the first of the *Strontium Dog* plays — *Down to Earth*.

Johnny Alpha was one of *2000 AD*'s most popular characters, a mutant with eyes that could see through walls, who roamed the galactic frontier as a Search/Destroy agent. The disinherited son of mutant-hating fascist Nelson Kreelman, Johnny was exiled from Earth, his only allies giant Viking warrior Wulf Sternhammer, timid alien fur-ball 'the Gronk', and unintelligible Scottish mutant Middenface McNulty.

Better known to new readers as the strip that spun off into the *Durham Red* series, the original Johnny/Wulf cast of *SD* has finally returned to the pages of *2000 AD* with the new *Roadhouse* storyline. To mark the occasion, *2000 AD*'s new owners licensed the characters to audio play producers Big Finish. Which is where I came in, because someone had to write the first one.

I pick my way through the drunks on Stockwell Road, negotiating the burnt-out cars on the council estate, to find the studio entrance next to a doorbell marked *Ladyboy*.

"It says Ladyboy on the bell outside!" I announce excitedly to the green room.

Everybody turns and stares at me.

"This is the writer," says director John Ainsworth, by way of explanation.

The actors are locked in a soundproof box, and I sit in the control room with the director and a gallon of coffee. We have eight hours to lay down 60 minutes of audio — not impossible, but it's going to be close.

Left to their own devices while waiting for their next cue, the actors chat among themselves, their voices coming across loud and clear through the studio speakers.

"What if," Pegg muses, "the aliens from *Aliens* got their own DVD commentary track?" The others rise to the bait, as the speakers in the studio immediately erupt in a cascade of hisses, screeches and wheezes. A technician looks at me worriedly.

"Don't worry," I say. "They're always like this."

Toby Longworth is thinking about his role. Tomorrow, he's going to be Judge Dredd, in the Big Finish audio *Death Trap*. But today he's going to be Wulf Sternhammer, a giant, blond, time-traveling Viking from the eighth century.

"Would I call Alpha *Johnny* or *Yonny*?" he muses.

"Oh no, *yoni* is Sanskrit for ladyparts," says a voice, unidentifiable because it's a perfect impersonation of Kenneth Williams. A heated debate starts up over whether it would work as a joke or not in audio. It is decided that, over many years in many pubs, Johnny has trained Wulf to pronounce his name properly.

Johnny Alpha is from Milton Keynes. He just works in outer space. But nobody is sure what a Milton Keynes accent is. Is it as much a non-entity as the town itself? Actress Fran Clarke has taken matters into her own hands.

"I rang WH Smith's in Milton Keynes and tried to get them talking," she says. "I got put through to the Cookery department and asked them to list all the Jamie Oliver titles they had. But they only had one book. And the woman who answered the phone was Scottish."

Luckily, the problem solves itself. Johnny Alpha comes from England and so does Simon Pegg. He steps up to the mike, and for the first time in twenty-five years, Johnny Alpha has a voice. It is gravelly, rasping, and tough, like it should be.

Midday and we're still moving very slowly. It's taken far longer than expected to record the first scene, a punch-up in an orbital casino, but things are picking up now. Over lunch, Pegg confesses that this is a dream come true for him, and that he has always cherished the idea of playing Johnny Alpha. In fact, it was the mention of the character in an episode of *Spaced* that led to Big Finish offering him the part.

I set a bad example by ordering a lager. Pegg has a coke. He's taking this very seriously — like he owes it to his childhood self. He heads back early, and I see him standing in the middle of the Stockwell Road, idly thumbing his mobile, scowling in intense concentration. He has a car chase to do this afternoon, followed by a sneak attack on the baddie's hideout.

Back at the studio, two actresses smoke a nervous cigarette.

"Was I enough of a bitch, darling?"

"I think you were a terrible bitch."

"But was I terrible *enough*? It's difficult to hit the right note."

"You think you've got problems? I've got two mouths and I eat metal."

"There is that, yes."

The director is herding the actors in for another scene.

"Does anyone have any questions before we start?" he asks.

"How do I get out of this chickenshit outfit?" I suggest.

There is a pause, and a lone voice pipes up on one of the speakers.

"I'd just like to say," says Pegg, "that I got the *Aliens* reference, just there."

"Okay," says the director. "Scene 23, into the salt marshes of doom, going for a take…"

(*Dreamwatch*, June 2002)

THE DILITHIUM CRYSTAL EFFECT
The Pitfalls of Translating Television

On the outside, May's life looks easy. She sits on the beach in Hawaii and watches the boys go by. Except that's not music on her MP3 player, that's the audio track to last night's episode of the American hospital show *Gorgeous Doctors and the Pert Nurses Who Love Them*. And May has until noon tomorrow to write it out in Japanese and email it to Tokyo.

GD&tPNWLT is a classic. Its creator is one of the most respected television producers in the world. You bet he wants residuals from all over. But for some reason, *Gorgeous Doctors* doesn't have much success in Japan. And partly that's because, while people like to think that translators work in some kind of Jedi temple, cut off from worldly concerns and attended by nymphs bearing grapes, a lot of them are like May, hacking out episodes at record speed, and hoping not to make a mistake.

It can happen. Translator paradise is a time-coded tape and a complete continuity script (with all the dialogue as broadcast) script. And *time*. That's what I insist on when I work from Japanese to English. But when working from English to Japanese, all May has is audio and a deadline. She still shudders at her worst mistake, a patient on the show admitted at "eighty years of age" whereas May thought they said "eighteen". The rest of the episode kind of stopped making sense, because it was about Alzheimer's disease.

May's predicament, and those of people like her, becomes a self-fulfilling prophecy. When faced with a barrage of noise like "Twelve amps of epi, and stat!" in audio form, she's lost without a script. She wings it. Science and technology in Japanese subtitles become so much nonsense. Carefully thought-out slang in cop dramas and hospital shows can transform in Japanese translation into "Blah Blah Blah. Reverse the polarity of the neutron flow." A whole generation in Japan grows up watching American TV with subtitles that make no sense. Some of them go on to become animators.

When Animator-san writes his first anime script, he figures he'll do it like the shows he loved as a kid. A bit of technobabble, maybe. Some vague comments about global warming and dilithium crystals. It doesn't *need* to make sense because none of those American shows do either, right?

And this is where I come in. Because when *Schoolgirl Milky Crisis* lands in my lap from Japan, and people are throwing pseudo-science and eco-rants at each other like something out of a bad sci-fi show, that's largely because the writer of *Schoolgirl Milky Crisis* thinks a bad sci-fi show is what the American public wants. Of course, not every series ends up like that, and not every translator has the same limited tools and easygoing lifestyle as my friend May Dupname.

Someday I'll pitch a towel next to her on that beach, and see how I do at translating in the sand. But right now, I still need my dictionaries, and a laptop on a table, and, you know, sunglasses, and sun-cream, and ultimately, it's easier to work indoors. Having a TV helps, too.

(*Newtype USA*, August 2005)

AD LIBERTIES

If Lawyers Argued About Anime Scripts...

[**T**ranscript continues] Members of the jury, there is a lot more at stake. We are talking about a new *precedent*. The defense has already argued that, in the original Japanese, *Schoolgirl Milky Crisis* wasn't all that. Our expert witnesses have *already* conceded that, with the additional gags and dialogue added by the American actors, it is actually *funnier* than the original. The question here is whether we, as anime fans, as anime industry personnel, have the right to interfere with someone else's script.

Ah! But whose script is it? You have heard the translator, testifying that the words "ad lib" turn up regularly on Japanese scripts: a blank space left for gags. When a Japanese actor makes up a joke on the spot, it becomes part of the "original" work. The gag might be so obscure that it requires scholarly footnotes to comprehend, which is fine if you are an academically-minded distributor like AnimEigo. But how would that play in a dub for TV? Is it right to translate what the Japanese actor ad libbed, or is it in the spirit of the original to let the American actor come up with something of his own?

You have heard the actor's testimony, in which he asked: if the original Japanese actor had leeway in the studio to make stuff up, then why not his American comrade? That if the original of, what was the anime called again? Ah yes, *Schoolgirl Milky Crisis*, thank you, Your Honor. That if the original of *Schoolgirl Milky Crisis* wasn't so great to start with, where was the harm in "improving" it with some homegrown humor?

We have cited Dario Fo's *Accidental Death of An Anarchist*, a stage play in which blank spaces are left for the actors to add timely comments from the headlines of the day. But, members of the jury, that is a *stage play*. It changes every night. Anime is set in stone. Translators get uptight about such *ad libbery* because if you let the actors go too far, the script isn't a translation at all. It's a return to the days when Japanese language was an unpleasant problem that needed to be "fixed" by making something up.

But wait, here's a modest proposal. Since we no longer live in a world where the original can't be available on the same disc, why not do *every* dub that way? Subtitle fans will still have their original audio track, and who cares what happens on the dub? It will, of course, turn American voice actors from the servants of the text into its masters. To anyone who values the meaning of the original Japanese, it will turn a lot of anime into just plain cartoons. But if you care so much about the original Japanese, why are you watching the dub in the first place?

Your Honor, I would like to call my surprise witness: the original writer of *Schoolgirl Milky Crisis*, flown in from Japan. Let's see what *he* thinks of the way his work has been treated in its translated form.

He'll be here any minute…

Just getting his stuff together, I'm sure…

What do you mean he's gone to a party? Well somebody find him! This is important! [Transcript ends]

(*Newtype USA*, November 2005)

FRIENDS IN HIGH PLACES
Anime in the Japanese Economy

I t was a rush job. One of those things that turn up at the end of the Japanese working day, when a Tokyo office calls it quits, and emails their backlog across a few time zones, hoping that someone can pick up in a country where it is still daylight. As they're shutting down, I'm waking up, and often I'll find a few things sitting in my email inbox. Recently, it's been the Tokyo International Film Festival, which has had me as one of many people making sure that the English translations are okay in their programs. This usually means helping the frustrated writers come up with things that actually make sense, since all they have to go on are publicity documents supplied by the usual suspects. Japanese press releases can be impenetrably obtuse. I still fondly remember how *Evangelion* and *Escaflowne*, in their original PR, were made to sound exactly the same. If left to their own devices, many marketers would be happy with "Boy gets robot in a heart-warming masterpiece with several girls who are demure and nice and a childhood sweetheart who is a mysterious girl." Go on, name that anime. I'll give you fifty tries.

But these were different. They weren't film listings at all, they were statements from politicians in support of the festival. Since the festival preparations were all but over, I wondered why they'd taken so long to file them. Then I realized they must have been waiting until after the Japanese election. But now the votes were counted, they knew they still had their posts. One was still the minister of economy, trade and industry. And the other was still Junichiro Koizumi, the prime minister.

Can you imagine George Bush showing up at an anime convention?

Confessing his love for *Naruto* and judging the masquerade? It's not going to happen. But Koizumi is a self-confessed manga fan. He relaxes by reading *Section Chief Kosaku Shima*. He won't be going to an anime con anytime soon, either, but you can bet he knows what he likes.

You can do a lot with 300 words. The Gettysburg Address, for example, or the combined plotline for every season of *Gundam*. You could say: "Hey guys, aren't movies great? Love that stuff you do with the car-chases and the strippers. We politicians wish we could see more movies, but, you know, we're running the country. Maybe see you at the première of *King Kong*. Good luck!"

Or you could do what these guys did. Don't worry, I'm not breaking the translator's oath. By the time you read this, the festival will have kicked off and their words will be in the public domain. They decided to acknowledge that film and "image content" (that's anime, manga, computer games and so on) are two of Japan's primary exports. Trade minister Shoichi Nakagawa went so far as to add the following: "Japan aims to establish intellectual property and the contents industry as key factors in economic revitalization. In particular, digital media and pro-active international initiatives are likely to cause rapid market expansion, contributing to related industries such as tourism and manufacture."

Does that get your vote? *Newtype USA* isn't just a magazine about cartoons any more. It's an insider view of new trends in Japanese economic policy. Yet another reason to take out a subscription. I think.

(*Newtype USA*, December 2005)

FOR GODDESS'S SAKE
A Little Linguistic Knowledge Can Be a Dangerous Thing

L ong, long ago, a man called Kosuke Fujishima wrote a manga about a boy who accidentally ended up with a divine girlfriend. We've seen the manga original in the UK, as well as the video spin-off, and now, at last, the 2000 movie directed by Hiroaki Gouda is out from MVM. And because they're nice like that, MVM have released an exact copy of the US release, with subtitles, dub, and a preview of the new spin-off. And because it's a copy of Pioneer's US release, it's called *Ah! My Goddess*.

Yes, this is the thing you know as *Oh! My Goddess*. That's the English title approved by creator Kosuke Fujishima himself, after years of controversy and pedantry in Western fandom. Unluckily for Kosuke Fujishima, his best-selling manga had a title (*Aa Megamisama*) that began with the very first letter of the Japanese syllabary, and that meant that after only a couple of minutes of Japanese class (in some cases, all they ever had or would endure), self-appointed experts were pointing at the Japanese covers and crowing: "See! It clearly says 'Ah!' and those translator idiots have written 'Oh!' I could do better than that, it's a conspiracy!" Etc etc.

Funnily enough, translators like AnimEigo and Studio Proteus have been in the business for quite a while, and they aren't as dumb as that. They are up to their necks in job applications, mainly from Asian Studies graduates with diplomas in hands and freshly-scrubbed brains, desperate to get a chunk of that translating work. But strangely, they're still short-handed, because most of those people get turned away. Studio Proteus have got high standards, you see. They recognize that just because someone says they speak Japanese, it doesn't necessarily mean that they do. And even if someone has put in the four years it takes to get a degree in Japanese, which is one of the most difficult languages in the world*, it doesn't automatically follow that they have a professional ability in English, which is the other, vital side of the translating coin.

Some translator must have thought long and hard about that "*Aa*" in *Aa Megami-sama*. They could have looked at it for days; mulled it over in the bath, speculated while shopping, let it mill around their mind when they were down at the shooting range. And one day, a penny dropped, and they realized that "*Aa*" wasn't just an exclamation, but a slang contraction of "*Anna ni*", which is, tragically for fandom, not one of the terms you cover in the reception class. When applied to Fujishima's title, it transforms it from the meaningless "*Ah Honorable Goddess*" to something like "*Goddess! The Things You Put Me Through.*" Or possibly "*What a Goddess!*" And our Proteus translator came up with an idiom of similar effect in English, that also had a bonus alliteration with the original. "*Oh! My Goddess*" — an excellent translation.

It was one of the textbook moments of smart, literate, and sharp translating, but it's still a popular target for that well-known expert, the Man in the Pub. And now it would seem that Pioneer, and their UK licensee MVM, have tired of arguing and translated the movie title with an *Ah*. Because at least that way, the fans will leave them alone.

When I've taught seminars on translating, the *Oh/Ah! My Goddess* decision is just one example among many others of supposed "truths" held to be self-evident by that sector of fandom that holds all professionals in contempt. I've seen distributors release shows with half-translated titles simply because it's too much like hard work convincing their detractors that they might know what they're doing. Some put out titles with deliberate errors, because following fan custom is easier than explaining where it's wrong. And the upshot is that anime becomes even more impenetrable to the public, who don't know the difference between a *Kimagure* and an *Urotsukidoji*.

Sometimes, admittedly, these failings *can* be laid squarely at the door of a distributor or their staff, but it's not always the professionals' fault. Some of anime and manga's most embarrassing errors have been at fandom's instigation, and have met with fandom's approval, in spite of their long-term ill effects. Do *you* know what the words *Kimagure* and *Urotsukidoji* actually mean? Wouldn't you rather translators had translated them for you?

(SCI FI channel (UK) website, April 2003)

---

* "According to the US Department of State's Foreign Service Institute, it takes 1320 hours of study of Japanese to reach the same level in speech that can be attained in 240 hours of Spanish (or Vietnamese) study."

Jack Seward, *Japanese in Action*.

FIVE GIRLS
NAMED MOE:
THE ANIME EROTIC

FIVE GIRLS NAMED MOE: THE ANIME EROTIC

Transcript of a speech given at the Swansea Animation Days, run by the School of Digital Media, Swansea Metropolitan University, Wales, 1st December 2007.

I have been asked to talk about animated porn.

[raucous cheers]

It's not my favorite subject, you know. Whenever the TV people are doing their Hundred Greatest Whatever, they always try and get various anime pundits talking, and they always try and bring the conversation around to porn, nudity, and erotica. Not because the Japanese are obsessed with it, but because TV producers and journalists all seem to be. So despite the fact that I would rather talk about Hayao Miyazaki, or science fiction, or romance, or something, erotica is often the genre that comes up most.

I guess we should call this lecture 15-rated. I'm not going to show you the worst stuff imaginable. Although Japanese animated pornography easily makes it into the R18 category, which cannot legally be sold anywhere outside a licensed sex shop, I don't think I am going to achieve anything by showing you things that will shock you. If you want to find them yourselves, by all means go looking. It won't take you long on the Internet. I'll also be talking today just about heterosexual porn. Gay erotica is a whole other area. I'll talk about it at the end if you like, I'll answer questions about it — I'll come back and do a whole lecture just on that subject — but today I'm talking about heterosexual erotica.

One of the questions, I suppose, is why we should bother? Haven't we got better things to do on a Friday afternoon? Well, one reason is because erotica is, to a certain extent, a patron of the arts. Many of what fandom call the 'fan favorite' titles, the niche interest material that only sells four thousand copies, to some extent, that sector is supported by the profits from pornography.

It's often assumed that all fans of Japanese animation are perverts...

[laughter]

The thing is that at the height of the video nasty scare, in 1997 — when the *Daily Mail* and the *Daily Telegraph* and the *Guardian* were going on and on about how these awful animated erotica were taking over the minds of our children — at the height of all that, the average British anime convention was attracting 500 attendees. Meanwhile, *Urotsukidoji: Legend of the Overfiend*, which was the most notorious of the anime 'nasties', sold 40,000 copies in Britain in that year alone. So anime 'fans' weren't buying it, it was selling to somebody else, in quantities far larger than the average sales for 'normal' anime. Believe me, the people who sell anime in this country would love it if every tale of magical girlfriends and silly princesses and talking animals sold as well as *Urotsukidoji*.

Another reason to look at it is that in all areas of the film business, not just in animation, pornography often shows you the first time that new technology is put to good use. Because pornography often operates at the edge of what is acceptable, it tends also to be on the cutting edge of technology, where legislation has yet to catch up and restrict it. Pornography doesn't necessarily *innovate* new technology, but it often steers how it is used.

For example, Betamax. There are all kinds of theories as to why Betamax didn't work, but one of the most popular is that the porn industry was already favoring VHS. And you're going to see this again with Blu-Ray and HDD. There are arguments now about which is going to be the big new format. But the argument can easily be settled by the US porn industry. If they suddenly all run for Blu-Ray, that's it,

HDD is dead.

Online ordering! The idea of having a shopping basket and you put stuff in and you give your credit card details to a secure server. Not invented by the porn industry, but embraced by it very early on, because of the opportunities it offered for mail order.

Have you ever wondered why your DVD remote control has got a Multiple Camera Angle Button...?

[laughter]

It's not that useful.

And you know, I've got this theory about Microsoft. On Windows XP, when you want to look at photographs, the menu has a Hands Free Slideshow option...

[laughter]

So as you can see, there is a secret market sector, there is a genre that is not spoken of, and it exerts an invisible pull on the mainstream. There are several reasons for this. One is that pretty much all of us would rather not talk about pornography. I'm sure none of the Swansea students started their course saying: "One day I am going to make an erotic cartoon and then I'll be famous." Understandably, we would all much prefer to work in what, for want of a better word, we'll call the mainstream. People in the pornography sector usually feel the same way, and they are very secretive about it. Porn is often excluded from the sales figures. It's not part of mainstream union rates. It's not counted in statistics, and that can be very misleading, because there are some companies in the Japanese animation business that are kept alive by pornography. There is always money in sex. But the way in which sex interacts with animation is a fascinating area, which I will try to explore a little bit today.

Pornography is the dark matter of the film business. People don't talk about it, and yet it's a place where some of the crucial experiments of the film business take place. If you want a clue as to how your industry will look in five years time, look at porn. Porn was first with straight-to-video distribution. Porn was first with bit torrents. Interactivity. Multiple camera angles. Pieces of computer software that you use every day were pioneered for their use in pornography. Seriously, everybody, if you get set a difficult question in your exams about applied uses of technology, don't just look in the industry journals — that's all theory. Go to a sex shop and see what's on the shelves. Pornographic consumers are wealthy, affluent men with nothing better to spend their money on than gadgets and pictures of naked girls. They're Early Adopters! Look in a sex shop and you'll get an idea of what the early adopters are already using. And in five years time, that's the format that will work.

And I will point out, as well, if any of you do end up writing about erotica, if you are going to be talking about cross-cultural comparisons, please, for the love of God, find out what your own culture is consuming before you start making generalizations about someone else's.

The reason I say this is that so many people, when talking about anime erotica, make these gross generalizations about what "the Japanese" like and what "the Japanese" do. And many of these people have never experienced the erotica of their own country. They've never been to a British sex shop and seen what's on sale there, for instance. And I think once you appreciate how our industry works, it becomes much more easy to appreciate both the differences and the similarities we find in Japan.

Anyway, the first pornographic anime *should* have been Hakusan Kimura's *Cool Ship* (1932, *Suzumi-bune*), planned as the first part of an erotic two-reeler, but it was seized by the police when only half complete. So nobody knows what happens in it, but whatever it was, it was very offensive!

[laughter]

After that, right the way through the 1930s, 1940s, and 1950s, cartoons are for children. There was nothing erotic until the very end of the 1960s, when Osamu Tezuka, the so-called 'Walt Disney' of Japanese animation, found himself in financial difficulty. Those of you who know the anime world will know of *Astro Boy* and *Kimba the White Lion*, of the huge boom in TV animation of the early 1960s. Tezuka is, rightly, remembered as one of the founding fathers of the Japanese animation business. But he was a creative. A creator. Arguably, many of his 1960s successes were based on novelty. *Astro Boy* was the first sci-fi cartoon. There were only two channels, and the other one was showing some crappy cowboy show. You bet *Astro Boy* got high ratings. But soon everyone was doing it, everybody was imitating his early successes. He went from being a big fish in a little pond to one of many fishes all scrabbling for the attention of the same number of viewers. He was running low on cash, the company was spiraling towards bankruptcy, and so he figured, "Hell, let's do something 'adult'."

The distinction here is quite apt. Tezuka did not set out to make pornography. I don't think he set out to make erotica. He set out to make a film that was aimed at an adult audience, but was animated. In other words, that perennial problem of the anime business, running up against the fact that the general public invariably assumes that all cartoons are for children.

If you watch Tezuka's *Cleopatra*, for example, in its entirety, it soon becomes very clear that you are not watching pornography. In America, it was sold as porn, under the title *Cleopatra Queen of Sex*. But everyone was equally displeased. The US distributors made the misleading, well, untrue claim that it was the first cartoon to get an X rating and nobody really cared. People who came expecting pornography got something too arty, and people going expecting a film for mature audiences just got a lot of nudity and titillation.

It's very interesting though, because in it Tezuka tries all kinds of innovations. *Cleopatra* starts off in the future, where everyone is live-action. They shoot it all live-action and put anime heads on everyone, which is very weird and a very interesting technique, kind of like *Clutch Cargo* in reverse.

So you end up watching a cartoon that is not for children, and that itself in the 1960s was an incredible idea, but it is not pornography. There are sex scenes which, frankly, would make it onto TV uncut these days, but at the time, it was something of a shock. Sadly, not enough of one.

There were a couple of attempts to copy it by other studios, but that was not because it was a success. It was because the other studios assumed that if Tezuka was doing it, then it had to be lucrative. But erotica does not work in mainstream cinemas, and the brief fad for 'adult cartoons' in the late 1960s soon faded away again. The problem is that pornography is a difficult thing to sell in an environment where movies are consumed in public theatres, because the consumption of pornography is usually, how can I put this? *A solo pursuit.* So unless you're in a theatre where nobody minds...

[laughter]

And that's not an invitation! It's very difficult to find your market. There might have been seedy places where you might watch nudie flicks in privacy, but basically, it's very difficult in a cinema environment to sell people something that frankly is better suited to a 'home cinema'. Now I know that some of you are thinking that can't be true of everything, because we're looking at the threshold of the 1970s, and surely that was a time of a great boom in mainstream pornography. For example, *Deep Throat* wasn't far away.

Deep Throat: supposedly the best-selling porn film in history, playing to packed theatres, and kicking off a whole boom in pornography. Well, I have a theory about it. It's not mine, it was first proposed by the film critic Roger Ebert. He said that the thing with pornography is that because nobody really looks at the statistics, and because they're reluctant to even discuss it, it can be a very handy way of laundering money.

So, let's just say, for example, that...

[picks audience member]

...let's just say that Shelley is running a prostitution ring.

[laughter]

And a gambling network, and a whole bunch of illegal things. And now she has a big pile of ill-gotten gains sitting in her room, but she can't spend that money. If she banks it or spends it, the tax man is going to notice it. However, if she sets up a cinema in a seedy end of town and shows a few dirty movies there, she has a new business that is both legitimate but difficult to investigate. Consumers of pornography like their privacy. They are often furtive. It means that people will understand if the business is cash-only, without any credit card receipts.

So she can then say, "Yeah, we showed a porno film six times a day. And they played to packed houses." Nobody needs to know that the cinema was empty. They can *claim* it played to a packed house. And if anyone asks for proof, well, here's a stack of torn ticket stubs. And every one of those ticket stubs is, I don't know, five bucks that you can claim to have legitimately earned. You run it through the system, you pay your tax on it, and it's yours! It's laundered! The side effect, however, is that a bunch of crappy films that nobody actually watched suddenly show up on the film business radar as really successful movies!

And this *accusation* — and it is an accusation, it's never been proved — but this accusation has been leveled at many aspects of the supposed boom in 1970s pornography, particularly in the United States. If you read between the lines, it suggests that pornography might not actually be as successful as people claim.

Anyway, so, nothing happened in Japanese animated erotica until the early 1980s, when the arrival of the video recorder changed everything. That's because tapes allowed companies to sell direct to consumers. Suddenly, any room with a VCR in it could become a little private cinema, and that had all sorts of bonus effects for pornographic consumption. Instead of waiting for a cinema chain or a TV channel, it opened up the market to new niches of fandom, and that included pornography.

The first anime released direct to video was science fiction, it was a show called *Dallos*. But the next *five* videos were all pornography. So if you look at the first few months of anime video in Japan, pornography is already there. Like I said, it doesn't necessarily *innovate*, but it moves faster to exploit a new niche that other sectors are still getting their heads around.

The sales, however, for pornography were very different in the VHS video business. They tended not to be bought by customers. Instead they were bought by video rental stores. So the average anime porn tape would retail for roughly a hundred bucks. It would be rented, on average, four times more often than a mainstream film. And because porn titles tend not to be serialized, if the customer is unhappy with what he rents, he can come back the next week and rent something else. So you don't have one of the difficulties that you have today with anime, where you can put out a TV show on DVD, and if the customer doesn't like episode one, he's not coming back for episodes two to twenty-six, and you're wasting everybody's time and resources.

What you get with pornography is that, particularly in this period, the market for the distributor was not the consumer, but the guy who ran the rental store. This has a really big effect on the numbers. For instance, I remember I was once on the phone to Edwin de la Cruz, one of the guys at, I think it was Media Blasters, an old American distributor. And I was being very irritating and telling him how crap I thought one of his titles was. And he let me talk myself out for about three minutes, listening to this insulting screed, and then he said, "You say that, Jonathan. But we sold ten thousand copies of that title to Blockbuster. Today."

You see, you are dealing with a very different market to the one we know now. The consumer's price point is very low, only a few dollars, and the tape is something they watch once and return. You wouldn't expect people to risk $100 on a single tape, but they might risk, say, *a dollar*. And if they don't like it, what the hell, they've only spent a dollar. The risk is low for the consumer, because they are only spending a few bucks, but it's also relatively low for the rental store, because every night they get their tape back and they can rent it to someone else.

But animated erotica is now, and always will be, constantly competing with live-action pornography for its audience. In general, the average porn consumer is going to want as realistic an experience as possible. He doesn't want to see cartoons. He doesn't want to see sex. He wants to have it. And the pornographic experience is never going to quite deliver.

Also, live-action is already there. The decision to watch an animated erotic work instead of a live-action one has to have a rationale behind it. In theory, you can simply argue that some people get off on cartoons. But even if that is your particular weird fetish, there aren't going to be enough of you to sustain a medium. Instead, as with *Urotsukidoji*, the bulk of your sales will always be outside the putative customer base. You are selling to people who are not buying your cartoon because it is a cartoon, but because it gives them something that they can't get from live-action.

So what is that? What is that special something?

Anime tries to find ways of reaching markets and fetishes that live-action cannot. Two people having sex in a hotel room is easy and cheap to film live-action. But not two people having sex on a spaceship, or in a medieval castle. So fantasy, science fiction and horror are important genres within animated erotica, simply because they do something that live-action can't.

Well, I say that live-action can't, but actually in recent years there has been a distinctive move towards more 'creativity' in pornography, particularly by a company called Private. *Private Gladiator*, for example, is one of their most notorious titles. It's like the Ridley Scott *Gladiator*, except a few minutes into the story, everybody takes their clothes off...

So actually a lot better in many ways!

[laughter]

No Russell Crowe though.

[groans of disappointment]

So anyway, let's go back to the 1980s and 1990s now. Forget Private and modern porn. Let's talk about a time when live-action pornography meant two people having sex in a hotel room. And when animated pornography meant sex in spaceships, sex in Dracula's castle, sex on the moon! That's what animation does best, so let's exploit that for all it's worth.

But even if you are going straight to video, you still need to worry about the Japanese censor, and that can affect your material. Japan actually has quite liberal censorship laws. Article 21 of the Japanese constitution specifies that *there is no censorship*. However, there is an *encouragement* to avoid "lewdness and the unnecessary depiction of genitalia", and so it has become the practice — not the law, but the practice — not to show pubic hair, and not to show any genitals at all. Policing this practice tends to fall to officers of the law who have been passed over in the promotional ladder, and they have become notoriously picky. During the 1980s and 1990s, they would even insist that animated pubic hair amounted to an "unnecessary depiction of genitalia".

This means that the Japanese porn industry, animated and live, finds ways to fetishize things which are representations of the actual images that have been banned. So for example, because of the restrictions on images of genitalia, it's easier to get a bondage film or torture film past the censor, because it doesn't involve genitalia. Characters become obsessed, for example, with white underwear, since this is acceptable, and an obsession with what is under the underwear is not — compare that to your own customs for wet T-shirt competitions. If you know what they are in Wales.

[laughter]

This also affects underwear. Frilly underwear is too fiddly to animate. Seriously, Studio Fantasia are particularly excited about this, and they made stuff like *Najica* that was basically just lingerie. Well, with people in it, obviously. It wouldn't just be underwear, that would be weird. But they got all kinds of complaints from their animators about the problems inherent in drawing all the fiddly little lacey bits in frilly underwear twenty-four times a second. So they experimented with a bit of variation and simpler underwear design. Colored underwear was tried, red, blue, green, but that actually was found to backfire. It lost its erotic charge because it tended to look like swimming costumes, so it wasn't something that the viewer was illicitly peeping at. So the default setting for anime underwear is plain, blank white knickers. Simpler to draw, and they look just enough like underwear so that the viewer peeping up a skirt or whatever gets to feel he is seeing something that he shouldn't be seeing.

The most infamous and productive bending of the censorship practices has been the use of the tentacle.

[scattered laughter]

I can tell exactly who the anime fans are in this audience!

By a process of facetious logic, you can argue that because it is a tentacle, it is not a penis, and therefore is not subject to any of the restrictions that would normally apply. You can show a multi-tentacled creature to the Japanese censor, and as long as he is *not seeing any actual genitalia*, he has nothing to complain about.

So in anime erotica, we get women penetrated by penis-shaped tentacles, women sucking penis-shaped tentacles, and views of penis-shaped tentacles, that seem to be ejaculating. And the Japanese censor is sitting there watching it saying, "Nope. No genitalia here. Nothing to see here, this passes without any trouble."

The tentacle is also an extremely useful device, because it allows the male partner in the sex act to be removed at a distance from the female, and consequently allows for better camera angles. But you need an excuse to have tentacles in your story, so erotic anime often drift towards tales of alien invaders or demon rapists.

I'm going to show you the kind of weirdness that this can generate. A show from Go Nagai called *Kekko Kamen*. A superhero who is almost entirely naked. Torture played for comedy, at a school. Naughtiness and sauciness to get it out of the sex shops, and legitimize it somehow. I'll give you a dose of the theme song so you get an idea.

> *We see her fanny but her face remains a mystery*
> *Her true identity is not to be disclosed*
> *Kekko Kamen! A girl with a plan*
> *Fighting for justice with a flail in her hand*
> *Guarding us from evil, protecting us from sin*
> *And if a teacher grabs her, she'll kick his bollocks in*

So I have here a sequence in which a schoolgirl is tied to a giant rotating swastika while a woman in a Nazi outfit throws knives at her to cut her clothes off. The point, however, is that at no point in this sequence do you see any genitals. You see bondage and torture and ludicrously comedic set-ups, but relatively tame nudity. So this makes it past the Japanese censor without any trouble, and then it reaches the British Board of Film Classification, and the first thing they think is, "Blimey, the Japanese are weird."

Erotic demands started to shift the interests of storyliners in the 1980s and 1990s. Anime enjoys a frankly undeserved reputation for strong female characters. Actually what it has is a predominantly male customer base and producers who pander to the interests of that base so much that character rosters started to become more female. The idea, I suppose, was that your audience didn't want to see five sweaty male astronauts, saving the world. Why not have five female astronauts, saving the world. In bikinis. Oh yes.

This kind of show has encouraged something which some call "moe" (*moeru*), a burning obsession. These obsessives are the market for much supposedly fan-favorite porn. However, "moe" may also mean *moeteru* (to sprout). Its emphasis being on young girls. Not for the usual reason men like young girls, that they are bendy, and have less baggage and lower standards. The girls tend to be the same age as the target audience, and the target audience is going to be a sixteen or seventeen year-old boy. Which is important. Because anime erotica is often ridiculed for being too childish. And frankly, it's aimed at children. It's something risqué for a seventeen year-old boy. It's not dirty mac nonsense. The emphasis is often less on the sexual act, than it is on eavesdropping on the world of a sixteen year-old girl. Girls are a mystery. They are unattainable. They are alien creatures. And we get an opportunity to just watch them hanging out. Naked.

Anime and manga have also enjoyed very close relationships with the world of computer games, for a reason that has remained constant. Whatever your format of choice for storing an image, a photograph, a digital file, whatever, a drawn anime image takes up less memory. And this has meant that the anime art style has become a regular feature in computer games, and indeed in erotic computer games. To the extent that we now have a generation who associate sexual desire with the anime image.

If you take apart the actual code of many Japanese erotic games, you discover that the decisions you make in the game don't necessarily have a direct effect on the outcome. Instead, they function really like a personality test. They put you in situations where the important thing for the game engine is not necessarily the answer you give, but how you give it. The computer is testing you. It wants to see if you are loyal, if you are patient, if you are sporty or intellectual. It takes all this information and it processes it to give you the love interest that it thinks you will be most pleased to have.

There are five of them. Actually six, but five for our purposes. The most obvious character is the Girl Next Door. She is the same age as the target audience; she is bland and inoffensive, she may even already be a friend of the lead character. Other characters include the Tomboy (sporty and aggressive), the Maid (demure and submissive), the Older Woman, and the Child (not necessarily in age, but certainly in attitude). Add to these five basic archetypes a lesser-known sixth type, the Disposable Foreign Female, and you have a roster of the kind of girls that are offered to gamer geeks as potential prizes in erotic games.

There's a happy end in every case. The choices made determine not the events that unfold, but what kind of girl the player most wants. Pundits have tried to argue that Japanese games are not so predictable, that there are more archetypes. But if you break down the code, that's what you get.

What you also get, of course, is merchandise. Sales figures, statistics, which start to tell you about what kind of girl is 'fashionable' in a given period. Modern developments in Japanese animation reflect a mildly disturbing trend in these dating sims and moe games. Which is that some girls come in and out of fashion. Fifteen years ago, the most popular kind of girl was a nerd. She wore glasses, and liked computers and was, frankly, grateful. Today, the fashionable girl reflects the increasing isolation of the audience. She is young, perhaps even underage, she is stupid to the point of being retarded, and hence goes along with everything. She is submissive, to the extent that she will fuss and cook and clean for a lazy boyfriend like she's some kind of doormat-mother substitute. And she is so shallow and so needy that she will have paroxysms of joy if her love object so much as says a kind word.

Although there's a new trend developing for Older Women. It's just turned up in the last eight months or so, a lot more Oedipal fantasies like *Stepmother's Sin*. So as you can see, the 'ideal woman' in the anime erotica field is not a concrete statement of fact, it's an ever-changing trend. Older women are coming back in, in Japan, apparently.

One wonders about the future potential for animated erotica — pornography thrives on the niches in what is not possible or acceptable, and animated pornography in what is not possible or acceptable in live-action pornography. But both access and content have liberalized in Japan — is there anything left?

The line between games and films is blurring all the time. And the line between digital and real is blurring all the time. The real interest for me in the modern state of pornography is in the delivery system. Issues in censorship are one thing, technology is another, but it's the delivery system that is most interesting. Modern Japanese pornography is centralized, on Japanese servers. Even in cases where the rights have been sold to foreign distributors, the Japanese have made every conceivable step they can to regain the rights. If someone defaults on their contract, they whip those rights away. If that doesn't work, one company has even resorted to buying back all of its shares, so that it can sell in an internal economy.

Modern pornography is characterized by direct downloads to computers and mobile phones, with some Japan-based distributors even providing English-language options direct to consumers abroad.

Since pornography is usually five years ahead of the mainstream in terms of its distribution and production techniques, I expect to see more mainstream anime taking similar routes to its audience by 2012. The next format is No Format. It's all digital, you buy it for your phone, or your home entertainment system, and it is delivered to you by the Japanese. This presents a very real danger to jobs in the middle, in the distribution sector, because many of the people who currently fill all the middle-men jobs, selling anime in Britain, in America, in France, will be surplus to requirements if the operations are all centralized back in Japan.

Your access to all anime material, erotica or mainstream, may well increase in the near future. It may become easier and cheaper to get it, but what worries me is that the Japanese will increasingly be masters of their destiny when it comes to deciding what to sell you. Considering the misreadings of other cultures' erotica that I have been discussing today, I wonder if new genres, and new media, will be taken out of context in much the same way as the tentacles, and the rotating swastikas, and the many other weird things we've all been laughing at today.

Thank you.

[applause]

I've been told that I have time for two questions…

[Q: Do you see there being a future increase in interactivity in erotic anime?]

Well, the thing is that the boundary between film and game is eroding all the time and it's eroding fastest in the pornographic sector. The dating sims, for example, that I was discussing today, at one end they are quite romantic, or rather, are regarded as quite romantic, but not at the other.

I translated two erotic games from Japan back in… oh… 1997. So they've already been around for quite a long time. I did one called *Timestripper*, which was about… well, basically, it was the *Terminator*, but Arnold Schwarzenegger was a beautiful lesbian. And another one called *Ring Out*, which was about the little-known world of underground lesbian wrestling. So these games are already in existence, but my concern is that, frankly, it's a bit fiddly. As I said, the average male consumer of pornography is not really interested in *seeing* a sexual act, he's interested in *having* one, and pornography is his means to a close approximation. Now, if we look at a modern trend in live-action erotica, the concept of POV [point of view] porn, where the male 'actor' is invisible and the female characters address the camera as if the viewer is the actor, then I can see that having a lot of application in the interactive world.

[Q: Such as teledildonics?]

Theoretically, I suppose, but what would worry me is console provision. Because, you know, I don't see there being much chance of Nintendo commercials saying, "Oh yeah, and by the way, you can plug in a dildo here!"

[laughter]

Many of the big companies, in anime and games alike, have subsidiaries that work in the porn area, but I don't see much likelihood of the mainstream console market openly supporting it. I mean, maybe there might be some sort of subsidiary they set up that makes some kind of unlicensed software that 'just happens' to plug into a Nintendo Wii. A Nintendo Wii-Hee!

[laughter]

But otherwise I don't know.

[Q: Are the Japanese approaching beauty in the wrong way, in their attitude towards nudity, for example?]

In the wrong way!? I think that's in the eye of the beholder, isn't it? Okay, that question requires a very long answer, and people have written entire books about the subject, but I'll give it a go. The idea that nudity was 'wrong', as imposed by Article 21 of the Japanese constitution, for example, was imposed as a result of Westerners' reaction to the Japanese. The Japanese were all very happy to jump in the bath naked together before Westerners turned up and told them they had to be Christian and covered-up, and taught them to be ashamed of nudity.

I think there are certainly very different attitudes towards beauty, which I don't really have time to go into, but in the erotic world, particularly the pink films of the 1960s, which were a kind of soft-core live-action erotica, the idea of what beauty was, was defined less by cultural traditions and more by attempts to get around the censor.

So, always follow the money. Never assume that "the Japanese", all 125 million of them, have a full consensus and a particular idea about what is beautiful. We could probably argue amongst ourselves about what *our* idea of beautiful is. And very few people would agree 100 percent with me about Nicole Kidman, dressed as a belly dancer…

Oh, did I say that out loud?

[laughter]

It's a very difficult thing to define, but I would suggest that you should always assume that censorship and technicalities come before any ideas of beauty, in the porn world. In the artistic world things might be different, but in the porn world you are trying to serve people sex, and sex always takes precedence in that sector over ideas of beauty.

Thank you.

[applause]

AROUND THE
WORLD

ENTER THE DRAGONS

Selling Anime to the Chinese

"**F**or too long have we waited," he thundered. "Now our time has come, to destroy them! To Destroy Them All! Forever!" And after chuckling to himself for a moment, he had another bread roll. I looked around the restaurant nervously. Luckily, I was in Italy.

Film festivals are not that different from anime conventions, except there's less chance of having to share an elevator with three grown men dressed as schoolgirls. This festival was very swish, packed with producers producing, directors directing, actors acting up, and writers on their mobiles, lying to their editors.

I was there as the Chinese animation curator, but Japanese attendees soon found out who I was and wanted me to hang out with them. I'd been to the same college as the Taipei contingent, which practically makes you related as far as the Chinese are concerned, so they wanted me to hang out with *them*. Meanwhile, the place was crawling with pretty Italian girls, and I did my level best to hang out with *them*, but they'd all brought their big brothers. So I did what any rational being would do. I sought political asylum with the Communists.

Which is how I came to share breakfast with Mr Lee (not his real name). Put in enough years coloring cels, handle enough minions and sign off on enough storyboards at a busy animation studio, and you get to collect the perks. And for Mr Lee, the perks meant a week in Italy on government money, getting shown round Venice by perky hostesses with surplus vowels, and occasionally setting up new deals.

Talking Japanese animation with the Chinese is no picnic, because they insist on using the Mandarin pronunciation for all the staffers' names. So you won't get anywhere with them until you accept that

Spirited Away was directed by someone called Gong-Qi Jun. But we were soon discussing the relative merits of motion-capture and rotoscoping, the ideal size of a studio, and how best to hold an audience's attention. Well, he was. I was trying to remember the Chinese for "pass the salt."

And then he hit me with it. He told me he liked my work and he enjoyed my critical insights. He was impressed with my comments on the anime business, and like De Niro in *Angel Heart*, he rolled a hard-boiled egg around his plate under the palm of his hand, watching absent-mindedly as the shell crazed and cracked.

"I'd really like it," he said, "if you would come to our studio in China for a few weeks, and teach us."

"Teach you what?"

"About the Japanese animation industry," he said, matter-of-factly. "And how we can destroy it."

Say it out loud in a hotel dining room, and see what people do to you. Luckily for me, Mr Lee's Darth Vader impersonation was in Mandarin and we were surrounded by Italians. His secret was safe.

Not something you expect to hear every day at breakfast. But he was serious. He was dead set on finding a way to stick it to anime any way he could. Anime, he explained, was just too damn good. And Gong-Qi Jun wasn't his only worry. There was that Gao-Qiao woman, and all those damn movies by Ya-Jing. And so on.

I bring this up now because of something that happened a few months later, after I had smiled inscrutably and said no (how could you have doubted me?). That's because there was no longer a need for me to fly over and tell Mr Lee's people all the Japanese trade secrets. The Japanese were doing it for me.

Next time I saw Mr Lee, he was negotiating on an international co-production, for a show we will call (by popular demand) *Schoolgirl Milky Crisis*. Japanese story, Japanese top brass, but the actual animation gets done in China. Which means that even though US distributors will swear on the Bible that it is as Japanese as cherry blossoms and Zen, it *kinda-sorta* counts as a local Chinese production as well, so the Japanese get to make it cheaply *and* bypass China's restrictive quota on foreign TV shows. Everyone's a winner, then?

Everyone, especially Mr Lee, who gleefully informed me that he and a party of select minions would soon be heading to Japan, where, as part of this happy deal, they would be shown around the studios of their partner, taught about How Anime Did What Anime Does and treated to some insights into what it was that made Japanese animation such a world-beater.

Which is a happy ending for everyone concerned… Unless you're paranoid like me. Because I have a suspicious mind.

(*Newtype USA*, March 2003)

SAUNA OF DEATH
Anime Fandom in Finland

I must have taken a wrong turn. The sun set around midnight, and suddenly the woods were dark. I was heading back to the seashore, but I'd forgotten the fork in the path. Now I was standing in a pitch-black forest, lit only by the stars, with no idea where I was. It didn't help that I was completely naked.

I started to regret all the bad things I'd ever said about Moomins. If you're ever in Finland and agree to do the midnight sauna thing, pack a flashlight.

Japanese pop culture still has a bad reputation in Finland. This May, the original *Dragon Ball* manga was whipped unceremoniously off the shelves when a meddling pressure group complained about sexual innuendo. The Finns still get the censored American *Dragon Ball Z* on TV, but if they want to read the manga, they have to settle for imports in Swedish or English.

Finland has no anime distributors. The only localized products they get are big-league items like the *Animatrix*. There's simply not enough demand in a population of a mere five million for someone to get off their butt and prepare a version in the local language. Finnish anime fandom relies on American imports and dedicated fansubbers, and holds out in vain for a moment when the TV channels show something more than

Pokémon and other kiddy fare.

Although Finland is off the beaten track for most travelers, it's a popular tourist destination for visitors from the Far East. As I get off the plane at Turku airport in the country's far southwest, the first sight that greets me is a giant white troll-creature, welcoming me in Finnish, Swedish, English and Japanese.

Between 1945 and 1971, Finnish author Tove Jansson created a long series of tales about the Moomins, happy hippo-like creatures that live in an idyllic land of islands and forests, modeled on the Baltic coast near Turku. By 1969, the series had gained an anime incarnation, and Finland remains a major Japanese tourist destination. The Finns look down their noses at the *Moomin* anime, which Jansson herself never really liked, but it worked as a magical advert for their country. Finnair planes are packed with Japanese visitors determined to see the magical forests and lakes for themselves.

They're not the only new arrivals. The day before the Finnish anime convention begins, the Baltic Tall-Ships Race turns up in Turku harbor, injecting half a million people into the town. It increases the population of Finland by ten percent for several days, and floods the town with bemused sailors and their families. One Russian lieutenant in full dress uniform even makes it to the convention itself, where he is mistaken for a *Silent Service* character, and mobbed by enthusiastic teenage girls.

The Finns are no strangers to computer graphics, not the least because their national airline likes to imply it is staffed solely by digital avatars. For reasons I don't quite comprehend, all the in-flight safety announcements on Finnair use motion-capture instead of real people to demonstrate the procedures.

I introduce the Finns to a different kind of CG animation when I give my guest of honor speech. The lecture hall is packed to capacity and there are eager Finns standing in the aisles. Though this is only Finland's second anime event, it already dwarfs the turnout at British conventions.

In the English-speaking world, a group of young people in a log cabin in a remote part of the woods is a recipe for a low-budget horror movie. In Finland, it is the national ideal of the perfect vacation. I decide that Finland needs a national stalk-and-slash movie, with teenagers menaced by an evil Moomin. I see people in the crowd making notes.

After regaling them with my ideas for a *Sauna of Death* anime, I talk the audience through the pros and cons of motion capture, and demonstrate it with a clip from *A.Li.Ce*. This obscure 1999 digital anime features a time-traveling Japanese idol singer who crash-lands in post-apocalyptic Finland. The sight of snowy wastes causes the crowd to burst into applause.

Back at Turku airport, I walk across the tarmac towards the propeller-driven plane that will ferry me to Helsinki for my international transfer home. I walk behind a family of Japanese tourists who dawdle with extreme reluctance. The father puts his arm around his wife (a highly unusual gesture of affection for the reserved Japanese), while the couple's young daughters skip around them and point at the plane. None of them realize that I am eavesdropping on their conversation. What are the chances of finding a Japanese speaker this close to the Arctic Circle, after all?

"Sayonara Moomins," says the younger girl to the pictures on the airport walls.

"We are leaving," says her sister, dolefully. "We are leaving this land of manga."

(*Newtype USA*, October 2003)

STEAMING

Picture Research for *Steam Boy*

Tower Records, Piccadilly Circus, London. 13:00 hours. I had no idea what Gichi looked like. All I knew about him was his girlfriend was a designer, and his sister was in the air force. Neither fact was much help.

Luckily, he stood out a mile. Thin as a manga pretty-boy, all dressed in black like Dracula's malnourished Japanese cousin.

"Are you...?" he said, pointing at me.

"You bet I am!" I replied.

"Cool!" he said. "Where's the gay place?"

I am sure that Piccadilly Circus has heard plenty of conversations like that before. In this case, though, it was anime-related. I took him down Old Compton Street, pointing out the rainbow flags. He ignored them and snapped the old buildings on a posh camera. He wanted more. I took him to Chinatown and pointed out a supermarket.

"It's Victorian?" he asked, taking out his camera.

"Yep. And it used to be a brothel!" I added.

"A WHAT?"

"A BROTHEL!"

"FANTASTIC!"

We were getting *looks* from passers-by. I dragged him up to Covent Garden. We made a strange couple — a spindly oriental cameraman and a towering gaijin, pointing excitedly at any building more than a hundred years old. Gichi snapped away like his job depended on it.

On that day, it did.

Steam Boy needed buildings. *Steam Boy* needed a realistic view of nineteenth-century London. *Steam Boy* needed Gichi photographing Victoriana, and a separate crew doing likewise up in Manchester. They were going to take it home, shove it on a wall, scan it in, whatever. And two years later, I hoped, I could watch Katsuhiro Otomo destroy my favorite pub.

"This place would be a fantastic building to blow up!" said Gichi enthusiastically, lifting his pint.

I smiled weakly at the barmaid.

"It's okay," I said. "He's in anime."

(*NEO* #3, 2005)

GLASGOW KISSES
Anime at the 2005 World-Con

C all me a romantic, but if I had next year's Hugo Award voters in one place, I'd damn well make sure they saw a Miyazaki movie. But there was no *Howl's Moving Castle* at the World Science Fiction Convention in Scotland. UK rights holder Optimum mysteriously forbade it, even though the same company was happy to see its own *Appleseed* screened at the event.

Far be it for me to feign knowledge of the small print — Optimum's hands may have been tied by its contracts. But anyone donating anime material to the World-Con was onto a winner. Ten years ago, at the last Glasgow World-Con, the BBC had gleefully handed over anything that the organizers requested, for free. This year, the Beeb insisted on a fee per item, and the World-Con was forced to reduce its screenings of TV material.

It was UK anime companies who cashed in on the gap, with an extensive donation for the video rooms. ADV Films was so keen to get *Voices of a Distant Star* into my 'History of Anime' lecture series that marketing chief Hugh David even ran a copy round to my flat the day before, in person.

For some people, a World-Con is a view of another world. For me, it's a view of Earth. It's the only time I get to see the world of conference centers and businessmen. I also get to see SF fandom up close, and it's not the impoverished students of newspaper lore. There were computer programmers, rocket scientists, and several hundred writers, many of whom were hungry to learn more about anime, and with disposable incomes to back up their interest. Five people alone told me that my talks about Japanese sci-fi had sold them Platinum box sets of *Evangelion*. Still more commented that seeing *Appleseed* had convinced them to buy the DVD. It was *Howl's* loss, but Miyazaki will survive, I'm sure.

(*NEO* #11, 2005)

ROAD TRIP
Teen Yearnings for Japan

This month's evidence that truth is stranger than fiction: two teenage French girls, apprehended in Poland, two days into an attempt to reach Japan overland. According to the newspaper *Libération*, the pair planned to ride the Trans-Siberian railway to Vladivostok, and somehow hitch their way across the Japan Sea, all so that they could reach the place of their dreams, the "land of manga".

Were they really that dumb? In this age of attention-seeking reality television, there is a part of me that senses a knowing gullibility — a selfish act of folly designed to generate media coverage, and, just maybe, the notice of a cunning marketing executive, who can make the girls' dreams come true so long as they wear his *Schoolgirl Milky Crisis* T-shirts. Or was there a shadowy corporate hand all along — can it be a coincidence that the news broke a week before Japan Expo in Paris?

Or is there something more sinister at work? How could two teenagers on the run expect to make it 6,125 miles across Asia? Do they have a history of mental illness or troubles at home? Did they steal the money? How were they going to eat? Were they *really* alone, or is a creepy Internet pen pal keeping his head down in Warsaw and hoping to entrap unluckier victims next time?

It's a manga plot waiting to happen. Your choice — a horrific tale of kidnap and slavery, as two innocent heroines are abducted by barbarians of the steppes and sold to a despot in Somethingstan; a comedy of daft adventure as our feisty Frenchies race across Asia in pursuit of an impossible dream; a heart-warming series of encounters with local people, their eyes growing progressively slantier, their skin gradually yellowing, until after a long quest, we reach the Promised Land.

There's a story in this. There's a movie in this. And despite my disbelief that they could be so utterly, utterly stupid, there's a part of me that understands. I was sixteen, too, when I decided to go to Japan. But my means of transport two years later was a university application form. It's safer, trust me.

(*NEO* #23, 2006)

LA CHEVALIEUSE D'ANIME
Japanese Cartoons and the French Presidential Election

As I write this it's the day after the French presidential election, in which a paltry 6.2 percent of voters swung Nicolas Sarkozy into power. But it's his opponent, Ségolène Royal, who gained the attention of the manga and anime world, particularly after a meeting with the leader of the Japanese socialist party, in which she blamed the position of women in Japanese society on the debilitating influence of "les mangas".

The Japanese were baffled by Royal's words, leading Foreign Minister Taro Aso to diplomatically suggest she might try "reading a few more". But there's more going on here than simple politico soundbiting after an easy target. The French language, despite its xenophobic policing of English "Franglais" slang, has long since allowed the Japanese word *manga* into general use, but usually applied to animation — the French having surrendered to the marketing guff of 1990s video corporations, all except a small village of indomitable *otaku*.

Nor was Royal's comment a bit of off-the-cuff punditry — in 1989 she wrote a whole book on the subject. In *Discontent of the Baby Zappers*, she directed both barrels of her invective against the way in which TV was rotting children's minds. She was particularly scathing about Japanese imports, which she regarded as "nothing more than fights, murders, heads ripped off, repugnant masks, horrible beasts, disgusting demons. Fear. Violence. Noise. With minimal animation. Stories reduced to their most simple expression."

Her thoughts on women, as repeated almost twenty years later, clearly apply not just to anime but also to the Japanese live-action world: "[Girls] reduced to subordinate roles, but also sadly used as victims seized by flying monsters and other robots, reduced to panicking observers (fainting, yelling, weeping, while the hero transforms himself into Bioman, Spielvan or another Metalder)."

And yet, while anime and manga fandom throws a fit on the message boards and calls Royal an idiot, it is perhaps worth mentioning that there are many Japanese, even within the animation business itself, who would agree with her, most notably Hayao Miyazaki, whose entire movie output was formed in reaction to the type of situations that Royal describes.

(*NEO* #34, 2007)

BUM NOTES

The Curse of Manga in China

To Beijing, where Tsugumi Oba and Takeshi Obata's *Death Note* manga has kicked off a local controversy. The manga, also an anime and live-action movie, features a magical notebook which will cause the death of anyone whose name is written in it. Originally a possession of a spirit of the underworld, it falls into the hands of a Japanese boy, who uses it for good — sort of *Ring* meets *The Equalizer*.

Except now Chinese junior schoolchildren have been found keeping their own *Death Note* notebooks, writing down the names of their classroom enemies, and putting curses on their teachers. This, say the powers that be, Must Be Stopped.

But there's more at work here. The Chinese press first began covering *Death Note* copycats when schools banned the manga in Shenyang. Shenyang is the capital of Manchuria, which was effectively *part of* Japan in the 1930s. This both predisposes the locals to follow Japanese media, and the powers that be to get huffy about it.

Death Note is also merely one of several horror comics implicated in the backlash, and many are pirate editions — could this be an underhand way of cleaning up illegal presses, rather than children's minds? The Chinese government doesn't believe in "superstition", so banning *Death Note* for its occult influence is the thin end of a controversial wedge that would end in recognizing the existence of the supernatural!

Speaking as someone who was reprimanded at school for employing sorcery in a hockey game (long story), I can attest that this is just children being silly. Children aware of their own powerlessness start looking for power elsewhere — in the occult, in religion, in music, in sports. Girls go through a teen witch phase, little boys decide they're Jedi. In Singapore, you can buy *Death Note* jotters in the local equivalent of Woolworth's. The *Death Note* controversy is less to do with the occult, and more to do with unruly children, an admittedly macabre fad, and yet another excuse to blame Japan for modern China's social ills.

(*NEO* #35, 2007)

POLE POSITION
The Power of Piracy

To Poland, where police have detained six individuals associated with the subtitling site Napisy.org. Much of their material comprised Hollywood movies, but to the American anime press, they were plain and simple fansubbers. They weren't pirating the movies, merely translating the scripts and giving them away, at least in the eyes of their global supporters. But this is a mealy-mouthed, facetious defense. The fansubbers "charitable" activities made illegal downloads accessible even to non-linguists, and encouraged the Polish grey import market. In what may turn out to be the crux of the entire case, the fansubbers' site also contained paid advertising. In a legal sense, this turned them from harmless fanboys swapping scripts to a self-made Internet TV broadcaster that wasn't paying for its content.

The legality of unlicensed translation has been an issue in the anime world for ten years. Its first catfight broke out after a low-ranking executive from a well-known American company infamously told a fan translator that she was free to watch any Japanese video on her own, but if she turned to a friend and began explaining the plot, she was taking the first step towards copyright infringement.

Of course, nobody is going to send the cops around if you do that, or if you lend a book to a friend. But if new technology allows you to make a perfect copy of that book and hand it over, not just to one friend, but to a thousand, and for them to copy it for ten thousand complete strangers, it's a bigger deal.

To some extent, anime companies' marketing departments have become their own worst enemies. They bombard fans with the constant refrain that anime is "taking the world by storm", that anime sales are huge and the industry is going great guns. But forget Poland, even here in the English-speaking world, it's not always as rosy as the companies pretend. Despite bestseller status for many titles (itself something that can often be readily bought for marketing purposes), many anime titles still have UK sales that struggle to hit high four figures. A thousand fans stealing a TV show for free, or even sampling it for free and deciding not to proceed, can spell the difference between life and death for some shows.

This is why UK anime's recent move into TV and legal downloads is such a good thing. For ten years, fans have been asked to put their hands in their pockets and pay for experiences that appeared "free" to Japanese viewers. By selling more directly, some anime companies may be able to get ahead of the fansubbers, and hence the pirates. They also stand to make a better profit, even on titles that would have been economically unviable on video. Most importantly for UK fans, such technology renders simultaneous worldwide releases more likely, effectively cutting off the demand for grey imports. Great days ahead?

(*NEO* #36, 2007)

TIGERS IN THE MUD
Anime in Smaller Countries

To Estonia, where anime was suddenly thin on the ground. Like you, I live in a world steeped in anime for the last decade. Its absence is noticeable and very strange. For those who follow the history of Japanese animation abroad, the story has been one of an inexorable drift eastwards from the United States, out into Europe through a video nexus in the UK, and direct from Japan through television channels in France, Italy and Germany.

But the small countries of the old Warsaw Pact have largely been left behind. Apart from a few subtitled releases on video, the southern Baltic states still live in a world strangely like the early 1990s. The only anime I caught in Estonia was *Digimon* dubbed into the local language and buried among a slew of American anime clones on a dedicated cartoon channel. Ironic for a country whose war heroes were once the subject of a manga by Hayao Miyazaki — 1998's *Otto Carius: Tigers Covered With Mud*.

Tucked in the northeastern corner of Europe, the medieval town of Tallinn enjoys an uneasy reputation as the perfect party city. The population is forty percent Russian, leading to easy exchanges with nearby former-Soviet states. Meanwhile, tourists and bachelor parties have turned it into the only place in the world where it is possible to eat a wild boar vindaloo, go to a strip club *and* test fire a dozen guns on a private firing range. Are people in Estonia simply having too much fun for Japanese cartoons?

And yet. And yet. I *know* anime fans from Estonia. I know they exist somewhere, but in a manner that mixes old-style small town isolation with modern Internet access. Like American *otaku* in the 1980s, the Estonian otaku lives in the sticks. He, for demographically it is still a he, sees dubbed kiddie anime but doesn't know it's Japanese. When he becomes a full-fledged fan, his main source is the Internet. Small language territories lack the allure of English, French or Chinese — publishing a manga or anime in Estonian simply cannot guarantee the returns from larger sectors. Still, you can watch Miyazaki in the morning and then head off for a crocodile kebab in the evening. Could be worse…

(*NEO* #40, 2007)

THE CARE AND FEEDING OF JAPANESE GUESTS
How To Treat Your Celebrity

Mr Matsumoto sipped politely from a Bacardi Breezer and tried to ignore the giant man in rubber dungarees who was whipping an enthusiastic girl tied to a rack. Loud music thumped and whined all around, while people in leather and chains cavorted drunkenly in the shadows. Another man pushed past me wearing a gas mask, leading a girl on a leash.

"I think," I said to the nervous Matsumoto, "that this is an unusual place to hold a convention party."

Matsumoto looked at me with bug-eyed amazement and a *get-me-out-of-here* stare.

"The safe word is *toucan*," he said.

"What does that mean?" I asked.

"I don't know!" he wailed.

The mild-mannered artist was having a bad experience, and not just because he'd been dumped in a fetish club against his will. A big name in the manga world, he'd traveled thousands of miles to a convention, lured by the prospect of meeting fans, signing autographs and seeing the world on someone else's checkbook. It was only on arrival that he realized he'd only been given an interpreter for his book signing, and not for the other fifteen hours a day he was awake. He wished he'd followed his gut when the invitation had arrived in *English*. His friends had warned him, he said. *Never leave Japan*, at least not to spend one's time in the company of SF fans.

Not every Japanese creator shares Mr Matsumoto's anxiety. I remember one who was ecstatic about going abroad.

"In America," he said, "people have *guns*!"

"Yes," I said, guardedly.

"Can tourists buy guns?" he asked. "Can they!?"

But for most Japanese creators, a foreign trip starts as a fantasy ideal of adoring fans and free goodies, which soon becomes a lonely waiting game in an anonymous Holiday Inn. Not every SF professional can spare the time to go to a convention and entertain strangers for three days for no immediate return except the fickle goodwill of fandom. If a Japanese guest is costing you his air fare, his wife's air fare, his hotel room, his travel, his days either side of the event and the inevitable interpreters' fees, that's a hell of a big investment for one speech and a signing. And when there is a language barrier as well, guests are in need of extra reassurance.

I've asked around for Worst Invitation stories, but there is no solid rock-bottom. Instead, low quality offers slide inexorably into white noise and half-mumbled queries so vague that they might not be an invitation at all. If you're pushy and fractious like me, you can just bluntly ask for clarification, but that's not the Japanese way. They wonder if they are paying for their own flight or hotels. They wonder if they can bring their spouse, and if someone will pick them up from the airport. They fret if it really is a convention at all, or some crazy stalker waiting for them with a chainsaw. In Japan, such events are usually corporate — but in the West, they are often run by *fans*... How does that work, they wonder? How *can* it work?

Eventually, with a few weeks to go, they panic and decide to stay at home, and etiquette demands that an excuse should be dramatic. The simplest explanation, that paying work is keeping them busy, sounds too brassy and callous to Japanese ears, so it needs to be something that evokes pity. Pneumonia, a car crash, falling down an escalator and breaking both ankles — these are all real excuses I have heard. In fact, I've heard them all from the same creator, who was so unreliable and his excuses so outrageous that his editors used to place bets on what he'd say next. They even drew his imaginary family tree, ticking off his seven sick grandmothers as they passed away and caused delays.

He would accept invitations in a moment of weakness, then agonize for months about whether he would survive. He spent all year animating in a dark studio, which made him jumpy outdoors even in safe, secure Japan. Suddenly, he was getting ready to travel to big, scary Abroad, his sole previous experience of which was limited to endless TV repeats of *Real Crimes*, *Police Stop* and *Death to Japanese Tourists*. Although I might have made the last one up.

This August, many English-speaking members of the science fiction community are going to find out first-hand just what it feels like for the Japanese when they travel thousands of miles to a convention in a language they have no hope of understanding. That's because this year's World Science Fiction Convention will be in Yokohama. Luckily, I think the Japanese will be able to put their past torments to good use making sure that everything runs smoothly for their foreign guests. Unless, that is, they are feeling vengeful.

(*SFX Total Anime* #1, 2007)

NO FUTURE FOR YOU

Wong Kar-wai Tries Science Fiction

In 1982, an anonymous Hong Kong estate agent realized that repayments on a new mortgage application would extend past 1997, the year in which the north part of the colony was supposed to go back to China. Nobody had mentioned this for decades, but he figured he ought to check, just in case it affected the contract. He queried it. The shit hit the fan.

Chairman Mao had supposedly revoked all treaties dating before his Revolution, but regaining Hong Kong was too good for the Communists to forget, and by accident or design, they also asked for Hong Kong Island itself, which shouldn't technically have been covered by the Handover. Britain's Tory government sold the people of Hong Kong out, denying them British passports and siphoning money out of the territory in a cleverly designed airport development scam.

The new Basic Law made empty promises about democracy, but the colony would never see 2000 AD.

There was no future. Science fiction was in short supply; Hong Kong's film industry drowned itself in a fairytale past of flying sorcerers and cartwheeling kung fu.

But the day after the Handover was the Hangover, when everyone woke up and realized that nothing had really changed. There might have been a nasty taste in some people's mouths, but they'd made it to tomorrow. The future was fair game.

Wong Kar-wai was in trouble. His *Happy Together* had scooped international awards, but the government wouldn't let him shoot *Summer in Beijing*, because he liked to make things up as he went along and that meant the censors couldn't see his script. Thanks to Wong's haphazard methods, a comedy about cookery had somehow transformed into the tragic romance *In the Mood For Love*. Now his production company was so strapped he was considering subletting his offices. He needed a new movie, and decided on *2046*, a sci-fi fable about a privileged elite and an impoverished underclass. But Wong was new to science fiction, and loved the people, not the megacity they inhabited — even in his contemporary movies, he focused on human drama.

His best work to date is still *Chungking Express*, in which unrelated love stories somehow intersect at a pokey noodle bar. He tried something similar for *2046*, drawing on images of sex-robots and bar girls for a doomed romance between a hostess and a nightclub drummer; an android who tries to commit suicide by doffing her power-supply shoes; a Japanese man (played by *Ichi the Killer* actor Takuya Kimura) taking a train to the future to be with a robot version of his lost girlfriend.

But while Hong Kong inspired other people's cities of tomorrow, it was too much like home to Wong. Instead, he upped stakes for Bangkok, which he thought was squalid and grotty enough for his purposes.

Like many who turn to SF without a safety net, Wong stumbled. With the future footage not quite matching, he returned to a previous character, a failed author from his earlier *In the Mood for Love* (played by Tony Leung). *2046* now takes place in the 1960s, as a heartbroken hack writer pines for a love that never was while churning out sci-fi stories. 2046 is the number of the room next door, where a bar girl was stabbed by a former lover, inspiring the writer to set a similar story in his imaginary future. 2046 becomes a year in which nothing ever changes, and which nobody has managed to leave, not even the time travelers who take their vacation there. Moments of Wong's original future break through his 1960s narrative like adverts for a movie that never was, and the audience is left to speculate on what might have been.

(*Judge Dredd Megazine* #232, 2005)

MORE MARTIAL THAN THOU
Or How I Met My Wife

Since there are thirty people in the hall and they can all kill me with their little finger, I decide to keep my head down. I sit on a chair near the back, affording me a view of the small storage area where the spare mats are kept, where someone from a rival discipline has surreptitiously scrawled "Judo is Best" on the wall. Oh, those wacky Judo guys. If the Shorinji Kempo club catch them, there'll be hell to pay. Or the Tae Kwon Do club. Or the Shotokan Karate club. Or the Chado club. No, wait, *Chado* is the tea ceremony. The Judo guys can probably take them. Unless their adversaries have just boiled their water, in which case my money's on the little old ladies with the kettles and spoons.

As the branch master counts out the punches for his students, I feel at home.

Ichi, ni, san, shi…

I've been here before. In the decade since I began learning Japanese, I have heard those words a thousand times.

Go, roku, shichi, hachi…

I have heard them in Taiwan and Scotland, in Norway and France. Today, I hear them in Finland. I know exactly what the Finns are saying when they are shouting war cries in Japanese. When they revert to their native tongue, they are inscrutable strangers once more.

Just hours earlier, I was teaching them about manga translation at the University of Jyväskylä. You can look round any Japanese class and pick up the Reasons. That guy there is doing it because he has a Japanese girlfriend. That guy over there, he's doing it because he *wants* a Japanese girlfriend. That girl in the corner with the black hair and the lip piercings — she's a gothic Lolita. Her friend with the garish pencil case? Hello Kitty hugger. And the anime fans of course — the guy in the faded *Nausicaä* T-shirt trying to push Ghibli DVDs at the skateboarder with an *Akira* decal. But back in the distant past, when I was sitting at those desks, the classroom population was much simpler. There was me, and there was a gang of martial artists.

It's changed. It used to be that Karate came first. Then you got into anime after you got into everything else Japanese. Now, you become an anime fan, and *then* you decide you want to kick ass like something out of *Street Fighter II*.

I've never been one of those kung fu sorts. Sure, I would love to run up walls like Keanu Reeves, but the groundwork turns me off. When I was young, the other kids wanted to be train drivers and ballerinas, I wanted to be a Jedi. In a pinch, I'd have settled for Shaolin Master. And I figured that somewhere near my hometown there was a mountain-top retreat staffed by super-powered monks who would teach me the ways of the Force and the Twisting Dragon Lightning Kick.

I wanted a training scheme like Luke Skywalker's. While his friends chased through an asteroid field and got captured by Darth Vader, he ran around a forest for a couple of scenes, and did a few push-ups. It took him about thirty seconds of screentime, and then he walked around inside a tree-stump. This, apparently, was almost enough to qualify him as a fully-fledged Jedi knight, with all the levitating powers, hypnotism stuff, and running, jumping shticks that I liked. I could do that.

So I figured real life martial arts would be more of the same. I'd find the dojo and get my angry white pajamas, and after a couple of weeks, tops, I'd have a black belt and the power to bend reality.

Life turned out different. For starters, there was no mountain-top temple near my house, because there were *no freaking mountains*. And what martial opportunities existed were to be found down the local sports hall. So there was none of that olde worlde charm I was hoping for. Instead, the whole thing smelled of sweat and dust like all the other sports halls I had been in. And the kung fu masters didn't look like Obi Wan Kenobi or Yoda; instead they looked like my Phys Ed teacher. Was I going to volunteer for that? I didn't think so. It was too much like hard work.

Outside the sports hall, it is minus ten. An elfin Finnish girl dumps a handful of snow on my head and runs off laughing.

This I understand. I scoop up some of my own, mash it into a ball, and fling it after her. She throws some back. So do I. Neither of us are very good at it, because the snow is powdery. It's more effective to just flick scattershot handfuls at each other, which entails getting closer. When she's in range, I figure I'll trip her up.

I grab her arm.

When I regain consciousness, I am lying on my back in a snowdrift, staring up at stars through the pine trees. She is calmly pressing snow against my bleeding nose and lip.

"I'm sorry," she says. "I keep forgetting I am a deadly weapon."

(*Newtype USA*, January 2004)

RUBBER

M O N S T E R S

SOME KIND OF MONSTER

The History of Godzilla

According to popular legend, the name *Godzilla* came from the mixing of two other words — 'gorilla' and the Japanese for whale, '*kujira*'. Special effects boss Eiji Tsuburaya claimed it was a nickname for a big lunk of a guy on the Toho soundstage, but director Inoshiro Honda's widow Kimi isn't so sure.

"The backstage boys at Toho liked to joke around with tall stories," she says. "But I don't believe that one. There has to be a better reason, one thought out after careful consideration. That particular explanation is, well... claptrap."

The future Mrs Honda was a lowly script girl at the time that the pages for Toho's secret project began circulating. At first, it was just a Big G.

"When I was given the script for the *Godzilla* movie," explains monster actor Haruo Nakajima, "my part just said 'G'... Just 'Item G', that's all. The actual name did not appear anywhere in it. When I read through the script, it seemed as if he was some kind of monster."

There were plenty of inspirations. The most famous is the Lucky Dragon V Incident — in which a Japanese fishing boat was too close for comfort to one of the Bikini bomb tests. When one of the sailors died from the aftereffects of radiation poisoning, it caused a huge stir in Japan. Project G, however, was already underway, inspired in part by director Inoshiro Honda's memories of ruined Hiroshima, which he passed through after demobilization in World War Two.

A lesser-known influence was animated — the first cartoon to be shown on Japanese TV was the Fleischer brothers' *Superman* series, which included an episode, 'The Arctic Giant', in which a thawed dinosaur rampages through Metropolis. With Toho Studios looking for something gigantic to fight the rising popularity of TV, Honda hit on the idea of a big monster that could only work on a big screen.

During the run-up to shooting, Godzilla actor Haruo Nakajima approached Eiji Tsuburaya for advice on playing a monster that didn't exist. Tsuburaya sat him down in front of a copy of *King Kong*.

Nakajima was hooked: "I found *King Kong* very interesting, but all that action was stop-motion; shot one frame at a time. I asked Mr Tsuburaya how long it would take us to film using that method. He said, 'About seven years, but we only have three months. And that is why you're getting in that monster suit!'"

But even as the special effects boffins toiled, for the actors in 'Project G' there was still little idea of how the mystery monster looked. So it was back to the zoo, this time for Haruo Nakajima, who looked for clues in wild animals. "I spent ten days at the zoo. I'd watch the way the elephants walked, the monkeys, the gorillas, but especially the bears. I used to take two lunches with me. One was mine, and the rest of it I'd throw to the bears. When one of them snatched it up and shoveled it into his mouth, I'd watch the way he did it."

But at ground level, the human actors in the *Godzilla* series were still largely in the dark. Akira Kubo remembers the problems with being one of the first actors to have to react to something that wasn't there: "There's just you and the camera. You have to trust the director. So it's a very different kind of acting from straight, mundane drama. It's extremely difficult because you have to react to nothing. That's how it is, just imagination. But you have no choice about that. You have to rely heavily on the director's cue to let you know when to be shocked or surprised or scared."

Actor Kenji Sahara agrees: "Our acting had to be psychological. Mr Honda had told us how he wanted our performances. He said if a monster appeared in front of us all of a sudden, if you suddenly heard a crash behind you or a claw suddenly reached out and grabbed hold of you, what do you think *you* would do? That's what he wanted us to bring across in our performances. So he wanted a doubletake where we'd just turn and say, 'What the hell is...? *Aaagh*!' He wanted that kind of shock. And he told us to draw on our own psychologies for that performance.

He didn't want us to over-exaggerate; he didn't want an unnatural reaction. He wanted a kind of naturalism.

"Because the monster was so big, they had this big pole, and at the top of it he'd tie a handkerchief. And he'd say that's Godzilla over there. And so we'd be looking at a hanky on the top of a pole and pretending it was Godzilla. But it helped us with the reaction. We'd look over and know where to look for the 'Aagh!'"

Safe inside the suit, Haruo Nakajima felt hot, sweaty and anonymous. But he had the last laugh when the film came out.

"I wouldn't be looking at the screen," he says, "I'd be looking at the people in the next seats. I'd be trying to gauge from their reaction what they were thinking. When the human actors were on screen, the audience would be talking or eating something. They'd just chat amongst themselves. But when a monster turned up on the screen, they'd be locked on the action with a glint in their eyes, especially the children. Back in those days, they'd never seen anything like it before. That's what I remember from those days."

But that still doesn't explain how the letter G eventually became Godzilla. And if she knows the real reason behind her husband's decision, Kimi Honda isn't telling.

"Inoshiro Honda was the kind of man who was too honest to be so haphazard," she says. "Probably only a handful of people knew the true origin."

She sips from her teacup and smiles to herself.

(*NEO* #5, 2005)

METHOD AND MADNESS

Behind the Scenes on the Godzilla Movies

The modern-period *Godzilla* films brought new technologies and a new kind of actor. Instead of lurking in the zoo like his predecessor, the new *Godzilla* actor Kenpachio Satsuma concentrated on a form of method acting. Already an accomplished martial artist, he tried to teach his body to move as if it belonged to a different species. "I'd go through some martial arts exercises, lift weights trying to move from the waist, to try and keep those lateral movements, keep everything facing forwards, trying not to move my shoulders. This would go on for an hour and a half before shooting. So I'd be doing these movement exercises until it came as second nature."

But getting your body to move like a giant lizard is one thing. Actually doing it while suffocating inside a giant costume is another matter. "The real problem is the lack of oxygen inside the suit," explains Satsuma. "And the heat. And the weight. And the fact you can't see. It's hard to walk... And that all gets combined! And on top of all that you have to act, you have to destroy things; you have follow very precise directions, and consider the lighting and camera angles. But absolutely the worst part of all is the weight you have to carry. The previous Godzilla actors told me that it's even heavier than the suits they had. Back in the old days it was all plastic, but these days the more recent Godzillas are even heavier because of all the animatronics. I don't open the mouth or blink the eyes, that's all mechanical and operated by somebody else. But of course I'm the one who has to carry it all around, and that makes it even heavier than before. On top of all that, there's sweat running into your eyes. Your natural reaction is to panic with all these gunshots going off. Your brain's saying, 'Oh no! What do I do? I can't see!' That's what it's like inside."

For Satsuma, one of the most dangerous moments came when he wasn't actually inside the suit at all. While preparing a scene in *Godzilla vs King Ghidorah*, in which the two monsters crash into the Tokyo Metropolitan Government building, the director strung up the suits with wires and pulleys. Hovering over the set like the sword of Damocles was the 300 kilo King Ghidorah, suspended from just a few wires.

"They were still finishing the set," he explains, "and they were going to use wires to move the suits around. But at the time there was nobody inside the suits, because they were going to swing them around and then start off loads of explosions around them. So we were all watching them from the sidelines when they were setting it up, and the director was saying, 'You'd better get this right first time!' So everyone's getting ready for it, and the director was going, 'Oh! Hang on! Just raise it a little bit...'

He was trying to get them to draw the monsters just a little further back to have a longer swing. So they kept on tugging and tugging; it was all to make the eventual crash look more impressive. The further they drew them back, the bigger the crunch when they met… So they're going, 'Yeah, just a little bit more, just a little bit more…' And someone goes, 'Uh-oh… it's going to break…!' And the wires all start going snappity-snappity… And everyone realized at once… The wires gave way! And the effects crew all go, 'Look Out!!' And it catapults them all forward… And they're all yelling and hanging on… And the people standing at the side were running out of the way going, 'Aaagh!' You could see the director's life flashing before his eyes, everyone else's too… And it was so heavy that it actually broke the piano wires. It destroyed all the miniatures. It took a whole week to rebuild the set."

Minoru Nakano is swift to point out that the Toho special effects division did more than stamp on model buildings. "Eiji Tsuburaya didn't just do effects for monster movies. He worked with Akira Kurosawa on the Macbeth remake, *Throne of Blood*. If you look for him on the credits, you won't see Tsuburaya's name there, it just says Toho Special Effects Group, but when the forest comes to life in the film, that was Eiji Tsuburaya."

"The enterprises we were involved in were not always special effects. We couldn't invest in stop-motion, mainly because there was more to our output than straightforward monster effects. If we had to do airplane

FORBIDDEN COLORS

Attention to detail is something that director Teruyoshi Nakano knows only too well, since one of his proudest moments is invisible to Western audiences who only see the Godzilla films on video. The tiniest details in the final film, *Godzilla vs Destroyah*, were the subject of hours of heated debate among Nakano's crew: "We even have to think about color differentiation because we have to set Godzilla up against an atrocious monster. It's come from space, it has to be unexpected. It has to be something out of the ordinary. If you look at Godzilla, he's monotone with shades of grey, he's a very dark creature, so in opposition we used lots of bright colors. Firstly, we thought, what is the most vivid color we can use? We started out with green, but it wasn't very interesting. We'd used gold on King Ghidorah before but we hadn't used it on any of the other monsters. But when we tried green and silver together, there was a wonderful gradation of color. But the trouble is, of course, that when you watch it on a TV screen, the cathode ray tube can't reproduce the rainbow-color gradation. It's a film for movie theatres, it requires a gigantic screen. The detail only exists on a cinema screen. The really fine points of the monster's coloring only come out at that point."

shots and if you want to turn a plane in the air, we wouldn't have been able to utilize stop motion there, and so it wasn't worth the time in our studio system."

But without the constraints of time and budget, the distinctive *Godzilla* style would never have evolved. The fact that the Toho team could accomplish so much with so little is a miracle in itself.

(*Manga Max* #3, 1999)

LOCAL HEROES!
The History of Japanese SF TV

Is it a bird? Is it a plane? No, it was a super-powered man from Krypton, star of the live-action series *Adventures of Superman*. George Reeves' monochrome outing as the Man of Steel was such a big hit in Japan that its peak rating was a massive 74.2 percent. Few TV shows have managed to match it, but that didn't stop the Japanese trying. They came up with *Moonlight Mask* (Gekko Kamen), a homegrown motorcycle-riding superhero. Other imitators soon followed, and before long, Japanese networks were fighting to snag the talent and the airtime for their own local heroes. One factor united all the shows. Every one of them tried to impress its viewers by using special effects — *tokusatsu*. The name for the effects soon became the name of a genre, and the rubber monsters and transforming heroes of *tokusatsu* TV would become known all around the world.

TV ownership in Japan skyrocketed during the 1964 Tokyo Olympics. When the athletics were over, the next biggest rating was for an American import, Rod Serling's *Twilight Zone*. It was so highly regarded by the new TV audiences that the TBS network even gazumped rival channel NTV for the broadcast rights, stealing the US show after one season. TBS also experimented with its own knock-off, for which it approached *Godzilla* special effects technician Eiji Tsuburaya. Tsuburaya was greatly relieved, since he had recently bought an expensive optical printer which was all but useless for anything except special effects work. When his previous development deal with Fuji TV fell through, he welcomed the chance to put his kit to use for TBS, but he would need plenty of excuses for effects.

First he had to deal with the network. The concept initially labored under the title of *Frightening Theatre Unbalance Zone*, in which a team of investigating youths (plus token girl) would meet up each week in the Unbalance coffee shop in Tokyo's Ginza district (that's Boardwalk or Mayfair on a Japanese Monopoly board) and delve into paranormal mysteries. Under the steady hand of Tsuburaya, the idea was transformed by 1966 into *Ultra Q*, the adventures of a Japanese airline pilot and part-time science fiction author who moonlights as a paranormal investigator in order to get ideas for his stories.

While the episodes featuring the flying author and his cohorts still aired under the *Ultra Q* umbrella, Tsuburaya and his people had much more fun playing to their strengths — and if you're sitting on an optical printer and an army of model-makers, there's only one way to go. In the wake of *Godzilla*, they knew that the thing they were best at was monster-men and miniature work. In one story, the *Ultra Q* investigators walked around a model cityscape inspired by *Land of the Giants*, and, inevitably, returned to the same set in a later episode to stomp it flat while dressed as dinosaurs.

THREE MILLION LIGHT YEARS FROM HOME

The final episode of *Ultra Q*, which was to have been a *Doctor Who*-influenced story about a train that could travel in time, was pulled from the airwaves in order to make way for an experimental episode of something else. The producers kept part of the name and the logo to slip it past audiences, and hit upon the name *Ultraman*.

Ultraman combined the paranormal investigation of the *Twilight Zone* with the legendary success of the old *Superman* series. But *Ultraman* also retained elements of *Ultra Q*, since the alien space hero that travels three million light years to help the Earth gets off to a bad start when he collides with a plane. Dying from an unexpectedly fatal reaction to Earth's atmosphere, Ultraman combines his life force with the mortally injured pilot Hayata (Susumu Kurobe). Hayata survives, but as an alien symbiote, with the secret ability to transform into Ultraman when his powers are required. And since Hayata's day job finds him working for the Science Special Investigation Team, most episodes feature him needing to transform at least once: into basic Ultraman form, or into a suitably giant variant allowing him to fight invading monsters on equal terms. This latter condition, however, has a time limit, ostensibly because of his power source, but really because the program makers wanted to keep special effects work down to a manageable number of minutes per episode.

SPIES LIKE US

Ultraman is one of the most important Japanese TV series of all time, widely seen all over the world (but not, bizarrely, in many English-speaking countries) and with an influence that extends all the way to the present day. Anime, in particular, are packed with *homages*, from the dual life form of *Birdy the Mighty*, to the power-related time limits of *Evangelion*. But the Science Special Investigation Team wasn't the only group to have a show on Japanese TV. The similarly named Science Research Institute were the leads in *Operation Mystery*, a group of suited men in a bubble-car, whose scientific sleuthing pitted them against adversaries that included killer moths and time-traveling archaeologists 'stealing' cultural artifacts for the benefit of future museums. Kids with psychic powers joined a secret society in the *Tomorrow People*-influenced *Infrared Music*, or fought supernatural crime with CB radios in *Emergency 10:4 10:10*. The forgotten *Unbalance Zone* concept was dusted off and given an airing as just plain *Unbalance*, while Eiji Tsuburaya was enticed back by his former employees at Fuji TV to make *Mighty Jack*.

Tsuburaya's love for the shows of Gerry Anderson was so great that he once blagged his way onto the *Stingray* set to watch the filming. Inspired in equal measure by *Thunderbirds*, 007's Japanese outing in *You Only Live Twice*, and the Japanese success of *The Man From U.N.C.L.E.*, Tsuburaya came up with a team of heroes for *Mighty Jack*, fighting to save the world from terrorist organization Q. Whenever Q's cat-stroking leader plotted a new attack, the team would launch in their titular flying battleship, assembling the kit they needed en route using the vessel's onboard factory.

But the early 1970s weren't only the era of the spy thriller; they were also the zenith of monkey mania as the *Planet of the Apes* movie spawned several sequels and an American TV series. Not to be outdone, Tsuburaya made *Army of the Apes* (a.k.a. *Time of the Apes*), in which an earthquake at a scientific research facility causes three youngsters to seek refuge in the cryogenics chamber. They are defrosted years later to discover that Earth has been overrun by talking monkeys, although the masks worn by the actors were not good enough to permit dialogue, so the apes' voices were added later by anime voice-actors.

THE RISE OF THE ANTI-HEROES

While Eiji Tsuburaya's take on sci-fi remained resolutely positive and heroic, some of his rivals took a much more downbeat view. Shotaro Ishinomori invented *Cyborg 009*, an enemy agent who turns to the side of good and whose dark adventures were limited to manga and anime during the 1960s. But with the early 1970s oil crisis and increased American involvement in Vietnam, TV was ripe for something similar, and Ishinomori recycled his story for NET (later renamed TV Asahi). With a dash of *Ultraman* and a pinch of *Moonlight Mask*, he created the *Masked Rider* — science student Takeshi Hongo (Hiroshi Fujioka), injured in a motorcycle accident, only to be resurrected as a cyborg by the Shocker crime organization. Resisting his brainwashing, Takeshi fights his former masters as the Masked Rider, into which he transforms by hitting a certain speed on his motorcycle.

Masked Rider's success spawned two obvious imitators. One, the anime *Casshern*, sank without a trace for twenty-five years before its rebirth as a live-action movie. The other, the *tokusatsu* show *Kikaida*, lasted for barely two years, but survived in reruns for an entire generation. Created by *Masked Rider's* Shotaro Ishinomori (thereby ensuring that if it looked too much like a rip-off, he'd have to sue himself), *Kikaida* is another cyborg warrior created by an evil organization. However, he manages to escape before his programming is complete, and fights his former masters in a series that achieved unprecedented success in American cable reruns and eventually returned twenty years later in anime form.

GO GO POWER RANGERS

In 1975, TV Asahi had tired of the anti-heroes and their spy-inspired forerunners and plumped for a new twist to the superhero format. Gerry Anderson was an indirect influence once more, but not in terms of special effects. Instead, the channel and their financial partners, the Bandai toy company, observed how convenient it was to have five color-coded heroes, thereby allowing for five vehicles, five actors forced to share the limelight, and five opportunities for merchandise spin-offs. Shotaro Ishinomori was called in again, and pitched a fighting team of five 'rangers'. The result was *Himitsu* (Secret) *Sentai* (Fighting Team) *Go* (Five) *Ranger*, five young warriors who helped defend the Earth from the invading Black Crucifix organization.

Ishinomori's ranger concept was recycled over the following decade with minor changes. In 1977, it was *Jaqk*, five heroes themed around playing cards. In 1979, it was *Battlefever J*, with an international taskforce who fought with the power of dance, then martial arts-themed *Denziman* (the first to introduce masks to make stunt-work easier to film), animal-themed *Sunvulcan*, and so on. But the most successful of all these 'Super Sentai' shows was 1991's *Zyuranger*. Capitalizing on the hype surrounding *Jurassic Park*, *Zyuranger* built its five-person team around dinosaurs, and somehow managed to make its way to America as the *Mighty Morphin' Power Rangers*.

The Power Rangers craze briefly brought a number of other *tokusatsu* shows to the attention of the English-speaking world. *Gridman* was retooled as *Superhuman Samurai Syber Squad*, *Spielban* and *Metaldar* were combined to form *VR Troopers*, and *Bee Fighter* somehow became *Beetleborgs*. Meanwhile, *Power Rangers* itself motored along and has yet to stop.

There are other elements that are common to most of these later *sentai* series. The color-coded set-up and predictable episode pattern were defined initially by the restrictions of the shooting schedule but also by the demands of a very young audience. Just as the Telly Tubbies will always say *eh-oh*, the Power Rangers will always suit up and transform, in a plot progression that seems predictable to older viewers but cozily comforting to the under-fives.

A distinctive element, also found in many anime, is the prospect of redemption for the bad guys, or if not them, their henchmen. On more than one occasion, the Power Rangers have enlisted the aid of one of their enemies, only to keep them around for the next season. Another element, common from the days when an injury forced the original Masked Rider to bow out mid-season, is that the leading characters are interchangeable. Not all actors can be so easily discarded, however, as US distributors Saban Entertainment discovered to their cost when the Green Ranger left the show. Protests were so high from anguished parents, forced to deal with sulking children, that Green Ranger actor Jason Frank was later brought back as the White Ranger in the next season, and the Red Ranger in the one after that. Public opinion was not the only factor that kept Frank in the show — as a martial artist, he was far better suited to the punishing schedule that even the American cast had to deal with. Watch the *Power Rangers* movie, and you'll see that his moves are sometimes slowed down, while those of Blue Ranger David Yost (a mere thespian) are speeded up to match.

Although the Power Rangers don't enjoy their early 1990s craze attention any more, they are still a regular fixture on children's television, currently enjoying their fourteenth year fighting alien invaders.

FAN SERVICE

Modern-day *tokusatsu* television builds on forty years of development. *Ultraman* soldiers on in a darker, grittier version informed by the very show that once paid tribute to it, *Evangelion*. Meanwhile, other shows hope to capitalize on the fact that the original fans are now parents themselves. Contemporary seasons of *Masked Rider* have become renowned for pretty-boy heroes designed to appeal more to lonely mums than their offspring, while several of the more recent productions from

SOUNDS FAMILIAR?

"For the next thirty minutes, your eyes will apart from your body, and going out into the mystery zone." Not the world's best English, but a fair attempt at imitating the creepy opening of the *Twilight Zone* from Eiji Tsuburaya's *Ultra Q*.

the Tsuburaya studios have migrated from the morning kiddy slots to the late-night schedules. There, they are free to entertain adult *tokusatsu* fans, such as viewers of *Bunny Knights*, whose pretty heroines had an animated transformation sequence to catch the otaku audience. There is also the notable case of *Cyber Girls Thelomea*, a trio of super-powered ladies in skin-tight latex who work for a genetic engineering project to create a master race and also battle monsters on the side, with much ripping of clothing. It might not be a 'special effect', but it certainly holds the attention of the late-night audience, while the descendants of the early *sentai* shows continue to battle monsters in the mornings.

Japan, and the world, are safe from monsters for as long as the *tokusatsu* heroes are here to protect us.

(*NEO* #7, 2005)

TRIUMPH OF THE WILL

Review: *Casshern*

As a fascist Asian superstate finally conquers Europe, a Japanese scientist works with DNA samples harvested from a 'primitive ethnic population'. His attempt to bioengineer human spare parts for the war effort is almost successful, but the experiment goes awry, allowing hundreds of mutants to escape from the lab. Almost as an afterthought, the distraught professor dips the corpse of his war-hero son Tetsuya (Yusuke Iseya) in the magic goo. Tetsuya comes back to life, at a price. His muscles are so over-wrought they risk tearing his skeleton apart, leading a second scientist to contain his destructive power within super-strong armor. The result, after far too much backstory, is Casshern, a genetically engineered superhero who resolves to fight the remaining mutants — although there are now only four of them, and they have somehow walked halfway around the world to find a deserted enemy flying fortress, which they've taken over... along with its attendant robot army... and... did I mention the rocket-powered suit? No, neither did they.

An hour of *Casshern* affords fascinating glimpses of what could have been a superhero epic made by victorious Nazis — Leni Riefenstahl's *Ubermensch*, set in Berlin after the fall of London. Another hour plays more like an al-Jazeera ninja movie, with evil soldiers from an industrial civilization stealing a priceless resource from impoverished third-worlders. Throw in a couple of bits of stop-motion, and some full-on CG cityscapes in the style of the anime *Metropolis*, and the result is a car-crash of a film, sometimes with two soundtracks and two plots running simultaneously.

Although it's based on a cartoon not a comic, *Casshern* should be considered alongside the latest slew of Hollywood adaptations like *Hulk* and *Daredevil*. It takes a relatively obscure hero from the 1970s and gives him a big-time upgrade in a new medium. The original *Casshern* was a kid's show from Tatsunoko, the people who brought you *Battle of the Planets* and *Speed Racer*, but it never really took off, perhaps because its protagonist was highly derivative of two earlier wounded-cyborg anti-heroes, *Kamen Rider* and *Kikaida*. But *Casshern* has just enough name-recognition to inspire a remake, particularly when it has already been done once before, as a slightly darker 1993 video anime.

In this flabby live-action sumo wrestler of a movie, director Kazuaki Kiriya takes a scripting credit for himself, although the more experienced scenarists Shotaro Suga and Dai Sato also appear as co-writers. It is they, perhaps, who tried to rein in some of the original's excesses — the 1972 Tetsuya had a canine companion, Friender the transforming wonder-dog, here given a touching cameo as an everyday pet. The anime Tetsuya also had to deal with a mother transformed into Swanee the electric swan, whereas in the movie she is kidnapped by the baddies, but given her own little place to live on the fortress, and it appears, gets the chance to do a spot of gardening.

Like Sly Stallone in the ill-fated *Judge Dredd*, Tetsuya leaves his trademark helmet off — fans get a couple of glimpses of it on a shelf, but someone clearly thought that Yusuke Iseya's star-power face was best not concealed. But he's no oil painting, and such headgear would have made stunt work easier to shoot — one of the film's major shortcomings is that the martial arts scenes are rather obviously lacking martial artists, for

calmly solved all problems." Honda's wife, Kimi, who met him in 1951 when she was a script girl on his directorial debut, *The Blue Pearl*, said that Honda regarded himself as a documentary film-maker, even as his career steered him into ever more fantastical stories. "He only returned to Japan once the war was over. At that time, he passed through Hiroshima, and saw the atomic devastation with his own eyes. That planted the idea. That fear influenced his work. Without the Bomb, there could not have been the monsters."

In 1953, Honda directed *Eagle of the Pacific* (a.k.a. *Storm Over the Pacific*, a.k.a. *I Bombed Pearl Harbor*), a film about the 'Reluctant Admiral' Isoroku Yamamoto, who planned the 1941 raid on Hawaii even as he warned his superiors that the attack would "awake a sleeping dragon". The production brought Honda into close contact with Eiji Tsuburaya (1901-1970), an effects technician who specialized in miniature work for re-enactments of great air and sea battles on film. Although Tsuburaya was skilled in many areas of cinematography — responsible, among other things, for the moving forest in Kurosawa's *Throne of Blood* — it was his mastery of miniatures that led to Japanese monster films' most enduring trope: men in rubber suits destroying intricate model cities.

The pair were reunited for their most famous work, *Godzilla* (1954), by producer Tomoyuki Tanaka (1910-1997). A native of Osaka, Tanaka graduated in economics from Kansai University and began working for Toho in 1940. His credits, however, list no films before 1947, suggesting that he was low enough in the pecking order not to be tainted by associations with wartime propaganda. Leaving Toho to become an independent producer, Tanaka was credited on over 200 films in his lifetime, but the ones for which he is best known are the Godzilla franchise and the '8.15' sequence about the end of World War Two ('8.15' referring to 15 August 1945), beginning with *Japan's Longest Day* (1967).

The Luminous Fairies and Mothra, an allegorical sci-fi story first published in serial form in *Weekly Asahi* magazine, was intended by its authors to create a 'new monster' for the 1960s. Whereas the 1950s had been dominated by the nuclear specter of *Godzilla*, the 1960s saw Japan crushed between the Cold War opposition of the two great superpowers, Soviet Russia and the United States of America — contracted into the imaginary land of Russirica in the original story, altered to Rolisica (or Rolithica) in the film.

The original *Mothra* story formed during a period when both Japanese left- and right-wingers had hoped for the end of an ignominious Security Treaty with America, only to have their hopes dashed in a scandal that would lead to a prime ministerial resignation. Riots broke out over Japan's controversial renewal of agreements made ten years earlier under Allied occupation, permitting American airbases to remain in Japan. It was a reminder to the Japanese that the legacy of World War Two still steered their daily life, and it suggested that the wider world, particularly the USA, regarded Japan as an entity still in a larval stage, unsuitable for political decision-making on an international scale, fit only to be colonized and commanded by the victorious West. Japan was supposedly demilitarized, but had already served as an 'unsinkable aircraft carrier' for the US during the Korean War and the tense nuclear standoff of the Cold War.

Like Godzilla, Mothra was born out of nuclear paranoia, but she is also a creature infused with hope. Radiation poisoning is not a fatal disease on Mothra's island — instead, the flora and fauna have adapted. Much of the inspiration for *Mothra* can also be seen in *King Kong* (1933), with its emphasis on mankind's attempt to tamper with the natural order, and with the exacting of an elemental revenge.

The mixture of Japanese and Polynesian characteristics in Mothra's home island drew inadvertent parallels with Japan's pre-war expansion. It is implied, but not stated outright, that Japan has a right and obligation to protect the native islanders in the face of unwelcome foreign expansion — a restatement of the Pacific Mandate claimed by Japanese imperialists in the early twentieth century. However, the Japanese self-image in the first *Mothra* film is one of guileless innocence — the Pacific idyll of Infant Island (Beiru Island in the English translation), disrupted by the greedy self-interest of foreign carpetbaggers like Clark Nelson (Jerry Ito). In a sinister touch, the twin fairies are transformed into a circus act, although the Malay lyrics of their seemingly harmless song contain the distress signal that will summon their protector.

The words were the work of lyricist Shinichi Sekizawa (1920-1992), who would go on to win a Japanese Grammy award in 1964. It was reprised in several later *Mothra* movies, but Sekizawa was a man of many talents at Toho, and had also received directorial and script-writing credits. As the adapter of the original *Mothra* story for the screen, Sekizawa kept to the concerns of several other second-string creature features he had written for Toho — a 'lost world' scenario, a fearful monster and a science fictional spin. But whereas it is possible to deconstruct the motivation of most Japanese monster movies into either revenge or escape, Sekizawa's *Mothra* is different — she merely wishes to rescue her beloved fairy 'children'.

Mothra was intended as a family film, released at the height of the school summer vacation and planned as an effects extravaganza to distract children. It was one of several monster movies made in imitation of *Godzilla*, but with a greater emphasis on spectacle. The *Godzilla* films themselves were soon to lose the serious, chilling tone of the original, and enter a realm of self-parody; *Mothra* was the shape of things to come. Noriaki Yuasa, who would go on to direct the flying turtle movie *Gamera*, identified a distinct change in the attitudes of 1960s cinemagoers. "Audience expectations were very different after television. We couldn't make a film for all age brackets that would appeal to every single member of the family. So the people at the company said, 'Okay, let's just try and appeal to the children, and the adults will have to bring them.' That was a major factor in the gradual drift towards a juvenile audience."

Television also had an indirect influence on the choices available for *Mothra*'s cast. The film displayed an invisible undercurrent of talent exchange between cinema and television at a time when the two media were supposedly mutually antagonistic.

The leading role of 'Bulldog' Fukuda was taken by Frankie Sakai (1929-1996). Born plain Masatoshi Sakai in Japan's southwestern corner of Kagoshima, the heavy-set performer began his career as a jazz drummer, before moving into comedy, most memorably in a double-act in the style of Laurel and Hardy, with partner Ishiro Arishima. His early film roles were characterized by light entertainment vehicles such as *Young Jazz Girl* (1953) and *Jazz on Parade* (1954) — it is perhaps his lack of an early 'serious' profile that allowed him to do the unthinkable and perform on television.

The Japanese film world had a deep mistrust of the new medium, and sought to discourage any positive associations for it, even in the language used to discuss it. Serious cinema actors were often contractually forbidden from appearing on the 'brown screen', as studios disparagingly called it. But Sakai enjoyed a popularity with the primetime TV audience that producers hoped would translate into increased ticket sales, allowing him to switch between the two rival media with impunity. He also dabbled in serious acting, beginning with his shock casting in the one-off teleplay *I Want to Be a Shellfish* (1958), in which he played a kindly barber who is arrested for alleged war crimes. The award-winning drama garnered praise for both its controversial subject matter and its innovative technology — it was the first time that videotape was used in Japanese broadcasting, allowing scenes to switch from pre-recorded outdoor locations to Sakai's live studio trial.

The impasse between cinema and TV actors would continue until 1963, affording Sakai the opportunity to grab several male leading roles on the big screen in the meantime, where producers might reasonably hope his TV profile would encourage parents to attend children's movies with their offspring. *Mothra*, released on 30 July 1961, was a chance for him to shine, although his fame rarely traveled far from his home country. The only one of his roles to reach general Western audiences was his performance late in life as Lord Yabe in *James Clavell's Shogun* (1980), although some fans of Japanese animation may have heard his performance as Kapi the dog in the cartoon film *Nobody's Boy* (1970).

The role of camerawoman Michi Hanamura was played by Kyoko Kagawa (b.1931), an actress unquestionably of the cinema camp at the time *Mothra* was shot. With appearances in Kurosawa's *Lower Depths* (1957) and a leading role in Mizoguchi's *Sansho the Bailiff* (1954), she was firmly regarded as a film actress, and would not begin appearing on TV until the 1970s. She enjoyed a long career in drama, variety and daytime TV serials, but returned to the cinema late in life, including an appearance in the international hit *Shall We Dance?* (1996). She is one of a rare group of actors to successfully navigate from the role of an ingénue, through a career as a leading lady, into character parts in old age.

The dastardly Clark Nelson was played by Jerry Ito (b.1927), sometimes credited as 'Jelly' Ito, whose greatest claim to fame outside cinemas was as a presenter on the TV language program *Let's Play With English*. A native New Yorker, Ito was the son of a Japanese artist and a foreign model, whose Japanese-speaking ability was, in the words of Ishiro Honda, "truly terrible". His last known film appearance was in *Golgo 13: Assignment Kowloon* (1977).

As Dr Shinichi Chujo, Hiroshi Koizumi (b.1926) continued a career as the voice of authority in a crazy world. After graduating university in 1948, he initially joined NHK as an announcer, and found fame with multiple appearances as the love interest in TV and movie spin-offs of the comic strip *Sazae-san*. He was a celebrity panelist on the game show *Quiz Grand Prix* throughout the 1970s and has continued to appear in Japanese film, most recently alongside Mothra herself once more in *Godzilla Tokyo SOS* (2003).

The most memorable human stars of *Mothra* are the *shobijin* fairies (literally 'small beauties'), played by identical twins Emi and Yumi Ito (b.1941). Known collectively as The Peanuts, the girls had found fame in their late teens as pop singers and hosts on the TV series *Hit Parade* (1959). They moved on to a ten-year stint hosting the variety show *Soap Bubble Holiday* (1961), and had hits across three decades before their official retirement in their mid-thirties. Their songs, both in their original forms and in cover versions, regularly reappear as the themes to TV dramas and commercials, and the girls' success story is itself being adapted into a TV series.

Their movie roles were considerably more limited. Their twin status gained them a dual role in *I & I* (1962), a remake of Disney's *The Parent Trap* (1961) in all but name, and they reprised their *Mothra* roles on several occasions, but they remained largely figures of the television world. Notably, they did enjoy a small amount of fame in Germany, where singer Caterina Valente performed a local version of their hit 'Koi no Vacance' ('Love Vacation'). This led to some coverage for The Peanuts in the German media, and may have played a part in the broadcast of *Mothra* on German television in 1994.

Composer Yuji Koseki (1909-1989), likened by some critics to a

'Japanese John Phillip Sousa', began his career in 1937 and worked throughout the war era on stirring martial themes for films such as *Mr Marine* (1944) and Japan's first-ever feature-length animated film, *Momotaro's Divine Sea Warriors* (1945). He composed many of Japan's wartime hits, including the old favorites 'Sink the British Pacific Fleet', 'To the Battle in the Sky', and 'Pray to the Dawn'. Beyond the film world, his compositions included well-known anthems for three baseball teams, the Chunichi Dragons, the Hanshin Tigers, and the Yomiuri Giants, and post-war singles such as 'Scarlett O'Hara' and 'The Nagasaki Bells'. His work on *Mothra* came late in his career, the 102nd of his 111 movie credits, although his greatest moment was still to come. His 'Olympic March' was heard around the world at the inauguration of the Tokyo Olympics in 1964. Soon afterwards he would leave film behind to work in television, where he stayed until his retirement in his late seventies.

Filming *Mothra* required several facilities available to the Toho Studios. Location shooting was conducted before the start of principal photography, with a camera crew dispatched to Los Angeles to get some exotic foreign imagery — stock footage that would be used in several Toho productions. Main photography was undertaken in Tokyo, along with the miniature effects work required to allow Mothra to attack both Tokyo and the fictional foreign metropolis of Newkirk City — a combination of New York, San Francisco, and Los Angeles. Later *Mothra* movies would use a larva-form that was either electronic or operated by hand and hence relatively small, but this first film used human actors inside the larva-Mothra costume, necessitating the use of what are now known as 'bigatures' — miniatures on a larger scale than standard, requiring more detailed construction but allowing for a more impressive visual impact. In a reversal of the usual Toho effects trickery, several over-sized sets were also constructed, in order to make the twin fairies appear true-to-scale when matted into normal footage.

In Japan, where studios and vested interests often have a stranglehold on the press, reviews are customarily toothless, with praise for the deserving often lost amid puff-pieces for the unworthy. *Mothra*, however, attracted unusual complaints when a Hiroshima-Nagasaki survivors' group protested that its radiation imagery was in poor taste. Decades later, this adverse reaction kept *Mothra* off laserdisc, reducing its chances of reaching foreign audiences in any form but the American dub, which dropped thirteen minutes of footage.

The English-language voice track was laid down at New York's Titra Sound Studios. The dubbing director, Lee Kresel, had previously worked mainly in the field of dubbing Italian films, although he had also previously helmed the English-language dub of the anime feature *Alakazam the Great* (1960). *Mothra's* English script, which clung closely to the Japanese original, was written by Robert Myerson, who would subsequently also work on the English dub of *Gamera*. The English-language voice cast went largely uncredited, although one of the dubbing actors was Peter Fernandez, who would become one of the leading lights of the English-language anime industry in the 1960s and 1970s, working on shows including *Marine Boy*, *Astro Boy* and *Speed Racer*.

The English-language version opened in US cinemas soon after the Japanese release, but was largely dismissed by critics. *Variety* dubbed *Mothra*: 'A ludicrously-written, haphazardly executed monster movie… too awkward in dramatic construction and crude in histrionic style… even cinemutation buffs should wince at this one… A pretty embarrassing effort on the part of the Toho people to duplicate a Western screen staple.'

The film was screened in American theaters on a double bill with *The Three Stooges in Orbit* (1962), a situation that may have led the *New York Times* to be more forgiving: 'For several seasons now the Tokyo studios have been turning out this kind of diversion, with some kind of monstrosity terrorizing the country and rattling the screen in an overpowering blend of scenic effects, ranging from the obvious to the striking. This one is different, if not exactly superior… Although the direction, acting and dialogue are clumsy and absurd… [it] smites the eye with some genuinely artistic panoramas and décor designs… Some of the special effects shots are brilliant… As touchingly bizarre as we've seen in years.'

Four decades on, Amazon Japan's editorial review rates *Mothra* as 'a first-rate fantasy movie', lauding it for its humor, its effects, and its pioneering use of the anamorphic CinemaScope process (or 'TohoScope', as the studio would have it). In his book *Japanese Science Fiction, Fantasy and Horror Films*, critic Stuart Galbraith acknowledges that *Mothra* is 'preposterous' but notes: 'I had the good fortune to watch these pictures with the innocence of childhood… I was a kid, and I wanted films like *Mothra*… one of the genre's finest entries.'

CHINESE

A N I M A T I O N

In 2002, I was the guest curator of a Chinese animation season at the Udine Far East Film Festival. The essay and reviews in this section appeared in a special 2002 issue of the Italian magazine *Nickelodeon*, which also served as a brochure for the festival. An edited version of the entry on *Grandma and Her Ghosts* was subsequently used as part of the sleeve notes for the Taiwanese DVD version of that film.

Hidden from view for much of the twentieth century, China's animation industry has still managed to influence the rest of Asia. However, the political situation in China has often conspired against animators and stifled their potential.

The earliest innovators in Chinese animation were the Wan family, twins Laiming and Guchan with their brothers Chaochen and Dihuan. Inspired by screenings of American cartoons in Shanghai, the brothers began experimenting with animation techniques, initially gaining funding from advertising — their earliest works were used to sell a brand of typewriter. Their first 'real' cartoon, *Uproar in an Art Studio* (1926), featured a character coming to life on an artist's canvas, in a similar fashion to the Fleischers' *Out of the Inkwell* series. The Wans continued to dominate early Chinese animation, creating anti-Japanese propaganda in *The Price of Blood* (1932) and the first Chinese cartoon with sound, *The Camel's Dance* (1935). With Shanghai under Japanese occupation, they then began work on their most influential movie, China's first full-length feature, *Princess Iron Fan* (1941).

Taking three years, 237 artists and 350,000 yuan to make, *Princess Iron Fan* retold part of the popular Chinese folk-tale *Journey to the West*, specifically the duel between the Monkey King and a vengeful princess, whose fan is desperately needed to quench the flames that surround a peasant village. As only the third feature-length cartoon ever to be made (after Disney's *Snow White* and the Fleischers' *Gulliver's Travels*), it was a triumph for Asian animation and swiftly exported to wartime Japan. Its influences were far-reaching, inspiring the sixteen year-old Osamu Tezuka to become a comics artist, and prompting the Japanese Navy to commission Japan's first feature-length cartoon, *Momotaro's Divine Sea Warriors* (1945).

Fleeing Japan in the closing days of the war, *Momotaro's* producer Tadahito Mochinaga adopted the Chinese name Fang Ming, and was instrumental in the founding of an animation studio in Shanghai. Co-opted into the Communist propaganda machine, animators were encouraged to make cartoons that conveyed party doctrine. Notable among the films of this period is Te Wei's cel-animation *The Conceited General* (1956), initially mistrusted as an old-fashioned folk-tale, but soon praised as a Party allegory, reminding audiences that even the highest in rank must be humble in their dealings with others.

Animation flourished as Mao's 'Hundred Flowers Campaign' encouraged artistic endeavors in all walks of life. Qian Yunda's *Red Army Bridge* (1964) glorified the Red Army while lampooning their Republican enemies, in a tale of a bridge destroyed by fleeing landlords but repaired by noble Communist soldiers and defended by a peasant collective. The film was also a triumph of the dying art of cut-paper animation, masterfully imparting character and movement with extremely limited resources.

The same period saw the earliest example of 'brush animation' in Te Wei's *Where's Mama?* (1960). An homage to the watercolor paintings of Qi Baishi, it featured a group of tadpoles in search of their mother, pestering chicks, crayfish, goldfish, turtles, and a catfish before eventually locating her. The unique style, which imitated an artist's brush work on a page, fast became a distinctly Chinese hallmark, repeated in *Buffalo Boy and the Flute* (1963) by Te Wei and Qian Jajun. The style would reach its creative peak with Te Wei's *Feeling From Mountains and Water* (1988), the simple tale of an aging musician, cared for by the young boatman who has just delivered him to shore. The sentimental story is dwarfed by its scenery — true to the tradition of the *shan sui* (literally 'mountains and water') watercolor paintings it emulates, humans are all but lost amidst striking images of hills, lakes, and waterfalls.

The Wan brothers were not inactive during this time. Wan Laiming animated the earliest chapters of *Journey to the West* under the title *Havoc in Heaven* (1961 and 1964).

However, the onset of the 1965 Cultural Revolution destroyed China's animation business for a decade. The animators were scattered across the countryside and forced to 're-educate' themselves by working on farms. After the fall of the Gang of Four in 1976, Chinese animation tried to pick up the pieces. The most famous result is A Da's *Three Monks* (1980), a simple tale of three squabbling Buddhists, made as an allegory for the lack of communication between neighbors during the Cultural Revolution.

Another parallel can be seen in China's first-ever widescreen animation, *Nezha Conquers the Dragon King* (1979), directed by Yan Dingxian, Wan Shuchen, and A Da. Retelling the Chinese myth of the child superhero Nezha's war against four evil dragons, the movie's subtext wasn't hard to spot — the real-world enemies of Chinese animation were not dragons, but the Gang of Four themselves, the instigators of the Cultural Revolution. Similar ridicule awaited the Mao era in *Super Soap* (1987), in which a canny businessman bleeds the town, and the film, of all color, before playing his trump card and playing on the people's desire for fashions and fads. Similarly, in Zhou Keqin's *Monkeys Fish For the Moon* (1981) a group of apes embark on a tough mission to obtain the unobtainable, bound to end in disappointment.

A sense of loss permeates many post-Cultural Revolution anime. Sometimes, as in *Nezha* and *Super Soap*, it comes out as a sardonic satire. Sometimes it is more bitter, such as the desolate parade of death and injustice in A Da's *Wanderings of Sanmao* (1984). The titular Zhang Leping comic character was a popular icon in A Da's youth, and also lent his name to Cantonese actor Hung Kam-bo, better known as 'Sammo' Hung. Starting as a light-hearted comedy, the sepia-toned cartoon soon slumps into tragedy, with A Da's frustration at the Party projected onto more acceptable enemies — invading Japanese soldiers.

Political and economic changes in the 1990s brought fresh

opportunities into the Chinese animation business. The gradual thawing of relations with Taiwan allowed for greater collaboration among Asian nations, particularly between the many smaller studios like Taiwan's Wang Films and Shenzhen's Jade Animation, which had formerly worked as subcontractors for American and Japanese animation companies. The acquisition of Hong Kong also made the People's Republic an overnight heir to decades of independent Cantonese animation. Released in the year of the fateful handover, Andrew Chan's *A Chinese Ghost Story: The Animation* (1997) was a remake of Tsui Hark's famous kung fu movie, but with an animation director poached from Japan. Its production exploited the links between Hong Kong and the PRC just over its borders, and was released in both Cantonese and Mandarin editions.

Despite being made in the People's Republic and loaded with references to Chinese myth, Chang Guangxi's *Lotus Lantern* (1999) owed its greatest debt to the Disney Corporation. Though the resulting mix of songs and knockabout comedy is somewhat chaotic. Better critical success was enjoyed by Lee Chooman and Wang Shaudi's Taiwanese-Korean co-production *Grandma and Her Ghosts* (1998). Drawing for inspiration on Hayao Miyazaki's *My Neighbor Totoro* (1990) and *Kiki's Delivery Service* (1989), the film is a crash-course in Chinese folk mythology, concealing several parables for children that both encourage kindness in this life, and affirm a strong belief in the next. In its portrayal of three very different generations of a single Chinese family (peasant grandmother, yuppie mother, and slacker child) *Grandma and Her Ghosts* manages to maintain its ethnic identity while speaking to audiences across the Asian region — a recipe for success that its successors would be advised to emulate.

As with animation industries all over the world, the future of Chinese cartoons is inevitably bound to the development of computer technology. In this arena, the People's Republic lags far behind, but the new 'Autonomous Region' of Hong Kong has led the way ever since the all-CG animation *Cyber Weapon Z* (1995). Computer graphics have played increasingly large roles in recent Chinese films, most notably the special-effects extravaganza *Storm Riders* (1998), and mixed live-action/animated films such as *Old Master Cute* (2001). Nowhere is the influence of CG more apparent than in Toe Yuen's *My Life as McDull* (2001), a feature-length spin-off from the Hong Kong comic and TV cartoon *McMug* (1991). A series of vignettes about a Hong Kong piglet, *McDull* was hailed by some critics as a uniquely Cantonese production, though it still bears the hallmarks of an international animation culture — originally inspired by writer Brian Tse's encounter with the works of Raymond Briggs, the style veers between Sanrio's super-simple *Hello Kitty* and Isao Takahata's *My Neighbors the Yamadas* (1999).

The next few years in Chinese animation are liable to build on the success of *McDull*, as the technologically-advanced Hong Kong region brings funding to the waiting animators of the Shenzhen and Shanghai economic zones. The cartoons produced by this marriage of complementary talents can now flourish in the world's biggest sales arena. With a potential audience of over one billion, Chinese animation has the opportunity to financially outperform many of its foreign rivals before it has even left the domestic market — a sobering thought for both the Disney kingdom and the emperors of anime to bear in mind.

PRINCESS IRON FAN

While on their Journey to the West, Tripitaka, Monkey, Sandy, and Pigsy cross a valley suffused with almost unbearable heat from the nearby volcano known as the Mountain of Flames. Monkey goes into the heart of the volcano, but is forced to retreat by local fire-demons. Instead, he decides to borrow a famous magical fan, whose first sweep can summon forth incredible winds, and whose second can call down massive rainstorms. However, the spirit princess who owns the fan refuses to cooperate, since Monkey is responsible for the death of her son. Instead, she uses the fan to blow him away.

After obtaining a magic pearl that negates the fan's effects, Monkey returns, transforming into an insect and landing in the Princess's tea. Washed into her digestive tract, he causes havoc with her internal organs until she agrees to give him the fan, but after he leaves her body, she fobs him off with a fake.

Meanwhile, Pigsy seeks the aid of the Princess's lord and master Buffalo, a demon who is understandably annoyed, not only because

Monkey has killed his son, but because Pigsy clearly covets his wife. Pigsy sneaks into Buffalo's palace disguised as a frog, and after accidentally getting inhaled partway up the nostril of Buffalo's pet stegosaurus, steals the animal. He rides it back over the hill and poses as Buffalo, telling the Princess that Monkey is in the vicinity and that he needs to borrow her fan to deal with him.

The triumphant Pigsy returns with the fan, but instead of handing it to Monkey, he is duped into giving it to Buffalo, who has adopted a Monkey disguise. The real Monkey and his traveling companions fight with Buffalo, who transforms into a real Buffalo and is trapped in a split tree-trunk. When informed of her husband's capture, Princess Iron Fan reluctantly hands over the fan to secure his release, and Monkey successfully douses the volcano's flames to allow the travelers to continue on their pilgrimage.

The first feature-length cartoon to be made in China, *Princess Iron Fan* exerted an incredible influence on the Asian animation market. Made in Shanghai during the Japanese occupation, it established many precedents for the Chinese animation industry, including the use of songs and bouncing-ball subtitles, and the popularity of *Journey to the West* as a source of traditional stories. It also inspired the Japanese to make their own animated feature, indirectly pollinating the early anime industry. *Princess Iron Fan* was cited as a major influence on Japan's greatest manga artist, Osamu Tezuka, who claimed to have been inspired to enter the field after seeing it as a boy in 1943.

Princess Iron Fan is notable for several bizarre moments of throwaway humor, in the comic style of later Warner Bros. cartoons. These include the opening scene in which Pigsy can be seen pulling off one of his own ears to use as a fan, before reattaching it without a word — a bit of pantomime business that may have made more sense in live theatre, where the part would more obviously be played by a man in a mask. This aspect continues in the depiction of the Princess's first use of the fan, which results in a local cat losing all its fur, a local maid losing her bedclothes, and a nearby house only hanging onto its roof with the aid of cartoon hands. It reaches the peak of surrealism when Pigsy steals the stegosaurus, which he does by sucking on its tail until it deflates, rolling the flattened creature up like a rug, and carrying it away.

The film makes heavy use of rotoscoping in an attempt to hide inexpert animation. This process of drawing over live-action footage of real human actors serves to make the humans' movements almost impossibly fluent and accomplished, while the non-human cast are noticeably less well-realized. Certain of the demonic and immortal characters, such as Buffalo and Pigsy have clearly been portrayed by live actors wearing masks, since the animators' skills do not quite run to adding realistic facial details to these cast members. Nevertheless, considering the resources available to the Wangs at the time, the film is a stunning achievement and contains some genuine innovations, such as the sparkling dress worn by one of Buffalo's wives — one can only imagine the shame and envy it engendered in an audience of Japanese propagandists, who hastily commissioned *Momotaro's Sea Eagles* (1943) and *Momotaro's Divine Sea Warriors* (1945) in an attempt to prove that Japan, too, could produce animation to a Chinese scale and standard.

RED ARMY BRIDGE

When news arrives of the approach of the Red Army, the local landowners in Hunan province flee for their lives, partly demolishing a rickety bridge to seal off their escape route. The feared Communists, however, turn out to be friendly heroes, who co-operate with the peasant locals to repair the bridge. The renamed Red Army Bridge appears imbued with the spirit of Communism — when the rich fugitives return, one of them slips and falls while crossing it. Soon, however, the area is invaded by the jack-booted, goose-stepping soldiers of Chiang Kai-Shek's Republican Guomindang (KMT) forces. Fearful of an ambush, the cowardly KMT soldiers argue among themselves about who should approach the bridge. The first soldier to do so barely escapes with his life when his hat is pierced by a crossbow trap. The commander decides he will tear down the 'Red Army' sign on the bridge, but falls through a loosened board and lands in the river. The wily peasants then scare off the rest of the KMT with firecrackers, which their enemies mistake for gunfire.

An entertaining eighteen-minute propaganda movie, all the more interesting for its accomplished paper-cut animation, often indistinguishable from more expensive cel techniques, Qian's *Red Army Bridge* juxtaposes ruddy-cheeked, plump peasantry with pallid, gnarled Republicans. It was released during the so-called "anti-Rightist" backlash to Mao's Hundred Flowers campaign, but although its revolutionary fervor seems obvious to this day, it was withdrawn from circulation in 1965 on account of its highly stylized artwork, deemed too "reactionary" for a modern audience. It was shown in Annecy in 1965 — director Qian previously studied puppet animation under Jiri Trnka.

THREE MONKS

An orange-robed monk is praying to Guanyin when he realizes that the plant in the offertory vase has run out of water. He must walk all the way down the hillside to the lake to get more water but the effort is worth it — the Goddess of Mercy smiles upon him. A second monk, this time clad in blue, comes to the temple, and water becomes an issue between them. Eventually they agree to help each other bring water up the hillside, but the compromise reduces the amount of water they can provide — one monk can balance two buckets on a single pole, but two monks carrying a pole between them can only put one bucket in the centre. A third monk, a fat man in yellow robes, brings even more discord to the temple, since he is constantly thirsty and very unreliable at drawing water from the lake.

Eventually, the monks are no longer on speaking terms, and sulk over their dinner. They all develop hiccups and, without any water to wash down his food, Orange actually drinks the water from Guanyin's vase. The temple mouse, tiring of their antics, starts a fire by gnawing through an offertory candle, and the monks almost see their temple burn down. They realize the error of their ways, and install a winch on the cliff-top, allowing them to exploit their strengths and bring enough water for all.

A Da's 1980 cartoon began as an allegory for the lack of communication between neighbors during the Cultural Revolution, but also contains some marvelous uses of caricature — each monk has his own personality, defined as economically as possible with movement and actions.

MONKEYS FISH FOR THE MOON

A group of forest monkeys become entranced by the sight of the moon. They clamber into the mountains in an attempt to retrieve it, and when it still proves to be out of reach, they stand on each other's shoulders. This, too, ends in failure, until the monkey leader notices that the moon is reflected in the waters of a nearby pool. They form a simian chain to reach into the pond, but the moon's reflection scatters when they try to grab it. Eventually, they scoop up the water in a discarded melon rind — the water remains calm in the bowl-like receptacle, and the monkeys believe that they have captured it at last. However, during their celebrations, they quarrel and the "bowl" is broken. The waters scatter and, looking up, the monkeys believe that the moon has escaped once more into the sky.

Made with paper-cut animation, with the famous artist A Da as art director — he is also responsible for the monkeys' victory dance.

HAVOC IN HEAVEN/UPROAR IN HEAVEN

The Monkey King watches his subjects practicing with their weapons, and is so excited that he grabs one for himself. However, no blade seems good enough for him. Hearing that the Dragon King (see *Nezha Conquers the Dragon King*, p147) has many excellent weapons, he bullies his way into his underwater palace. The Dragon King shows him the fabled Gold-Banded Cudgel, and jokes that Monkey is welcome to take it if he can carry it. Much to the Dragon King's annoyance, Monkey discovers that the cudgel obeys orders. He shrinks it to a portable size, and makes off with it, causing the wily King to complain to the Jade Emperor that Monkey has stolen it. It is decided that Monkey should be offered a sinecure position in Heaven to keep him out of trouble — ministers select Master of the Heavenly Stables as suitably small fry. Initially affronted at such a lowly post, Monkey soon begins to enjoy his new job, though it causes chaos in the stables. Proclaiming himself to be the Great Sage Equal of Heaven, Monkey returns to Earth to sulk, where he is pursued by the heavenly warriors Lijing and Nezha. He defeats them, and is offered another minor post, this time in charge of the Peach Orchard. Insulted that he is not invited to a banquet of immortals, he causes the attendees to fall asleep, and drinks the wine himself and drunkenly eats the forbidden Peaches of Immortality. He flees home once more, and is pursued by the three-eyed Erlang and his dog (see *The Lotus Lantern*, p152). They defeat him and the gods decide to burn him in a furnace, but he is now immortal and untouchable. He returns to his Fruit and Flower Mountain, where he hopes to live in peace.

Originally released in two parts (1961 and 1964) Wan Laiming's cel animation retelling of three early chapters of *Journey to the West* was to become the signature cartoon of the Shanghai Animation Studios. Making strong use of Beijing Opera motifs, particularly in music and movement, the brightly-colored film also received Party approval — at the time, it was regarded as a metaphor for the "havoc" caused in bourgeois China by the young, dynamic Chairman Mao. Shown to acclaim in Locarno in 1965, its lead character's distinctive theatrical-simian features have made him the logo-animal for the studio, and inevitably led to his appearance in several other Chinese cartoons, from the semi-sequel *Monkey Conquers the Demon* to less accomplished cameos in *Lotus Lantern* and *Dingding vs the Monkey King*.

NEZHA CONQUERS THE DRAGON KING

After a long gestation period of three and a half years, General Lijing's wife finally gives birth. But instead of a child, Lijing finds a strange fleshy ball like the closed petals of a plant. Slicing it open with his sword, he finds a tiny finger-sized boy inside. The immoral Taiyi arrives on a crane, bestowing Nezha (for so he is named) with the Cloth of Celestial Confusion and the Cosmic Ring. The boy soon grows up, but the land of his birth is constantly troubled by the predations of four dragon kings who bring storms, floods, fire and ice to the humans.

One day, tiring of the animal sacrifices hurled into the water to appease him, Aoguang, the Green Dragon King, instructs his goblin attendant Ligen to bring him a human child to eat. Nezha is playing at the water's edge with two of his friends, one of whom is dragged beneath the waves by Ligen. The angry Nezha strikes the waters with his cloth and ring, causing shudders to resound through the Palace of the Dragon King. Ligen tries to stop him, and in the ensuing duel, Nezha's ring turns him into a toad. Enraged at this insult, the Dragon King sends his son Aobing to punish Nezha, but Nezha proves too strong for him. The demonic Aobing tries to escape by returning to his true dragon form, but Nezha kills him and rips out his spinal cord to use as a whip, discarding the corpse in the sea, where the Dragon King swiftly finds it.

The Dragon King demands that Lijing punish Nezha suitably (an eye for an eye and a son for a son), and Lijing has trouble arguing, since Nezha happily admits that it was he who killed Aobing. Nezha tries to return the spinal cord, but the Dragon King goes back on his word and tries to report the incident to the Heavenly Court anyway. Nezha fights the Dragon King in front of the court, tearing out some of his scales before he surrenders. However, as soon as he is safely back in his undersea pavilion, he summons his three brothers to fight back. The four dragons create a succession of natural disasters, and demand that Lijing kill Nezha in atonement. Lijing, however, cannot bring himself to do so, and the dutiful Nezha eventually takes his own life.

While the four Dragon Kings celebrate at a lavish undersea banquet, Nezha is brought back to life by Taiyi. He goes into battle against them, accompanied by a Fiery Phoenix (not dissimilar in shape to the one in *Battle of the Planets*!), which sucks up the fire blown at him by the Red Dragon, and then uses the heat it stores to melt the ice blown at him by the White Dragon (with additional wind-chill provided by the Black Dragon). Eventually, Nezha defeats them and saves the day.

The first widescreen feature animation made in China (artlessly panned and scanned in this VCD presentation), *Nezha Conquers the Dragon King* combines several elements from *The Creation of the Gods* (*Feng Shen Ban*), a Ming Dynasty chronicle of ancient myths, itself later animated in Japan as *Soul Hunter*. As with many other Shanghai Animation productions, there is an inevitable connection to the Monkey King, though this one is distant — Nezha also appears as one of Monkey's foes in *Havoc in Heaven*. This might make him seem like a strange choice for a feature, but the movie's subtextual appeal takes on new meaning in the light of the earlier fall of a very different Gang of Four in 1976 — the real-world enemies were not Dragon Kings, but the instigators of the Cultural Revolution.

The folk-tale is well known in the rest of Asia, and is the remote inspiration for the anime *Legend of the Four Kings*. In the anime series *Gundam Wing*, Nezha (in its Japanese form *Nataku*) is the name given by Wufei to his giant robot. There was also a live-action Chinese movie, *Nezha* (1982).

MY LIFE AS McDULL

When she gives birth in inauspicious circumstances, Hong Kong sow McBing decides it would be arrogant to name her son McNificent as planned. Instead she calls him McDull, and the piglet grows up with a humble name to match his humble nature. He attends school with a collection of other animals, including fellow piglet McMug, cat Darby, cow twins May and June, Fai the turtle, and Goosie the goose. Despite the incompetent antics of their teacher Miss Chen, the young animals do just fine. When McDull is taken ill, his mother rashly promises to take him to the Maldives when he recovers, but realizes that she can't afford it. Instead of "breaking her promise", she engineers a long journey to the Hong Kong hinterland, where some carefully placed fake signs convince her gullible son that they really have flown to the Indian Ocean. During their vacation, McBing is inspired by a news report of a successful Olympic athlete. She encourages McDull to take up sport, and the piglet soon begins training in the new sport of bun-snatching. However, his Olympic hopes are dashed and he returns to his former life, taking time to discuss with the audience his love of Christmas turkey and his hope for the future.

My Life as McDull is based on *McMug*, a 1991 comic strip by Brian Tse and Alice Mak. Tse was a Hong Kong writer who discovered the works of British illustrator Raymond Briggs while studying in Sydney. Mak was the artist who transformed Tse's work into a simplified art style redolent of *Hello Kitty*. Naturally, merchandising spin-offs soon beckoned, and the *McMug* menagerie soon got their own magazine, *Yellow Bus*, as well as the first animated TV series to be commissioned, produced and broadcast as a solely Hong Kong production.

This movie spin-off continues the spirit of director Toe's TV series, with a dizzying array of techniques jostling for attention, including 2-D cel animation, pencil work, paper-cuts, fully-rendered CG, and even unadulterated live-action. Despite its claims to be a wholly Cantonese production, it remains tempting to draw parallels with several foreign works. In particular, the loosely linked vignettes and washed-out colors strongly resemble Isao Takahata's *My Neighbors the Yamadas*. Designed for an audience with the attention span, linguistic ability and love of repetition of the very young, the script nevertheless conceals many in-jokes for the parents in the audience.

GRANDMA AND HER GHOSTS

When his mother goes to visit his father abroad, city-boy Doudou is dumped in a south Taiwanese fishing village with Grandma, a fish-ball vendor and sometime spirit-medium. Grandma has little time for him because it is the height of summer and there are ghosts to appease in two local festivals. The gate to Heaven will soon close for the year, and lost spirits must be guided through to their next life. Grandma must feed hungry ghosts, keep genuinely evil spirits at bay, and provide restless souls with floating lanterns. Sulking at the lack of urban comforts, Doudou peeks into a forbidden outbuilding, and accidentally frees an evil spirit that possesses Grandma's cat Kulo.

Kulo convinces the homesick Doudou that he can go home if he sells his Grandma to the devilish rag-and-bone man, a deed which involves making her weep three times. But Grandma's tears also give Doudou the power to see that spirits really *are* wandering the village. Local boy Ah Ming has befriended the gigantic ghost of a beached orca, and the children help it learn to swim again. Doudou also promises to help Flat, a ghost snake squashed in a car accident, and Apple, a shy schoolgirl ghost, the circumstances of whose tragic death are discreetly kept off-screen. However, the possessed Kulo is eating up all the souls in the vicinity, and must be stopped.

A crash-course in Chinese folk mythology, *Grandma and Her Ghosts* conceals several parables for children, preaching kindness in this life, and affirming a strong belief in the next. Its attitude towards death is refreshingly straightforward — a girl is advised not to cry at a funeral, and tartly asks if it is better to be laughing, while the film is confident enough in the afterlife to make a character's death the central joke of the final scene. Buried even deeper is something for the adult audience, a yearning for the innocence of youth (the ability to see ghosts fades with age) and a gentle nudge that it is not only the kids who should work harder on others' behalf.

The film excels at portraying the generation gap through its characters. Grandma is a working-class, Taiwanese-speaking widow who must actively concentrate to speak Mandarin to her grandson, while her daughter is a well-spoken urban yuppie, resigned to long months without her husband while he works abroad to raise money for a house. Asides reveal that she married without Grandma's approval, and that they have barely spoken for six years. Doudou is a cosseted only child, used to designer sneakers, gaming consoles, and air-conditioning, for whom Grandma's leaky seaside cottage at first seems like Hell on Earth. And yet, by the time the closing credits roll, Doudou has learned new respect for others, his mother has swallowed her pride, and Grandma is yammering into a mobile phone.

Comparisons are inevitable with Tsui Hark's animated *Chinese Ghost Story* (1999), which similarly imposes modern mores on the spirit world, but does so with an appreciably higher budget. Both films must have begun production at around the same time, but *Grandma and Her Ghosts* wears more obvious influences from two *Japanese* cartoons released in Taiwan in the early 1990s. With an urban child sent to the countryside because of parental illness, eventually coming to love and respect the rural tradition, it owes a clear debt to *My Neighbor Totoro*. Both films also feature a wrinkled, knowing crone in a supporting role, and moments in *Totoro* foreshadow the dawdling mushroom mini-ghosts that Grandma shoos from the house, as well as the Cheshire-cat grin adopted by the possessed Kulo. Taiwan's local dialect is still awash with Japanese loanwords fifty years after the colony gained its independence, but black cat Kulo and white dog Shilo have Japanese names *and* pedigrees, resembling similar animal characters in *Kiki's Delivery Service*. Anime influences extend further, with Super-Deformation in sequences that portray the characters as diminutive caricatures of themselves, and one sweet moment in which the guardians of Hell assume Super-Deformation form in order not to scare the timid Apple. The inescapable influence of

Japanese pop culture also appears in a couple of in-jokes, such as when Doudou's guilty conscience causes him to dream of his grandmother as a character in a *Tekken*-style computer game or a doll attired as *Sailor Moon*.

THE LOTUS LANTERN

In a time when gods still ruled directly over men, Sang Shengmu chooses to leave Heaven and renounce her immortality, preferring instead to remain on Earth with her human lover. Seven years later (the lover having disappeared without a trace), Shengmu's brother, the chief god Erlang (also seen in *Havoc in Heaven*), kidnaps her young son Chenxiang. Tricked into meeting with her brother to discuss ransom, she is imprisoned beneath a mountain. Wandering the halls of Heaven unattended, Chenxiang befriends a little monkey (called, unsurprisingly, Xiaoyi — Chinese: 'little monkey'), and hears the tale of Sun Wukong, the legendary Monkey King, from a kindly old man who claims to be the God of the Earth. When Chenxiang hears that the Monkey King was once also imprisoned beneath a mountain, he decides to seek him out and ask for advice on rescuing his mother. Stealing his mother's divine lantern back from Erlang's treasury, Chenxiang meets Gamei, the daughter of a human chief, held hostage in Heaven until her father completes a statue in Erlang's honor. Back on Earth, Chenxiang must rescue Xiaoyi from Fashi, an itinerant swindler (with a strong Beijing accent!), and evade an old woman who is really Erlang's dog in disguise. Then, after two pointless musical interludes (which spring suddenly upon the audience after a song-free first half), Chenxiang has now become an adult, and finally meets the Monkey King. Now a Buddha and uninterested in the affairs of mankind, Sun Wukong does not desire to help him, until Chenxiang reminds him that he is the Buddha of Fighting and honor-bound to combat injustice. He also plays a parental card, noting that Wukong was born from a stone and hence could never understand the depth of his pain.

Relenting, Wukong gives him the white Dragon-Horse once ridden by his former master Tripitaka, and tells him that if he pushes a certain magical rock into a lake of fire he will gain a stone axe that will allow him to defeat Erlang. Unfortunately, the rock in question is the statue being carved by Gamei's tribe. In the interim, her father has died, and she has been released from imprisonment to complete the work. Although her entire tribe will be imprisoned if the mission fails, she agrees to help Chenxiang, and the villagers push their statue into the nearby volcanic pit. Chenxiang rides in on the Dragon-Horse and retrieves the magical axe. He almost loses his final battle with Erlang, but Sun Wukong turns up at the last minute and lights the Lotus Lantern, thereby imbuing Chenxiang with supernatural powers. Chenxiang frees his mother from her prison, and the two are reunited on the crest of a rainbow.

Despite being made in the People's Republic and loaded with references to Chinese myth (the film grinds to a complete halt for several minutes while the Earth God recaps the story of *Havoc in Heaven*), *Lotus Lantern's* heaviest influence is the staunchly capitalist Disney empire. Featuring half-hearted power ballads, a love-story between a demigod and a chieftess, a central cast inspired by *Aladdin* and shots pastiching *The Lion King*, *Lotus Lantern* seems reverse-engineered to import a little American magic to China, and even comes with a reference to the opening of the Barcelona Olympics, at which an archer lit the torch with a fiery arrow. Meanwhile, the Monkey King appears like a reluctant superstar in a contractual cameo — talked about for much of the film, but of relatively little importance, his appearances seem judged purely to draw some sort of continuity between *Lotus Lantern* and earlier Shanghai animations such as *Havoc in Heaven*.

The plot is a mess from start to finish, and sawn into a succession of vignettes seemingly to showcase animators' talents, though not necessarily for the good of the movie as a whole. The songs are crowded unceremoniously into the second half, while the first is preoccupied chiefly with knockabout farces in the Warner Bros. *Looney Tunes* tradition. This is most noticeable in the scene where Chenxiang breaks into the treasury to steal the lantern, causing two giant stone guards to come alive and chase him around the oversized room, complete with set-ups and sound effects redolent of the *Tom & Jerry* cartoons.

The print supplied by the Shanghai Animation Film Studio is distinguished by excellent English-language subtitles from uncredited translators, who even make a brave stab at the songs and Fashi's rhyming-couplet dialogue.

INDUSTRIES

AND MARKETRIES

EXCUSES, EXCUSES

Adventures in Manga Editing

Manga creators, particularly young ones who have yet to hire their assistants and work out a good schedule, are surprised by the daily grind of creating a comic. You have theoretically limitless time to create your perfect opener. You can hone it, refine it and remodel it as often as you like. It can take years for the idea to gestate and take full form, and for you to find the time to put it on paper. You have your whole life to write Chapter One.

But if you sell it to a Japanese weekly, you have *seven days* to write Chapter Two. Seven more to write Chapter Three. Want a holiday? Forget it, Chapter Four's deadline is already looming. You've got everything that you wanted, but suddenly you're on a treadmill with no end in sight. You drag in help from outside, you cut corners, you extend single fight scenes to last twenty pages so you don't have to think up more story, and when the deadlines start to loom, you manufacture an alibi. Dead relatives, strange afflictions, sudden crises... some of them true.

People in the manga business are used to weird excuses. Which is why the manga publishers have 'editors' on their staff whose job it is to ride shotgun. Charming ones who suggest meeting up for a drink to hand over those last pages. Caring ones who phone to check you're okay, coincidentally on the day before the deadline. And then there are the heavies, who will camp outside your letterbox and shout persistently until you feed the pages out, one by one.

Some manga creators can react badly to such pressure. An editor of my acquaintance was once forced to dart back and forth in a Tokyo street, dodging speeding traffic, to pick up the pages floating down from the rooftop, where an angry author was hurling them into the air.

And you thought being a manga editor was a desk job?
(*NEO* #20, 2006)

FEAR FACTOR
TV Programming For Beginners

I n my anime dungeon, where I torment fans who displease me, there is a special chamber for people who think that getting anime on TV is easy. Fans are locked in a room until they come up with their idea of a perfect evening's anime viewing. Then I make them name the other eighteen hours they haven't considered yet. Then I make them do it 365 more times, without once including a show that they wouldn't want to watch themselves. After the wailing has finished, when their schedule is finally written in thirteen color-coded inks, I walk in and take away half the titles.

"Sorry!" I say. "It turns out that everything beginning with letters N through Z is already sold. You'll have to pick something else! Oh, but look here, *Legend of the Four Kings* is available, and here's something about the daily life of the starfish…"

Program buyers get a rough deal from fans, because everyone always assumes that they can pick from everything that's been made. But buying television programs is like some terrible game show where you have to fish jelly off a merry-go-round, blindfolded. And where does this terrifying spectacle take place? Cannes, France, just before the famous movie festival, when the place is packed with buyers and the evil creatures that ply them with alcohol and then try to make them pay good money for bad shows.

Rights are available for a limited period. You have to snatch them before Fox renew or Cartoon Network take out a two-year deal. So I'll be shouting, "There! *Escaflowne*! Get *Escaflowne*! Now! Left a bit! No! It's the cut version, back off! Oh wait, wait! Here comes *Blue Gender*!" Meanwhile the programmer is getting covered in jelly, and tripping over 157-episode packages of *hentai*, while ducking big *Overfiend* mallets that swing down from the ceiling, and an audience of anime fans chants: "We don't watch your channel but we want *Schoolgirl Milky Crisis*!" over and over again.

TV markets can be triumphs of faith over reason. I've lost count of the number of times I've seen sales sheets offering twice as many episodes of a show than actually exist. The rationale, one drunken executive inadvisably confessed, was that if an American company was prepared to pay for 200 episodes of *Schoolgirl Milky Crisis*, then the producers would damn well run back home and *make* some more.

TV rights kick in at different points, and out again when you least expect it. There are grace periods after video release and before the release of sequels, and some distributors only have video rights, so you must buy the show from the Japanese, who *can* sell it to you, but *can't* sell you the dub because that belongs to someone else. And in the case of one well-known series about girl-vigilantes, the people who sold the rights came back later and confessed they didn't actually *own* them. Sorry!

One Korean company realized the buyer from one British distributor only ever watched the first five minutes. Accordingly, they stuffed most of their budget into an awesome opening sequence, and the buyer signed on the spot, only to get the film home and discover that the rest of it was distinctly… substandard. But he sucked it up, he did his dub, and the next year he was back at Cannes, trying to sell it on to some other poor schmuck.

That's business…!

(*Newtype USA*, June 2005)

THE THIRTY-FOUR-MINUTE HOUR
Why It Pays to Recycle Animation

Previously on the Far West… The producer of *Schoolgirl Milky Crisis* had it all worked out. He wanted to go straight to video, but he wanted to do so in imitation of old kids' shows. This was because:

(A) "Fans like that," we are told, by people who have never met any fans.
(B) A TV 'half-hour', minus commercials, is only twenty-five minutes.
(C) It saves tons of cash.

There was a time in the late 1980s when cancelled TV shows had their unscreened episodes released on video. They would often be cut into 'movies' to make them look less like TV. These days, straight-to-video productions are more likely to be cut to look like TV. Here's why.

On American TV, opening sequences are short and sweet — the momentary stylized Seattle panorama of *Frasier*, or the frenzied piano of *Will & Grace*. Advertising is king, you see, and someone at NBC observed that a long credit sequence might lead people to see what's on the next channel.

Not so in anime. Credit sequences can stretch one or two minutes. This showcases the theme song, coming soon to a store near you. It also allows the animators to use the same piece of animation over and over again. Opening (OP) sequences often recycle scenes from the show, and do so every week. Ending (ED) sequences can be even simpler, and sometimes comprise a single still picture, with the credits rolling over the top. It sure beats drawing twenty-four pictures to fill every second.

There are other ways of chipping away at the work. The best in cartoons is the transformation sequence. It doesn't matter if it's *He-Man* shouting "By the Power of Grayskull", *Transformers* combining or *Pokémon* attacking, it amounts to the same thing. You will have recyclable footage. If they last a cumulative two minutes per episode, you will get a free episode every season, and your animators can have a week off.

You can also just pause. Because a still image only has to be drawn once. As budgets stretched and snapped on *Evangelion*, one moment simply ran music over a single still frame for forty-five seconds. But *Evangelion* wasn't saving money for the sake of it. Often, its moments of stillness allowed the animators to re-allocate budget to places where it would do more good: the battle sequences, or recording one more version of 'Fly Me to the Moon'. Because the world needs another one, right? But post-*Evangelion*, some producers forgot this, and simply slashed budgets to the bone. The savings were reallocated, not to better battles, but to bigger lunches.

Digital animation has given us a new variant of the pregnant pause. Once a scene is up on the screen, it costs little more than RAM to keep it running. Hence the recent trend for over-long 'beauty passes' — that SF moment when a ship passes before our eyes, and keeps going, and keeps going... and keeps going just a little bit longer. Add it all up, and an 'hour' of new TV anime only lasts for thirty-four minutes of new animation.

Then of course, thirteen episodes in, you will have a recap episode in which, for some reason, the characters will talk over what has happened in the previous season. With lots of recaps.

Where was I? Oh yes, *Previously on the Far West...*

(*Newtype USA*, September 2005)

ASTRO TURFING
Guerilla Marketing in the Anime World

Tonight I have another hat on. Tonight I'm a friend of a friend, Just Some Guy in the kitchen at the party. Which means Sarah (not her real name) is talking to me, because she has no clue who I am. If she suspected for a moment that I'd be writing these words, she would have run a mile. But Sarah never bothered to ask me what I do for a living, because she thought I was Just Some Guy and because Sarah likes talking about herself.

"You wouldn't believe me if I told you," she says coquettishly.

"Try me," I suggest.

"Well," she breathes excitedly, "I'm sort of like a secret agent."

She pauses for effect, but I have long since learned that saying absolutely nothing gets a lot more out of people than saying something.

"You see," she continues eventually, "do you know anything about Japanese cartoons?"

"No," I say. And many Internet lurkers would agree with me.

"Well, they are big news with the kids," she tells me. "And that's where I come in."

"As a secret agent?"

"Absolutely! It's not all about microfilms and assassinations. Sometimes it's about grass roots."

"Grass...?"

"Roots! Yes! Because *anime* — that's what it's called, you know — because anime is really like an underdog. A lot of the kids, you know, they like it because it's not Disney!"

"Like *Spirited Away*?" I suggest unhelpfully.

"Er... well, that *was* Disney, sorta," she concedes. "But a lot of the other stuff, well, it's not. You know, it's different. And that's why the kids like it."

"And where do you come in?"

"Well, a lot of anime's fanbase is, kind of, grass roots based," she says. "It spreads by word of mouth. You know, some girl on MySpace will say that she's big into *Schoolgirl Milky Crisis*, and suddenly ten boys are into it too."

"I see," I say, because so far, I do.

"So that's what I do."

"What is?"

"The grass roots!"

"Er...?"

"I do the grass roots! I make the grass roots *happen*!"

She giggles, and I try to contain my excitement. Because for ten years I have always suspected that there were shills at work in the anime business, but I had never found one before. Oh, there were a lot of false prophets. There were hundreds of fans with websites, keen to suggest that they had (*wink-wink*) friends in high places, but that didn't make them secret agents. That made them *fans* — fanatics about a particular medium or genre or show, keen to spread the word with evangelical zeal.

No, what interested me was the possibility of paid barkers. Wolfish non-fans who would wear sheep's clothing for a few hours a week as part of viral marketing campaigns.

"You're the girl on MySpace?" I ask.

"Sometimes! Or I'm the new poster who gets all excited about *Who Dat Ninja*!"

"You're a sock puppet?"

"Well, that's kind of a negative phrase. I like to think of it more like artificial grass roots facilitation."

"Artificial grass roots?"

"Yeah."

"Like astro turf?"

"Kinda..."

(*Newtype USA*, May 2007)

THE COLD EQUATIONS
The Sharp End of Anime Sales

"**H**ere," says Steve the Seller. "That's the cover for *300*. There's a special edition with extra Iran-bashing."

"Cool!" says Bob the Buyer. "My vast chain of video stores will take ten thousand."

"Great. And this is a mock-up of the cover for *Blades of Glory*. There's a free ice skate with every disc."

"Wow, so you have to buy two to—"

"You got it, everyone will have to buy two to complete the set."

"Yeah, but that's gonna be lumpy on the shelves. I'll take a thousand."

"Okay, got it," says Steve the Seller. "And this is coming out the same month. It's *Schoolgirl Milky Crisis*!"

"It's what?"

"*Schoolgirl Milky Crisis*! Come on! You remember, with the stamping on buildings and the really cool theme song. It's from the director of *Devil Devil Beast Beast*!"

"Meh…" says Bob the Buyer, and now Steve's worried.

"It's got a great price point!" he says, his voice rising in panic. "It'll have foil lettering on the cover."

"I don't know," says Bob. "I think the market's kinda peaked on these. We still haven't sold all our copies of *Pointless Harem Boy*."

"Hey!" says Steve. "Forget that! That's a completely different director. That's a completely different movie. You can't compare the two!"

"Well," says Bob. "Sometimes our customers do, and it's their nickel."

"But!" shrieks Steve, clutching at straws. "You gotta take this! It's got–" He has to think fast. He's got to think of something that he knows is within the bounds of possibility. There's no time for a director's commentary. He can't offer a free ice skate, because that bird has flown. He can't offer chapter selection as a bonus extra, because nobody takes that seriously any more.

"It's got a featurette!" he says excitedly. "Oh yeah, a little featurette about the whole thing, how it was made, what its fans think of it, all that kind of stuff."

"Really?" says Bob the Buyer.

"Really!" says Steve the Seller.

And Bob signs up right there for five thousand copies, and all Steve has to do is make sure that there is something on those discs that justifies his idle boasts. With five thousand copies shipping in a couple of months, he knows that there will be some money to pay for it, but they need to find someone to make it happen. They never planned on making that extra, but now they are committed to one.

You think this sounds unlikely? A company that shall remain nameless once rashly promised a Special Edition of *My Girlfriend is a Wolf Girl* to stores, only to realize that they didn't have anything to make it, you know, special. And only last week, I had a call from the producer of *Schoolgirl Milky Crisis* asking me what it would take to make "some fifteen-minute thing" that would get him out of a rash promise made to a video store chain in a moment of weakness. Y copies ordered leaves X money available to make… *something* on the disc.

Which makes me wonder. If you really want to change the anime business, work your way up until you're Steve the Seller, and then promise everyone *your* dream editions. Or become Bob the Buyer, and demand them. And then the cold equations will crunch into motion, and they'll have to *make* them for you.

(*Newtype USA*, June 2007)

SCREENING
Decisions in Dark Rooms

It's ten o'clock in the morning on a rain-washed street in London's Soho district. The clubs are dark and closed. The Thai Cottage restaurant won't open until lunchtime. The coffee shop on the corner sells early morning caffeine shots. Yes, for the London media set, this is early morning. This isn't the up-with-the-lark early birdism of sunny California. In media London, nobody's at their desks before ten. They're all out late at night partying, sorry, *having meetings* in popular local venues. And then the next day they sidle into the office after the rush hour is over.

I am the only one standing outside the screening rooms. This isn't your afternoon or evening Event, with nibbles and wine and smiling marketing girls. An earnest, dapper Japanese man, still on Tokyo time, hands me a single glossy card about *Schoolgirl Milky Crisis: The Movie*. He has a stack of twenty. The cinema seats maybe fifty, in plush super-luxury.

Another five people arrive. They are young and bored. None of them really wants to be here. They are the newest workers in their respective offices, dumped with the worst of the pre-MIP tasks — watching a Japanese cartoon at ten in the morning.

All the real action will happen in France, at the Cannes MIPCOM fair. That's where the buyers from the distributors are being wined and dined by the distributors. That's where the goodie bags and perks are. That's where people are splashing out on lunch. That's where, in a week's time, the higher-ups will be living it up. But before the movie world converges on France, there's the pre-MIP screenings.

Nobody has time to watch movies in Cannes! They're too busy being "entertained". So the week before, they send out the expendable soldiers to catch film after film at special screenings so they can turn up in France knowing what they want. Or rather, what they *don't* want.

If a film is really huge, if it really has buzz and momentum and Tom Cruise, then you don't need to revise for it on a wet October morning. These screenings are for the wallflowers — the ones that didn't get invited to the ball. And yes, that usually means the Japanese cartoons.

Pro audiences are the worst in the world. Within twenty minutes, I am alone in the cinema. The others waited just long enough to make sure this wasn't another *Paprika*, another *Akira*, another *Howl's Moving Castle*. As soon as they confirm it isn't, there's no need for them to stay. They don't want it. They walk straight out without a backward glance. They will write a single line email to their boss, and that's another meeting he won't be taking in France.

I stay to the end. I'm only here because I was genuinely interested in seeing the film. Outside, the Japanese exhibitor grabs me.

"You're Jonathan Clements," he says.

I ask him how he knows.

"You stayed to the end," he says with a sad smile. "And you laughed at the Kurosawa joke."

He stacks his remaining cards and looks at his watch. He knows who I am. Which means he knows I don't actually have anyone to report to. Nobody's buying *Schoolgirl Milky Crisis*, not today.

(*Newtype USA*, November 2007)

RUNNER BEINGS
Starting Out in the Animation Business

Matthew Sager is head of recruitment at the Moving Picture Company. Last month at the Swansea Animation Days, he stared down at an audience of undergraduates, and told them they were probably going to be teaboys. A "runner" position is now the default setting for most first-time media jobs.

"The average lifespan of a runner," Sager confesses, "is six to eight months."

Don't worry, they don't spontaneously combust. They stop being runners because they turn into something else. You know, like butterflies.

I still remember the first runner I gave a job to. Her name was Sam, and she was a tall, statuesque girl with cropped blonde hair who could have been a model. One day, I stopped her as she was dashing out of the *Beast Warriors* dubbing studio, making sure that we all had coffee and toast.

"It's like this," I told her, "we sent an actress home by mistake. We can't get her on her mobile because she's on the Tube. By the time she's above ground, it'll be past six, and we only have twenty minutes to wrap it up."

"Okay," Sam said. "What do I do?"

I handed her the script.

"Microphone number three," I said. "You're the invading alien general."

I think it was her sole anime performance. Runners are badly paid, and work crappy hours. But they do it because it puts them on the spot when the real jobs come up. I don't know what happened to Sam since 1995, but I bet she isn't making coffee any more.

A girl in the Swansea audience asks Matthew Sager what it takes to be a runner.

"Enthusiasm," he says. "And you need to be over eighteen."

But although a smile and a good attitude will get you through the door, runners don't become directors by magic. Then again, runners with degrees in Animation don't make coffee for long.

(*NEO* #15, 2006)

AFTERLIFE
The Future of Second-Hand Manga

While statistics show that the size of the manga market has steadily decreased in Japan over the last decade, that doesn't necessarily mean that the Japanese are reading less manga. The figures only refer to *new* manga — serialized in magazines and bought in shops as graphic novel compilations. In the past, the vast size of the Japanese publishing industry was often over-estimated by pundits who counted the same title twice, once on its magazine publication and once when it was reprinted in book form. This only matters if you are an accountant, not a fan.

But it's these book forms that are weighing heavily on the industry now.

Anthology magazines the size of phone directories have built-in obsolescence. The ink comes off in your hands, the paper is often colored to hide the fact it has been recycled several times already. You're supposed to read it on a train and then dump it at the next station, thereby allowing creators to sell the same thing back to you later on in book form.

But books are much more enduring. In Japan, you can shell out for new editions of the complete works of Masamune Shirow or Osamu Tezuka, or you can just pick them up second-hand for a fraction of the price. Ex-bachelor fanboys are forced to sell off their collections by irate spouses. Old-time fans die off, leaving their collections to go back on the market. Second-hand manga are great news for impecunious fans, but they can cause the entire market to depreciate in value. It's going to be an interesting question, over the next few years, if UK manga sales also develop a second-hand afterlife. Then again, there are some companies whose products are so shoddily assembled that they won't last long enough to make it to the second-hand stores. Poor print quality, weak glue… was this a cunning plan to build in obsolescence, or just low quality from the start?

(*NEO* #24, 2007)

RAT IN A HAT
Selling *Ratatouille* to Rata-phobes

R*atatouille* was a problematic title from the start. In many cultures, including the epicurean United States, the film was advertised with a pronunciation guide for the title, so that people wouldn't get laughed at in cinemas when they bought their tickets. In Finland, a *–ille* ending inconveniently indicates the allative case: in other words, that someone is trying to climb inside a rat. And in Japan, well, they just don't like rats that much.

Like every other Disney/Pixar movie, *Ratatouille* made it to Japan in record time; the first concession to the local audience coming in the form of a local language dub for the kiddies. The lead rat, Remy, was voiced by Daisuke Nishio, now playing the voice of Pinocchio in *Gunslinger Girl*.

But that wasn't the only change. In Japan, *Ratatouille* is called *Remy's Delicious Restaurant*, a deliberate attempt to associate the film with the gourmet genre of the affluent 1980s, as seen in works such as *Tampopo* (the quest for the perfect noodle), and similar foodie tales such as *Delicious Liaisons* (the quest for perfect consommé), *Sommelier* (a maverick wine waiter who doesn't play by the rules), and *Antique Bakery* (in which an ex-boxer gets a job in a cake shop). But *Ratatouille* also got a new name because the Japanese audience, said someone with a clipboard, just wouldn't go for the idea of a movie with a rat in it. Whatever next… cartoon mice!?

Ratatouille already boasts a rat who is more fastidious than usual — Remy walks on his hind paws so that he doesn't get his food dirty when he handles it. But for Japanese audiences that wasn't enough. My mole from the Japanese market tells me that focus groups reacted strongly against the very idea of a rodent near a place where food might be prepared.

What are we going to do? You can't de-rat *Ratatouille*! There would be nothing left! Instead, advertisers experimented with some new footage and discovered that their scores for test commercials went up if they tried one little thing. Apparently, if a rat is wearing a chef's hat, he is no longer perceived as distasteful vermin, but as a cartoon chef who happens to have fur.

Problem solved. Print adverts for *Ratatouille* in Japan give the movie a new title, and give its ratty star a posh looking hat at all times, in order to make it clear that he's not your everyday rat. Which is nice.

(*NEO* #47, 2008)

NO FORMAT
The Delight of Downloads

Somehow I find myself at Dessloktoberfest, a *Star Blazers*-themed annual party for the great and not-so-good at Anime Weekend Atlanta. There are balloons, and streamers, and sausages (this latter as food, not decoration, although nothing would surprise me with these guys). And Bob is holding a small plastic cup of mysterious blue punch.

"I've come to talk to you," he says, "because you're not holding a small cup of mysterious blue punch, and so I guess you must know something I don't."

In fact, it's Bob who knows something ahead of everyone else. The punch might make him feel ill, but he's celebrating. He's seen the future.

Last time I met Bob he'd been in anime video. In a way, he still is, but his card has a new title on it.

"I'm getting out," he says. "I'm moving sideways while I still can."

Bob has realized, like a number of other players in the industry, that arguing over new formats is a sucker's game. He doesn't much care whether Blu-Ray replaces DVD, or HD DVD, or some other format nobody has thought of. He's realized that whatever happens, someone will end up investing in new machines to make the discs, or widgets, or chips, but that it doesn't have to be him.

As ever, anime is software. It doesn't matter if you're using a tape or a disc or anything else, you'll still need something to put on it, and that means that the blue-chip investment is anime itself.

Bob's getting into TV, and into the ownership of broadcast rights, because to him it's the perfect business. He has something, he sells it, and then he still has it. Let other people come to him and put their hands in their pockets for video rights or mobile phone distribution deals, he still sits on the product itself, and if the format changes, he can change with it.

"The next format," he says sagely, "is No Format."

Several major duplication houses around the world, the people who make the physical tapes or discs that your anime come to you on, have already gone bankrupt or shut their doors. One, the factory that once made ten thousand DVDs of *Schoolgirl Milky Crisis*, caught fire just before all its old mastering machinery became obsolete — a happy accident considering the cost of renovation.

Over in Japan, the first signs of "No Format" have already shown up. TV stations and some distributors have already been offering direct downloads. The most impressive developments have been in *hentai* — the erotic movie business is usually the first to experiment with new technology. In *hentai*, some Japanese companies are clawing back their rights, jumping eagerly on American clients who fail to keep to contracts, grabbing back their titles along with the subtitles that go with them ready for hosting on local servers. "No Format" means no middlemen, too. It means that the Japanese can start selling directly to you someday soon, down the Intarwebnet.

The only people who are safe in America are those who already own pieces of anime as they are being made.

Bob smiles and takes another sip of his mysterious blue punch. He's put all his money into the remake of *Geek Gets Girls*. In two years' time, when you and a million others each pay the Japanese your dollar to download, Bob's already on twenty percent.

(*Newtype USA*, April 2006)

COMING OF AGE

The *Pokémon* Generation Grows Up

Mike is a giant bear of a man, gentle by nature, scary by necessity, charged with making your anime convention a fret-free experience.

From what I can see, the frets are just re-assigned. Every time you walk down a hotel concourse and *aren't* pelted by bottles, attacked by stick-wielding morons or pestered by non-fans who have somehow wandered into the wrong part of a hotel, you have convention security to thank. Back in the day, it could be someone's mom. In these times of huge attendance, it's more likely to be hired guns, maybe with a few volunteers like Mike, who know anime fans, and know it's all in fun.

But this is Mike's last stint running security at an anime con. Next year, if he goes to a convention at all, he's decided to do something literary. You know, with books and stuff.

"It's not that I don't like anime," he says. "I love it! There's always something new." Mike isn't an aging cynic who thinks that anime was better in the good old days. He doesn't diss *Naruto* or stick pins in effigies of American voice-actors. He loves anime as much as he did fifteen years ago when he first got into it.

In which case, I have to ask, why's he getting out?

Mike points at the costumers that surround us, stomping and glomping and waving into each other's phone cameras. A dozen characters from *One Piece* and *Dragon Ball*, a couple of Inu Yashas, a whole platoon of Vash the Stampedes, all giggling and friending and connecting in bizarre faux-gangster text-speak. They look harmless to me, but Mike has seen the future.

No matter what we oldies may say, anime fandom outside Japan before the 1990s was a false dawn. The old-school fans might have started up the magazines, and ran the first conventions, duped the first videos and gen-locked the first fansubs, but there just weren't enough of them to make a real difference in financial terms. Do you know how many people were at Anime Expo in 1993? Just under seventeen hundred.

Blame *Pokémon*, blame a whole bunch of things, but anime went mainstream in the late 1990s. Kids' anime were sold to *kids*, on TV, in vast numbers. To some extent anime stopped attracting fans because it was different, and started attracting fans because it was *the same* — an art-style familiar from Nintendo and Sega. Go us, anime was a melting pot! Number of attendees at Anime Expo in 2005? Thirty-three *thousand*!

The *Pokémon* generation represented a huge wave of new fans. Their youthful purchases helped fund more obscure anime. Their snapping up of DVDs created whole new concepts — American voice-actor fandom, truly huge conventions, manga print-runs large enough to flood bookstores. They are part of the rich tapestry of anime fandom as it exists today. You, dear reader, are probably one of them.

"I know," says Mike. "And that's great and all. But next year, or the year after, or sometime soon, that whole generation… they're going to be old enough to drink. And after that, con Security ain't gonna be so much fun."

(*Newtype USA*, August 2006)

BUBBLE FICTIONS
Anime and the Credit Crunch

It is a scene straight out of *Evangelion*. At the offices of a secret government project, a stern-faced leader informs a reluctant young protagonist that the world is about to end. A clock on the wall counts down the seconds until disaster, unless… unless someone climbs into a dangerous, untested prototype machine, and does battle with the fates themselves.

But Japan is not under attack from avenging angels. The countdown clock is financial, ticking away the moments until Japan's debts spiral completely out of control, and the country comes crashing down — collapsing banks, armies of starving ex-workers, and considerably less anime in the stores.

This year's big Japanese sci-fi movie was the satirical *Bubble Fiction*, in which Ryoko Hirosue is catapulted back to the boom year of 1990 in a last-ditch attempt to save the Japanese economy. The effect is not unlike *Back to the Future* as written by accountants — Japan's modern woes are tracked back to a tiny loophole in a proclamation by the Finance Ministry, and high jinks inevitably ensue.

There are sly digs at the fashions of yesteryear, and cameos from whichever future stars the producers could persuade to play their younger selves. Most notably, Ai Iijima, the future author of *Time Traveler Ai*, can be found dancing at a discotheque. Phones are the size of bricks, shoulder pads the size of helipads, there are tight ruffled dresses on body-conscious Tokyo ladies, and men wear suits two sizes too big for them. Written by *Bayside Shakedown*'s Ryoichi Kimizuka, *Bubble Fiction* presents a fantasy view of the 1990s, in which people literally give money away in the streets, taxis need to be hailed with a ten thousand yen note, and champagne flows freely among the party set.

But there is also a sense of impending doom. It's here, as Tokyo land prices soared to silly heights, that the seeds were sown of economic collapse. The Bubble, warned some pundits, was sure to burst, bringing disaster on the hedonistic Japanese.

Creatively, the Bubble years have a lot to answer for. Outside Japan, the economic might of Japan led Hollywood to make *Black Rain* and *Rising Sun*. The great growth in wealth among the Japanese turned them into the owners of video players, and hence helped drive the modern anime industry. The idea of a future economic implosion even gave us the name of a famous anime, *Bubblegum Crisis*. Deep pockets nurtured the garage kit and figurine industries. The largest disposable income of all turned out to be in the hands of the charmingly named "parasite singles", twenty-something women living rent-free with their parents, hence a similar emphasis on bespoke cute. *Hello Kitty* might have been around long before the Bubble, but she certainly achieved megastar status with the help of all those yen with nowhere else to go.

But let us also remember the indirect effects of the crash. With profit margins constricting in Japan itself, producers and publishers became more amenable to foreign sales. Anime and manga abroad, particularly in America, are another side-effect of the boom and bust, and a generation on, the fact that the American market plays such a great part in Japanese business decisions is, at least in part, a result of deals done in the Bubble period.

But what if the American economy starts to slump...? Who's going to pay for anime then? Sub-prime days ahead, my friends?

(*Newtype USA*, December 2007)

THE THIRD DIMENSION
Is 3-D Anime the Next Big Thing?

C inema always needs to be one gimmick ahead. You can watch stuff at home... ah, but if you want to see color, you have to go to a cinema. You can watch color at home... ah, but if you want amazing sound you have to go to a cinema. You can watch movies at home... ah, but if you want to see them earlier you have to go to a cinema. Every generation has its cinema-TV tensions, and two decades of consumer electronics have given many modern fans the chance to replicate much of the cinema-going experience in their own homes. The risk remains that audiences simply won't leave their houses to go to see a film. With movie-going manners at an all-time low, are we really surprised?

The reintroduction of 3-D, stereoscopic movies, usually for big event blockbusters at IMAX theaters, seems at first like a rather desperate, 1950s-style solution to a twenty-first century problem. But it's not just about stereoscope, it's about delivering an experience that people can't replicate at home. It's about keeping cinema special, not just with 3-D pictures, but also with mind-blowing sound and giant screens.

I hear rumblings from inside the studios. I've overheard creatives at Pixar and DreamWorks, commiserating with each other that they are being asked to twist plots to incorporate 3-D "moments" like the super-long tracking shots in *Beowulf*. Budgets at Warners have been allocated to take certain old movies and give them a new lease of life with a 3-D effect. And *everybody* saw Disney release *Meet the Robinsons* in 2007, not in a few gimmicky showings, but all over the United States in a "Real D" format. Steven Spielberg is reputedly tinkering with a 3-D projection process that doesn't require those silly eyeglasses — but what it does require is a special plasma screen that people will not have in their home systems.

If you're wondering what this has to do with Japanese animation, the answer is apparently nothing. And that's your problem, right there. I don't hear similar stories coming out of the Japanese business. If the Japanese are conducting similar experiments in 3-D, I'm not hearing about them.

Behind the scenes in the American industry, creatives are already debating how to use 3-D properly. They are determining how the technology will serve the art, and not vice versa. People in the industry are already plotting the films you will see in 2011 and 2012. Some of the plans revolve around the implementation of technology that doesn't really exist yet. Maybe stereoscopic movies will be a flash in the pan like they were in the 1950s, but if their time has truly come, it's going to change the nature of film in the next few years. The credibility gap in styles and execution between 2000 and 2010 might loom as wide as that between *Steamboat Willy* and *Fantasia*.

Are the Japanese ready for this? Are they going to be left behind? Are they confident that 3-D will be another passing fad they don't need to worry about? Or do they already have something even better up their sleeves?

(*Newtype USA*, February 2008)

NEW! IMPROVED!
On Getting Better Anime, Slower

This month's conundrum: check discs of *Schoolgirl Milky Crisis* are sent to reviewers and one writes a piece citing errors. The distributor complains because it was a *check-disc*, not yet finished. He shouldn't have called it an error, he should have told them about it so they could correct it. The reviewer says: wait a minute, is he reviewing this DVD, or is he unpaid quality control? Lines are drawn in the sand. People scowl.

Step inside my wayback machine. Come to a sunny 1950s day

somewhere in the mid-West. There, lurking in the supermarket aisle, hearty and homespun, with an alice-band in her hair and a clipboard in her hands, is The Researcher.

"Excuse me, ma'am," she says to a passing shopper, "if I could have a moment of your time, I have been sent by the Lords of Marketing to test some stuff. And it would help me very much if you could answer a few questions. It will help us in the fight against Communism, you see.

"Imagine there are two packets of soap powder. One is the one you usually buy. The other is almost exactly like it. But it has the words 'NEW! IMPROVED!' written on the side. Which do you buy?"

The housewife wonders if this is a trick question. But then she shrugs and says, "The new one, I guess."

And with that, or probably with a representative sample of several thousand other conversations like that, our fates were sealed. Because despite being a statement of the blindingly obvious, a silly answer to a misleading question, one of the laws of marketing came into being.

New is good. New is great. Old is so last year. And if you were wondering what the heck this has to do with anime, anime started getting old twenty-three years ago.

Before 1983, anime was ageless. Kids saw it on TV and loved it, played along with it, enthused about it with their friends, and then grew up. There was little repeat viewing — anime was the way you remembered it through your rose colored spectacles. But you became a teenager, you put away childish things, and that was that.

Video changed all that, turning anime into a commodity that could be sold. Video gave us repeat viewings, it gave us fandom, not just in Japan, but in places where anime had never been broadcast. It helped anime grow up. But it also made it something that needed to be sold for dollars instead of given away free on TV, and that meant finding something to put on the package. "New" sells.

Newness is an obsession of our age, an addiction we can't seem to shake. It's no longer enough to see a show we like. We have to know it is new, and then we want it before everyone else. We want a company rep to tell us when he's bought the rights and when it's coming out, and once we know, we'll whine in agony when it's delayed.

Can something be *too new*? Can it be rushed out unfinished, its translation unfinessed, its dialogue not quite synched? In our clamoring for swift releases, we might be getting the New. But do we risk sacrificing the Improved?

(*Newtype USA*, September 2006)

MANGA

S N A P S H O T S

GOLF LESSON COMIC

Issue # 211 • **Debut Year:** 1990 • **Page Count:** c.250
Publisher: Nippon Bungei Sha • **Price:** 380 yen (c.$3.80)
Cycle: Monthly

Japan is not known for its wide-open spaces — instead, it's internationally renowned for the sheer lack of flat, empty ground. Surely a golf course would be an obscenely extravagant folly? With the media full of stories of solitary play and digital gaming, console-related injuries and capsule hotels, the Japanese obsession with golf can seem at first like a contradiction in terms. But it is golf's sheer exoticism that has made it such a sign of affluence among the Japanese middle classes. In a country whose hinterland is largely mountains and forests, where so much habitable space has had to be wrested bodily from the sea, the idea of eighteen stretches of land set aside for a mere game is the height of conspicuous consumption. Even more so than in the UK, a golf course is a sign of land for the use of a tiny elite. Membership of a golf club is the ultimate status symbol among Japanese upper management.

The higher level of wealth required to participate in golf in Japan has led to a difference in the daily routine. (Unless you fancy crazy golf or a putting green, the Japanese simply don't have lower end, cheaper facilities.) Japanese golfers are often up before dawn for the long trip to a distant course. Once there, they eat a large breakfast before taking their time on the first nine holes, and stopping for a long, luxurious, and often rather liquid lunch. In the afternoon, it's time for a leisurely and perhaps slightly inebriated stumble around the last nine holes, and a posh dinner in the evening. Compare this to many British courses, where the best you can hope for is a sandwich bar or pub grub. For the Japanese golf *otaku*, it's a long, long day, but if you're paying all that money to be a member, why not take your time?

And how does a would-be golfer advertise his affiliation? Why with a manga magazine, of course, published on the first of every month, just after payday, when the club-buying wallet is at its thickest, and the boss is most liable to look with approval on the sight of junior staffers sucking up.

Golf Lesson Comic began life in 1990, right at the height of the Bubble Economy. With Japanese prosperity climbing to ludicrous levels, the bespoke sports industry sought to imitate the great, sweeping greens of the American business world. Japanese money snapped up real estate as far afield as Australia for golf enthusiasts, with golf tourism in Hawaii and Guam forming a large part of Japan's foreign travel boom. In the wake of the collapse of the Japanese economy, derelict golf courses became one of the signs of the recession, along with the abandoned theme parks that form part of the eerie background of films like *Spirited Away*. But golf itself remains an aspirational activity. Multi-tiered driving ranges still exist all over Japan for golfers to practice their swing, in the vain hope that one day they will be permitted access to one of the dwindling number of proper courses — many of the boom-time links having been swiftly repurposed for housing.

PRACTICALITIES

As with manga anthologies for the older man like *Big Comic Spirits*, the cover story on *Golf Lesson Comic* is not an image from one of the stories within, but a picture of a person from the real world. For example, on issue #211, it's certified "golf babe" Momoko Ueda, the twenty-one year-old woman who became the youngest player ever to win a paying title in the Japanese professional golfing association. In 2007, she won five Japanese national tournaments, and became the first Japanese player to win the Mizuno Classic in nine years. Ueda is perfect cover-girl material — a nice young player to take all the old granddads' minds off their stuffy sport, and sure to encourage more women back into the game. Although, to be honest, last time Japanese women started playing golf in large numbers, they were hardly welcomed by the establishment. With their plaid clothes and their silly shorts, they were soon dubbed *oyaji gals* ('old-man girls') by other players. By all accounts, Ueda has more of a chav-casual chic that is sure to ruffle even more feathers.

Features in *Golf Lesson Comic* favor slightly more text stories than the manga world usually allows. These include Maiko Wakabayashi's gossipy *Golf Locker Room*, and a cunning quiz, *Golf Brain Training*, that scores multiple-choice answers with a sliding scale of bogies, birdies and pars.

Mike Aoki's Rule Navi is a cartoony series of questions on golfing law, each demonstrating a possibly thorny issue, and then answering with Mr Aoki's best guess at the right way to deal with it. Where appropriate, it then follows with real-world examples, ready for players to see for themselves on YouTube.

As in the Western world, many sporting stories come with a named player affiliated to the title. The modern golfing girl is encapsulated in the form of Tomoko Kusakabe, whose photostory *Golf! Take it Easy!* reaches its third installment in this issue, but Masaki Tani lends his name to a bona fide manga strip in the form of *Sense Up Score Up*. A published author on golfing theory, Tani takes a back seat in the manga strip, which begins with a few photos of him in action, before replacing him with a manga demonstration prepared by third parties. Author Hirotoshi Nomura and artist Elliot Goto provide the actual comic pages, in which a workmanlike likeness of Tani guides a daft novice through the dynamics of a golf swing. Even though the pupil is named Mr Suzuki, he is drawn with the features and hair of a foreigner, imparting a cunning and rather obvious subtext to Tani's supposed mastery of the sport.

Writer Nomura is back, this time with illustrations by Tetsuya Nemoto, for the putatively deep and thoughtful *Golf Awakening*. As with almost every other strip, it comes attached to a celebrity brand, in this case aging pro-golfer Akira Chiba, and features a series of migraine-inducing fashions. Coming to an end this month is Kazuhito Komura's *Art of Golf*, in which, you guessed it, a bunch of guys get together and play golf, while talking about golf-related matters, with plenty of golf advice for the golf-loving reader.

More advice awaits in *Slice Clinic*, in which the spectacularly bequiffed Doctor Slice lectures us on the "amateur golfer's worst enemy." *Shinichi Yokota's Easy Golf World* focuses this week on the difficulties of getting out of a bunker. Which is all very well, but this magazine has been running for nearly twenty years! Has the subject really never come up before? One wonders, when looking at this 211th issue of *Golf Lesson Comic*, how many people have been reading it all along, and how much it relies — like so many manga for readers in other age brackets — on being able to recycle old material every couple of years.

A mildly more entertaining approach comes in the form of Shinichi Ikeuchi's *That Golfing Feeling*, a light-hearted series aimed at the "single golfer." Now on its 157th chapter, it charts the tribulations of Masashi Kanda, a handsome player with a handicap of eighteen, who nevertheless experiences the same trials as any other player. This month's episode finds him stuck in the rough, and wondering how best to chip back onto the green.

Ikeuchi returns in the same issue for *The Dignity of Golf*, in which golfers from all conceivable walks of life compete in a tournament with all the melting-pot conflicts of an episode of the *Wacky Races*.

GETTING WOOD

Takeshi Kawasaki writes *Hana's Highschool Girls' Golf Club*, a comedy in which three golf-playing girlies barge their way onto a local course. High jinks inevitably ensue, the emphasis less on the ladies' terrible prospects than on their guileless self-assurance and their undeniable love for the sport. Somewhat pretentiously, the artwork is billed as *gekiga*, 'dramatic pictures', as if by calling it such, artist Tatsuo Kanei turns it into Shakespeare. As in so many sports manga across all genres, the ladies succeed through their purity of heart and their hard work behind the scenes. When a brash, portly rival player with a foreigner's face and Rod Stewart's haircut chooses a seven-iron to knock a ball the full 163 yards to the eleventh hole, our plucky heroine delivers an impassioned speech on smaller being more beautiful, and selects a lighter six-iron for herself. Her ball also reaches the green, but does so a few feet ahead of her enemy's — a vital benefit on a three-par hole! Hah! Take that, America! Who's laughing now? Well, nobody as it happens — the comedy seems somewhat absent, at least in this chapter.

The Single Road, drawn by Sugar Sato, is more baffling. It seems to set itself up as another tale of female golfing, perhaps even with a pun on the single player and the singleton, in the style of *Bridget Jones's Diary*. However, our heroine spends most of the episode rushing to the golf store while apologizing on the phone for her tardiness. Meanwhile, the story cuts away to the punctual men who have already arrived and who are busy practicing with their drivers.

A different sporting style is presented in Reigo Izuki and Kazunari Matsuda's *Partner*. Drawn with a stern, manly boldness of line that recalls the martial arts comics of other genres, it depicts golfing matches as dynamic competitions of strength and smarts. The educational angle is nestled carefully in the background, with the reader afforded long opening shots of each hole in order to invite speculation on how our hero is going to approach it. Like the martial arts genre, there is often an emphasis on lateral thinking. In this one, our hero plucks a tuft of grass from the rough and casts it in the air in order to get a better sense of how the wind is blowing. This issue sees our guys competing for the ultimate hole, a peninsula almost entirely surrounded by water, and clearly inspired by the infamous seventeenth hole at Sawgrass Stadium in Florida.

Best Score Syndrome, reaching its final installment in this issue, is the tale of a golfer whose desire to increase his handicap has become an obsession. However, considering that he feeds this burning pathology by putting on some loud trousers and going round a golf course, it is difficult to see how his experience differs all that much from everyone else's in the magazine.

Ten years ago, a carbon driver would set you back $200. Nowadays, even with the favorable exchange rate, adverts in *Golf Lesson Comic* can put the price of a single golf club as high as $700. But if you can afford membership of a Japanese golf course, you can afford to blow the price of a small car on a set of funny-shaped sticks. *Golf Lesson Comic* knows this, and its pages make for a fascinating glimpse into another stratum of Japanese society — people who are very rich, have nothing to prove, and an appalling sense of fashion. One also gets the sense, dare I say it, that the reader of *Golf Lesson Comic* is rather dull. In the 1990s, the magazine tried to broaden its appeal by working golf themes into more traditional genres. It ran a detective mystery, *The Hole-in-One Murders*, lessons in putting green etiquette for the nouveaux riches, and the bawdy sub-*Caddyshack* comedy of *Golfman*. While those stories have long gone, the current roster of titles continues the discreet effort to pep up golf's repetitive nature. Its modern incarnation sticks just as closely to the nuts and bolts of golfing — even though it packs several manga strips into its page-count, they are less "stories" than they are lessons, living up to the bluntly pragmatic title of the magazine. It does, after all, deliver exactly what it promises: golf lessons, in a comic. It is certainly a fascinating prospect for the manga reader, not necessarily for what it contains, but for the example it presents of an industry that will truly publish a story about literally anything — well worth remembering next time someone tells you that manga are nothing but sex and violence. But it still leaves me with the feeling that, even when ambling around a golf course looking for their balls, this magazine's readers are all work and no play.

(*NEO* #42, 2008)

HARLEQUIN®

瞬

Issue # 100 (ish) • **Debut Year:** 1999? • **Page Count:** c.540
Publisher: Ohzora / Harlequin KK • **Price:** 630 yen (c.$6.25)
Cycle: Monthly

Although the name may not be immediately familiar to English readers, Harlequin Enterprises is the current owner of a label still often thought to be quintessentially British. The company was founded in Canada in 1949, and specialized in women's publishing from its earliest inception. Ten years later, it began licensing titles from the famous Mills & Boon romance brand, and found many more lonely hearts and incurable romantics in North America than in Mills & Boon's British home. By 1971, Harlequin had done so well that it was able to buy its former supplier. While the Mills & Boon name is still a popular brand in the UK, its romance products are better known around the world under the Harlequin moniker, in twenty-seven different languages, including Japanese.

TISSUES AND ISSUES

Harlequin Japan was set up in 1988 to translate romantic fiction into Asian markets. Faced with unprecedented competition from well-established romance anthologies like *Hana to Yume* (*Flowers and Dreams*) and *Margaret*, the Tokyo office soon fought back with its own manga magazine, translating English-language novels into Japanese, and, crucially, using Japanese artists.

That makes the output of *Harlequin* a bona fide part of the manga world. As with Mills & Boon and Harlequin novels in our own world, opening one of its publications is an entry into a puzzling subculture of hearts and flowers, of trembling lips and dewy eyes, as handsome princes are tamed by the will and sacrifice of their elegant ladies, who might start off as girls next door, but scrub up nicely to become princesses in waiting.

On the subject of which, the adverts and incidental articles in *Harlequin* magazine provide similar rollercoaster passions. Here, the reader finds an ad for bust enhancement, since apparently one's handsome prince will simply not come until one's boobs are bumped up from a C to an E. The competition prizes this issue are a grab-bag of classy cosmetics, including a Prada make-up pouch, Givenchy scent, and a Coach scarf. A diet supplement pill with the unfortunate name of Fat End occupies two pages of advertorial, complete with charts, a message from a Scientist in a White Coat, and before/after pictures of Ugly Sisters who have become Cinderellas. Meanwhile, the horoscopes offer a bewildering array of consumer advice to get the reader through the month. Eye shadow is, it seems, the only way that Geminis will get lucky over the next thirty days, while Cancers are exhorted to festoon themselves in designer goods, and Taureans are advised to get themselves a mirror ball. One almost wishes that more Japanese girls took such advice seriously, as it would surely brighten up a shopping trip to Shinjuku if one girl in every twelve was dragging around a disco lighting array, while every Sagittarius was on the lookout for "a masked angel". But then again, that does pretty much describe Shinjuku anyway. And on the back cover, Kleenex clean up with an advert for tissues.

MY FAIR LADY

As for the stories themselves, *Harlequin* has significantly less than the average manga anthology. This is because it eschews the usual serialization element of most Japanese comics. Its tales begin and end in a single issue in page counts of more than a hundred pages each, which is great for the occasional reader, but limits the number of titles that can fit.

ALL AMERICA WEPT!
"Zenbei ga naita!"

Japanese romances and tragedies are often rated for modern audiences by the number of tissues required to sob one's way through. A single-tissue production might feature a single unfortunate accident and half-hearted reunion. A two-tissue affair could involve a major accident, star-crossed lovers and possibly a small pet pulling through. Triple-tissue warnings only apply to major surgery, doomed love, and tragic ponies.

However, advertisers saw their gimmick backfire in recent years with the use of the term "*All America Wept*". Originally intended to refer to a movie that had held US audiences enraptured, the term became so overused by eager marketers that it is now something of a joke. If a Japanese person says "All America Wept" in the cynical twenty-first century, it is liable to be translated as a dismissal of unnecessary emotion – tantamount to "Nothing Special".

The Prince's Tutor by Nicole Burnham was published in English text form in 2003 and is the most recently published story to feature in this issue. Its plucky yet unsure heroine is Amanda Hutton, a governess hired by the obscure European monarch Eduardo diTalora to teach his wayward son Stephano the ways of protocol. Amanda is initially reluctant, since she is used to schooling children, not spoilt youths. Prince Stephano is an unabashed cad, devoted to skiing, yachting and other jet-set pursuits, and determined to give his unwelcome tutor the run-around. One doesn't need to be a rocket scientist to see where this is going, particularly when the cover of *Harlequin* magazine loudly proclaims: "All stories self-contained, and with happy-endism."

But Japanese readers are less interested in the original than they are in the artist of the manga version. As the unusually strong backstory of *The Prince's Tutor* implies, it is part of a larger series — Amanda's best friend Jennifer has already got her own handsome prince, by marrying Stephano's elder brother in the earlier *Going to the Castle*. But such details need not trouble Japanese readers, who are expected to be far more interested in the home team: it's artist Soraha Himura, not Burnham, who gets top billing on the cover. Himura's work has graced many other Harlequin translations, with bodice-ripping titles like *Turbulent Covenant*, *The Playboy Sheikh* and *The Wife Next Door*. But who is this masked stranger? The artist's name is quite clearly a pseudonym — the mysterious Ms Himura could well be another, better known manga artist drawing such adaptations for pocket money.

READER, SHE MARRIED HIM

Notably, the uncredited translators and adaptors of the stories make only small concessions to the local readership — part of Harlequin's appeal in the Japanese market rests on its foreign exoticism. Stephano was tall, dark and handsome on the original American cover of *The Prince's Tutor*, suddenly, in the manga version, he has long blond hair.

While the stories themselves are translated faithfully, the titles are often altered for extra emphasis. Emma Richmond's 1999 romance *The Reluctant Groom* is transformed in Harlequin manga form into *The Winds of Gibraltar*. Twenty-eight year-old virgin Abby Hunter is a gawky, hapless girl who feels extra awkward around men. Imagine, then, her surprise when she is propositioned by blond tycoon Sam Turner. A heartless cynic who doesn't believe in love or marriage, the impossibly handsome Sam is clearly in need of some education, and Abby is the one who provides it, clinging to her heartfelt moral position, rebuffing his daring advances, and going weak at the knees at the merest prospect of a snog. It's a foregone conclusion that Richmond's story will end with its heroine marching up the aisle — what suspense there is lies in *how* she gets her man. Will this be an old-fashioned Mills & Boon, or one of the more modern ones with a bit of sex thrown in? Artist Kakuko Shinozaki supposedly uses her real name, although she only shows up on Japanese databases drawing other Harlequin stories. She sprang fully-formed into the manga world, drawing racier romances such as *Mission to Seduce* and *Mackenzie's Pleasure*, in similar light, airy styles, low on shading and backgrounds, with all the artist's energy concentrated on the faces and emotions of the passionate characters. She also works under other pseudonyms, as 'Yoshino Shinozaki' and 'Neneko Pochiko', but it's Harlequin that seems to put food on the table in the Shinozaki house, with the other names appearing only infrequently.

POPPY LOVE

The Harlequin line is itself divided into several mini-brands, including the Red Dress imprint that apes Bridget Jones's neurotic self-regard, and fantasy novels under the Luna imprint. But by far its longest running sub-genre has to be medical fiction, with less emphasis on bone-saws and bodily fluids, and more on pert starry-eyed nurses and the handsome doctors they adore. Tales such as Helen Shelton's 1997 *Poppy's Passion*, remade in Harlequin manga-form as *Don't Call It First Love*.

Artist Atsumi Ryo has never worked for Harlequin before, but has previously drawn manga adaptations of murder novels, most notably Mitsuhiko Asami's mystery *A Letter From Hoichi the Earless*. But there's no murder here, as pink-haired intern Poppy breezes into work late, only to discover that the newest recruit at her hospital is the tall, dark and handsome Tom Grainger, a man she adored from afar six years ago. Before he went off to study surgery at Oxford (where else? Mills & Boon heroes never graduate from Scunthorpe Poly), Tom was also the subject of Poppy's most embarrassing teenage incident, when he literally crushed her hopes. It was Tom who came back one night from a night on the town with Some Blonde Floozy, diving onto his bed with The Wavy-Haired Slut Who Isn't Good Enough For Him, only to almost squash poor young wallflower Poppy, who had been lurking beneath the sheets, hoping to surprise him.

"Of course I love you, Poppy," he had said later on. "But I love you like a brother." *Oh, the agony!* And that was before Tom's indiscretion with the Evil Blonde Tart turns out to be with the wife of a fellow doctor, leading to his dismissal from Saint Joan's Hospital, and his disappearance from Poppy's life.

Which brings us to the here-and-now, with Poppy realizing that she still has feelings for Tom, and that she is no longer the daft naked teenager hiding in his bed, even if she is still open-mouthed in awe at his rich doctor's life, with open-topped car rides around exotic, foreign London town, bottles of New Zealand Sauvignon Blanc (that's right, no expense spared!), and a passionate confession in the lounge.

"I'm not a cold, heartless surgeon," confesses Tom. "When I am with you, I am *just a man...*"

And with such a statement, it's only a matter of time before Poppy is all dressed in white for her wedding at a country church, where artist Ryo attempts to depict her glowing with love for her man, although the unfortunate omission of pupils from her eyes in the final frame make it look as if she has been brainwashed and sent off to married life as a Stepford zombie.

A MATCH MADE IN HEAVEN?

A Fine Romance

Romance manga have been obsessed with royal romances throughout the modern era, in part because life was ahead of art. In the 1950s, when girls' manga were still finding their feet, twenty-three year-old Japanese everygirl Michiko Shoda met a handsome young man on a tennis court — a man who turned out to be the dashing Prince Akihito. Actually, it's not all that rags-to-riches — Michiko's dad was president of the massive Nisshin Flour Milling company, and Akihito's love match was only approved after prolonged negotiations between government representatives. But to the Japanese people, that fateful tennis match was a sign of fairy-tale romance — supposedly the first time that a Japanese prince had married a commoner. The former Miss Shoda is now Empress Michiko of Japan.

THE DARK HALF

Harlequin romances are also unable to resist the allure of the past, hence the brand of Harlequin Historicals, set in times without adequate plumbing or broadband internet access, when men were apparently men and women were bafflingly grateful. All, that is, except for Chiara di Paradini, a half-gipsy fortune-teller in eighteenth century Venice, who is determined to seek revenge on Luca Zeani, the wealthy aristocrat who ruined her sister's reputation. Except that when Chiara uses her psychic powers to look into Luca's soul, she sees nothing but good in him. Has she misunderstood the handsome, rich Mr Zeani after all? Surely it could not be that the blond, beautiful, and did we mention, *rich* Mr Zeani has an evil twin, who looks just like him, but has all the morals of a bounder and a cad? Such frustrations form the central plot of *The Shadowed Heart*, a 1998 historical by 'Nina Beaumont' (a pen-name for Nina Gettler), highly regarded by romance readers, and given the manga treatment here under the new title of *A Venetian Fantasy*. But artist Karin Miyamoto has also drawn many more modern *Harlequin* stories, including *The Sudden Bride*, *The Edge of Paradise*, *Playboy Doctor*, and *Bodyguard Lover*.

And that's your lot in this month's issue — just four stories, albeit fully self-contained, and with the promised "happy-endism". And as one final note, the *Harlequin* manga is printed on noticeably better quality paper than most other anthologies, with stain-free production values we haven't seen since *Kiss*, another girls' mag.

(*NEO* #31, 2007)

ROSE MYSTERY

瞬

Issue # 1 • **Debut Year:** (Aya: c.1987) • **Page Count:** 534
Publisher: Ozora • **Price:** 600 yen (c.$6.00)
Cycle: Monthly

Ozora are the company behind the popular *Harlequin* magazine, but their publishing slate extends much further into the romance world. Take *Love Comic Aya*, which, the publisher's website informs us, "is a magazine with the message that if there is love, then the life will be happy. This is a magazine that delivers innocent but stimulating love to the 'grown-up' ladies."

Well, there's no arguing with that. More of the same old Mills & Boon, you might think. Except that *Love Comic Aya* still likes to shake things up. Like *Harlequin*, it has an editorial policy that likes to keep stories self-contained in a single issue. No tuning in next month for the demanding *Aya* audience, instead they get their beginning, their middle, and their end all delivered in one chunky story. But, someone must have realized, if everything starts and finishes in a single issue, then the chance arrives for special themed editions.

Hence *Rose Mystery*, an issue of *Aya* but with the magazine's real title in teeny-tiny print in the corner. Hitting the bookstores around Halloween, and with a distinctly vampish girl on the cover, the emphasis is on "love, madness and mystery" — detective comics for lonely goth girls!

The sparse advertising offers a glimpse of the *Rose Mystery* reader's self-image (or at least what the advertisers imagine it to be) — smarter than the average teenager, alienated and in search of alternative paths, an Ugly Duckling hoping that posterity will prove her to be a majestic black swan, quite probably with an Anne Rice novel tucked in her handbag and a pale, interesting boy on her arm. The incidental pages are packed with vicarious dark tales, magical remedies for ailments both real and imagined, and even a loan shark company offering to help pay for it all. There is a 'healer' who promises to sort out unspecified issues, crystals for sale and a magic pendant. There is also a phone line on which the *Rose Mystery* reader can listen to tales of luckless heroines who are tied up by criminals, exploited by media moguls and felt up by family members.

One thing's for sure, if you aren't wearing black and scowling at passers-by before you read *Rose Mystery*, you certainly will be by the time you've finished!

The *Rose Mystery* reader is confident but scared, darkly ostentatious but secretly vulnerable. The advertisers know this, and unsurprisingly seek to exploit it, but the magazine does not. In fact, the magazine treats all this with the same resolute, positive ambition as Ozora's plain vanilla romantic sister-titles. The message is simple and winningly charming: goths need love, too.

OTHER WORLDS

Creeping Corridor, by Kaoru Oikawa, features Kotoido, a girl whose home burned down when she was in primary school, taking her family with it — creating an archetypal manga orphan and a mystery worth solving in a single incident. The sound of sirens still makes her nervous, but she manages to hide it well from the boys who are already vying for her attention. Until one fateful day when she meets a dark, handsome, pony-tailed stranger with a mysterious way of speaking and a dapper manner — she is convinced that she remembers him from her childhood. The stage is set for a tale of haunting and shadow worlds, and although the whole story is tied up in seventy crisp pages, it ends on a mystery chill, with enough loose ends to be regarded as a pilot chapter for a longer-running story.

In *Kaguya's Sound Rains* by Kaori Takesaka, protagonist Kazuya is a handsome musician from "N city in N prefecture" — the town is not identified, but the chances are high that it is supposed to be Nagasaki. But when he takes a path home that he hasn't used before, he finds a flute in an abandoned house, and is suddenly whisked back in time to 1952. There, the confused youth befriends Monaka, a local girl who isn't ready to believe that he is a time-traveler, but still can't explain his strange clothes and mannerisms. The whole tale is a gentle, science fictional variation on the story of Kaguya (see the Paper Moon boxout on p196), a princess in Japanese mythology whose home world is the moon. Takesaka excels at presenting 1950s Japan as a place that is no less alien to a modern teenager — elegant, beautiful but also savage and, in a bittersweet moment of closure, unendurable for our hero.

Hiroko Kawasaki offers another tantalizing pilot in the form of *Mystery Shopper Ichiko's Report*. The bizarre set-up has the titular Ichiko, a private investigator who likes to camouflage her office as a hairdressers or clothes shop, whichever aspect best helps her next case. In this regard, the story mixes the chameleon tactics of the *Transformers* with an episode of *Miss Marple*. The device, however, is not well used here. Its purpose seems simply to be a means of encouraging the reader to imagine adventure and scandal lurking around the corner wherever she may find herself, even if it is reading the magazine while waiting to have her hair done. Ichiko is a 'mystery shopper' because she goes out looking (i.e. 'shopping') for trouble, and she finds it here when she foils an assassination attempt by a man's jilted lover.

THRILLS AND CHILLS

There are no chances of a sequel to *Staccato* by Ginko Arishima, which begins where other tales might end, and artfully tells a detective story by concentrating solely on what would be the final chapter of an Agatha Christie whodunnit — that climactic drawing room confrontation when a murderer is unmasked. Old-time noblewoman Yuriko suspects that her late mother has been poisoned. With the aid of her would-be lover Shozo, she thinks through the evidence, but only uncovers a new and unexpected scandal. In a deeply Gothic twist, the more she discovers about her mother's secret life, the more she ruins her own, until a fateful, shocking denouement when she turns on the man she had previously hoped would bring her happiness.

Nor is Arishima's story the only gory one in *Rose Mystery*. Noriko Yamauchi's *Your Gentle Hand* begins with a chilling jolt — a close-up of a man's bloody hand, clutching at a weeping woman. Yamauchi builds the suspense for all it's worth, cutting right from the close-up into a sunny, romantic story. The reader is left guessing throughout — whose blood will we see? Whose hand? Who's weeping? She ramps up the tension all the way through by repeating the motif of zooming in on human touches. Hands clasp each other in pleading, in love, in argument, and every time the reader wonders if this is when things are going to really kick off. It's a triumph of the manga medium — using the 'camera' angles and trickery of cinema to tell a story in comic form that mixes romance and suspense.

A different kind of chill is on offer in *Bird Charmer* by Rika Harada, which begins unapologetically with the designer grab-bag of a game-based or fantasy manga. A talking rabbit? A life-sized Pierrot doll walking down the street? But Harada is playing with the reader's expectations — this time the circus really has come to town, and the reader is thrown into the carnival world of itinerant performers for whom clowns are an everyday sight. And in a nod to many classical misunderstandings, there are two teens from different worlds, both called Mizuki — one from the carnival, and one from an everyday town. The circus folk have their own rules, customs and homes, but exist constantly on the move, imparting their momentary respite in the hometown of young Mizuki with all the magic and mystery of a doorway to another dimension. Should he join the circus? And if he does, is he making a pact with dark forces? Harada's tale cunningly uses the tropes of fantasy to tell a very everyday story.

TWISTS IN THE TALE

A similarly clever attitude informs the art style of *Wife in a Box* by Kei Kousaki. The plot is deceptively simple — a harassed housewife gets caught in a supermarket fire. But the execution is just genius: a trip to the high street is presented as a dark fairy-tale. The supermarket has suspicious accidents and ominous cobwebs in aisle four. And when an assistant claims to have the right item "out the back", the storage room smells funny, and suddenly leads our heroine to scream at him, "DON'T OPEN THE BOX!" Throughout the story, Kousaki draws her heroine's

MYSTERY LETTERS: SCHOOL M IN TOWN B

Many of the stories in *Rose Mystery* add a note of authenticity by feigning identity protection. Universities, schools, hometowns are often identified by single letters, as if the story being told is true, and innocent victims need to be protected. It's not a device found solely in Japanese storytelling, but it occurs surprisingly often in Japanese horror and detective fiction. The idea is to add a frisson for readers, who can believe that if something is being kept secret, it is because they are reading a story that involves real people. It also saves writers having to think up names for everything.

hair with the same energetic billows as clouds of smoke — sure enough, by the end, one mixes with another. The tale is perfectly mundane, but the execution is a wonderful example of how *Rose Mystery* can twist basic stories into adventures that will hold its target readership enraptured.

In *The Witness* by Kimiko Ohmasa, a man cannot believe his eyes when he walks through a park at night. He sees a pretty blonde woman who stabs a homeless man to death when he approaches her. The sole witness to the crime, Ono refuses to believe there is not more to the story. He begins to investigate, and in the course of stalking the killer, a minor TV actress, he falls for her. The two become lovers, and she explains the truth behind the sordid event, only to turn on him herself. As he lies bleeding on her floor, incapacitated by an attack with a golf club, she pleads with him not to die… He's found a right one here — she tries to kill him so that her secret doesn't get out, but then begs him to stay alive. The ending is the darkest of all in the magazine, leaving the reader's imagination to decide whether our hero's adoration offers redemption to his beloved, or if we are witnessing the last moments of a serial killer's victim.

Rose Mystery is a strange discovery; a test issue for what could be a whole new sub-genre. If it is an experiment, then it is a resounding success — its stories breathe new life into old clichés; its authors find innovative ways of appealing to a new set of readers. Unlike many of the magazines aimed at gothic-Lolitas, it lacks the objectified pretty boys and man-on-man action that particular audience seems to crave. Instead, it aims squarely at an audience of girls who are thoughtful, tasteful and Tiffany-twisted.

(*NEO* #40, 2007)

PAPER MOON: THE ORIGINAL LUNAR PRINCESS

The *Tale of the Bamboo Cutter* (*Taketori Monogatari*) is one of the oldest folk-tales in Japan. It tells the story of a beautiful girl who is found inside a piece of bamboo (prime flute-making material in the Far East), whose original home is thought to be a fantastic city on the moon. Lunar princesses can be found all over the manga world as a result. Updated versions of the story can be found in the works of Leiji Matsumoto, in *Sailor Moon S*, *Please Save My Earth*, and even in an erotic variant in *Rei Rei: The Sensual Evangelist*. In *Gundam Seed*, a mass driver on the moon is named Kaguya after the same legendary figure.

SUPER PACHISLO 777

Issue # 282 • **Debut Year:** c.1992 • **Page Count:** c.230
Publisher: Takeshobo • **Price:** 370 yen (c.$3.70)
Cycle: Monthly

After World War Two, much of Japan's surviving military manufacturing sector was retooled to create new items for the recovering population — fridges, cars and televisions. But in the immediate aftermath of the war, particularly in the 1940s when the population had yet to prioritize luxuries beyond food and shelter, factory management found a temporary stopgap to keep the factories busy. It was in Nagoya, so the legend goes, that a factory owner with a surplus of military-grade ball-bearings decided to move into the lucrative market of pinball machines. The advantage here was that although a machine would cost the same as a fridge, it need not be sold to private consumers, but instead to bar-owners and amusement arcades, who could recoup the cost from the users. But because this was Japan, with space at a premium, the pinball machines were set on end, vertically. This was the beginning of *pachinko*, so named for the sound the silver balls make as they bounce and carom around the noisy, flashy machine innards. Gambling machines, sellable to arcades not families, could relieve consumers of their money one coin at a time. Japan was soon awash with slot machines and their local variant, the pachinko vertical pinball games.

One-armed bandits soon grabbed the attention of working class gamblers, with parlors opened near stations and factories, where workers could industriously gamble away their earnings before they got home to wiser spouses. The media soon began to associate such gambling dens with Japan's gangsters. In the 1950s, government crackdowns made it illegal to win large cash prizes at pachinko. Instead, winners would receive daft tokens like teddy bears and chocolates, which they could then redeem for cash money if they knew the right people.

By the 1990s boom time, pachinko and slot machines were a $200 million industry in Japan, a big enough niche to attract the interest of manga publishers hoping to cash in on the *pachislo* (pachinko and slots) market. *Super Pachislo 777* is still running today, a manga magazine in which the comics take second place to acres of statistical charts, number analyses and tips.

Clues to the *777* reader's mindset are on the prize giveaway page. Among a smattering of DS and PS3 games are a weight-loss belt, toilet paper that looks like 1,000 yen banknotes, and a novelty pillow shaped like a pair of breasts, on which the weary slotter can rest his head after a day at the machines.

The adverts are sparse and follow a pattern that is familiar from other manga magazines for the older man. Pert young ladies offer to disrobe in front of a webcam for negotiable fees. Photographs are on offer of pneumatic idols in impractical bikinis. An intriguing advert offers temptations of a "no fee" phone club — until you read the small print. There is no fee for getting profiles of the ladies, or even for their contact details, but it's made clear later on that they are unlikely to waste much time answering their phones unless the caller is prepared to go out on a "date", which is where the meter starts running.

The hypothetical *777* reader who avails himself of such services can look to other adverts for assistance. White-coated American doctors promise dilatory miracles for the down-belows, if only the readers will take a course of their erectile wonder-drugs. Quack clinics promise no scarring for wart removals, zit zapping, and, perhaps more usefully considering the tone of the other commercials, discreet treatment for sexually-transmitted diseases.

When not chasing hookers, the *777* reader swims in a sea of slot machine trivia. Woe betide the noob who sidles into a pachinko parlor expecting to just feed the machines and try his luck. *777* is loaded with cunning tricks, such as a way of feeding multiple coins into the slot, liable to overload the machine's primitive counter and force several free turns. The magazine is loaded with printouts of the drums in the slot machines, so that any regular reader will know exactly how many nudges will take him from a losing two melons to a winning three.

SLOT FOR LIFE

There are enough hardcore slotters to keep *777* magazine alive, and even professional players. Several of them have collaborated with manga artists to tell their stories in *777* — or so the magazine likes to imply. One such success story is the pseudonymous 'Yukki', who writes the regular *Y-Style* manga drawn by Masashi Manabe. Yukki is every aging slotter's dream, a shapely Hokkaido-born twenty-something in a baseball cap and tight jeans, who spends her days in the Tokyo pachinko parlors and her nights, it seems, stretching mournfully on her sofa and waiting for that special someone. Yukki's specialist area is twenty-two-bit pachinko, machines with little interactive movies or animations on a central screen, which alter along with the player's success and time playing. Yukki's manga contains screen shots from the animation, and finishes with her dressed as a schoolteacher (this means a tight blouse, spectacles and a pointy stick, in case you were wondering), lecturing her fans on this month's discoveries, which include the revelation that a *Certain Death III* pachinko machine will pay out, on average, once in every 308.5 balls. It might sound silly, but such observations earn Yukki five million yen a year (c.$49,500).

'Ichiru' is another pro player, who writes *Ichi Oshi* with the artist Keisuke Tsukamoto. But *Ichi Oshi*'s manga component is only small. The bulk of it is taken up with Ichiru's observations on his conquest of the month — the *Fist of the North Star 2* slot machine, which pays out big-time one pull in every 336.008.

PRO SLO

This issue's cover story pro is 'Gari Zo', who teams up with a manga artist to write *Pro Slo* (Professional Slotter). Fifty-eight chapters into the story, Gari is a bespectacled chap with a five o'clock shadow, who leaves his apartment with a telling admission to his long-suffering wife, "Long time no see!"

His 'working' life is a seemingly endless round of bleeps and clicks, as he feeds money into the slots, preferably at new parlors where he is not yet recognized. Just to make his life more difficult, every machine has a counter, advertising to punters and staff how many times it's paid out Big and Regular, in how many spins. This week, Gari's obsession is the new *Evangelion* machine, which allows the artist to intersperse the dull sight of spinning melons and cherries with some of the artwork from the in-game mini-animations.

How does a pro slotter make his living? According to Gari Zo of *Pro Slo*, last month he spent eight days doing absolutely nothing, seven days cracking the *Evangelion* machine (of which only one day paid significant winnings), four days writing his manga and accompanying column, another week earning real money by playing machines he'd already cracked, a couple of days traveling, and one day "helping out" at a friend's pachinko parlor (likely to have been a handy way of getting a look inside certain machines). His total haul from slots in those thirty days was a net profit of 272,000 yen (c.$2,700). He probably earned at least that again by telling you all this in a chapter of his thirty-one-page manga, which means he earns annually... er... more than us.

Professional slotting, it seems, requires a combination of autistic obsession, mathematical genius, and never-ending days sitting in front of one-armed bandits in insanely loud amusement arcades. Gari lives in an apartment and drives a Toyota (at least according to the manga), when his career choices would make one rather expect him to be sleeping under a railway bridge. Perhaps realizing that he will face scorn, his section of the magazine includes a day-by-day breakdown of his activities for the entire month. Other contributors to *777* magazine follow the same pattern, daring doubters to scoff when they are prepared to offer such exacting accounts. This is also part of the magazine's wish-fulfillment appeal. It offers the vague glimmer of hope to its readers that wasting their lives gambling is not a slow spiral into penury, but the first steps of a new and glamorous career in which they are paid a living wage to do what they love. It is, however, interesting to note that the contributors to *777* magazine can barely scrape a subsistence-level salary by slots alone. The real profits, ironically, come in writing the manga and magazine articles telling everyone else how to do it.

PINBALL WIZARDS

Not every contributor is quite so statistically minded. Matsuhi Nakayama's *Magical Heroine Mahi Mahi* is a gag strip that tries to superimpose the adventures of a "magical girl" onto life on the slot machines. Romance and social interaction is of more interest to the characters in *Slot Evolution*, written by Hiroshi Nakazawa and drawn by Yuna Takanashi, although the creators still find the time to talk about the latest releases. As seen in many other manga in this issue of *777*, the big new thing is the *Evangelion* slot machine, which several of the pros have been trying to crack this month — I bought this issue of *777* in Japan in 2007, in the wake of the new *Evangelion* movie. But whereas others treat it simply as a flashy interface over the same old Type Five drum system, the *Slot Evolution* team use it as a chance to push anime fanboy buttons, treating us to the sight of an attractive girl getting excited over a series of *Evangelion* buzzwords.

"Oh no!" she wails. "Samiel is attacking Neo Tokyo! The Type Two Eva isn't enough!"

Sadly, almost exactly the same plot appears in this month's *Positive Slotters*, with another young lady getting similarly excited about the same game. Here we see one of the pitfalls of *777*'s subject matter. The slot world moves fast, and has a limited number of new releases each month. Given that it takes a week or more to master a new machine, that readers always want the newest information, and that *777* is on a monthly turnaround, it is only to be expected that many of the authors end up covering the same material each month. The *Evangelion* machine crops up in half a dozen of *777*'s titles as the professionals scramble to crack it first.

DIFFERENT SLOTS

More frivolous fun can be found in Makoto Sogami's *Together With Sister*, a pastiche of Go Nagai's *Kekko Kamen* in which two sailor-suited schoolgirls mix ludicrously tough classroom life with their love of slot machines. At school they are tormented, stripped and tortured by a teacher in a mini-skirt. After class, they try their luck on the one-armed bandits, with the assistance of Slo Rich Mask, a tracksuited superheroine who offers frankly useless advice about beating the odds.

As if that were not boggling enough, *777* also offers *Deccult Five* by Hiro Touge. This bizarre manga follows the lives of a group of teenagers who have combined their love of "data" (computery things) and the "occult" (witchy things) to become the titular group — a bunch of geeky goths, if you will. So it is that a kimono-clad schoolgirl, a handsome hero, and their specky mate hang out with a man dressed as a professional wrestler and a feral child. And where do they choose to hang out? Why, in the place that combines the magic of blind hope with the heartless data of spinning wheels — an amusement arcade.

Understandably, some strips turn away from the slots themselves into the lives of those who work among them. *The Manager of Fire* by Hiroshi Natsume is a sarcastic portrait of an amusement arcade owner, depicted as a maniac with gangland connections, determined to rig his machines for the best possible payout... to himself.

Mimi's Tales of Bad Slotting, by Mimiko Matsumoto, is a series of short strips designed to warn players of ways to avoid "amusing" others. This month the emphasis is on fashion faux pas, with admonitions aimed at girls who sit in mini-skirts on high pachinko stools, affording passers-by a view of their knickers, as well as those who go braless and tight T-shirted into the air-con cool of a pachinko parlor, and then wonder why everyone is staring at their chests. Mimiko saves a smidgen of ire for big-nosed, loud foreigners, who have a habit of wandering into pachinko parlors and cluelessly feeding coins into random slots. Ha! Look at the stupid foreigners with their Japan T-shirts and their enthusiasm — a little dose of Japanese anti-charm, just in case you'd started to believe that they were nice all the time.

Not everyone in *777* has had a lucky month. Chobi, the protagonist of *Chobi's Work*, is a fat pro slotter who spends this issue failing to bring home the necessary high scores, and slopes off home dejected. In *Chobi's Work*, he confesses that this last distraction has accounted for a slow month and some botched days. A note at the end of his column reveals that, despite his self-effacing attitude and slacker styling, last year he earned six million yen (that's about $59,500 in real money) from his profession. However, Chobi's attitude seems a little less dedicated than his fellow pros. He doesn't even write the manga based on his life, instead farming out the writing to 'Yudai' and the art to Shinsuke Koga. Nor are his stats as detailed as anyone else's, which might help explain why he ends this issue slouching off empty-handed, hoping for better luck another day.

(*NEO* #45, 2008)

LEGALITIES

LIGHTBOXING

The Trouble with Tracing

Swiping is one of the guilty secrets of the art world. A comics artist, pressed for time, will slap an image on the lightbox and trace around it. Bad lightboxing is often easy to spot — I see a depressing amount of it from proud art teachers who think their little darlings have done an original "manga" image, and I have to tell them that little Albert has just traced the cover of *Princess Mononoke* and given her a Viking helmet. That takes your grade from an A to an F in one easy step.

Now the lightboxing scandal has hit Japan, with artist Yuki Suetsugu accused of tracing images for *Flower of Eden* from the manga of Takehiko Inoue. Only a few weeks later, Inoue himself was accused of stealing images and poses in his basketball manga *Slam Dunk* from NBA photographs.

Why is this news? Lightboxing other people's art might be morally questionable, but using photos for reference is hardly the same thing. Artists have ripped off photographs for the last 100 years. One famous illustrator of my acquaintance can always be found browsing through the porno mags for "reference material" — a steel bikini and a sword drawn over the top, and he's got his fantasy femme fatale, without having to pay a model to hold *that* pose. Manga art is famous, indeed often celebrated for its photo-real backgrounds. It's not rocket science, it gets them from photos! Then again, the Japanese can be very funny about image ownership — permissions are much stricter in Japan. It wouldn't surprise me if a lawyer was preparing a case in which the subjects of photo-reference sue for a cut of profits made with the aid of their images, or at least their general outlines.

Ironically, this has already been satirized in a manga, the wonderful

Patlabor, in which robot pilots discovered their movements in civilian machines were being recorded for use in military robots. The pilots got indignant because they were sure *something* was being stolen from them... they just weren't sure what.

In the meantime, draw your own images, don't just trace other people's. (*NEO* #19, 2006)

STUDIO 60
How Many Assistants Does an Artist Need...?

This month's news — manga creator Mayumi Kurata is forced to cough up six million yen in tax arrears. That's $58,000 to you, incurred over the three-year period that the artist and her sixty-strong studio have been cranking out *Damen's Walker*, a manga about women who always fall for the wrong guys, which has recently achieved greater fame through the presence of a live-action TV adaptation.

Wait a minute... a studio of *sixty* people? A manga artist with *sixty* assistants?

While there most certainly are solo creators who labor in their studios over every detail of every page, they are not the norm in the manga business. Oh sure, they'll be the people you're most likely to bump into at conventions, because they are most likely to be the ones with enough spare time to go to conventions. Once true success arrives, they're on a treadmill, and that means hiring staff.

At first, assistants just do the dull stuff. Scanning, coffee... lettering. But as a creator gets a name for themselves, assistants take over actual art tasks. They'll drop in brickwork and fabric patterns, they'll shade in the sky and add clouds... soon, they're drawing complex machinery like cars and helicopters. That can change the nature of a title. Some authors start to favor scenes that will take work off their hands, leading to many manga crammed with photo-real depictions of machinery or city architecture, because assistants are using real photos as reference.

The time can come when a truly successful artist is barely drawing at all. Instead, she's managing a staff of 'assistants'. Titles start to be credited not to Artist X, but to Office X or Atelier X. The creator has set up a company to own the manga instead of herself. And in this case it's the company that the taxman has come after.

And yes, I suspect it is the tax*man* we're talking about here. Something tells me that *Damen's Walker* struck a nerve in one of its rants on table manners, or drinking choices, or etiquette, and someone decided to be extra-careful in scrutinizing Kurata's tax returns. But if she now uses the experience as inspiration, does that make it tax-deductible...?

(*NEO* #29, 2007)

VOICES FROM THE PAST
Where Do Old Dubs Go to Die?

Unless foreigners are putting money into the production itself, a Japanese company is only really *leasing* an anime to them, for a fixed period of years. When the license period is up, the Japanese get their show back. American Company A might have made some money on *Schoolgirl Milky Crisis*, but if they didn't renew their license, then there was nothing wrong with the Japanese selling the title to someone else. In fact, any Japanese company worth its salt would have to be crazy not to. Enter Company B, a new group of anime-loving American businessmen, ready to buy the property.

But what happens to Company A's translation, subtitle script, or English-language audio track? Nobody really cared all that much twenty years ago, but now anime has a history and a tradition it's becoming more of an issue. If Company A lets its license lapse on *Biker Boy Bomb Boogie*, who owns the dub track?

Some old contracts assign such material back to the Japanese. After all, what use is an audio track to an anime if you don't own the visuals? It's so much dead tape, so why not let the Japanese do what they want with it? Lucky Company B; if they want to buy *Schoolgirl Milky Crisis* now, they will get a free audio track to sweeten the deal. A dozen of my own anime translations have reverted back to the original copyright holders. In theory, that means that if a company buys *Pointless Harem Boy* these days, presumably it will receive a copy of my script as a bonus extra.

Unless, of course, it's a Ghibli film. I'm not privy to the contracts on Miyazaki dubs, but something tells me that Lauren Bacall and Christian Bale don't act for a flat fee. They're probably on residuals, which means they stand to gain or lose money on what happens to that audio track should Buena Vista's license in *Howl's Moving Castle* ever lapse. A company that takes over the rights would also take over the obligation to pay royalties to those that are entitled to them.

But if Company A has kept its rights to a dubbing track, it could then try to sell it to Company B. This has already happened several times, as new anime owners suddenly hear a knock at the door, to find a man with a DAT tape offering to "save them thousands of dollars" by selling them a ready-made dub.

Which leads to the suggestion that has soured so many meetings. Old dubs are a buyer's market. Company B will smile sweetly and say, "Yes, that's very nice, but there is a high chance your dub wasn't that good in the first place. If it were, you'd have made so much money that you would have wanted to renew your rights instead of dumping them for us to pick up. So, no, we'll make our own dub. But thanks for asking."

That's not always the case, of course. Sometimes Company B thinks they can make a new dub cheaper than buying the old. Sometimes, nobody *knows* who owns the old dub any more, and it's legally less trouble to simply make a new one. Sometimes, people just forget Company A had a dub in the first place.

(*Newtype USA*, February 2007)

GAIJINS AND DOLLS
Language School or Dating Agency?

You're going to have to lie if you want a job teaching in Japan, my friends told me. I didn't believe them, and so had no success for two months. The problem is that Japan is full of foreigners who come for a few months to teach in the vacations. The language schools know that, but for the sake of appearances, they have to be 'surprised' when the *gaijin* (foreigner) ups stakes and goes home before the year is up. Otherwise, the clients of the schools would think it was the schools' fault and take their business elsewhere.

There are plenty of elsewheres to choose from. In the Osaka region, where I have been based for eight months, I counted at least 250 major English language schools, all scouting for native 'teachers'. The appalling standard of English teaching in the high schools, even though English is of prime importance in securing a university place, guarantees that every year there will be a horde of applicants for the night school programs. Furthermore, the snob value of being able to afford private English lessons is a draw for many older customers.

It's not English lessons per se that the customer is paying for, as the billboards demonstrate. They proclaim that "English conversation" is available, alongside a photograph of a foreign girl staring seductively into the camera. A set of commercials aimed at women depicts a handsome gaijin in a tuxedo, looking as if he's just got back from the opera.

The chance to boast that one is learning English in one-on-one lessons with a genuine foreigner ranks pretty high with middle class Japanese. The fact that you might have very little to show for it after a term doesn't enter into the equation.

Most of Japan's language 'schools' are more social institutions than places of learning. At one interview I was told that I would only teach for about half the time for which I was employed. For the rest I would be in the ominous-sounding Voice Room. It was actually a coffee lounge, where I was expected to make polite English conversation with whoever turned up.

A qualified English teacher would never get involved in such a farce, which is just as well, because the schools don't want qualified English teachers. Their idea of a perfect teacher is a fresh graduate (the discipline doesn't matter), since that makes him/her just old enough to be older than most of the pupils, and still young enough to be beautiful and sexy. The degree is required, since the clientele insist on some form of credentials, although the schools themselves only require you to pay lip service to this.

"Do you have a degree?" "Yes, of course." So went my screening, and I was in.

My English grammar test consisted of one question: "What is a gerund?" When I replied, utilizing the stunning word power of my failed Latin A Level, I was told that I was the first person for fifteen years who'd got it right.

When I eventually found a job it was with a smaller language school that turned out to be nothing more than a telephone in someone's flat, bolstered with impressive-looking business cards. I'd ring looking for students, and students would ring looking for teachers, and the lucky man in the middle would take money in advance from them, hold onto it for a month or so, take a sizeable cut and pass the rest on to me.

Everybody is ripping everybody else off, except for the poor students, who don't even realize that they aren't getting their money's worth. What makes it worse is that the Japanese university at which I was supposed to be studying started life in the same way, as a phone number that promised English lessons. It has grown over thirty years into a college with 4,000 students, including foreigners who are supposed to be learning Japanese. However, upon our arrival we discovered that our real purpose was little removed from that of hundreds of other gaijin (except they were paid and we weren't) — to talk to the students and look nice in the ads.

(*The Guardian*, 28th July 1992)

THE USUAL SUSPECTS
Tragedies and Tabloids

An attractive English teacher, apparently strangled by a student stalker, Lindsay Hawker was front-page news last month. As I write, Hawker's murderer is still at large, and her grief-stricken father proclaimed that the death had "shamed" Japan. Hawker's murder is heartbreaking and horrifying, but if Japan should feel ashamed, it is at the fact that a fugitive, barefoot homicide suspect can elude trained police. Somebody knows where he is, and I don't know how they sleep at night.

The Hawker case has other elements to occupy pundits. She worked at a language school that discourages its teachers from 'fraternizing' with students after hours — a controversial policy that led a disgruntled employee to seek legal action in 2005, but which could have saved her life. The school's motives revolved around its simple desire to control the purse-strings for the lessons and to avoid classroom romances that might turn sour through misunderstandings, but such things are easy to say on paper. When I lived in the Far East, I often went to teach at strangers' houses — back then it seemed innocent and everyday, now it seems silly and sinister. I was just as trusting as Lindsay Hawker, but not so unlucky.

What does this have to do with manga? If you're lucky, nothing at all. But there are already whispers that Hawker's alleged killer fancied himself as something of an artist. Supposedly, he had a collection of 'manga', although reporting has been so vague and full of insinuation that it has been unclear so far if journalists are referring to *hentai* games or pornography or, you know, comics.

None of which automatically turns anyone into a killer. The usual tabloid suspects have been quick to dust off their anti-manga tirades, going so far as to suggest that the killer may have been inspired by a comic, without a shred of evidence.

By the time you read these words, maybe he'll be in custody. If he says "manga made me do it", get ready for the backlash. If they haven't caught him, yes, shame on Japan.

(*NEO* #33, 2007)

BAN THIS FILTH?

On Illegal Lolitas

This month I have been mainly reading a government paper with the snappy title of *Consultation on Possession of Non-Photographic Depictions of Child Sexual Abuse*. This concerns the controversial UK Home Office proposal to make it illegal to own images, even if drawn, of children being sexually abused.

What controversy there is lies largely in the eyes of an anime and manga fandom convinced that this will somehow infringe their civil liberties. However, the paper's three authors, Vernon Coker, David Hanson and Cathy Jamieson, present a reasoned and detailed argument that is worth reading. Let's be ultra-clear here — they are not trying to stop you reading comics. They are trying to make it difficult for people to get hold of pictures of children being abused. Not because they think you will be corrupted, but because they know children can be.

Freedom of speech, freedom of fantasy — these are a separate debate. The problem, when one is talking about criminals and perverts, is that one is often too innocent to see what they are up to. It was initially a shock to me, some ten years ago, when I heard the BBFC ruling that *Overfiend IV* might be used "by pedophiles to entice children". The concept of 'grooming' wasn't one I'd ever heard before. Whatever you may think of the censor, movies are classified for a reason. There are things that we would really prefer children not to see. Not just because it might give them nightmares (actually, I still have nightmares about the Slitheen on *Doctor Who*, and I'm thirty-six!), but because books are not simply entertainment for children. We hope our children will develop a love and respect for the written word. We hope that they will take books from us and teach themselves. It is why some countries (sadly not ours) refuse to allow advertising amidst children's TV programming. It's why worthy organizations want children to find books that say nice things about Muslims, gays, divorce, brushing your teeth. It's why you really, really do not want some nonce showing *hentai* pictures to children and using that as a means to convince them that what they see is normal, acceptable, and indeed encouraged.

(*NEO* #39, 2007)

FOXY BOXING
When Can You Sell Something to Yourself?

The big news this month, although it seems to have sailed stealthily past the pundits, is over in Japan, where the Bandai-Namco conglomerate has embarked on a bizarre, and at first sight faintly loopy enterprise. The company has sent agents out into the stock market to *buy back* third-party shares in Bandai Visual and Bandai Networks. In other words, the parent company of some of anime's biggest shows, not least *Gundam*, is trying to take over *itself*!

Now, what on Earth, you might ask, is the point of a company repurchasing its own shares? Surely only an idiot would sell something one year, and then turn around to buy it back again, at a loss? But I suspect something much cleverer is going on behind the scenes. If Bandai-Namco owns its subsidiaries in their entirety, the company won't have to please any external shareholders. Instead, it can make some wacky decisions of its own, like, let's just say, selling an entire anime series to a Bandai-owned TV channel for just one dollar. With anime prices spiraling downward, Bandai's best chance of competing in the 'content' market is by arranging things so that its own content is cheaper than everyone else's, and it can do that by literally making it possible to give it away… to itself.

But if that's what Bandai's planning, the corporation should know that someone tried this once before. There were ructions in Hollywood a few years back when Fox, the maker of *The X-Files*, decided to sell *The X-Files* to a Fox-owned channel at a knockdown rate. But if you're the star of the show, your fees are calculated on a percentage, and if the deal is lower, so is your cut. Some of the cast and crew didn't like it, and kicked up a storm.

But here's a thought for the canny investor. What if you owned the last free Bandai Visual share in the world, and Bandai had to come up with whatever you wanted to get it off your hands? Now there's an anime plot waiting to happen!

(*NEO* #41, 2008)

FRIENDS FROM AFAR
Celebrity Visitations, Welcome and Otherwise

Confucius says, "It is a pleasure to learn, and to put your learning to its appropriate use. It is a delight to receive friends from afar. It is a quality of the true of heart that they are not mindful that they are not famous." But let's put that in context — when Confucius said that, he was living in exile. Nobody liked him, nobody knew who he was. It's not a wise epithet, it's a plea from someone imposing on your hospitality.

And I bring this up because of a man we're going to call Kazuhiro Domu, who was the creator of a best-selling manga and anime about psychic teenage bikers, which we are going to call *Schoolgirl Milky Crisis*. And for some bizarre reason, he had decided to spend a vacation looking at steam trains, and while he was in a foreign country, he figured he would drop in at his local publishers.

Tee-hee, he thought. Imagine the looks on their little gaijin faces when I roll in and surprise them. They will be so pleased to see me. They will jump for joy, and show me round their offices, and have their picture taken with me. They will interview me for their magazine and get me to sign copies of the manga and stuff. They can take me out for lunch, and tell me how great I am. It'll be like Christmas.

It never occurred to Kaz that his foreign publishers might not have translators lurking around the building at all times. He figured that *someone* in the building would speak Japanese, right?

So he wasn't quite expecting the welcome that he got. The receptionist dimly comprehended that a man with oriental features mumbling something in Japanese about manga might be something to do with her company's product, and she eventually called the only person in the building who spoke a foreign language. Unluckily for Kaz, the language was French, which was about as much use as a dog filled with sand. Kaz got increasingly irate, and the receptionist called Security.

Don't be too hard on the Company That Shall Remain Nameless. They'd had their fair share of nut-jobs in the past. There was the boy who set up camp outside because he "just wanted to look at the place where they made *Schoolgirl Milky Crisis*." There were the fans caught rummaging through their trash in search of discarded videos. And then there was the unpleasant day when they were raided by police who had received an anonymous tip-off that there was porn on the premises. You know, the tentacle kind.

Fortunately, this is where I came in. Because, even though I didn't work full-time at the company, I had a meeting there about some daft anime — *Geek Gets Girls* or *Emo Ninja Boy*, or something like that. And so I strode obliviously into reception to behold the remarkable sight of what passed for "Security" — Doug from Marketing and Steve from Accounts, sitting on top of a loudly protesting Japanese man who was quite unmistakably the world-famous Kazuhiro Domu.

At last someone was able to translate his words, which at that moment, comprised, "Get these morons off me!" along with a few obscene Japanese epithets for which not even several years translating *Urotsukidoji* had fully prepared me.

"He's not a tramp," I advised them after a brief exchange. "He is someone who is going to sue your ass if you don't let him go in the next ten seconds."

The Visiting Dignitary Unpleasantness passed into industry legend — I can tell you about it now because none of the guilty parties are still working for the company involved. But it got me thinking — what are the chances I could run a scam based on the experience today? What if I got a friend of oriental extraction, put him in the *faux*-casual slacks and polo shirt that seem to be an anime creator uniform, and pushed him at the doors of an unsuspecting anime company. He could put on a funny accent and pretend to be someone camera-shy — Hajime Yadate perhaps, Izumi Todo or Saburo Yade, "just passing" their UK distributors, and dropping in to say hi.

Maybe the true scam doesn't lie with the distributors. That's just a laugh and a slap on the back and a chance to lose work with an entire corporation forever more. But how much is in it for me if I try the ruse with an anime convention? Signings, public appearances — just how far could my anime celebrity fake it?

Hajime Yadate, Izumi Todo and Saburo Yade don't actually exist. And I don't mean I just made them up for this column. I mean that they really are artificial entities created by big corporations to hold copyrights. You see them on anime credits, but you're never going to meet them in a pub, because they're made-up people. But the studios aren't going to admit they're not real people, are they? I could bring an impostor along to a convention and get him to sign stuff for a fee… Who'd know?

Ask yourself this: on those very rare occasions when a Japanese celebrity does turn up in the UK, what evidence is there that they *aren't* a paid impersonator? I think I've just found a way to please everyone… Fans get to say they met Director X or Designer Y, and the UK distributors get to save on an air fare. It'll be our little secret. *Ssh…*

(*SFX Total Anime* #2, 2007)

RADIO DAYS
Mugged by the Mainstream

The girl who met me in reception had a badge that said Emma. She didn't actually tell me who she was, but sulkily informed me that she was here to take me upstairs. She didn't show an iota of enthusiasm until the elevator reached the designated floor, at which point she practically pushed me into the green room.

"Someone will be with you," she mumbled, before disappearing.

Someone soon was. Coincidentally, her name was also Emma. But Emma #2 displayed little interest in me. Instead, she was running through the questions with the people who were just about to go on-air before me. A nervy girl whose dog could play the bongos, or something like that. Emma #2 whispered her way through the questions she was going to get, just to put her at her ease.

That's nice, I thought. I imagined that for a lot of people, appearing live on the radio was quite nerve-wracking. I've lost count of the number of times that I've done it, and it's still pretty nerve-wracking for me. There is always that little devil at your shoulder, whispering that now would be the ideal moment to have a Tourette's Syndrome outburst. And the thought of it makes you giggle. And then it's too late.

Except Emma #2 didn't bother to tell me what questions were coming up. Instead, she pushed me into the studio where Emma #3 lay in wait. Another Emma — what were the odds? I began to suspect that this wasn't going to quite be the discussion of manga's broad genres that I had been promised.

With a proud flourish, I pulled a selection of manga from my bag.

They'd asked me to grab a few titles from around my office: *Ironfist Chinmi*, which I translated many years ago, Yoshihisa Tagami's Wild West manga *Pepper*, and *Shooting Stars in the Twilight* by Kenshi Hirokane.

"What's this?" said Emma #3, wrinkling her nose in scorn.

"Oh, that's my favorite," I said. "*Shooting Stars...* is a series of love stories and thrillers for the elderly."

"The elderly!?"

"Yes. I did say that manga catered for *everyone*. This particular series is for people in their sixties."

She turned through a few of the pages with an unhappy look on her face, and then handed it back to me without a second glance.

"Don't you have any porn?" she asked.

"Er... no," I said.

"It's just, I was hoping to see something shocking."

"I'm not all that sorry to have disappointed you," I replied. Then I remembered there was one more manga in another part of my bag. It was a copy of *Princess*, an anthology magazine for teenage girls.

I stuck *Princess* on the table, too.

"Is it porn?" said Emma #3.

"No," I said, beginning to get a faint idea of where this was all going. "It's for teenage girls!"

"Do they like porn?" she asked.

"You do realize," I began hesitantly, "and I did tell you on the phone, that manga is not just porn. It is kids' stories, and adventures, and thrillers, romance and drama, science fiction and detective stories—" But she cut me off with an upraised hand.

"By the way," she said, just as the light changed from happy green to ON-AIR red, "we've had to drop a few of the questions. It was kind of boring. Instead we're going to talk about changes in Japanese porn legislation."

And with that, I was in the line of fire, lured on-air to talk about the Japanese comics that I loved, and, once more, forced to become a spokesman for and defender of an entire nation's erotica.

Not that I mind that so much. There have been some fascinating developments in Japanese legislation recently. The Japanese government has spectacularly bowed to American pressure over obscenity regulation. Japanese law infamously rates obscenity on the basis of harm — in other words, it has long argued that if a sexual act, however unpleasant, is shown in a drawn image, nobody is actually being harmed and so the image should not be kept from consenting adult readers. This position has increasingly come under fire, both from UNICEF and from pressure groups like Cyber Angels, who have argued that manga should be subject to the same restrictions as "real" images, since they could be used to "groom" susceptible children.

Remarkably, the Japanese government has been prepared to listen to this. Instead of telling the Americans to leave them alone, the Japanese Cabinet Office issued a Special Opinion Poll on Harmful Materials. They discovered that a surprising percentage of the Japanese population agreed that "harmful" manga images should be censored. 90.9 percent in fact, said that they thought Internet images should be regulated. 86.5 percent said that they thought child porn in manga should be regulated. Interestingly, however, a massive 72.7 percent admitted that they didn't actually know enough about the materials under discussion to say for sure whether someone would be harmed, or how they would be harmed, or what was harmful.

This is a fascinating legal area. Obscene materials, like green politics, cross international borders in a wired world. They require international agreements, not local fixes. Despite complaints about the slowness of Japan's response, its willingness to listen to American arguments on the subject has been unprecedented.

And what does this have to do with manga? Not a whole lot, particularly if it's the only thing you get to bring up, and your time to talk about it has been slashed to less time than it takes to boil an egg. A runny one.

"Manga cover every conceivable genre," I pleaded in vain. "So, *of course* there are erotic manga." But that doesn't mean that every discussion of Japanese comics should turn into one about pornography. And it's ironic that Emma, Emma, and Emma's desperate desire to be shocked should have caused them to discuss Japanese pornography on national radio, giving it far wider coverage than it ever had in the Adults Only section of a comic store.

But that's what you get in the mainstream media. A promised fifteen-minute slot dwindles to five because someone has a dog that plays the bongos, and before you know where you are, you might as well not have bothered getting up early. It had cost me ten bucks to get into the studio that day. I was already wondering if I shouldn't have just stayed in bed and used the money to buy cheese.

On my way out of the studio, Emma #1 realized I might be angry about my treatment. She finally tried to make conversation.

"Does my name mean anything in Japanese?" she asked.

"Yeah," I said. "You're the ruler of Hell."

(*PiQ* magazine, July 2008)

MUSICAL STINGS
How *Gunbuster* Lost Some of Its Groove

It was, to some, a sign of lost innocence when the new version of *Gunbuster* jettisoned one of its musical jokes. A ninety-second piece redolent of the main theme from *Chariots of Fire* once played over the shots in the first episode of Noriko's training regime. Time has moved on — the tuneful gag was just that, a gag, but the makers of *Gunbuster* didn't dare hope that American lawyers would all be anime fans with a sense of humor. They pulled the original cue and replaced it with something else — if you've never seen *Gunbuster* before, you probably won't even notice, but even so, it's still a smidgen different from the original release.

This happens a lot. *Gunbuster* may be the most prominent case at the moment, but music rights snag up a lot of media productions. Radiohead's 'Paranoid Android' was a superb ending to *Ergo Proxy* in Japan, but likely to be absent from most non-Japanese releases. Duran Duran's 'Girls on Film' won't be gracing *Speed Grapher* in many non-Japanese territories. It's simply less hassle to replace the music with something cheaper.

But this is not news. It's not even *new*. And let's take a moment to remember what happens when the music is not replaced — the show can disappear altogether. Such issues ruined the chances on video of the anime serials *Goshogun* and *Srungle* when they were combined in 1985 as *Macron One*. The hybrid was spiced up with several US pop hits, which increased its appeal but made it a legal nightmare to renegotiate all the musical moments for other formats.

The thing is, music's worth a lot of money. Internet downloads aren't just a haven for pirates, they are a motherlode of new income for the rights holders of pop tunes. If you write a pop song, and someone wants to use it in a commercial that will air 200 times a week for a year in 300 markets, or as the opening theme of a cartoon show that will sell a hundred thousand copies on DVD, you bet that you want a cut of that. But if someone tells you they only need it for Japan, that's fine, and cheaper for them... until the day that the 'Japanese' series is sold to anime fans in America, in Australia, in Belgium, in Germany...

Nor is this problem limited to the anime world. Hugh Laurie in *House* gets a different theme song in some countries, because of the cost of the music rights for Massive Attack's 'Teardrop'. Fans like me of Taye Diggs in *Day Break* were briefly deprived of that serial's post-cancellation Internet conclusion because of what the broadcaster called "an unforeseen complication in music rights."

This is good news for creators. It affords them the kind of protection and job security that we all wish for the media business in the twenty-first century. You can't rip off *Gunbuster* without paying for the privilege, although sadly, this also seems to mean that *Gunbuster* can no longer tip its hat to Vangelis.

(*Newtype USA*, April 2007)

HIGHBROW
SKILLS
IN A LOWBROW
MEDIUM

HIGHBROW SKILLS IN A LOWBROW MEDIUM: TRANSLATING JAPANESE ANIMATION

Transcript of a speech given at the British Centre for Literary Translation at the University of East Anglia, 30th October 2001.

My name is Jonathan Clements, and I am a scriptwriter, author, and translator, in that order. I've always seen myself as a writer who happens to understand Japanese. Writing comes first. I spoke English before I learned Japanese. I was selling my writing before I was selling my translations. And that's the way it should be. In this country, Japanese speakers are very thin on the ground. The UK still only produces about 120 Japanese graduates every year, and they all earn far too much money in business or banking to worry about translating Japanese cartoons. And merely speaking the language isn't enough. Sixty million people in this country speak English, or claim to, but they're not all writers. You don't just pull someone in off the street and ask them to write a novel, and I don't think mere linguistic ability is enough to get someone hired as a translator.

[murmurs of reluctant assent]

One of my favorite translation companies, Studio Proteus in San Francisco, have this great policy. They're in America, where every year sees hundreds of new Asian Studies graduates hammering on their door and demanding work in this field. And they say, quite rightly, "We can pick and choose. Why should we hire you? We've got award-winning writers working for us already. Go away and sell a novel or sell a screenplay in your own language, then come back and tell us you can do a Japanese writer justice." Yes, translation is a craft a lot of the time, like writing is a craft. But they're also arts, and you would want someone serving your work as well as it could be served in another language.

[muted mumblings of very reluctant assent]

You're all post-graduates on the translation course here, so I imagine we share very similar qualifications. Like yours, my Bachelor's degree was a four-year language course. I studied Japanese and Mandarin at Leeds University. Gave up Mandarin in my third year so I could do a year of Cantonese. After that, I got a British Academy scholarship to do my Master's at the University of Stirling — I specialized in anime (that's Japanese cartoons) and manga (that's Japanese comics), and the routes they took into other languages. Then, after five years in the tertiary education system, after slogging my way through my early twenties still at school, after learning three of the world's most difficult languages, I found myself in London working on an anime dub... and while I was going through the budgets, I saw how much everyone was getting paid. I said to the producer, "You know, I can't help noticing this actor is getting paid more to simply read out my script aloud than I was paid to write it." And she said: "Oh, well, of course. Actors have to go through all that training, don't they?"

[stunned silence]

And that's the kind of attitude you can all expect in this line of work. Don't think for a moment that I'm going to complain about what actors get paid, they earn every penny. But the attitude of this industry towards translators can be quite shocking. Part of it, I'm sure, stems from the film industry's attitude towards writers themselves. Writers are notoriously badly treated in the film industry, but a lot of that stems from the way that they work. Their job is done before shooting begins, so they're not usually part of that whole social whirl of cast and crew. They also find themselves in the position of having to work with words and story, but *for* people who can't string two sentences together themselves.

In the film business, where everyone has a horror story about how poorly writers are treated, you can imagine how much extra difficulty there is for a translator. Creativity is a very difficult thing to evaluate. A degree in Media Studies proves nothing. You can become a producer simply by waving a check book. People like that can get very nervous and jumpy around someone with a genuine skill. If you're lucky, you will be regarded as some kind of bizarre freak who can speak Foreign, and only that. Nobody likes to admit that you can actually do anything they can do, but do it in another language.

I should point out here that I love my job. I'm not complaining. I do enjoy films like *The Player* and *The Mistress* or TV series like *Action* that ridicule the Hollywood system. But I only get a kind of guilty pleasure from it. That's because I believe the film industry is much maligned. Yes, it can be creatively impoverished, and run by people with the morals of goats, but it's also a great patron of the arts. I can work for four weeks on one script that will pay all my bills for the rest of the year. It makes it possible for me to get on with the work I really want to do. This book [holds up *Anime Encyclopedia*] was a full-time, seven-day endeavor over a whole twelve months. If it wasn't for the money I made from writing some episodes of something called *Halcyon Sun*, I wouldn't have been able to put that kind of time in, I would have had to do it on weekends. It would have taken 'til 2005. The media business might waste your time, but it *pays* to waste your time, and it pays handsomely for the privilege.

The stuff I'm going to talk about today, however, is from the *video* business, and that can make a big difference. I'm going to show you an example of my work, so you can get an idea of the kind of thing I do. This is a show called *Sol Bianca 2*, which I translated for the UK market a few years ago. This tape sold about 4,500 copies, which is average for this sort of material. With the best will in the world, that means the distributor can't have made a profit of more than $35,000. That's peanuts in the film business, and that kind of nickel-and-diming attitude rolls down on through the system. The translator is normally the one who feels it the hardest.

So what have we got here. This is sci-fi from the eighties. Even if you couldn't read the copyright statement, you could guess from the fashions. Three girls are trying to set up a deal on a space liner. They want to buy a shipment of a valuable element called "pasha", and they want to buy it from a group of interstellar arms dealers.

[chortles of disbelief]

I'm glad you think that's funny, because it's about to get worse. Looking around me, I'm guessing that *[points]* you speak Japanese, am I right? And the rest of you don't? These girls in this video, they all speak different varieties of Japanese. The leader, Feb, is very feminine and graceful, she speaks a very feminine dialect. Janny, the one with the short pale-blue hair, she speaks a very butch, male dialect. It's very unsettling to hear that with Japanese ears, and it's even obvious if you don't speak Japanese that there's something not quite right about this one. April, the one in the trilby, is kind of in between the two. Anyway, this is what I do…

[Shows sequence from the beginning of Sol Bianca 2.*]*

And we'll leave them there in the middle of the firefight. Now the first thing you might notice about that scene is the neologisms. People are throwing terms around like "nanoviral bombs" and "necrograph". You're going to need a science fiction sensibility if you're going to be able to translate terms like that. You can't turn up after you've read nothing but Jane Austen and *Bridget Jones's Diary* and expect to work out how a science fiction author would coin these terms. Luckily, you people already have policies to handle this sort of thing. The Equal Frequency Rule gets you out of this one. Those terms are written using Chinese characters — in other words, they use Japan's classical language, so you do the same. You put the characters into Latin: "*Mor-Scriptor*"… Nope. Okay, Greek: "*Necro-Graph*". Oh yeah. Until you find something that's going to fit.

But a bigger problem, I think, comes from the fact that science fiction, by its very nature, bends language in new and unexpected directions. Because I was working for a cheapskate company on this one, I only had the tape to go on. Contractually, these days I always insist on a timecoded tape and an ADR script, because imagine how much trouble I would have had if I didn't see the pictures that went with the words. A lot of film companies don't think of this. They think that lines like, "You can tell us after you're dead," and "Get under the floor," will be self-explanatory when they're just sitting there on the page. Well, they're not. Particularly in science fiction and fantasy, when literally anything can happen on screen, you need to be watching that screen.

So how does this all look on delivery? Firstly, I assume you know how a script is supposed to be formatted: directions, explanations and dialogue. As a translator you might expect to have to translate the whole thing. On rare occasions, when I've translated a script for investors, so they can see how an unmade film is *going* to look, this is how a script would appear. But anime companies in this country don't want that, they want something that drops most of the description of events, and sticks almost completely to straightforward dialogue.

This is going to get shoved straight into a computer and shunted onto the screen. The numbers here at the left are rough timecodes in minutes and seconds (the timecode is that black numbery thing that you see at the top of preview copies, to make sure that everybody is looking at exactly the same moment on the screen). Always, always insist on a timecoded tape. Don't ever make the mistake of assuming that little clicky-counter thing on your VCR will be good enough, because we're often dealing with NTSC/PAL conversion here, and that's going to change the frame rate. Make sure that when you say something happens two minutes and thirty seconds in, it's happening right where you say it is.

Those little lines down the left-hand side denote changes in shot. They establish a very vague sense of timing so that you can count your way through changes in angle. They're really not that important to a subtitler, but we'll come to why they're really there later on. Characters' names are self-explanatory, and the lines themselves follow after that. If all you're doing is shoveling the dialogue onto a subtitling screen, this is all you're going to need. This system is absolutely, completely idiot-proof, unless you are Labyrinth Video, who once harangued me down a phone for ten minutes, telling me that my translation was crap, before they realized they were watching the wrong tape.

[laughter]

If you can, try and find out how wide your subtitling screen is. A good company should know. Whether they're laying stuff out in a font that fits twenty-five letters on a line, or thirty-five, if you fit your dialogue to the size of the screen, the subtitler isn't going to screw around with it. If you run over, he's going to look at the page and cut something, and you don't want him deciding what goes. He's not a writer. He's not even a typist. But he will have the power of *life and death* over your dialogue if you make any mistakes during delivery.

Subtitlers have done some whacked-out things to my scripts over the years. On *Sol Bianca* they cut over a quarter of my dialogue and decided that they would have one of the space pirates doing "homework", as if she were a schoolgirl. On *Plastic Little* they added a line which I had specifically told them to leave out, while cutting a crucial sentence a couple of seconds before it. On *The Cockpit* they changed the Zero-Sen fighter plane's name to "Zero-Zen", presumably because it sounded more 'foreign', and even altered the date of Hiroshima. I think they moved it to some time in 1953. If only the American air force had done that too, everybody could have got out of the way.

Eventually I got so pissed off with the little, pointless, and often counter-productive changes that they were making to my scripts, that I did something about it. I wanted to find out what it was that made these people think they knew what they were doing. So I called them.

In the spirit of gutter journalism, I called up one particular company which shall remain nameless *[names company in a loud voice]*, and I said, "Hello, I'm a very rich film producer, and I need a film subtitled." And they said, "Bloody marvelous. We'll do it. Send us the script, we'll translate it, we'll shove it up on the screen, and then we'll send it to you for checking. We can do absolutely any language." "Can you do Japanese?"

"No," they said. "Er… What we do for Japanese is, you send us the script in English, and then we take it from there."

So I said, "And there's a discount, right?"

And he said, "No… Er… You see… these translators, they don't know what they're doing half the time… we have to edit their dialogue, and that's what you're paying for."

So this 'translation' company was taking money from people for translating Japanese scripts, the only proviso being that the scripts had to be in English first.

[shocked gasps]

So I was pretty unimpressed with that. And I can see you are, too. And I did wonder, as you are probably wondering, exactly what it is that causes a supposedly reputable company to behave in such a way. And I wondered about it for a whole year, until I saw what's known in the trade as a spotting list, in this case from a little show called *[names show]*.

I would show you the scene on tape, but to be honest, the distributor was too cheap to send me a copy, and I couldn't bring myself to buy it with my own money. Let's remember, folks, Japanese is a rare language. According to the US State Department, it takes eight times longer to reach a competent level in Japanese than it does in something easy like French or Vietnamese. And with this in mind, some of the Japanese film companies try to jolly things along by promising to provide their *own* translation if you buy it. Now I don't know who does this stuff, but I'm guessing it's the guy in the office who says he's got an English degree, and we all know how useful they are.

[hearty guffaws]

I've seen companies in this country try and get away with saying, "Ah… We shouldn't pay you as much money for this job, because it's only editing… It's in English already." Bear in mind that this is just after they've told you to screw yourself, and then come sidling back a couple of days later when they realize that they don't understand half the shit on the page, and that they're going to need a Japanese speaker after all to translate the so-called translation. And if you're sitting on a spotting list, the chances are pretty high they won't have bothered to send a Japanese script as well, so it's actually going to be harder if you can't hear what people are saying on the tape.

On the left-hand side you see the helpful so-called translation that the Japanese supplied. It's almost nonsensical, but I've seen companies say, "We don't need a translation, we got one from the Japanese already. Ha ha ha, you suck!" and actually stick this kind of stuff up on the screen. Now, as you can probably guess from the notes I've scrawled on the right, this spotting list is not what I would call 'up to professional standards'. This is just brilliant, because you can see here from the annotations on the page, that there are twenty-five lines on this sheet, and twenty-three of them are wrong. You can see the tell-tale signs here, and here, of someone who hasn't worked out how to use definite and indefinite articles, and certainly someone who isn't fluent enough to know when to break the rules in dialogue. In other words, the guy who wrote this is a native-speaker of Japanese, using English as a target language.

[shocked gasps]

And he's just taken your job.

[laughter]

So what? He's translating out of his native language. It's a mess. The first line of the spotting list, "I'm all wet, I was in the storm of war," is actually relatively faithful, but this passage, as you might have guessed, is actually a song. It *should* be: *[sings]*

Through the storm of battle
My clothes are dripping wet.
Now I need my baby
To help me to forget (do doo doo doo).
Now all I'm wanting (do do doo doo)
Is to be sleeping
Wrapped within your loving arms.

There's another four stanzas, but I won't make you suffer any more.

You'll notice that my translation at least makes an attempt at rhyming. I know we're always told to stay away from rendering verse as verse, because it invariably comes out as doggerel, but pop songs are pretty easy. You've got your meter and your scansion, and I normally cruise through for one line which fits perfectly in both languages. In this case, it's this one: "Wrapped within your loving arms." I use that to set the tone for the way the rest of the song is going to work out. Even if you're not going to rhyme the song, at least italicize it to somehow separate it from the rest of the dialogue. I recommend you try and get it to scan with the music as well; it's kind of jarring for the viewer to have the beat rolling in front of him, getting the tune but reading words that don't fit.

If in doubt, I'd like to mention that Michael Jackson's songs have had consistently shitty scansion and dodgy para-rhymes since he finished the *Bad* album. If in doubt and your line doesn't fit, and you're up against the clock, just stretch a couple of syllables. He does it all the time, and he calls himself the King of Pop.

[laughter]

Okay, talk of fitting your lines brings me neatly onto the final topic I'm going to go over with you today, and that's dubbing. Japanese cartoons are synched to animatics, which means, in other words, they record the dialogue to a very rough, but completely timed animated storyboard. This means that whatever the actors do in the studio can be stuck on screen by the animators after the fact. If they were animating me talking right now and I suddenly went WUGGAWUGGAWUGGA, that wouldn't be a problem 'coz they'd have it on the tape and they would just draw it. There's a separate track called the 'M and E' (Music and Effects). So if we're doing a dub over here, we don't need to do music again, we don't need to do foley, like footsteps and so on, we just need to do the words. But, here's the thing. We're doing words to pictures that were done to match the Japanese voice recording. There's nowhere near as much scope for improvisation, and we've often got a real lip-sync problem.

The item in front of you is a page of the Japanese script from my first ever translation job, something called *KO Century Beast Warriors*.

[writes on blackboard]

KO 世紀 ビースト 三獣士 KO Seiki Biisuto Sanjushi

This is the title in Japanese. This is the f... flipping title! The Japanese use four different writing systems, and they're using three of them here. This here [世紀, "Seiki"] is 'Century', this here [ビースト, "Biisuto"] is 'Beast', the English word 'beast'. Here at the end, these three characters [三獣士, "Sanjushi"] are 'Three Beast Warriors'. There's a prize for anyone who can spot the pun.

[silence]

Okay. 'Three Beast Warriors' — that's "San Ju Shi". But if I change this "Ju", to replace it with this character:

銃

I get another "Juu". I get "San Juu Shi" — 'Three Rifle Warriors' which is Japanese for 'three musketeers'. So some people call this *Three Beastketeers*...

[laughter]

...which is a pretty good translation.

Nobody knows about the "KO" part. "KO" has eighty-four different meanings in Japanese. It could be this one — 'Child', or this one, 'Ray of Light'. Turns out it's actually "K.O." — 'Knock Out'. *Knock Out Century Beast Three Beastketeers*. And that's the title.

We haven't even got off the title page and you're looking at me like I've just set fire to my hair.

[laughter]

So anyway, where was I? Oh yeah, the script. Mmm… lovely… squiggles. You'll notice that, even though the population of Japan have more word processors than they can realistically expect to use, they have kindly sent this script in hand-written Japanese. This is quite rare these days, but I did not enjoy seeing 150 pages of handwritten Japanese like that turning up in my mail box, I can tell you. For those of you who persist in learning boring old languages with alphabets, I'll talk you through it. Firstly, it reads from right to left, of course. Top row is the shot number, you'll see that changes in shots are denoted by a line right the way across the page, which is the Japanese equivalent of those little dashes I showed you on the *Sol Bianca* script. That's how we used to do it in English too, until some underpaid translator realized he was paying for his own ink to draw them.

So, I'm going to go through these lines so you can follow them. I'm actually going to show you this scene later on, but I want it to fester in your minds for a while. This is a show about Wan, a boy who can turn into a tiger, and Meima, a girl who can turn into a mermaid. And they're mutants on the run from evil humans. And this is the big fight at the end of episode one, where they're trying to get off the humans' battleship, and the human's leader, V-Daan has just beaten up the hero. And here we go, shot 314, on the far left: Wan hits the ground, and Meima looks worried. That's the action, written here along this upper portion.

Then in this lower portion, that's where the dialogue goes, so as you can see it's very different from a traditional script layout. But handy, though, because it allows for simultaneous action and dialogue. As Wan falls to the floor we get "SE" (Sound Effect), "Dosa!"

Okay, there's a line on the page and we're into shot 315, which is V-Daan chuckling contemptuously and saying, "Ore wa na, hikui yatsu o ijimeru no ga daiiiiisuki nanda yo." Or, "Oh how I loooove kicking weaklings around."

See here on shot 316, the little girl, Yuni, gets a line which is simply an exclamation mark. These are dotted across the page. See here, there's another one, and another one, and another one. They're effort noises, subvocalizations, little moments of grunt or groan that need to be scripted because they're not on the Music and Effects track.

These are relatively easy to deal with in the dubbing studio. You put the words "[effort noise]" on your script, and the actor will just synch it to pic on the day of the dub. More troublesome are these puppies: the words "ad lib". Now, these are relatively commonplace in anime scripts, not least because the Japanese actors love improvising.

They've also often got better experience of their characters, often because there's already been a radio play version before they've done the anime, and because anime actors tend to get typecast, and often know exactly what kind of character they'll be playing because it's the one they play all the time. But how do you translate these ad libs in an English dub? In my first job, I assumed the actors would want the same free rein, and I just wrote the words "ad lib". But it fast became apparent that the actors we were getting in for the English dub often couldn't come up with something quite so good — they couldn't just pull new lines out of their asses on the spot. They didn't have the time or the inclination. I ended up writing the so-called "ad libs" for them and putting them in the script, either as faithful translations of whatever the Japanese actors had come up with, or as my own creations. Quite simply, the English actors weren't being paid enough to put the effort in themselves, and they'd often only just seen the script when they walked in.

This was a surprise to me. I wondered if it was the same all over the voice-over business. I got the chance to find out one day when the studio caught fire…

[nervous titters]

No, it did; the studio caught fire. All the fire extinguishers went off, and the place was full of particulate, and we were told to piss off over the road to the coffee place while they sorted the problem out. So I found myself with one of the professional actors with half an hour to kill. I got him to tell me his Perfect Dubbing Day. And this isn't some luvvie fantasy, either, this is how he often worked.

He's dubbing a Dutch movie, and he turns up with the other actors for the morning session. Then, they get their cigarettes, their coffee and their munchies, and they all sit down and watch a subtitled print of the movie with the director. They work out who's playing what part — which can be important, you don't want to end up having to interrogate yourself like poor Rupert Degas on *Adventure Kid*. They try out some voices, and, most importantly, they know what the film is about. Then they have lunch. Then, in the afternoon, they run through the film. They've seen it already, they know how it works. They also use an ADR system like a giant piece of toilet paper...

[laughter]

No, really! The actual script is written by some poor sap on a long roll, like toilet paper, and it winds in real-time underneath the screen itself. So not only can you read your lines right off the paper, but if you're going to be interjecting, you can see your interjection coming up, and yell out at exactly the right moment. You don't have to wait to see the character's lips move or second-guess the timing. You work in that way, and you can do a ninety-minute film in a day. Compared to an anime dub when you're lucky to do forty-five minutes in a day.

Now at my first anime dub, *Beast Warriors*, I was stupid. I was working under the impression that the actors would all get copies of the script in advance, and subtitled copies of the tapes so they could watch it before they turned up. I grew up around actors, I know that they like to "run lines" and, well, not "get into their parts" as such, but just get an idea of what they're going to be doing. But the company I was working for didn't do any of that. They just handed them their scripts as they walked through the door, pointed them at the screen, and started on page one.

To put it bluntly, the producers thought that the actors were too lazy to give a shit. And the actors in general *didn't* give a shit, because they weren't being paid enough to care. $500 might sound like a lot for a morning's work, but not if that's the only work you see for three weeks.

So with all this in mind, I'm going to show you this sequence from the end of the first episode of *Beast Warriors*, where the beasts are trying to get off the humans' battleship, Professor Password is killed, and the big fight starts. You'll notice effort noises in the wrong place, a sobbing girl whose chest doesn't move, some drifting lip synch, and a couple of other things we'll talk about later on. This is about another three minutes of footage, so don't lose the will to live, it'll be over soon. And if any of you do get bored, you can entertain yourselves by listening to me playing the baddie.

Here we go…

[Shows sequence from the end of Beast Warriors 1.*]*

And we'll leave it there. Something that only just occurred to me watching that again was the haphazard nature of the casting. Professor Password, there, that poor actor was only told as he walked in that he'd be doing an Irish accent.

[Irish audience member: "That was an Irish accent!?"]

Er… well, Irish/Scottish/Celtic Fusion Sound System. I don't know. The point is that he got treated just the way translators get treated. People either think you can't do a thing. Or they think you can do everything. My grandmother got pissed off at me once because I couldn't read the instructions on her Russian vacuum cleaner. I tried to point out that I hadn't actually learned Russian, but she wasn't listening. Same with this guy, Tim Block, his name was. He never claimed to be able to do the accent, he just had it dumped on him and did his best. And maintaining an accent makes it that much harder to actually act, because your mind's on something else.

Also note the children's voices were real children. Normally, in Japan and the UK, we just draft in a woman who can do a kid-voice. Here we had real kids, which made a nice change, but obviously they have a lot less experience. In fact, you were just watching the results of the first day of their first professional job. Apparently they were going to get some kids from a drama school, but they called the week before the dubbing started and told us that they weren't going to let their students take part in "one of them there Japanese Porno Videos."

So anyway, there you go. That's the kind of work I do, and some of the things I wish I'd known about seven years ago when I started in this business. Not all of it's going to be directly relevant in your language areas, but I hope you've got some idea of what it's like. And you've seen a transforming chicken, too.

[laughter]

There's one other thing I wish I'd known when I was younger, and that was how much I was worth. Does anyone here know what the Writers Guild minimum is for translation?... That's right, there isn't one. Okay, if I gave you a script for a production below a $2 million budget and asked you to rewrite it, the WG minimum is $18,000. That's for taking someone's script and translating it from English to *English*. I hear there's a guy in America who does anime scripts at a hundred bucks a time. Big difference.

It can be very easy to forget how much you are worth, particularly if you spend four years at a university sitting with thirty people who are all smarter than you. I wasn't a particularly stellar student at my college, but I was the one who found myself in this business. I had no idea how much my time was worth. I didn't know if I spent two weeks working on a script, how much I should be paid. I let myself get conned, a lot. I can't tell you how much you're worth, but I can guess it's probably more than you think. If you ever find yourself in my position, always bear one thing in mind: the guy who *fixes your toilet* charges 100 bucks an hour.

And thank you.

[applause]

[question: "How do I get to translate films?"]

The field is very small in every language. In Japanese, about half a dozen people in Tokyo have got the whole deal sewn up between them. It's not that they're a clique, just that there aren't that many films that really need the treatment. It'll be the same in most linguistic groups, even those where there's more call for English into... You're Italian, right? Right.

English into Italian. The trick is to make yourself known. Be known. Be famous. I got my first translation jobs because I was already writing about Japanese cartoons for magazines. Make yourself available. Get to know these people. Who you know is important, because I would never recommend someone I didn't know unless I had a particularly in-depth knowledge of their work. Don't get a complex about "who you know" — quite often, you get to know *who* you know, because of *what* you know anyway. It's not a cop-out.

Have any of you heard of *Princess Mononoke*?

[murmurs of recognition]

That script was nominated for an award as 'a work by Hayao Miyazaki and Neil Gaiman'. Neither of those men was the translator. Hayao Miyazaki was the writer, but he doesn't speak English. Neil Gaiman performed a function which you as professional translators might call editorial, but he doesn't speak Japanese. Best as I can work out, the people responsible for the actual translation were either Ian McWilliam or Steve Alpert, who do speak Japanese. You may well ask, what the hell was the company doing hiring translators who couldn't write dialogue, meaning it had to hire an editor for the script, and one, I might add, who threw in a few semantic drifts of his own? The point here is that Neil Gaiman got that job because Quentin Tarantino recommended him. He got that job because he is a famous writer with a body of his own work, which can give the average producer an immediate idea of what kind of work he's going to turn in. You don't want to be Ian McWilliam or Steve Alpert. You want to be Neil Gaiman. You want to be the one that they go looking for. I've been there. I've been asked to "translate" something, and then my agent got me extra money for the job, because I *actually spoke* the language I was translating!

[hysterical laughter]

You think that's insane? Yes, it is. But stupid people are never going to appreciate you for being a translator. Being a translator isn't going to be the thing that snags you the real money. You need to be something else. I know you probably don't want to hear that when you've picked translation as your specialty. But remember what I said when I came in. You can do this in at least two languages. Don't be a wallflower off someone else's fame. If you think you can rewrite other people's books, get a track record in writing your own as well.

[question: "In translating anime, is there any consideration of the target audience? Is it different in Japan and England?"]

Actually, these days, the audiences aren't that different. A combination of events in the wake of a show called *Evangelion*, coupled with the rise of *Pokémon*, have effectively destroyed the old anime audience. In 1995, the anime audience was under-twenty-fives. Today, in Japan as well as England, you're lucky to find a fan who can *remember* 1995. The average fan is now fifteen years old. In fact, if you want the full profile, he's fifteen years old, he lives in a kind of Fertile Crescent across the Midlands from Birmingham to Bradford, he lives with his parents, he doesn't have a girlfriend, he has a console (not a PC), and he would rather buy trainers than books. That's the audience demographic Manga Entertainment were playing to. And, rather handily, that's the audience demographic that the Pokemaniacs are going to turn into by 2003. So a lot of the old stuff can be dusted off for DVD and thrown back out there. Does that answer your question?

[question: "Is there money to be made in the business?"]

In theory, though I wouldn't recommend that anyone goes looking for work in the anime business. I imagine there's more work in computer games at the moment, which utilize similar skills, but with much chunkier scripts. The biggest script I ever translated was a computer game — it was 30,000 words!

I will warn you, though, computer games bring their own problems, most notorious of which is the number of times translators are given scripts to translate with no idea of what's going to come up on the screen.

If you ever wondered what was wrong with the dialogue in *Resident Evil*, it was the translator having no clue whatsoever what would eventually be going on onscreen around his lines.

I was doing one game script once that mentioned 'the door of the tree'. Or it could have meant 'the wooden door'. Japanese can use the genitive case as an adjective on occasion, there was no context, and this was a fantasy game, so damn right there could have been a door in that tree. Be ready for that kind of hassle.

[question: "If you're translating games, do you need to know about localization?"]

Is everyone here familiar with the term localization? No? Oh, excellent! You're going to love this. Because so many translators don't actually translate. Because so many of them just move it into a rough facsimile of English and hope that someone else will turn up and wave his magic wand over it. Because of this, the word translation has shifted in meaning. People will say things like, "I don't just want a translation! I want something that is the same in English as it was in Japanese."

[confused mutterings]

Yes, I know! Charlatans like that well-known agency, The World and His Japanese Girlfriend, have actually demeaned the word itself. Which means that people who really do translate have been forced to come up with new words to describe what they really do. My favorite is the odious "trans-creation".

[groans of disbelief from the audience]

Now *localizing* is something from the computer and Internet worlds. It implies that you will translate the words, but also fiddle with all the technical aspects of the webpage, say, so that all the signs are in the right place, and the arrows point in the right direction. And to answer your question, no, they won't expect a translator to have enough computer knowledge to do the actual coding or shifting, though you may be asked to sit in and make sure all your words get put in the right place. I recommend you do so, since web work is very lucrative. Dotcoms are dripping with cash, and you can make a lot in that world. It might be below-the-line, but it can fund some of your more literary endeavors.

[question: "Is there an environment where the translators can communicate with each other?"]

Yes, the Crown on New Oxford Street.

[laughter]

["I mean like the newsgroups."]

[conversation devolves into a discussion of Italian and French newsgroups and their value for fact-finding, which is as good a place to leave this seminar as any].

KOREA

MISTER VENGEANCE

Old Boy's Path to America

After a drunken night on the town in Seoul, Oh Dae-su (Choi Min-sik) just wants to get home and give his daughter her birthday present. But on the way... he simply disappears. In the ensuing fifteen years, he is drugged, hypnotized and locked in a single room. He fails in an attempt to kill himself. When he is finally, inexplicably released, his only desire is to locate his captor, Evergreen. Evergreen, however, offers him a deal — he has until 5 July to discover *why* this has all happened. If he gets it right, Evergreen will commit suicide. If he gets it wrong, Evergreen will kill every woman Oh Dae-su has ever loved.

Western critics seem flummoxed by *Old Boy*. They see influences in *Angel Heart*, in the works of Sophocles, in revenge tragedies like *Titus Andronicus*. God forbid that they might investigate its original source material, a 1997 comic from Japan, drawn by a mah-jongg fan. The artist of the *Old Boy* manga, Nobuaki Minegishi, specializes in off-the-wall gangster tales, and, bizarrely, a long-running epic that retells the path to success in mah-jongg (think gin rummy with chunky plastic cards) as if it is a martial art. The eight-volume *Old Boy* manga was a relatively minor element of Minegishi's output, so minor in fact that he was prepared to sell the film rights for a measly $10,000.

The bargain-priced rights for *Old Boy* ended up in Korea, hence the sudden relocation of the story's action from Tokyo to Seoul. The Korean movie business is flourishing, thanks in part to its local talent and its willingness to dive into co-productions, but also to an unforeseen effect of globalized electronics manufacture. If Korean companies are producing the cameras, kit and equipment for film-making, where do you think is the cheapest place it to buy it all? This is why English movies are still My Bollywood Gangster Wedding, and Koreans can afford CG ants crawling out of Oh Dae-su's skin, giant insects appearing on the subway, and super-cool opening credits that rotate with the relentless ticking of clockwork.

Director Park Chan-wook is an unrepentant fan of British gangster movies of the sixties and seventies, counting *Get Carter* among his all-time favorites. Outside Korea, his best-known work is *Sympathy for Mr Vengeance*, a tale of escalating, tit-for-tat atrocities between two driven psychos. In his homeland, his most popular movie is *Joint Security Area* (*JSA*), a superb detective drama set in the demilitarized zone between North and South Korea. One of its most iconic images, a dead body sprawled on the borderline between two feuding authorities, was the main inspiration for the *Judge Dredd* audio drama *Solo* (and I should know!). At the time, *JSA* did the biggest box office in Korean cinema history, but *Old Boy* was to wipe the floor with it, also outperforming *Matrix Revolutions* and *Kill Bill* in Seoul.

Kill Bill's director, Quentin Tarantino, didn't seem to mind. That year he was head of the jury at the Cannes Film Festival, and fought hard to get *Old Boy* the prestigious Palme d'Or. His fellow jurors said they would rather cut their ears off, and handed the prize to Michael Moore instead, but *Old Boy* gained a respectable second place by snatching the Grand Prix du Jury. It also got a fifteen-minute standing ovation.

"I used to think that the Cannes dress code was ridiculous," Park told *Sight and Sound* magazine, "until I saw all those people in black ties standing up and applauding. It felt ten times better than if they were wearing T-shirts."

(*Judge Dredd Megazine* #229, 2005)

IT'S A WONDERFUL DEATH

Review: *Christmas in August*

When Jung discovers he only has weeks to live, he does what any self-respecting Korean man would do. He goes back to work at his father's photo shop in Gunsan, where sassy meter maid Darim makes him rush her negatives through the machine. But as they fall for each other, Jung cannot tell her that their relationship is doomed, in a film that is by turns funny and tragic, but always moving.

The dying writer Dennis Potter once described a tree in his garden as having the "blossomest blossom". Every single frame of *Christmas in August* is suffused with a similar hyper-reality. Mundane family events, dinners, workdays, are shot with the intense appreciation of the condemned. This is nothing new, of course; Akira Kurosawa's *Ikiru* also portrayed a cancer-ridden man who befriends a pretty girl, but Hur Jin-ho's direction is sublime. There are also echoes of Hirokazu Koreeda's *Afterlife*, particularly in the concentration on lives captured on film — an old lady sneaks back after a family photograph, asking Jung to snap her for a "death picture" to adorn her coffin. Poignantly, this was the last film made by cinematographer Yoo Yong-kil.

Han Suk-kyu and Shim Eun-ha are superb as Jung and Darim, with an instant, unfakeable rapport that goes beyond flirting, as if they have only just met but still been married for years. Nor are they merely two-dimensional romantic ideals. Darim transforms a frumpy traffic warden's outfit into sexy uniform chic, but she can be willful and self-regarding, ignorant of Jung's plight. He, meanwhile, is stoic and tight-lipped, but also scared, unable to express his feelings unless smashed out of his brains with friends who think he is joking. The result is two very human people, falling in love and clinging to every moment, in a film that urges its audience to do the same.

(*NEO* #10, 2005)

BROTHERS IN ARMS

Taegukgi and National Trauma

Before the 1950 Inchon landings famously save the day, South Korea fights a desperate holding action, a series of savage battles with guns, bayonets and eventually bare hands, as seemingly unstoppable forces from the North roll down towards the coast. Eventually, with their backs to the sea near Pusan, out of food and low on ammo, the South Koreans make one last heroic stand.

Drafted against his will, former shoeshine boy Jin Tae (Jang Dong-gun) volunteers for a series of highly dangerous missions, hoping thereby to win the Medal of Honor and allow his younger brother to escape the draft. But his actions are misinterpreted as foolhardiness by a brother who does not understand his true motives.

Brotherhood (*Taegukgi*: the original name actually refers to the Korean flag) is a monster of a war movie, over two hours of color-drained footage and stirring combat, lifting elements of *Band of Brothers*. Nor will it be the last time a nation visits its martial past in Spielberg style — the Japanese epic *Clouds on the Hill* is due in 2009, and set to blow everything else out of the water. *Brotherhood*, however, is Korea's entry in the genre, a blockbuster in its home territory that out-grossed *Troy* and Harry Potter.

The opening is deliberately evocative of *Saving Private Ryan*, a movie-within-a-movie in which modern-day archaeologists unearth the trenches at the scene of a famous battle. But because 148 minutes is a long time to fill, a *second* prologue sets up life in 1950 Seoul, just to make it clear what people are fighting for.

Scratch the surface of many Korean movies, and you will find a nation at war with itself, torn by the prospect that the enemy is not only within, but also a relative. World War Two literally sliced the country in half; if you were raised on the good-and-evil spy stories of the Cold War, Korea is the last place on Earth where you can still have them. If you yearn for a return to the dividing lines of Smiley's Berlin, see the Korean movie *Joint Security Area*. For dastardly Communist sleeper agents plotting the downfall of civilization, look no further than the time-traveling espionage of *Lost Memories*, or *Shiri*, the superb action movie from *Brotherhood* director Kang Je-gyu.

Duty looms large, both as a feature of this national trauma, and also in the steps taken by South Korea to fight it off. Korea still has military conscription, creating a ready-made market for such tales of valor. Sadly, this can also hamper it; the Koreans' battles are not our own (the four divisions of American soldiers who fought at Pusan are not mentioned here), and it is difficult to appreciate some of the mind-boggling achievements in *Brotherhood* without an understanding of the big historical picture, or a good map. Nor does it help that the supporting cast are a collection of stereotypes who might as well have Dead Meat tattooed on their foreheads, introduced at great speed, clutching photographs of their family, and lining up to die before we've got to know them.

Brotherhood turns away from a straightforward battle into the territories of espionage, revenge and redemption. But its later stages introduce an unexpected twist that wrenches it free of much of the gung-ho excitement of its fellow war movies. Most ask Why We Fight, but *Brotherhood* asks if it's really worth it. Despite its heroism, its final answer is more ambiguous.

(*Judge Dredd Megazine* #233, 2005)

THE SKY IS FALLING

Review: *Sky Blue*

I n the year 2142, the human race is either dead or living in savagery, except for the inhabitants of the advanced Ecoban mega-city on the Sisil Atoll in the Pacific. There, humans live in super-clean splendor, supported by a miraculous power system that runs on the Earth's one widely available resource: pollution itself.

But after a century of prosperity, the Ecoban power system has done the unthinkable. It has consumed all the pollution. Unless the ruling council does something quick (like torch an oil field), the Earth will be reduced to its natural state and all the machines will turn off. Meanwhile, dark, handsome eco-terrorist Shua is determined to bring Ecoban down, unaware that his childhood sweetheart Jay is now a lieutenant high up in Ecoban's security division.

Korean animation has yet to see its fiftieth birthday; the first cartoon made on the peninsula was an advert for Lucky Toothpaste in 1956. Like many other sectors of Korean life, animation was protected behind a series of import quotas as part of the country's status as a "developing nation", which left it indolent and sluggish in international competition. Apart from a couple of local efforts, panned for slavishly imitating the Japanese, Korean studios chiefly worked as low-echelon animators on foreign productions like *The Simpsons*. When the restrictions were lifted in the mid-1990s, it was suddenly a case of sink or swim for the young Korean animation business. Mainly, it sank.

Most local efforts were uninspired copies of anime, like the basketball story *Hungry Best 5*, or the martial arts adventure *Red Hawk: Weapon of Death* (as opposed to what? Weapon of Nice?). Others were sneakily misleading; my favorite being *Armageddon*, whose opening five minutes was an all-singing, all-dancing CG spectacular, which then collapsed into shoddy nonsense as soon as the film-makers could be sure that foreign rights-buyers had reached for their checkbooks. Korean animation in the last decade has chiefly comprised a succession of high-minded initiatives, collapsing into cutbacks after poor box office.

Sky Blue has not broken this pattern. It was a flop in its homeland, although its technical achievement is remarkable. It isn't anime (since anime is Japanese by definition), but influences are clear in its muddled eco-worthiness, and the cel-and-CG look pioneered in Japanese shows such as *Blue Submarine Number Six*. It also makes excellent use of its computer graphics, alongside traditional cel animation and inserts of both live-action and model work.

Some story elements strike less impressive notes, with irritating children shoved unceremoniously into what is otherwise an adult drama, the soullessly mawkish attempts at injecting romance, and Korean film-makers' predictably hackneyed attitude towards character relationships. It also, as usual for Korean film, splits the world into two — a society of consumerist insiders with gadgets, cool clothes, and sophistication, facing a foe whose people live like rats in squalid deprivation. These are not merely the haves and have-nots of Wells's *Time Machine* or Lang's *Metropolis*, but also have an origin closer to home.

Once stripped of its impressive widescreen elements, *Sky Blue* is little more than the 'good-hearted terrorists conspiring against a future metropolis' familiar to all fans of *Akira*, but it shines in the little touches it brings to its world-building. Director Kim Moon-syang has an artistic eye for tiny details in puddles, shadows and rain, but also a boldness at depicting big sci-fi allegories. That doesn't just show up in the eco-ranting storyline, but in moments like the protagonists' first fateful encounter as adults, a Tarantino-esque homage to the two Koreas: handcuffed to each other, held at gunpoint, in a museum full of artifacts neither appreciates.

(*Judge Dredd Megazine* #234, 2005)

TRAVELS IN TIME

Review: *2009 Lost Memories*

26th October 1909. On a crowded train platform in Manchuria, Japanese statesman Ito Hirobumi is *not* assassinated by a lone gunman…

Fast-forward a hundred years… In a Korea that is a province of the Japanese Empire, Japanese Bureau of Investigation officers Sakamoto (Jang Dong-gun) and Saigo (Toru Nakamura) hunt down a fanatical group of terrorists. At first, they believe that their enemies want to regain their country's lost independence. But the troubled Sakamoto discovers that they want to restore something much more important — time itself.

The potential in *2009* is truly exhilarating — a Japan that entered World War Two on the Allied side, a world where the first A-bomb was dropped on Berlin, where Japan became a permanent member of the UN Security Council, and Seoul is dominated by a statue of a Shogun.

The premise is the perfect excuse for a Japan-Korea co-production, without opening old wounds like *Killing the Target*, or resorting to the sappy intercultural love stories of *Friends* or *One More Kiss*. Instead, it pits two screen idols against each other, drawing in both the usual movie-guy crowd and extra box office from the female TV drama audience. Toru Nakamura is no stranger to mind-bending storylines, having starred in some of the most twist-laden serials on Japanese TV, including *World of Ice* and *Sleeping Forest*. Co-star Jang Dong-gun is a TV drama heart-throb in his native Korea, who crossed over when his newsroom drama series *All About Eve* played on Japanese TV.

However, *2009* merely puts a slick, high-budget sci-fi gloss on an everyday Korean thriller. It presents a nation at war with itself, but this is little different from the real-world North-South tension that informs other recent blockbusters like *JSA* and *Shiri*. After the irresistible opening sequence, it soon lapses into standard clichés — torn loyalties, doomed male bonding, fiery patriotism, and several trucks full of small-arms ammo (according to the *Making Of*, roughly 20,000 rounds). This still beats much of what Hollywood has to offer, so few will complain, particularly since the UK release is the lean International version that loses twenty minutes of unsightly flab.

2009's sci-fi elements are forgotten for long periods, only to be reinstated with a magical twist towards the end. Its alternate reality becomes disappointingly self-referential — as in Philip K. Dick's *Man in the High Castle*, the characters realize they are inhabiting a world that is a wrong-turn from reality.

The alternate history is a little shaky, too. In our timeline, when Ito Hirobumi died on that station platform in 1909, his last words were: "What an idiot..." He cursed his assassin for killing the one man who could have *stopped* Japan annexing Korea. Director and co-writer Lee Si-myung must have realized this, because halfway through he dumps a load more factors into the equation, jettisoning Important Event time paradoxes in favor of Temporal Meddler ones that owe more to *Back to the Future Part II*. But in the Big East Asian Time Travel Movie Stand-Off of this year in the UK, *2009* still wins out over its Japanese rival *Returner*.

(*Previously Unpublished*)

ARMAGEDDON
Lee Hyun-se and Korean Animation

I t's business as usual for schoolboy Hyesong: falling asleep in class, playing truant, and running for his life from time-traveling assassins. They've been sent from the year 2150, where the last remnants of humanity face imminent defeat at the hands of the Eidian invaders, and only Hyesong holds the key to survival. Luckily for him, his pink-haired sweetheart Marie Kim is another time traveler, sent back undercover to protect him.

Strictly speaking, this isn't 'anime' at all; it was made in South Korea. Lee Hyun-se adapted his own comic and directed it in what was effectively a showcase for the abilities of the Korean animation business. So much of the laborious, hands-on graft of the animation business is done by Korean colorists and in betweeners that it's possible to claim thirty percent of the world's cartoons are, to some extent, made in Korea. The major Korean studios have long busied themselves with the dog-work on supposedly American shows like *Batman*, *Spawn* and *The Simpsons*, but also with many Japanese productions. *Tenchi Muyo*, *Tokyo Babylon*, *Ghost in the Shell* and *Macross Plus* are just a few of the famous anime that employed Korean studios. While the Japanese bosses insist that the top production ranks (from director down to key animator) remain Japanese, the Tokyo labor shortage has resulted in many lesser jobs going to studios in Seoul and Pusan.

This film, however, still reflects their shortcomings in the animation world. Korean key animators (the human links between the director's commands and the in betweeners' actions) are relatively inexperienced, but their role is vital in preserving the pacing and fluidity of the animation. Hence there are some scenes in *Armageddon* where the animation jerks around, where perspective wavers or where the director takes the easy option of a tracking shot over onscreen animation. The time-consuming task of animating speech is occasionally dumped altogether in favor of a far cheaper option: unmoving mouths.

But the main problem with *Armageddon* is that it tries to cram too much into a single story. There are enough plots and subplots in the original comic's 2000-plus pages to make a dozen cartoon serials, and this feature-length movie version tries to encompass them all.

It begins eons ago with a civilization of mysterious aliens, who begin a search for intelligent life. Finding none in the universe, they resolve to create their own, and set up bioengineering projects on distant worlds. At that point, they disappear from the story, which then continues with the tale of one particular world, Omega Phi 8988, known to its inhabitants as Earth. The first project fails miserably with the annihilation of the dinosaurs. The second, using enhanced mammal evolution, almost fails too when the great civilizations of Atlantis and Mu wipe each other out in a nuclear war. The last survivors of the Mu empire (who call themselves the Elcan) go underground as the shattered Earth rebuilds itself and the human race starts over in the Stone Age. Then and only then does the story fast forward to Hyesong's high school high jinks in 1996, but even then, Lee's *Terminator* homage is not the end of the story. In fact, at this point in the film we've only sat through twenty minutes. The schoolboy Hyesong turns out to be the new messiah, the living embodiment of the Earth's guardian computer 8988. He is whisked into the future to protect the world, and discovers that the invading Eidians are the servants of another computer called 6666, which it is his destiny to destroy.

On the way, he dies (twice), ages ten years in a day, transforms into a symbiotic lifeform, loves and loses the agent sent to protect him, undergoes a grueling training program, falls in love (again) with his girlfriend's twin sister, and embarks on a bloodcurdling vendetta against Castlerose, the admiral of the invading fleet. Meanwhile, the aliens reveal themselves to be honorable individuals at the mercy of a computerized conspiracy, fleeing a doomed world in a desperate search for a new home.

Perhaps it wasn't such a good idea to let Lee Hyun-se direct the adaptation of his own work, since an artist's love for his creation sometimes comes at the expense of sensible, objective story editing. Lee could easily permit himself eight (!) separate prologues in the long comic version, but many of these plot elements merely weigh the film version down. But in his home country, Lee has considerable clout. An artist who was once so poor that he gave up comics to work in a bank, he found plenty of his own money to count when he wrote *Terror Team*, Korea's best-selling comic ever, in 1982. Since then Lee has produced many of Korea's landmark comics in the manga style, including *Blue Angel*, *The Last Acrobat*, *Abaddon* and *Fifth Season*. None of these are available in English, but many have been translated into French, and may be found at more esoteric comic stores. If there's something about *Armageddon* that takes your fancy, Manga Entertainment have released another Korean animation, Sang Il-sim's *Red Hawk*.

A final note: *Armageddon* is often confused with *Harmagedon* (1983), a genuinely Japanese animated movie directed by Rintaro and featuring character design by *Akira's* Katsuhiro Otomo. However, the latter has never been released in the UK.

(SCI FI channel (UK) website, 1999)

PUNDITRY

WHAT WERE THEY THINKING!?

Anime's Maddest Ideas

They come to you and they suck out your brain. "Hi, my name's Chad Vuttmunch, and I work for SuperCash Incorporated. I was told you knew all about this here Japanese animation, and we'd like to buy some shows. What would you recommend?"

I'd recommend leaving me the hell alone, because I long ago grew tired of giving free advice to company executives. Particularly when I knew they weren't really listening. They'd do what they always did — take a preview tape from whoever bought them the biggest lunch, watch the first five minutes, and then call to say, "Thanks for the advice JC, but we've decided to ignore you completely and buy *Schoolgirl Milky Crisis*. Hope we didn't waste your time 'n' all." So I got even. Next time I got brainsucked, I fought back.

Shiken Kaado Senshira! Five alien girls who save the Earth from peril. You won't have heard of it because it doesn't exist — it's a made-up title I used to get people like Chad to ask Japanese studios for when I was bored, and it means *Warriors of the Test Card*. It was fun to think of important executives blundering into a meeting and saying that they'd heard the Test Pattern was the best thing on Japanese TV. But I gave up tormenting them after a while, when I found out just how mad some of the real anime series were.

Made two decades before *RoboCop*, *8-Man* featured a Japanese police detective injured in the line of duty and brought back as a cybernetic crimefighter. He was a role model for the kids of his day, fighting for justice, and... er... recharging his batteries by smoking cigarettes loaded with radioactive isotopes. When the series was shown on American TV, the distributors were understandably keen to downplay that aspect. But

8-Man wasn't the most carcinogenic of anime for kids. Pressed for time one day in 1981, the harassed animators at the Tatsunoko studio couldn't think of a unifying concept for their new team show. So the people who gave you five ninja dressed as birds in *Battle of the Planets* emptied their pockets and tried to see if their contents inspired them. And so was born *Gold Lightan*, the pyromaniac tale of a giant robot who hides inside a Japanese schoolboy's cigarette lighter, leaping out to battle evil whenever duty calls, and — wait for it — assisted by his brave lieutenants, who hide inside the lighters of four other school children. Encouraging eight year-olds to play with fire must have seemed like a really good idea at the time. Especially considering the Japanese love for paper walls. The same year saw Studio Pierrot's *Shame on Miss Machiko*, the everyday story of a schoolteacher whose pupils set elaborate traps to strip her clothes off. Broadcast on Japanese TV, the show sent the Japanese Parent-Teacher Association into fits of rage. The kids, however, loved it.

Writers' hasty decisions can often come back to haunt them. Someone, somewhere, must have thought it was a sweet idea to give the crime-fighting heroine of *Super Milk-chan* a snot-encrusted, talking nostril-hair for a companion. Somewhere in Japan is the man who thought the best place for *Luna Varga* to hide her giant dragon-steed was up her ass. When looking for an undercover occupation for the mean assassins of *Weiss Kreuz*, somebody thought it would be a smart idea to make them all florists. These aren't half-baked drunken ideas thought up in a bar… well, actually, they probably are, but they are also real-life anime plots. Someone actually paid for that! Someone wrote it. And a bewildered audience sat down to watch it.

One of my personal favorites is *Fly Pegasus*, the tale of a blind football team who win the championships by playing with a ball that emits a loud noise — disability as comedy, must have had them rolling in the aisles. But not even its bumping, tripping soccer players seriously compete in the what-were-they-thinking stakes of *Variable Geo* (martial arts combat between rival waitresses), the crime-fighting train *Hikarian* (think *Thomas the Tank Engine* meets *Transformers*), or *Miyuki-chan in Wonderland*, which retold the Lewis Carroll 'Alice' classic, but with all the cast wearing bondage gear.

Who knows what possesses the Japanese to come up with these concepts? I suspect it is the sheer volume of material they have to think of every year that inevitably makes a few of their shows seem a little crazy. But it all made my *Test Card Warriors* seem positively sensible by comparison. I tried to come up with something even sillier sounding, like, I don't know, an entire rugby team of transforming machines that combine to make a super-robot... but, the Japanese didn't see the joke. That's because they'd already made *Dairugger XV* in 1982.

(*Newtype USA*, December 2002)

GHETTO HEAVEN

Anime at the Oscars

Hooray for cartoons. There's an Animation Academy Award. For too long, we've been regarded as a second-class medium while live-action Hollywood pap scoops the accolades. But we're still out there in the cold, we're just in a different kind of cold.

Magazine schedules being what they are, as I write I don't know if *Spirited Away* has even been nominated for an Oscar. But whether it has or not, it's being considered in the class of Best Animated Movie, a new category whose inaugural appearance in 2002 was won by *Shrek*.

Around the time that *Shrek* was getting the Best Film That's Not A Real Film Award, last February's big news was the richly deserved success of Hayao Miyazaki. After the disastrous performance of *Princess Mononoke* in Germany, many local critics didn't even bother to go to the Berlin Film Festival's screening of *Spirited Away*, a decision they came to regret when the international jury unexpectedly gave it the prestigious Golden Bear. While German pundits tried to bluff their way through interviews ("Err... *ja*, ze movie is very good. But I don't know why, because I have not seen it!"), the film's staff were on hand with some thought-provoking comments.

Producer Toshio Suzuki, the man for whom the word "canny" was probably invented, laid part of the credit at the door of the American Motion Picture Academy, thanking them for raising the status of all cartoons with the newly-created Animation Oscar. Well, that's what he might have meant, but Suzuki is also the joker who presented Harvey Weinstein with a samurai sword and a note that said "No Cuts." The fact is that the German judges were prepared to praise *Spirited Away* simply for being the best *film* they'd seen, whereas America's Oscar voters are obliged to stick it in the cartoon ghetto. Was Suzuki having a little chuckle at the Americans' activities — changing their own rules to keep a mere Japanese cartoon from threatening Hollywood on its home turf...?

There was once a time when the Japanese seriously considered submitting Isao Takahata's *Pompoko* as a contender for Best Foreign Movie at the Oscars. Did you see that? Best Foreign *Movie*. Not Best Foreign Cartoon, not Best Thing That Isn't A Real Film, not Runner-Up Prize For Not Having Christopher Lee In The Cast, but Best Foreign Movie.

Movies have always been about artifice, the creating of new worlds, and finessing our own reality. Short actors are made to look taller, tall actors are turned into hobbits, doddering oldsters have backflipping stunt-doubles. Long years lived breath-by-breath are snipped and chopped and edited into their visually-appealing highlights. Animation does it in a different, hyper-real way, but it is a way that is still legitimate. Defenders and apologists of the Animation Oscar will tell you that the new category is an admission of that, a "two thumbs-up" to the entire animated medium. Don't get me wrong, there are people in and outside the Academy who genuinely feel that this is an incredible victory for animation. There are people who fought tooth-and-claw to get that category accepted, and deservedly bigged themselves up when it finally was.

But do *you* think this is a victory for animation? At a time when Hollywood films use unprecedented amounts of special effects, and so-called 'live-action' movies comprise vast digital sequences? With *Final Fantasy: The Spirits Within*, we got our first glimpse of movies in the twenty-first century, with the supremacy of the actor eroded by the onslaught of the "vactor." Ben Affleck got to sit in a movie theater, popcorn in his lap and his arm round J-Lo, and see a virtual actor who looked remarkably like him in a movie that he'd never actually worked on. Entire cast members (Yoda, Gollum, Dobby) now only exist in computers. For a long time, producers have told us that films are real, and that actors are real people, and irreplaceable. But with every doubling of computer power and every leap in digital software, the boundary between real and virtual slips away. Just exactly how much of *The Matrix* is real?

Here, take this red pill.

There's never been a better time for taking animation *out* of the ghetto, but instead, the Academy have built a wall around it. As the last bastion of the movie musical, cartoons already sew up Best Song on almost every occasion. Nobody disputes the quality of their writing — *Shrek* was also nominated for Best Adapted Screenplay last year. But with Miyazaki on the American scene, "cartoons" are now officially giving "real" movies a run for their money in the big-hitter categories. There are people who want to see that threat neutralized, before it defeats them in the publicity stakes.

You think I'm mad? Why is it the Germans get to call *Spirited Away* a great Film, while we get to say it's a worthy Cartoon?

(*Newtype USA*, February 2003)

DISCONTENT OVER KONTENTSU
Sampling Anime Statistics

I quite like the research. It feels a bit like spying. It's not like someone is going to shoot me to get the microfilm. I don't end up anywhere more dangerous than the British Film Institute library or the Video Association. In a world where every website has an opinion on the anime business, you'd be surprised how much real information costs. When Dave from Marketing meets you at a convention and tells you anime sales are "going great", do you honestly think he would say anything else? If you want to know how well he's really doing, it'll cost you. Sales figures are available, at $50 a title. Charts of video sales can be bought per territory, at $100 per year. One long-gone company once tried to pay $10,000 for all the names and addresses from Manga Entertainment's fan club database. That was the bribe they were prepared to offer me, at least. Who knows how much the information was really worth to them? When a million American children each buy a *Pokémon* plushie, that's a lot of money.

Teru is late for dinner, but he has an excuse.

"Sorry," he says offering a limp hand for me to shake, "I was buying half a TV network in Malaysia."

He's not lying either. Teru doesn't use the word *anime*, he uses a new Japanese buzzword, "*contents*". To him it's all software, all *kontentsu*. His business is officially advertising. If you want to sell your widgets, you go to his office, and they'll do the complete package. Go to him, and he'll open your product in twenty countries. He'll get you discounted ad space in national newspapers, magazines, cheap spots on the radio, and primetime commercials on television. He can do this because his company part-owns the broadcasters and publishers.

This is what's known as vertical integration. If a movie is shot on a Sony camera, edited on a Sony desktop, burned onto Sony DVDs using Sony hardware, distributed by a film company that's owned by Sony, and shown in Sony theaters using projectors made by Sony, I think you can see where most of the money ends up. You can also see why companies like Sony and Matsushita moved into Hollywood in the 1980s, so that they could make their movies with Sony actors on a Sony payroll.

But why is Teru's company, which shall remain nameless, suddenly interested in the territory-by-territory sales of *Schoolgirl Milky Crisis*? It's because they've run out of things to integrate. They've been playing Monopoly with real people for ten years, and now they've got the lot. They're looking for another game board, and that brings them... here.

Why sell their *kontentsu* to an American company, when they could set up their own American subsidiary? There's less waste that way. Which is where I come in, because when people are playing with real money, they want real facts.

Teru flips open the file I give him. His smile fades as he reads, turning into a scowl. *Schoolgirl Milky Crisis* isn't doing nearly so well as people think. I see his plans for international expansion collapsing before his eyes.

"Well," he says with a sigh, "at least we know the Americans aren't hiding royalties from us."

(*Newtype USA*, March 2006)

FIFTY-FIFTY
The Rise of the Foreign Audience

The cinema is silent, with row upon row of plush, empty seats. I can hear the muffled hubbub of the crowd outside, but in here there's just me, some guy called Sam, and a huddle of engineers fussing around us like hairdressers, miking us up for the discussion to come. Sam stares at me sideways, like he's trying to remember who I am. I'm pretty sure that we've never met before, but the gaijin world can be shockingly small.

It's a première screening of his company's latest, which we're going to call *Schoolgirl Milky Crisis*. So while the technicians faff and fiddle, I ask him where he's from. How he got into this. And the $64,000 question: his involvement with the show.

Originally, the venue was expecting a Japanese body on the stage. They, at least, were hoping for someone with a name like Matsumoto or Yamada, someone with a racial identity that said "anime exclusive" to the crowd. Sam is disappointingly white — if I wanted Caucasian, I could get that at home. I agreed to be onstage because I was expecting someone who'd actually, you know, worked on the production. I'm worried that Sam is a last-minute replacement when a shy industry figure pulled out of what could be a difficult question-and-answer session.

"I'm not being rude," I plead. "It's just that I wanted to make sure that you're not some guy from marketing that they've shoved onto the stage at short notice."

Because if you are, I think, *I'm not going to ask you any difficult questions.*

"Well," he says with a smile, "actually I *am* that guy. But don't panic, I know what I'm doing."

To my great relief, Sam's seen the production from the inside. He knows the players involved and he was in the room when the decisions were made. Like all the best studios, the people who made *Schoolgirl Milky Crisis* are now trusting in foreign talent to sell their stuff abroad. And Sam might still be a crazy fanboy, but he's got an MBA and a diploma in Japanese.

Onstage, when the questions start flying, Sam answers with Numbers.

It's unprecedented in anime punditry. But he's got nothing to hide on this one — *Schoolgirl Milky Crisis* doesn't have a local distributor yet, and he's happy to give evidence of how well it's done in Japan. So I figure I'll ask something for myself. For myself and for anyone who reads *Newtype*, anyway.

"Twelve years ago," I say, "an anime producer told me that the foreign market was only worth ten percent of a Japanese company's interest. Can you put a number on it now?"

"Sure," says Sam. "It's fifty percent of our business. Half of our plans, half of our selections, are geared directly towards foreign markets, specifically America. And it's worth fifty percent of our profits."

There's your tipping point. If Sam's numbers are repeated across the other companies, modern anime is only half conceived with a Japanese audience in mind. There's still a domestic market, but you can expect to see increasing numbers of anime made for foreigners. That's us, probably. Nobody yet knows what this actually means — more European fantasies perhaps, or more samurai with afros. Whether this is a good thing depends on what you want from your anime, and how the companies interpret that in their plans and productions.

Like I said, I can get Caucasian at home.

(*Newtype USA*, January 2008)

THE GRAVEYARD SHIFT
Anime After Midnight

Where's the real anime on TV? Where's the primetime slot for *Cowboy Bebop*? Why is there nothing but graveyard shift re-runs on the SCI FI channel?

2005 is the tenth anniversary of *Evangelion*, when Japan went crazy over one of the best anime series ever, and *nine* years since a bunch of producers lost their shirts trying to copy its success. The anime industry's still recovering, and budgets are noticeably smaller than they were in the good old days. I don't mean your big-name movies, your *Howls* and your *Steam Boys*. I'm talking about TV — that thirty-five hours a week of new material that forms the bulk of all Japanese animation. These days if it's not a kiddie cartoon, they dump it on air when everyone's asleep.

Back in 1997, the Japanese magazines made a big deal out of the fact that the catgirl detective anime *Hyper Police* was on at one in the morning, saying that it was the ideal way to "give fans what they want." That phrase is marketing shorthand for "tits and ass," and yes, you can get away with a lot more of it on late-night television.

Late-night anime isn't what the fans want, by any means. But it was a cunning way of cutting costs — selling to a TV channel, not direct to fans. The graveyard shift was the last redoubt of that 1980s phenomenon, the straight-to-video anime. Except then you brought your own video. Nobody stayed up that late, they just taped the show and watched it the next day, saving the distributor an estimated quid a throw by not having to stick the anime on a tape and send it to a store to sell. The net result? A lot of short TV serials that didn't make much sense, with a bit of nudity and crappy animation… Sound familiar?

(*NEO #1*, 2004)

TALKING HEADS
On Television Polls

Much as I loathe the lazy pseudo-democracy of the format, for my latest bout of UK TV on-air punditry I'll be on Channel Four's *100 Greatest Cartoons* this Easter.

The public voted from a pre-selected list of 300, chosen not by viewers, but by a bunch of giggling students in a pub. At least, that will be the horrified suspicion among many anime fans. In fact, Channel Four's list is perfectly reasonable. If it is ignorant of over 2000 anime titles, it's only because of the voters they were expecting — people whose animation knowledge stops with *Captain Caveman*. I don't need to tell you that anyone with an *Anime Encyclopedia* can come up with 300 vote-worthy anime titles in a trice. But that's the problem with democracies. You have to displease all the participants equally.

However, as I write, what you see on the night is still subject to change.

One well-known studio refused to cooperate, indignant that there was any hint of a *need* for a vote. Surely their half-witted mascot critter was a shoe-in for the top slot? Two other distributors argued that their productions weren't "cartoons" at all, but rather live-action movies that... er... used 100 percent motion capture and CG special effects. This is a symptom of a war behind the scenes in Hollywood, as "real" actors fight to have CG movies barred from the "real" Oscars and lumped in that new *cartoon* category. Another studio claimed their fully animated TV series was not a cartoon but a comedy. You know, like *Seinfeld*.

As for me, I did my part. I glorified Miyazaki. I lionized Otomo. I demanded to know why *Urotsukidoji* was there at all — yes, it *sells* well, but that doesn't make it the greatest by a long tentacle. I pleaded the case for anime yet again, and if you didn't vote, don't whine...

(*NEO #4*, 2005)

HIGH JINX
Conniptions Over Commentaries

"Hi," I said. "I see you're advertising a special edition of *Schoolgirl Milky Crisis*. And I wondered what was going to be in it that wasn't already in the two-disc box you released last year?"

At the other end of the phone line, Fiona (we'll call her Fiona) was Very Enthusiastic.

"It's going to have a commentary track by Jonathan Clements," she said earnestly, which was news to me.

Commentaries are a gift of the gods, a spin-off of late twentieth-century media that can effectively double the running time of a film. And they're cheap. I tell you, even adding up appearance fees and studio time, they cost less than a two-page advert or a posh-looking menu screen. So what is it about the punditry business that puts Murphy's Law into action? I have never done a DVD commentary that hasn't involved some kind of disaster. The start delayed by seven hours because an actress decided (on a whim!) to move house that day; the producer who sat within range of the microphone and kept farting; not forgetting Fiona's faux pas, advertising my involvement before she'd actually hired me. I once turned up at Manga Entertainment to record a commentary for *Appleseed*, only to discover that a minion (no longer with the company, I hasten to add) had forgotten to get any recording equipment. Or even a VCR. It should be simple. The film plays, you talk. It's not rocket science!

But then there was one producer who fretted about my booking for a movie-length commentary.

"What time will you stop?" he demanded to know.

"Well," I said, "we're on schedule, so assuming everything goes to plan, about seventy-four minutes after I start."

"Oh no!" he said. "I don't want you to rush it!"

(*NEO #7*, 2005)

EXPLANATIONS
The Search for Deeper Meanings

Have you noticed how everyone seems to want to *explain* manga? It's not enough to say that there are comics from Japan — everyone wants an origin story delving back into the mists of time. For a specialized magazine such as this, that's fine — I'm sure you want to know everything there is to know. But out in the mainstream world, such explanations can backfire. People want to know why the Japanese read more comics. Actually, the Japanese read more of everything. They have one of the largest publishing industries in the world, and comics are only part of that.

Have you ever wondered how a Japanese pundit might sound, holding forth on our own culture with the same kind of attitude?

"Aha! The comic. Yes, the *komm-ick*. Contracted from the German for 'come with me', the traditional invitation of the medieval storyteller. A comic, or in parts of Europe, a *comique*, is by definition, comical. You see, they have to be funny. If it's not funny, it's not a comic. The first comic was invented in a cave in France by a nameless Stone Age man. It was about a reindeer hunt, but the guy in the cave next door drew his own about a bear hunt, and eventually there was a crossover. DC have recently released it as *Reindeer Hunt Reloaded*, with two collectible covers. Then came the Bayeux Tapestry, which wasn't actually a comic, but looks a bit like one. In Europe, comics are usually read by children, as they have more time on their hands. Adults don't read at all, unless it's *Harry Potter*, or fan fiction they downloaded for free off the Intarwebnet. Comics often have square panels in order to create cruciform shapes in the spaces in between, a reference to the European cult of Christianity..."

It might sound silly, but the paragraph above is perilously close to many real-world errors I've seen in writing about Japanese comics. Pundits should always proceed with caution.

(*NEO #17*, 2006)

REALITY CHECKS
Unwelcome Facts and Figures

Every now and then, instead of occasional monthly rants on the state of the business, someone will pay me to give them hard facts. I've learned to live with the inevitable disappointment, since so many only want to hear what they want to hear.

A couple of years ago, I was asked to report on the state of the British anime and manga market, by a government-affiliated organization that wanted to promote new investments. They wanted all the details — who bought what, where and why. They wanted future sales forecasts, gender parity projections, marketing demographics and untapped niches.

I gave it to them.

They sent me my money, and I waited expectantly for the report to be published.

After a year went by, and my figures had started to go a little stale, I bumped into one of the commissioners in a pub and asked him what was going on.

"The thing is," he said, "we want to *encourage* investment. We want to encourage investors to buy rights and get stuck in. But your report, well, it kind of said that anime and manga weren't doing as well as everyone thinks."

"That's right," I said. "They're not. Dave from Marketing is always going to tell you that manga is taking the world by storm. He's never going to tell you that sales are down, that they weren't all that 'up' to start with. He's going to lie. I can name you the companies that are doing well in the UK business, and I can name you the ones who've cocked up. And I can tell you why."

"You see," he said, "this is why we haven't published your report. We're protecting Dave from Marketing."

"But," I said, "surely you would protect him more if you *warned* him about the danger areas in manga: if you told him what's worked and what hasn't, so he didn't wade in with false expectations?"

"Please," he said. "If we paid you double, would you stop talking about this?"

(*NEO #22*, 2006)

TOP OF THE PICKS
The Trouble With Top Tens

This month sees the Discovery Channel's run down of the top ten comic characters of all time. Viewers and Internet surfers all over the UK have had the chance to vote for their favorite, from a roster that includes Batman, Wonder Woman, and Superman. So, in other words, the usual suspects. It would be churlish to complain too much about the list, since the program makers are obliged to include faces they can expect the audience to know. Not much point in pushing for Barbarella, when most viewers don't even realize she started off in a comic. You can't broadcast an English show without an English creation, so Judge Dredd is flying the flag this Jubilee week. You've got to acknowledge the European business, so there's guaranteed to be at least one from Asterix and Tintin. And since the still frames of comics don't make for good onscreen action, something that's actually got a TV presence (be it in cartoon or live-action form) is bound to be a producer's preferred choice, like Hulk or Witchblade.

But where does that leave Japan — a nation whose comic industry is staggeringly large? Could it be Astro Boy, the original Japanese superhero who's still got a profile to this day? The robot warriors of *Gundam*? Or, surely, at least *something* from the prolific pen of Hayao Miyazaki?

No. There *is* a Japanese entry in the Discovery running, but it's been chosen for its chances in the wide world of *non*-anime fans. In this anniversary year, so soon after its triumphant return to DVD, the story that has been chosen to represent everything Japanese is an understandable, if problematic choice — Katsuhiro Otomo's Akira.

Most voters won't even know who *Akira* is. They'll probably have hazy memories of "that kid on a bike" or "the guy with the metal arm", and won't realize that they're actually Kaneda and Tetsuo respectively. Akira actually only turns up for a few brief moments in the film that bears his name, and if the director had had his way, he wouldn't have appeared at all. Still, there's something to be said for a superhero whose sole ability is to blow himself up. Coming soon, the adventures of Explodeyman...

But what would the Japanese make of this choice? Last month, the Japanese channel TV Asahi ran its own cartoon character contest, based on viewers' votes from all over Japan, and listing their Top 100 Titles. The number one slot went to Doraemon, a blue robot cat still unknown in the UK. The two and three slots went to anime characters with a distant European pedigree: master-thief Lupin III and pigtailed Tirolean tearaway Heidi. The fluffy, fun-loving Totoro was at number four, and at number five was Sazae-san, a hapless housewife whose weekly show remains the highest-rated anime in Japanese history, and has been running since the 1960s.

And where's *Akira* in this list? It's way down at number eighty-eight, jammed in between two obscure children's shows. That's still a good showing for a cartoon that's older than most of the voters, but it's nowhere near the top-ten focus of the Discovery Channel. The reason: *Akira* might be a recognized classic, but it's old news in Japan. Its days in the popular magazines are a decade in the past. If you're a fifteen year-old Japanese kid, the chances are high that *Akira* is a comic that your *dad* used to read when he was a teenager.

One of the reasons that the Japanese love foreign money is the way that we'll take something after they've finished with it. Just when they think there's nothing left in an old favorite, we turn up and grab it for ourselves. Most of the popular UK shows of today, from *Dragon Ball* to *Evangelion*, are all but forgotten in their home country. The mega-successful *Pokémon* only made it to number eighty-six. How times change.

So something to bear in mind when the voting comes in: whoever UK viewers decide is the most popular character, it'll only be the tip of the iceberg of possibilities. The Japanese can, and did, come up with a completely different list of their own, as if Superman, Batman and Wonder Woman never even existed. The highest-ranking non-Japanese cartoon in the TV Asahi poll only scraped in at number thirty-nine. It was *Tom & Jerry*.

(*SCI FI channel (UK) website*, June 2002)

WRONG ABOUT ANIME
A History of Incorrect Assumptions

Anime is taking the world by storm. We know this because roughly every eighteen months, the British newspapers tell us so. Fresh crops of journalists looking for a way to get 'down with the kids' are soon drawn to the press releases and marketing of anime. But it's all doomed to go wrong, as one might expect from any attempt to encapsulate an entire medium in an easy sound bite.

Japanese animation is an entire medium, like film itself — from the Academy Award-winning genius of Hayao Miyazaki to straight-to-video T&A quickies by pseudonymous hacks. It is not, as some journalists still believe, one big series with the same characters, that begins with fluffy bunnies and summer meadows, before devolving into a cavalcade of filth. Filth, they would say, that Must Be Banned.

NOT JUST FOR KIDS!
A futuristic thriller by a first-time feature director who ran way over budget by faffing with his color palette, *Akira* started the anime business as we know it simply by being so impressive that a Japanese origin for a cartoon stopped being something that distributors wanted to hide.

Akira's UK distributor, Island World, even confusingly changed its name to Manga Entertainment, hoping to tie itself to the things that it would have liked everyone to refer to as "manga videos".

But although early hype implied that *Akira* was typical of the anime business, and that there was plenty more like it back home, that wasn't actually true. Expensive movies like *Akira* were actually quite rare. Much of what followed *Akira* was made straight-to-video. This was great news for Japanese science fiction fans, who got to ignore the silly TV sci-fi of old in favor of more serious stories like *Mobile Police Patlabor*, which first saw the light of day on video. But in the UK, the video material often meant disappointing follow-ups that clogged shelves but didn't measure up to the movie that first caught people's attention. Seeking to keep the new UK fad alive, distributors played up the fact that these cartoons "weren't just for kids any more" — a recurring cliché in anime journalism.

Investors had flocked to Japan in search of the next *Akira*, but came back instead with a load of old rope. The cheap video world had whole bins full of filler, some of which were more like promotional videos for works in other media, showcasing big moments or important subplots from novels such as *Psychic Wars* or *Legend of Arslan*, early stages of famous manga series like *RG Veda*, or big scenes from games like *Panzer Dragoon*. When exported out of context to the UK, they made no sense. A glut of them gave anime a bad reputation in science fiction circles for boggling plotlines and thin characterization, often marred still further by starting in the middle of a story and lacking a proper ending. Which is wrong, obviously.

TITS & TENTACLES

Many British distributors assured themselves that plot wasn't that important to their customers anyway. *Akira* might have been subtitled and sold to the art-house crowd, but internal company memos secretly identified the core audience as uneducated teenagers in search of inarticulate, brassy thrills, while marketing sheets openly courted a group that came to be known as the beer-and-curry crowd.

Selling to them proved difficult, particularly when the spread of available titles crossed every conceivable BBFC certificate. Read the early press on anime, and you'd be forgiven for thinking that everything was 18-rated filth, but the spread of 18, 15, 12 and PG titles in the anime world has remained relatively constant for ten years. Some companies tried to get a higher certificate by f***ing swearing a f***ing bastard lot in their English dubs, leading one BBFC examiner to point out that they were deliberately making their titles seem ruder than they were.

One of the most successful films in the wake of *Akira* was the notorious *Urotsukidoji: Legend of the Overfiend*, a saga of rape and demonic apocalypse, in which tentacled monsters fight for control of the multiverse. It was just one story out of thousands, but it was the one that swiftly gained attention — not the least because opinion-formers were sent press packs outlining just how shocking it was. Inevitably, someone took the bait. MP David Alton (now Lord Alton) initiated one of the government's regular debates on media influences, and decided to include a mention for those Japanese cartoons he kept reading about.

"Outraged Members of Parliament are calling for a ban on horrific 'snuff cartoon' videos which show scenes of child-rape, mutilation and murder," gasped a shocked *Daily Star*. "These sick Japanese-made Manga films have reached cult status over the last two years among youngsters in Britain… A recurrent theme is sexual assault on young girls by supernatural beings."

The British Board of Film Classification also repeated some of the sillier propaganda about anime. "In Japan, it seems," said a report with all the authority of a man in a pub, "these films provide sex and violence for men, who watch them after work in male clubs where sexual favors are bought and sold." But behind the scenes, the censor treated anime with much greater respect, according cartoon images the same weight as live-action film. While the tabloid press wrung its hands about "filth", none dared admit that everything had already been passed by the British censor. In those genuinely rare cases of "sick" content, the British censor had already ordered its removal before an anime was released.

Later episodes in the *Urotsukidoji* franchise lost great chunks of their plot alongside BBFC excisions, leading to yet more incomprehensibility in the storylines. Meanwhile, the franchise's new distributor, Kiseki

Films, sent out press releases detailing just what had been cut, so that journalists could be disgusted all over again, at things they hadn't even seen.

BATTLING SEIZURE ROBOTS

Parliamentary concern wasn't only directed at anime. The reason for the debate in the first place was the Jamie Bulger murder of 1993, in which two children — misleadingly alleged to have been inspired by scenes in the American movie *Child's Play 3* — savagely murdered an abducted toddler. Anime played no part in the case, but as anime's own distributors had repeatedly insisted, anime was the sickest thing you could buy on the High Street, and so it was soon dragged in. Such boasts were designed to play right to the beer-and-curry teenagers, but also tarnished the medium's reputation elsewhere.

But anime's pitch as the brash hardman of the High Street was ruined by new developments. Much to the annoyance of then-Home Secretary Jack Straw, the BBFC began certifying live-action porn movies that were far more explicit than before. Faced with competition from "real" pornography, anime's shock value faded away — it remains a rare sight indeed in British sex shops, where clientele have many more live-action temptations to distract them. The UK's anime distributors had cherry-picked all the available plain vanilla erotica, and the BBFC had slapped a ban on everything that was left. Anime needed a new means to stir up some controversy and some much-needed wrongness.

Thank God, then, for *Pokémon*, which made waves in 1997 with a highly publicized incident back in Japan. Cost-cutting measures and poor quality control had left a strobe-like effect onscreen in one episode, which caused a number of Japanese children to feel unwell. Others jumped on the bandwagon with lemming-like abandon — ironically, many of the 'casualties' of the event were kids who'd watched the program again to see what would happen. No long-term harm was done, but the word *Pokémon* was a playground sensation: a cartoon that could make you feel ill!

The litigious American legal system soon dragged *Pokémon* back into the headlines. As Pikachu's fortunes increased, several cases attempted to milk Bandai's yellow cash cow, over the use of a person's likeness (Uri Geller), performance rights for the Poke-rap, and the tragic case of a child who choked to death on a Pokeball. In UK playgrounds, the story was rarely about the anime — a child was stabbed over his *Pokémon* collectible card, but it was an anime image that accompanied the story.

I'D LIKE TO THANK THE ACADEMY...

At the turn of the twenty-first century, anime's profile changed again. Buena Vista, the distribution arm of Disney, struck an historic deal to sell the films of Hayao Miyazaki, the creative genius whose Studio Ghibli had produced many of the best anime ever made. Throughout the period that UK distributors were squabbling like children over demonic rapists and ninja schoolgirls, Miyazaki and his colleagues had been back in Japan steadily cranking out heart-warming family films about growing up and living a good life — such as the magic-realist middle-aged angst of *Porco Rosso*, the teen witchery of *Kiki's Delivery Service*, and the gentle summer pastoral of My *Neighbor Totoro*. With Disney behind them, the films suddenly leapt to the forefront of the international cartoon world.

Anime fans complained, and are still complaining, that Buena Vista all but buried its Studio Ghibli acquisitions, but the movies single-handedly rehabilitated the medium. Suddenly, anime was art-house again, with *Spirited Away* snatching the Best Animated Feature Oscar. Hollywood studios all started acting like kids themselves, with anime as their oversized *Pokémon* cards. If Disney had Hayao Miyazaki, then DreamWorks wanted the works of Satoshi Kon, and Columbia scrabbled to acquire anything by *Akira* creator Katsuhiro Otomo. The rights rush of the *Spirited Away* era didn't make fortunes for anyone, but it inundated many countries with a lot of really good Japanese cartoons. The UK was no exception, and for a brief few months, anime was flavor of the month again. It's not just kids' stuff, gushed the newspapers. It's Art. It's high quality. Sadly, of course, the equation of all anime with Hayao Miyazaki's cinema masterpieces was just as silly as claiming it was all video porn.

FALSE FRIENDS

Anime comes from Japan. This inconvenient reality has inspired canny investors to try to grab something that looks like it but isn't. Cartoons from Korea, China or even America, with a few big-eyed girls and explosions, have become a new sector in anime wrongness. They're not anime, but their marketing will seek to imply otherwise.

But bona fide anime has gained some big-name fans in the modern film world, and some of them have money of their own. This has led to the creation of anime made to order, often reflecting foreigners' ideas of what anime should be, rather than what anime actually is. Manga Entertainment helped create an anime classic in this way as early as 1995, by stumping up part of the cash for the superlative *Ghost in the Shell* — now acknowledged as a masterpiece. Meanwhile, Quentin Tarantino showed his grindhouse credentials in *Kill Bill* by commissioning an anime sequence from the celebrated Madhouse Studio. Although shot using state-of-the-art digital animation and motion capture, the seven-minute *Origin of O-Ren* was treated to look as if it were one of the gory, cheaply-made nasties of old — a throwback, perhaps, to Tarantino's video store days.

Perhaps the film world's most famous anime fans were Larry and Andy Wachowski, who peppered *The Matrix* with nods to anime sci-fi, and made up for it by commissioning *The Animatrix* from an international roster of creators, including *Ninja Scroll* director Yoshiaki Kawajiri. Anime was the new cool... and... er... not just kids' stuff. Even Murphy's Bitter got in on the act, with a cinema advertisement called 'Last Orders', portraying a bunch of samurai in a future metropolis, rushing to get to a pub. It looked like anime because it was — made by Production IG, and directed by *Blood's* Hiroyuki Kitakubo.

BACK IN TROUBLE

Ask an anime fan which distributor is the biggest in the UK today, and they will probably say Manga Entertainment. A passing Miyazaki enthusiast will tell them to shut up, because it must surely be Studio Ghibli's UK distributor, Optimum Releasing. Supporters for 'fan-favorites' like ADV Films and MVM may then enter the fray, pointing out that both companies sell a lot of TV series, and each one has half a dozen discs. But they'd all be wrong. The biggest anime company in the UK for the last five years has actually been Warner Bros., which distributes both the *Pokémon* movies and *The Animatrix*. Warner remains entirely aloof from the specialist anime arguments, preferring to link its Japanese properties to cinema releases and not to get involve in the bickering about erotica or children's entertainment.

But the scuffle goes on, and anime could be due for another ban-this-filth campaign. Recent press insinuations that the Japanese murderer of British teacher Lindsay Hawker is a "manga fan" have already set true fans' teeth on edge. Meanwhile, anime is back on the political agenda. The current debate is not about anime at all, but about whether British television channels are obliged to make children's programming. John Whittingdale, the Chairman of the government's Culture, Media and Sport Select Committee, recently warned colleagues that if UK channels were not forced to make local programming for local people, "There will be a growth of the likes of Japanese anime cartoons..." And that sounds just... wrong. Right?

(*SFX Total Anime*, 2007)

TOY
STORIES

STATE OF PLAY

Behind the Scenes at the Big Toy Company

The room was packed to the brim with toys. Robots and dinosaurs, tanks and action figures. It was every boy's paradise, and there was enough here for Santa to supply the entire East Coast without ever leaning on help from his elves. A small huddle of intense-looking European market analysts and designers faced me from across a small table. Several of them had notebooks in hand and pens poised at the ready. They watched me expectantly.

"Okay," I said nervously, "I'm here, like you asked. What do you want me to do?"

The Europeans conferred for a moment and seemed to elect a spokesperson, a spectacular German brunette with eyebrows that went on forever, Spock-style.

"Ve vant," she said with Teutonic precision, "to vatch you play."

My life has always been pretty surreal, but being paid great lumps of cash to revisit my childhood had to take the cake. But I have spent the last week debating the relative merits of *Gundam* and *Godzilla*. I turned into Tom Hanks in the movie *Big*, holding up a transforming building and asking the designers what made them think it would be fun to play with.

I was there as a writer, as one of several ideas-people being consulted by a major corporation for tips on toys and stories. But I was also there as a Japan specialist, as someone who knew my *Pokémon* from my *Monster Rancher*, and was able to quote TV ratings to back it up. Because when these people talked about *Sailor Moon*, they didn't just want to know about who wore what color. Nor did they merely want to know more in-depth fanboy trivia like how the season one ending differed in

English and Japanese. They wanted every *scrap* of information I knew about the series, couched in diamond-hard business terms, from Bandai's need to find something new for their US *Tamagotchi* factories to make in the mid-1990s, to Studio DIC's loss of the optimum timeslot, to Bloomsbury's decision to drop the manga translation after the series bombed over most of Europe. And so I talked and talked, draining my mind of everything it knew, from sales figures to pin-up preferences, while a row of Czechs, Americans and Frenchmen made dutiful notes like earnest Olympic judges.

"Am I boring you?" I said, when someone asked me to explain how *Digimon* related to *Tamagotchi*.

"No! No! No!" said the German girl. "Zis is all verrrry interesting. If ve had known zis two years ago, it vould haff saved us…" she made a brief mental calculation, "fifteen million dollars."

It was the moment that I realized this was all for real, and that these people were spending Big Money. It also gave me another reason to love my favorite anime of all time, Hideaki Anno's *Gunbuster*.

In *Gunbuster*, we have Noriko, a heroine who remains a perpetual schoolgirl, decorating her cabin with posters for *Star Blazers* and *My Neighbor Totoro*, while she heads off to her day-job piloting a giant robot. Noriko quite literally stays eternally young, playing with toys while her friends grow old around her. Thanks to time dilation and relativity, she is still in her teens when her former school friends are hitting middle age. There is a telling moment in the last episode when she is given a photo of a girl who was only a toddler when she last saw her. Though only a few weeks have passed for Noriko, back on Earth her "niece" is already nearing her twenties. It's when it all hits home, and Noriko bursts into tears.

Those of us who work in the entertainment business get to have fun for a living. We don't pack sardines in factories or saw bits of wood in half, we get to fly spaceships and shoot bad guys and race hotrods. There are people here at *Newtype* who are *paid* to watch anime all day, or sit down and go right the way through a computer game. What you do for fun, we do for a living. And I'm not complaining.

But when fun is a full-time job, you tend to become a workaholic. And your friends, the people you know with real lives, can drift away. It starts to irritate them that they have to save to buy something for their kids that you get given for free. They get annoyed when you get paid to watch a movie that costs them money. And sometimes, they can get resentful that they had to stop playing with spaceships when they were seven, but that you still get to do it at thirty-two. Trust me, people can get really snitty about that. They tell themselves that you're still a child while they've grown up and faced their responsibilities, which is why Gainax's observations in *Gunbuster* are so on the nail.

And when your mom calls to ask how your week's been, you have to tell her that you spent much of it chasing a pretty Norwegian girl around a room with a model pterodactyl, making *"ARK! ARK!"* noises. And she thinks you're joking.

(*Newtype USA*, September 2003)

THE SECRET LIFE OF HELLO KITTY
The Story of a Merchandising Icon

She was born in London in 1974, where she still lives with her beloved sister Mimmy. She weighs the same as three apples, and enjoys baking and being nice to people. She is Hello Kitty, the most successful creation of the Sanrio Corporation, and sometime star of her own anime show. Kitty has appeared in a Fairy Tale Theatre, retelling Cinderella, Snow White, and Alice in Wonderland (a particular favorite of one of her early designers). She has presented How To... videos for timid toddlers, showing them how to go to the toilet in a grown-up fashion or avoid talking to strangers. Not that she takes her own advice — in one of her anime adventures, she and her sister mistook a couple of jewel thieves for alien visitors, and almost became accessories to a robbery. In Japan, she has appeared in retellings of Japanese myths, alongside other, less successful Sanrio creations like Bad Batz Maru the naughty penguin, Cathy the bunny, Jodie the dog, and Tippy the lovelorn bear. But Kitty brings in more sales each year than the rest of them combined, thanks to her simplicity, her owner's razor-sharp head for business, and the inexplicable worldwide affection that certain people feel for cats.

HELLO GIRLS

Hello Kitty was not born in a vacuum — the Sanrio Corporation had long been licensing products from others, including the characters from the *Peanuts* strip. Kitty's ancestors include the Smiley Face, the dots and curve of that plain "Have a Nice Day" icon that later achieved notoriety in the acid house era, dating back to a US corporate campaign in 1963. Other influences include Charles Schulz's similarly simple Snoopy, born in 1950, and Disney's infamous Mickey Mouse. But the ever-happy Kitty was born out of the frustrations of Sanrio's manager, Shintaro Tsuji, who was losing his patience with other people's intellectual property. For every Snoopy product he produced, he was paying money to Charles Schulz. He decided it was time to make something of his own.

Tsuji was never going to choose something weird. Sanrio today might have a menagerie of 450 characters, including humans, birds and frogs, but the company's most successful design was never going to be Hello Ocelot or Hello Wolverine. Nor did he want something that would have unpleasant connotations, a bird that might seem too flighty, or a plague-carrying insect. There was no Hello Ostrich or Hello Mosquito. Instead, Tsuji looked for an untapped animal mascot — bears were out because of Winnie the Pooh, dogs because of Snoopy, Mickey made a mouse unlikely, Bugs banished bunnies, and Donald did for the ducks. But there was no big mascot franchise for a cute little kitty cat.

Nor did Tsuji want to cough up for one of his usual artists. Takashi Yanase, for example, a manga creator who did much work for early Sanrio, was kept out of the loop on Project Kitty, because he would have demanded a cut of the profits. Instead, Tsuji farmed Kitty's design out in-house, to draftswoman Yuko Shimizu, a company employee on the Sanrio payroll. Shimizu, and after her, Setsuko Yonekubo headed the teams that created Kitty. Her London origin, which still surprises many British Kitty fans, was chosen simply because England was *cool* that season in Japan.

Japan lacks the greetings-card traditions that made so much money for

Tsuji's idol, Hallmark founder J.C. Hall. Instead, Tsuji needed to find ways to get the Kitty logo on other people's products. He had discovered as a young employee at the Yamanashi Silk Centre that consumers were more likely to buy flip-flops with flowers on them than flip-flops without. He began selling the idea of Kitty to other companies, offering them the chance to cutesify their products with the addition of the little cat. Then, as now, Sanrio's main business was in selling the icon itself, not the items it appears on. Hundreds of other companies now pay money to Tsuji for the right to adorn their umbrellas, notepads, erasers, and pottery with Hello Kitty icons — icons designed by women.

The early 1970s found Japan stuck between the old-fashioned, male dominated world, and the first arrivals of women in the workplace. Educational reforms left many Japanese girls graduating from Japanese colleges, only to hit sexist barriers in the workplace. Yuko Yamaguchi was one of this new breed, a graduate of Joshibi University of Art and Design, who knew she would never get to be an art director for a male-dominated advertising company. Instead, she signed up to work as a designer at Sanrio, and would eventually become Kitty's chief designer in 1980, shepherding the cute little cat through two decades of changes and rebrandings.

The cat's growth in Japan saw the rise of a new post-feminist icon in Japan, the *Parasite Singles* — women in their mid-twenties with huge disposable incomes because they have a job but still live with their parents while waiting for Mr Right. These are the women who boosted Japan's tourist industry in the late twentieth century, who bought all the Chanel and Gucci duty frees, and who played up their forever-child status by buying products that had once been aimed at little girls.

Needless to say, Kitty herself is hardly an icon of feminist achievement, particularly not in Puroland, a Sanrio theme park, where Shintaro Tsuji called for the dancers' skirts to be shortened so that there would be something for the dads in the audience to ogle.

HELLO OSCAR

Kitty's sister companies also achieved some surprising successes. Shintaro Tsuji became the first Japanese producer to win an Academy Award in

1978, when his movie *Who Are the DeBolts and Where Did They Get 19 Kids?* won the Oscar for Best Documentary. It was the only really noteworthy achievement to arise from the establishment of Sanrio Communications in Los Angeles, an ill-fated production house that produced several cartoons, none of which really garnered the acclaim for which Tsuji was hoping.

His first, *Little Jumbo*, was released in 1977, but had sat completed on the shelves for over two years — its distributor's lack of interest likely to have something to do with who owned the copyright. The titular elephant was created by Takashi Yanase, and consequently was less likely to reap direct rewards for Sanrio. Tsuji's biographers also claimed that he wrote the script to the serious, feature-length *Sea Prince and the Fire Child* (*Sirius no Densetsu*), although Japanese sources credit Chiho Katsura with that job. Tsuji's magnum opus, however, was *A Journey Through Fairyland* (*Yosei Florence*), his attempt to outdo Disney's *Fantasia* with the tale of a violinist who helps a begonia in distress, and is whisked away to Flower Land by way of a thank you. Some of Tsuji's productions used so many American staff that they fail to qualify as "anime" at all, and he was one of the pioneers of stunt-casting, finding voice roles in some of his movies for, among others, Peter Ustinov, Katherine Hepburn and Roddy McDowall. Other Sanrio productions were less significant, except perhaps the creepy *Ringing Bell* (*Chirin no Suzu*), in which a lamb teams up with a wolf to kill sheep.

HELLO WORLD

Late twentieth-century kids in the Chinese-speaking world came to see Japan as the place where all the cool things came from, to the extent that these *harizu* ('Japan nuts') formed a massive new market for Kitty products. In January 2000, an international promotion that featured free wedding doll Kittys with McDonalds Happy Meals went disastrously wrong. Up to 350,000 people in Singapore crammed into McDonalds ready for the first ones to become available, their cars jamming the roads near drive-ins. Millions of burgers were discarded in the streets, as consumers bought multiple Happy Meals just to get as many dolls as possible. Crowds at one McDonalds were pushing so hard that the plate-glass windows shattered, with seven people injured in the stampede, three seriously. Eventually, the Singapore government called in the army to maintain control, although there were still incidents of men fighting over who got the last doll in certain restaurants. A year later, when McDonalds tried a similar promotion with Hello Kitty in regal costume, Singapore restaurants were staffed with police officers to keep order.

Many tourist destinations have their own tourist-bait — a Hello Kitty dressed up in local finery, or clutching a local delicacy. You can buy a Kitty doing the hula in Hawaii, a Kitty of Liberty in New York, and even a black Kitty in one Japanese resort, where her coloring reflects the volcanic-boiled eggs of a local hot spring.

But some of Kitty's relatives don't make it out of Japan. Dakko-chan, a comedy Negro — one of whose products features the legend 'Even I can count 1-2-3' — was kept out of foreign sale for fear it implied to American buyers that those of African descent had lower IQs.

HELLO NURSE

Who knows whether they were being ironic or not? But when pop stars began proclaiming their love for Kitty, it generated a whole new wave of popularity among the younger generation. Christina Aguilera, pre-dirty phase, announced in *Seventeen* magazine that she adored her singing Kitty doll and the 'Hello Happy Song' it would play when she pressed its paw. Mandy Moore was spotted with a Hello Kitty bag at the Billboard awards, while Mariah Carey was spotted flashing a Hello Kitty CD player at a record signing. Bespectacled balladeer Lisa Loeb took things even further, posing with a specky Kitty doll on the cover of one of her albums. Its title, unsurprisingly, was *Hello Lisa*.

Reputedly, Sanrio will happily consider literally anything as a place to stick Hello Kitty. Its only stipulation is that a product should not be able to cause harm in any way, since the last thing Sanrio wants is for a child to be traumatized for life by an unlucky encounter with a Sanrio product. Children "bond" with brands from a very early age; modern marketers talk of influencing future consumer behavior from the age of eighteen months onwards, hence the paucity of Hello Kitty paper knives or staplers. The company, however, does have some sense of proportion. It is perfectly possible to injure oneself with a toothbrush, for example, but the chances of doing so are considerably less than doing so with a Hello Kitty chainsaw (*not a real product*). But Sanrio's definition of "harm" also extends, in true Japanese fashion, to shame — Hello Kitty's face is not permitted to appear on any product that a mother would be ashamed of showing to a visitor. However, some have found loopholes in the instructions; that, at least, is the only possible excuse for the Hello Kitty "massager", which is quite clearly a dildo.

HELLO 'ELLO 'ELLO

A predictable downside of Kitty's popularity in Asia has been the proliferation of Chinese knock-offs. Sanrio fights these copyright infringers by taking out regular adverts in the Chinese press, pointing out the marks of distinction of a true Sanrio product. The company also liaises on a regular basis with Singapore's intellectual property cops, and has conducted raids on pirate outfits.

Kitty consumers who think that they have found a fake product are encouraged to shop the copyists to Sanrio, for which they are rewarded in Sanrio goodies. Sanrio can take legal action where required, but sometimes takes a cuter approach. In one case, the company made seven Singapore stores take out a full-page advert in the local newspaper, apologizing for their shameless stealing of the image of Kitty and her little animal friends.

Not all stories end so happily. In 1999, three unemployed would-be gangsters in Hong Kong kidnapped a twenty-three year-old bar girl, held her prisoner for a month in their flat, tortured her to death, and then cut up her corpse. When police officers in Tsim Sha Tsui raided the scene of the crime, they found her rotting internal organs in a plastic bag, but no sign of the rest of her. They might have been strapped for evidence, were it not for the last minute confession of one of the murderers' girlfriends, an underage girl who could not bear the guilt any longer. She revealed that the dead woman's skull had been sewn inside a Hello Kitty mermaid doll for safe-keeping, giving the police the crucial piece of evidence they needed. Sanrio rode out the scandalous storm amid press coverage that could not resist referring to it as the Hello Kitty Murder. But after the murderers were sentenced to jail, Sanrio was forced to fight its corner once more, when Cantonese director Yeung Chi Gin decided to make a film about the incident. It was only after considerable pressure from Sanrio that Yeung agreed not to include any mention of Kitty's role in the movie *There's a Secret in My Soup*. Watch it now, and the precise identity of the doll is concealed behind digital blurring.

HELLO SATAN

Not all of Kitty's fans have been quite so respectful towards the mild-mannered cat. California resident Jim Yousling created his own version, *Hell* Kitty, a satanic creature with horns, a pitchfork and intimate piercings. An even more evil variant turned up in the anime *Tamala 2010*, in which a cute-seeming cat turns out to be the earthly incarnation of an ancient god of death, who lays waste to the human race by encouraging a pointless cult of consumption. Ouch.

But despite such detractors, Kitty continues to soldier on. She celebrates her thirty-first birthday this November, making her old enough to be the mother of some of her youngest fans. She appears on 22,000 products of varying quality and usefulness, everything from DreamCasts to toasters. In 2004 she even gained her own debit card, a Hello MasterCard designed to teach young girls how to slap down plastic to pay for really important items like lucky gonks and Hello Kitty toasters. Be afraid.

(*NEO* #11, 2005)

ONE TO TANGO

Japan's Dwindling Child Population

The Big Name Toy Company designed everything from the ground up, creating toys and cartoons in tandem. They had me working on six concepts for a TV series, that would be whittled down to three, then two, then one single idea that would be taken to the central office. There, it would compete with ideas from six other offices around the world, until the company put maybe a billion dollars factory time, animation, and advertising behind a single winning concept. They planned four years ahead. The toys in your stores this Christmas? They were decided in 2002.

I got to see The Book, a giant tome of psychology reports some six inches thick, containing what amounted to racial profiling of children around the world. Children in South America were more likely to play outside, German kids liked mechanical things earlier, and so on. When I turned to the Japanese section, two words jumped out at me: "Solitary Play".

I started hearing a strange little tango song in my head, a Japanese novelty hit from 1999 about three dumplings on a stick. It began as a joke by commercial director Masahiko Sato, but for some reason it took off. Kids liked the catchy tune, but the main audience for it was the parents. The single sold more than three million copies in Japan, and before long, an anime followed. It, too, was only little — three-minute inserts as part of the series *Watch With Mother*. But *The Dumpling Brothers* anime ran for five years, only coming to an end in 2004. Let's put that in perspective — an anime for the fan audience is considered a roaring success if it lasts for five *months*.

The Dumpling Brothers caught the mood of the time. Japan doesn't have a draconian one-child policy like that enforced in parts of China, but sometimes capitalism can exercise its own constraints. Single offspring are increasingly common, and that severely limits family dynamics. After two generations of belt-tightening and downsizing, fewer Japanese children have brothers or sisters. Moreover, they are increasingly less likely to have any uncles, aunts or cousins. Much of the interest in *The Dumpling Brothers* seemed born of parental nostalgia, looking back to when they had siblings to play with, and with a sense of regret that their own children would never have the same experience.

The same period saw *I Love Bubu Chacha*, an anime series about a boy who discovers that dead pets and circus animals have been reincarnated as his toys. The only 'human' friend he has is a neighborhood girl who pretends to be his sister, although she is actually a ghost. The viewers who watched these shows as children are now old enough to buy *Angel Tales*.

Some modern anime seem made specifically for viewers that are not part of any community; solitary shut-ins with few if any friends. But anime toys have always been ready to fill the breech, and to exert pester-power on a workaday dad returning home to his nuclear family, and searching for a way to buy his kid's affections. You hear it several times a day in anime for children.

"My father gave me a robot. My father gave me a robot. My father gave me a robot."

(*Newtype USA*, January 2006)

HOT COFFEE
On Rotten Easter Eggs

I picked up the trail in Australia, where the Australian Office of Film and Literature Classification began investigating *Grand Theft Auto: San Andreas*. The US Entertainment Software Ratings Board was already looking into claims that there was a hidden sequence within the game in which the player gets to go home and get naked with his digital girlfriend. For a while, it looked as if Rockstar Games would get away with it. The software developer disavowed all knowledge of the offending 'Hot Coffee' sequence, and it looked as if the whole thing was a very cunning bit of fanboy improvisation. It was claimed that the entire 'Hot Coffee' business was an amateur alteration of the code, a downloadable patch created by thirty-six year-old Dutchman Patrick Wildenborg, which rearranged snatches of pre-recorded dialogue and redressed pre-existing sprites to create the offending sequence. In other words, it wasn't *in* the game, it was something that someone had done with it, like the Homer Simpson respray of *Doom*.

Then, the 'Hot Coffee' sequence turned up in the PS2 version, and on the Xbox. Oh dear… Turns out that while Wildenborg's patch helped unlock it, it *was* part of the pre-existing code, a bit of programmer fun that had backfired. The game was re-rated for Adults Only in the American market, and Wal-Mart took it off the shelves. Rockstar's stock dipped eleven percent. The only place where it didn't seem to be affected was the UK, where the game had always had an 18 certificate, which meant the newly-discovered sequence made no difference.

That's computer animators for you. They love their little in-jokes. Be it initials appearing in puffs of smoke, tiny little freeze-frame gags in the middle of *Macross* battles, or flashes of the female lead's underwear when she falls over, they have always lightened the mood in the studio with their little additions. Nor, it has to be said, are fans all that different. Back in the days before DVDs, we all knew someone who wore out his VHS tapes pausing it at the nudie scenes. These days, you don't have to look far to find screengrabs taken out of context and mash-ups of famous characters in compromising positions.

There was a moment in the 'Hot Coffee' incident when it looked as if law enforcers would have to make some interesting legal decisions. When it still appeared that the code was nothing to do with the original games, nobody was sure how to stop its author from distributing it. It's just a series of letters and numbers after all. It was, in its intention if not execution, no more insidious than loading up *Tomb Raider* and running Lara Croft into a wall, just to hear her grunt and moan (and yes, I know someone who did that, too).

But with anime becoming increasingly interactive, and having less to do with cels and more to do with sprites, the potential for unwelcome 're-imagining' becomes ever more likely. In the erotic anime market, we have already seen innumerable thinly-disguised versions of famous mainstream shows, often by the original animators using pseudonyms: the all-nude *Schoolgirl Milky Crisis*, and the *hentai* version of *Geek Gets Girls*. As anime ditches its linear stories and becomes more of an environment in which pre-programmed characters move, as it becomes more like computer games, how long will it be before we start to see *hentai* patches traded for the most innocent of titles? And more's the point, will the studios be able to do anything to stop it?

(*Newtype USA*, October 2005)

SLEEVERY

THE EYE 2

Sleeve notes to the UK release from Tartan Video.

In the Pang brothers' first collaboration, *Bangkok Dangerous*, it is we who are the ghosts — unheard, distant creatures in the peripheral vision of a deaf hitman. Their next film, the first *Eye* movie, leaned heavily on cinema folklore, its plot device part *Blink*, part *Eyes of Laura Mars*, with a woman who inherits the corneas of a suicidal psychic. The movie's Chinese title, *Jian Gui*, translates more literally as 'Seeing Ghosts', a shift in emphasis away from the ocular concerns of its lead's transplant operation, and towards its true cinematic ancestor, *The Sixth Sense*. This goes some way toward explaining how *The Eye* can have a follow-up despite there being no direct relation: *The Eye 2* is not so much a sequel as another movie set in the same world. It is not about the same characters, but about the same attitude towards the supernatural. It also lifts several narrative and filmic devices from *The Sixth Sense*; its twists smaller, subtler, but ultimately just as shattering for its protagonist.

Since completing the film, the Pangs have gone on to another collaboration, *Eye 10*, the title referring to the number of ways a ghost can be rendered visible. The first two *Eye* movies mark methods one and two: inheriting a psychic's corneas and attempting suicide while pregnant. *Eye 10* crams in the other eight.

The Pangs occupy a uniquely international place in modern film, with backgrounds straddling the vibrant cities of Bangkok and Hong Kong. Like their earlier movies, *The Eye 2* takes place in multiple languages; it begins in a Thailand where service personnel can communicate in their native tongue but are obliged to use stilted English as a *lingua franca* with their clueless clientele. When Joey (Shu Qi) runs for home in Hong Kong, the medium of communication shifts immediately to rapid-fire, earthy Cantonese. When she seeks religious advice from a spiritualist (played by Philip Kwok), the language transforms again, this time into Mandarin, the cant of Buddhist sutras and Qing Dynasty ghost stories. Like Wong Kar-wai before them (who famously used four languages in a single scene in *Chungking Express*), the Pangs luxuriate in this globalized, multicultural Asia, stressing not only the melting-pot of modernity, but its potential for confusion and misunderstanding. When Joey asks the Thai hoteliers what is going on in her old room, the best they can do is mumble in broken English, "Buddha Ceremony!"

The Eye 2 has similarly international ideas informing its folklore, drawing on traditional Chinese ghost-tales but also modern variants popularized by recent Japanese horror movies, particularly the *Hanako* series. *The Eye 2* refers explicitly to two Hong Kong urban myths, a ghostly girl whose plaited hair covers her face, and a haunted bus stop where a disembodied voice demands to know the time, hoping to damn anyone who is foolish enough to answer. When, in brief but chilling moments, we are permitted a glimpse of the invisible waiting dead that surround the cast of *The Eye 2*, they stand motionless, hunched and expectant, like Romero zombies.

Throughout the movie, we are teased with the thought that this might not be a ghost story at all, but a realistic approach to what could be Joey's real-world mental decline, a view of madness from inside the mind of a disturbed individual, in the fashion of Satoshi Kon's *Perfect Blue* or Alan Parker's *Angel Heart*. But since the ghost lore of most cultures may have its ultimate origins in psychopathology, this neatly brings *The Eye 2* full circle.

Despite all appearances to the contrary, *The Eye 2* does not concern itself with the vengeful spirits that congregate in most Hong Kong chillers. Its central premise owes more to the gentle Buddhism of Thailand, a sense of karma that ties all living beings to the consequences of their actions. Joey may be driven to hysterical fear by the ghostly goings-on around her, but the spirits she sees are ultimately benign, albeit unpleasant in their appearance. True to Buddhist convention, everything that happens to Joey is ultimately her own doing; she causes her own problems, and is left alone to invent her own solutions. When we first see her, she is sullen, resentful and self-regarding, an attitude which not only sets up her fall from grace, but also confronts her with the need to transform herself for her ultimate, bloody redemption.

MY GIRLFRIEND IS A DEADLY WEAPON
Sleeve notes to Manga Entertainment's DVD release of *SHE, The Ultimate Weapon*, known as *Saikano* in some territories.

From the days of *Astro Boy* and *Gigantor*, many anime have rested on the idea of a genius inventor who gives a boy the gift of a superb sci-fi toy. But *SHE, The Ultimate Weapon* instead looks back to *Frankenstein*, a tale in which another scientist wrestled with nature and his own morality, and ended up creating a monster.

Chise, of course, is neither a monster nor a toy. Her name comes from a word in the language of north Japan's native Ainu people. It means 'home'. Our hero, Shuji, wants Chise to be the perfect Japanese girlfriend, only to discover that she has a life and a secret that threatens to ruin their relationship before it has even begun.

Ever since 1973's *Limit the Miracle Girl*, a robot created by a broken-hearted scientist after his real daughter's death, anime girlfriends have often come with time limits attached. From *Key the Metal Idol*, who needs an audience's applause to stay alive, to *Video Girl Ai*, who will only be in her man's life for the duration of the single-play tape she inhabits, these genies have haunted teenage boys in anime. They lurk in their dreams and tease them on dates, but always there is the sense that these girls are not quite right — they are aliens, they are ghosts, they are time-travelers, they are goddesses; the one thing they aren't is normal, and in many such anime, there may also be a girl next door or childhood friend of the hero who is the real marrying type. Anime's dream women are often literally that, fantasy objects for those lonely nights when a boy doesn't have a real girl to hold; their existence a temporary puzzle that waits for him to realize that real life, and real love, is right under his nose in the schoolyard or at the sports meet.

Modern anime often draws inspiration from boys' fascination with girls, depicting them as wondrous creatures with some special, incredible skill or ability, yet still mysterious and inscrutable. In the late twentieth century, they were telepaths and were-creatures, vampiric vamps and superheroines. But today's teens, the first generation to grow up with Microsoft and the Internet, see it in a new way. These days, the difference between the sexes is more likely to be portrayed as a software conflict or a hardware installation error. In *SHE*, as in *Chobits*, Chise's 'machinery' sometimes malfunctions, causing her to react to stress in unpredictable ways.

In *SHE The Ultimate Weapon*, we see all these elements and more — Chise at first seems so perfect for Shuji, but her surface appearance of demure Japanese womanhood hides something more sinister that Shuji can't really handle. Chise isn't the first girlfriend with a health warning, either. She shares the self-destructive potential of *Evangelion*'s Rei Ayanami, and the military training of *Mahoromatic*.

At the beginning of our story, Shuji decides that he wants to be with her. But when he is brought face to face with what Chise can do, he is forced to question the assumptions he made. In this element of *SHE*, we find ourselves looking back even before the days of anime, to the time when many misogynistic folktales suggested that women might have a demonic side. To this day, Japanese brides wear a headdress designed to hide their horns.

WAR ALL THE TIME

Tokyo scenery is the default setting for Japanese animation. Anime rivals argue on the roof of a school without a real yard. On their way home, they might stop at level-crossings to let trains pass right through the centre of their street. Anime lovers bike along hefty stone levees, built to stop ancient rivers from meandering through the town. Steep roads slice through terraces in the Tama Hills to reach houses perched on perilous scraps of land. From this vantage point, we can see the skyscrapers of Shinjuku, and know that at their base is the famous multi-directional zebra crossing. But *SHE The Ultimate Weapon* deliberately shifts its action far from Tokyo, to the fields and greenery of Hokkaido, Japan's northernmost island, and still its most untamed.

SHE The Ultimate Weapon still has urban settings, but the countryside is never far away. During preceding centuries, Hokkaido was something of a wild frontier, as Japanese culture and colonists rolled ever northwards, pushing aside the Ainu natives. In the television era, Hokkaido became Japanese drama's answer to the Wild West, where exiled samurai would duke it out in a lawless land of farmers and herders — Hokkaido is one of the few places in Japan where farmers can still stretch out and afford pasture land for sheep and cows.

Hokkaido is also a symbol of the Cold War. In the closing days of World War Two, Soviet Russia declared war on Japan, hoping to seize as much of it as it could before the inevitable Japanese surrender. Fighting in the north was minimal — although a group of heroic young radio operator girls famously committed suicide rather than surrender to the approaching Russians. To this day, two islands off Hokkaido's north coast remain disputed territory, home now to a Russian submarine base and oil prospectors.

Hokkaido is not merely the place where the Cold War looks Japan right in the face, it is a reminder that the Russian advance could have proceeded closer to Tokyo, dividing Japan into a communist north and capitalist south, like Korea. For the Japanese, it brings the most unpleasant thought of all — that the horrific devastation of Hiroshima and Nagasaki, in speeding a Japanese surrender, may have saved millions of Japanese lives from division and conflict. The captured islands remain such a hot topic in Japan that the country has still not officially signed a peace treaty with Russia. In Hokkaido, at least on paper, World War Two is still raging.

In 1945, war's devastation was visible all over Japan. Now it is often impossible to see, ancient temples have been rebuilt, cities remodeled. Japan often seemed cut off from the rest of the world; its language unknown outside its borders, its position often like a bubble at the edge of Asia — allegorized in anime as the sealed cities of *Heat Guy J* or *Megazone 23*. It is thus perhaps no surprise, post 9/11, that modern anime should so suddenly grapple with the idea of what it is to have a normal life disrupted by conflict, and to choose Hokkaido as the location to do so. In setting *SHE The Ultimate Weapon* in the one place where old conflicts touch directly on modern Japan, creator Shin Takahashi reminds us all just how precarious modern existence can be.

THE LAST LOVE SONG

SHE's director, Mitsuko Kase, has worked on a small number of prominent anime. Early work on giant robot shows saw her come into her own as a storyboard artist, drawing shot-by-shot outlines, in the style of a comic, in order to show animators what their cameras should be doing from moment to moment. Kase storyboarded episodes of the robot show *Patlabor* and time-traveling fantasy *Inu Yasha*, but such a hands-on treatment was not so necessary on *SHE* — this is because *SHE* was originally a comic, written and drawn by Shin Takahashi.

The anime version of *SHE* retains elements of Takahashi's original style, including the soft, pastel, almost watercolor tones in the artwork. It also studiously avoids most of the battles, this tale of wartime deprivation cunningly omitting much of the war in a truly original storytelling decision. The character designs also retain simple elements of Takahashi's comic, such as the strangely bestial look of Shuji's eyes — even his workmates at the fishery call him "Kitsune", or "Fox".

Modern Japanese computer gamers talk of a "Naki Game", a game guaranteed to make its player cry, his love-object sure to suffer from some blindness, consumption, or cancer. Such sentimental stories are commonplace in Japanese culture, from the modern-day TV dramas in which widowed fathers struggle to rear ungrateful offspring, right back to Japan's Romeo and Juliet, Chikamatsu's *Love Suicides at Sonezaki*, which ends with a man showing his undying love for his girlfriend by stabbing her in the throat.

One of Japan's all-time karaoke classics is Yutaka Ozaki's 'I Love You' — the story of a couple who have eloped, and now occupy a seedy one-room apartment, with nothing but each other and their debts. Elements of it run right through this final part of *SHE*, as Chise and Shuji embrace in their hideaway, and she implores him to say that this is what love is. Online fans of *SHE* posted warnings to each other that the closest thing to a happy ending came in episode ten, with the *Blade Runner*-influenced flight from the troubles of the world. From then on, it's a spiral into heartbreak, as Shuji nurses an ailing girlfriend with cold skin and no heartbeat.

Tragedy has been slowly chipping away at *SHE* since the very first episode. It's only now that we can look back and see how our perceptions were gradually eroded. Every chapter has contained some sort of subtle revelation that removes one more modern luxury. Shuji's friends tell him he might as well get on with the quaintly 1950s notion of an exchange diary because "right now we can't get on the Internet or use cell phones" — a terrifying prospect to Japan's 'Thumb Tribe' generation, who communicate solely in text messages. Then we discover that civilians don't have meat in their meals, the television often rolls with static, and that Hokkaido's famous summer festival has been cancelled. One day, as in the classic nihilist anime *Grey: Digital Target*, we hear there are no more fish. In *SHE*'s quiet apocalypse, the urban Japanese gamely try to muddle through, going about their lives as if nothing is going wrong. The result is a familiar world of Japanese high-school romance, slowly transformed into a desolate wasteland.

"Cheer up," they always say. "It's not the end of the world."

BIGGER THAN BIG

Sleeve notes to Manga Entertainment's UK release of *Tetsujin 28: The Movie*.

Mitsuteru Yokoyama (1934-2004) was born in the Japanese port town of Kobe. After leaving school, he worked for four months in a bank before quitting to become a comics artist. He was only twenty-two when he published the story that would make his fortune: *Tetsujin 28*, a contemporary of *Godzilla* and a rival to *Astro Boy*.

The story features the plucky young Shotaro Kaneda, a 1950s schoolboy whose late father leaves him the world's most amazing toy, the giant radio-controlled robot Tetsujin 28. But Tetsujin is only one of a series of military prototypes thought to have been destroyed during World War Two, and an evil terrorist organization has obtained the others.

In a post-war Japan only just freed from Allied occupation and the threat of further involvement in Korea, *Tetsujin 28* was a bold and controversial tale. The country had just won the chance to host the Olympics in 1964, placing a heavy emphasis on scientific progress and urban renewal. But Yokoyama's story contained a single underlying theme: the idea that technology was neither good nor bad, but at the mercy of whoever controlled it. With the Cold War turning super-weapons into the new super-threat, Yokoyama's story confronted the science fad head-on.

Yokoyama's story of a boy who could call upon a giant robot exerted great influence. Even Osamu Tezuka, the creator of *Astro Boy*, was to create his own pastiche, the Nazi experimentation drama *Big X*. *Tetsujin 28* defined sci-fi for an entire generation of Japanese children, with its schoolboy hero forming the template for many later protagonists, most notably Shinichi 'Jimmy' Kudo, the hero of *Conan the Boy Detective* (known in Britain as *Case Closed*). *Tetsujin's* immediate successor was Yokoyama's own *Giant Robo*, which would itself be adapted into an animated series. During the 1970s, as Yokoyama experimented with tales of psychic powers and historical epics (such as *Water Margin*), other creators would refine the *Tetsujin 28* concept, introducing first robots that could be piloted, and then robots that could transform. *Tetsujin 28* is the original giant robot, without which there would be no *Gundam* and no *Transformers*. It received its strangest accolade in the 1980s, when manga creator Katsuhiro Otomo used it as an inspiration for his landmark *Akira* — which similarly features a boy called Shotaro Kaneda and a forgotten super-weapon called Number 28.

Tetsujin was better known as *Gigantor*, screened in America and Australia but absent from UK television. Acquired by Fred Ladd and Peter Fernandez — the ground-breaking team that also adapted *Marine Boy*, *Astro Boy*, and *Speed Racer* for the English language — *Tetsujin 28* acquired a catchy theme song, proclaiming that he was "bigger than big... stronger than strong, ready to fight for right, against wrong."

His adversaries ranged from the evil Ugablob, who orchestrated UFO attacks on Tokyo, to Mr Nefarious, a bearded crime lord in a turban. One of his greatest enemies was Black Ox ('Toro Nero'), a single-minded robot utilizing alien technology, designed by the evil Franken organization with the express aim of being stronger that Tetsujin. In the original series,

Tetsujin's conflict with Black Ox was famous for one particular element: Tetsujin was unable to best his opponent alone, and required the active assistance of Shotaro and friends.

Despite its immense influence on Japanese science fiction and its classic status, this 2006 release of the movie is the first incarnation of *Tetsujin 28* to receive British distribution. It brings the Tetsujin story up to date with a series of modern techniques, including state-of-the-art computer graphics in place of cel animation or men in suits. It also replays the 'ultimate toy' angle for a new generation, with a control system relying more on virtual reality.

He's at your command…

SIGNS OF THE TIMES

Sleeve notes to Manga Entertainment's UK release of *Tokyo Underground*.

We are still experiencing the after-effects of the population explosion after World War Two. In Japan, as in the Western world, the baby-boom generation grew up radically different from the generations before it. It had new concerns, new slang, a new attitude that often put it at odds with its elders. In America, it led to rock and roll, and hippies. In Japan, it led to the New Breed.

It started as a joke — the older generation wisecracking that kids today were like alien life-forms. Japanese kids were growing up different — taller, sometimes fatter. They were reading Western books and comics, which made them ruder, and less 'Japanese'. They had their own fashions, their own language. Science fiction authors began to wonder if they might literally be a new form of humanity. The "New Breed" of 1960s tabloid headlines became the telepaths, wizards, aliens and cyborgs of 1970s Japanese science fiction. The people who make anime today grew up watching the anime versions, the "newtype" telepaths of *Gundam* and the destructive psychics of *Akira*. Now they are in the directors' chairs, they have their own take on teenage life — an underground world of great, hidden power, which is connected to the Japan of their parents, but somehow different from it.

Tokyo Underground is typical of early twenty-first-century television anime. Despite the Japanese setting and production, it was partly made abroad — animation assistant Shim Hyunok overseeing a crew of Koreans who "in betweened" the key drawings provided by the Japanese. Its colors are bright and often flat, reflecting the modern trend in computer animation that finds almost all anime being produced digitally — even Hayao Miyazaki's *Spirited Away* was animated in a computer, although it retained the look of traditional cel animation. *Tokyo Underground*'s origins lie in a comic by creator Akinobu Uraku, but it was published in a magazine owned by a conglomerate of computing and advertising corporations. This is not some long-running manga series, adapted at its end into a new medium. When published in print form, it was already intended as part of a multimedia franchise.

Tokyo Underground's director Hayato Date has been involved with some of the landmark television titles of recent years. He explored the underside of modern life in the *Vampire Princess Miyu* series, and was a key member of the team that made *Naruto*, a fan favorite of the early twenty-first century. He also made the lesser-known *Bubu Chacha*, a kids' show for the very young that subtly revealed the strains of modern life. Its lead character is a Japanese boy in a Tokyo suburb, an only child with no playmates, born of parents with no siblings of their own. He thus has no brothers or sisters, no uncles, aunts, or cousins, and lives in a self-absorbed world where only his toys talk to him. Even the girl next door, it transpires, is a ghost.

Tokyo Underground explores similar aspects of modern life. Its love interest, Ruri, is not merely a damsel in distress, she is a girl reared in a hermetically sealed world, cut off, as characters in the show observe, from the sun and sky. Like Japan itself, the fantasy realms of anime are often isolated from the rest of the globe. In the hidden worlds of *Tokyo Underground* we see a similar distant, unjust conflict to that in *Howl's Moving Castle* (2004), and a nation-under-siege like that of *Heat Guy J* (2002) — all works made in the aftermath of 9/11, a terrorist attack that claimed over a hundred Japanese victims in New York, much to the nation's collective horror. *Tokyo Underground* also reflects the iPod generation's general apathy towards the real world. In a reversal of the twists of *The Matrix*, our intrepid heroes face a completely new environment, unlike anything they have ever encountered. Their first thought, however, is how much it reminds them of a film set.

Like the protagonists of *Gantz* (2004), they find it hard not to treat everything as a big computer game. Even in moments of danger, our would-be hero Rumina comments that this is like some great big RPG; while specky sidekick Ginnosuke thinks that any problem can be solved with a little computer geekery. Today's kids are obscure, forgotten, powerless in the real world, and yet have immense potential. Their areas of expertise are so mysterious to adults that they might as well be magical — computers, the Internet, consoles, mobile phones. If you see a five-year-old child operating a DVD player for granny, you see the same brave new world that underlies *Tokyo Underground*.

VITAL
Sleeve notes to the UK release from Tartan Video.

The body has long been an obsession with Shinya Tsukamoto. He has taken it over with metal viruses in the two *Tetsuo* movies. He transformed it through violence in *Tokyo Fist* and *Bullet Ballet*. With his last film, *A Snake of June*, he announced that he was renouncing violence, but while *Vital* may be gentler in its execution, it is still very much a part of Tsukamoto's corporeal corpus.

Where *Tetsuo* seemed to allude to J.G. Ballard's *Crash* (1973), with its bodies distorted through meshing with metal, *Vital* seems to owe more to the same author's *Kindness of Women* (1991), in which Ballard recounted the stirrings of his emotions as a medical student for the woman whose cadaver he was dissecting.

Vital also references the elusive Blue Bird of Happiness, both in the theme of its title song and in the tattoo of its ghostly female lead. Maurice Maeterlinck's 1908 play is perhaps better known in Japan than in the UK, both through translations of the original and its use in the late Hisashi Nozawa's *Blue Bird* (1997), a TV drama series about a criminal on the run who finds refuge in the tropical island paradise of Saipan.

Tsukamoto's actual inspirations for his film are more prosaic: a terrible back twinge that left him bedridden for days, and a chance viewing of Leonardo da Vinci's anatomical sketchbooks. Tsukamoto first saw the books at the house of Alejandro Jodorowsky in 1992, where he had been perusing the director's sketches for his abortive *Dune* project.

"I looked at many of da Vinci's drawings," he told biographer Tom Mes, "and I could really sense his curiosity for the interior of the human body." Tsukamoto's research led him to witness actual hospital dissections, not with the ghoulish voyeurism one might expect from the director of *Tetsuo*, but with a curiously reverent respect.

For his film, he utilized both old and new talents. Leading man Tadanobu Asano is a familiar face in Japanese film, and previously appeared in Tsukamoto's *Gemini* as a vengeful samurai. But Tsukamoto and Asano had also worked together as actors in *Quiet Days of Firemen*, an obscure Japanese workplace-oriented movie from 1994. Asano welcomed the chance to work with Tsukamoto again, and was surprised to discover a personal association with the movie's location. Sensing something familiar about the abandoned Yokohama hospital where Tsukamoto shot the bulk of his real-world footage, Asano called his own mother, to discover that the very same Aiji Centre had been the place of his own birth.

Asano's female co-stars are less well known as actresses. Tsukamoto cast the model Kiki for her vulpine eyes, and ballerina Nami Tsukamoto (no relation) for her homespun spontaneity and her ability to dance in the role of Ryoko. As an unknown in the film world, she was also less likely to voice complaints about her role, which would require a full-size cast to be made of her naked body.

Ryoko's scenes are largely shot in a dream-world, for which Tsukamoto elected to use Japan's southern island of Okinawa. Other islands are equally idyllic, but only Okinawa offers direct flights to Tokyo for a film unit working against the clock. The island was also the prime location for Takeshi Kitano's *Sonatine*, and its use in *Vital* would lead Tsukamoto to take drastic steps in production. Regarding natural beauty as a crucial element of the film, Tsukamoto elected to shoot on 35mm, a lavish choice for the notoriously low-budget film-maker, and one which required an airtight seven-week shooting schedule to preserve the budget. To shorten the period of post-production, Tsukamoto used digital editing methods for the first time.

In *Iron Man: The Cinema of Shinya Tsukamoto*, the director discusses *Vital* as a continuation of his earlier work: "When I finished [it], I somehow felt refreshed, like I'd found a new environment for myself. In *Tetsuo II*, *Tokyo Fist* and *Bullet Ballet*, the protagonists hurt their own bodies trying to find out whether they are living in a dream. In *Vital*, the protagonist is confronted with a dead body and enters it. In the end, he crossed through the gate, from the agonized, suffocating life of the city; he emerges in the vast realms of nature. One day I would like to make a movie that would take me even further and deeper into nature, far away from that gate. For now, though, I would like to keep exploring just outside that gate, the way I did with *Vital*."

"WATCH IN AWE":
THE WORLD OF STAND ALONE COMPLEX
Sleeve notes to Manga Entertainment's UK release of *Ghost in the Shell: Stand Alone Complex*.

The year is 2030. The must-have modern accessory is a cyberbrain, a powerful computer installed inside the user's own head. Cyberbrains permit wireless access to other computers; memories can be stored digitally, people can communicate telepathically with other cyberbrains. And there is a whole new world of crime. Memories can be hacked, brains can catch computer viruses, and worst of all, all users are at risk from cyberbrain sclerosis, a fatal hardening of the brain tissue for which, allegedly, there is no cure.

Masamune Shirow stands alone and apart from the Japanese comics industry. Although he is one of its most famous proponents in the English-speaking world, his life and career are very different from the norm. As with his most famous creation, Motoko Kusanagi, his public name is an alias, adopted in his youth when he published amateur comics for fun, while holding down a job teaching art at a night school.

As with his most famous criminal creations, the Puppet Master and the Laughing Man, he is a loner in a teeming world. For many years, he enjoyed a reputation as a recluse, although he was no such thing — he kept himself invisible to the media, and continues to walk among crowds oblivious to his fame.

This is partly due to geography. Shirow was born and continues to live near Kobe, a port city on the coast of Japan's Inland Sea. The heart of the Japanese comics industry is more than two hours away by bullet train, in Tokyo. Shirow enjoyed success so quickly, and at such a young age, that he never got to experience the Tokyo art community for himself — while other artists worked as apprentices for more famous comics creators, and eventually hired assistants to speed up their own workload, Shirow remained a solo creator.

Shirow's isolation and relative success have made him a notoriously slow artist. This, however, has played to his advantage; as others rise to fame, they tend to spread themselves too thinly, diluting their talents by hiring too many assistants, cranking out work too fast, in order to get greater returns (most Japanese comic artists are still paid a flat fee per page).

LUCKY BREAKS

In the wake of the success of Katsuhiro Otomo's *Akira*, several of Shirow's comics were picked up for anime adaptation. *Black Magic* was the first, although Shirow did not enjoy seeing the compromises forced on his work by a production schedule, and eventually handed the production reins over to his co-director, future big-name Hiroyuki Kitakubo. When *Black Magic* was finally released, it was a mere fragment of the original, dressed up as a pastiche of James Cameron's *Terminator*. Shirow had little to do with the following year's adaptation of his *Appleseed*, and other productions merely used him for occasional design work — such as *Landlock*, *Gundress* and the game *Blue Uru*.

The only film to truly capture the depth and complexity of Shirow's work was 1995's *Ghost in the Shell*. As Shirow's big comic of the 1990s, *Ghost...* was always going to be adapted to anime; the difference this time came with foreign involvement. Manga Entertainment, determined to head off rival bidders for foreign anime rights, invested directly in the

Japanese production, increasing the available budget by thirty percent.

The cash injection helped transform the production into a genuine movie, made with cinema, not video audiences in mind. It featured innovative experiments in animation techniques, and laid the foundations for anime in the twenty-first century. It also featured a crew that did Shirow's work justice for the first time, many of whom had learned their trade on a famous series of the 1980s.

LABOR DAYS

Japan is often ahead, not with new technologies themselves but with their mass usage. It was affluent Japan during the late twentieth century, for example, that first saturated its business market with mobile phones and fax machines, leading to the promotion of equivalents for private use. The home of the video recorder was also the home of the straight-to-video cartoon — allowing creators to bypass television or movie theatre distribution after 1983, and make stories destined for video stores. The idea revitalized sci-fi, and made it possible to make anime for an older audience. This was the environment that saw adaptations of Masamune Shirow's *Appleseed* and *Black Magic*, but also one of *Stand Alone Complex*'s true ancestors, the *Patlabor* series.

Patlabor was years ahead of its time, a future policer in which the science and the fiction were equally weighted, the product of a fan collective called Headgear, two of whose most prominent members were director Mamoru Oshii and writer Kazunori Ito. It showcased life in an underfunded police unit with special responsibility for robot offences in a future where global warming had led to the accelerated development of giant robots for use in construction... and crime.

Patlabor mixed everyday glimpses of the future with a bigger story about industrial espionage, as the cast became unwitting pawns in a plan to use civilian pilots to test army battle-robots. Data theft was the order of the day, as programmers lifted the movements and reactions of skilled pilots to insert them into the programming of their new machines.

Stand Alone Complex retains elements of Masamune Shirow's original comic, but also owes a great debt to the *Ghost in the Shell* movie, itself heavily influenced by *Patlabor*. Incorporating such moments as the rogue *tachikoma* plot in episode #2, 'Testation', is an obvious nod to the first *Patlabor* movie. Although Mamoru Oshii himself was not involved in the first *Stand Alone Complex* TV series, he would return to the franchise as a story outliner on the second season.

OLD FRIENDS

Stand Alone Complex is not a sequel to the *Ghost in the Shell* movie. It is a re-imagining of the same basic story, centering on Section Nine, an elite unit within the Japanese government for policing computer and robot crime. Whereas the movie and the comic largely concerned themselves with crimes committed by the Puppet Master, a self-aware computer virus seeking asylum, *Stand Alone Complex* drops him in favor of a new enemy, and a broader, deeper introduction to Shirow's future world and his Nii-hama ('New Port') City — presumed to be in Tokyo Bay, but partly inspired by Shirow's native Kobe.

The Stand Alone Complex is a mental condition where the sufferer must choose between being an individual or submerging their identity in a massive, multi-minded crowd — compare to the "AT Fields" of *Evangelion*. But in the real world, many of the episodes 'Stand Alone', that is they are weekly installments of a futuristic cop show in which Section Nine fight crime in New Port City. However, twelve of them (episodes #4, 5, 6, 9, 11 and 20-26 to be precise) are 'Complex', part of the main story-arc, the tale of the entity or entities known as the Laughing Man.

UPGRADE

Stand Alone Complex uses Shirow's work as a foundation, but is a collaboration between a team of writers led by director Kenji Kamiyama — that same "KK" whose initials can be seen inside a cybernetic eye in the first episode. In a rare move, Kamiyama dragged his writers out of creative isolation to live in a hothouse environment more like that of American television, bouncing ideas and integrating their story concepts to create multiple layers.

There are many moments that allude to or revisit scenes from the comic and movie. Kusanagi's lieutenant Batou still nurses an unrequited crush on her. Her hen-pecked henchman Togusa is still attached to an antique handgun that Kusanagi regards as inadequate; although unlike the Togusa in the movie, he has embraced cyberbrain technology. The *fuchikoma* robots from the original comic are remodeled here as the *tachikomas*, intelligent tanks with the firepower of a helicopter gunship and the minds of ditzy schoolgirls — voiced in Japanese by some of the most famous actresses in anime in cameo roles.

There are, however, additional revelations, particularly about Kusanagi's early life. The comic had always implied that she had once had another body, and possibly another name: 'Motoko Kusanagi', in combining an everyday name with that of a legendary sword, is a pseudonym as conspicuous as 'Jane Excalibur' or, for that matter, 'Masamune Shirow'. The movie included a scene in which Motoko sees another version of herself working as a secretary — her body, we realize, is just a mass-produced shell. But it is not until *Stand Alone Complex* that we get another tantalizing scrap of information: that Motoko was only six years old when unspecified events caused her to swap her original body for a shell. This, then, is what must make her so good; she must have been one of the first humans to undergo full cyborg remodeling, not out of choice, but necessity. When we see a hand unable to hold a doll in the opening credits, we are watching one of Motoko's oldest memories, as she struggled to control her new body.

FIGHTING THE PHONIES

Stand Alone Complex makes recurring references to the work of legendary American recluse J.D. Salinger, whose judgmental Holden Caulfield in *Catcher in the Rye* bears some similarity to the Laughing Man, and even supplies the quote for his logo. The tune, 'Comin' Through the Rye', is a regular feature of daily life in Japan in everything from elevator doors to pelican crossings, and has cropped up before in the anime *Vampire Hunter D* and *Grey: Digital Target*.

Salinger's short story 'The Laughing Man' was first printed in the *New Yorker* magazine in 1949, and featured a tale within a tale, about a boy kidnapped by Chinese bandits, and vengefully tortured by having his head partly crushed in a vice. Left with a gaping hole where his mouth should be, he takes to obscuring the lower part of his face with a mask.

He proves a fast learner, even comprehending the language of wolves, and becomes a bandit with skills he had learned from his former captors. But his whole existence is a case of misdirection, for the story is actually about something else entirely, the tales of banditry and derring-do merely the means employed by a character to distract the reader from the *real* story going on around him, a thwarted romance.

À BOUT DE SCI-FI

There are other tips of the hat to pop culture, including references to a Disney theme park ride in 'Jungle Cruise' (#10), and a character modeled on Nurse Ratched from *One Flew Over the Cuckoo's Nest* in 'Portraitz' (#11). Episode #3, 'Android and I', is an extended homage to the works of Jean-Luc Godard, whose *Alphaville* also featured an investigator taking on an artificial intelligence over the control of a future society. The episode's titular android seems modeled on Jean Seberg, who famously starred in Godard's *À Bout de Souffle*, a copy of which can be seen in the episode alongside *Vivre sa Vie*, *Made in USA* and *Pierrot le Fou* — the latter also supplying the title of a famous episode of the anime *Cowboy Bebop*.

Most impressively of all, as with much other science fiction, *Stand Alone Complex* is not really about the future. Its closest foreign relatives include the allegorical America-under-siege of *Battlestar Galactica* and the complex political maneuvering of *The West Wing*. Twenty years ago, Masamune Shirow envisaged a future threatened by terrorists and pseudo-terrorists, of information super-highways and designer plagues, brainwashing and recovered memory, a future of data farms, identity theft, and twenty-four-hour surveillance, where corporate greed would steer nations into distant wars, and government assassins would gun down suspected criminals in the street. Welcome to his world.

LIVING
MANGA

UNDERDOGS

Japan's Volleyball Heroines

1964 was a watershed year in the history of Japanese television. Home set ownership hadn't had a significant boost since the Crown Prince's wedding a few years earlier, but suddenly the Japanese had a new reason to buy one of those new fangled TV devices.

For Japan, the Tokyo Olympics was an excuse to rearrange urban road systems, to inaugurate the fabled Shinkansen bullet trains, and most importantly, to demonstrate that World War Two had been forgotten. The lavish opening ceremonies, televised in full color, were watched by 89.9 percent of the sets in Japan — it remains the highest ever Japanese TV rating, and is unlikely to be beaten. The Tokyo Olympics also witnessed an underdog story that has so often been repeated, refashioned and retold that many modern viewers do not even know that the cliché was once real news. The 'Witches of the East', a group of athletic Japanese girls, somehow made it to the finals in the women's volleyball contest. Amid nail-biting hysteria in the Japanese media, buoyed up by local support, the Witches snatched the gold medal.

Japan went volleyball mad. If it happened today, jiggling female athletes would be packaged as entertainment for *boys*, but in the 1960s, a girls' sport was sold to a female audience. Shiro Jinbo and Akira Mochizuki created *The Sign is V* for *Shojo Friend* magazine, in which high school volleyball star Yumi (played by Kaai Okada in the TV adaptation) learns to hate her chosen sport after a harsh training regime kills her older sister. But Yumi is tempted back into the sport when she and her former teammates are hired as ringers by a corporation that wants to win glory in inter-company amateur games. In everything from off-court rivalries to the girls' conflict over their handsome male Coach, *The Sign is*

V had everything we expect to see in a modern sports drama; it was remade as a movie in 1970, and you can see something like it every season. The sport may change, but the plot remains the same — even *Shall We Dance?* merely swaps the sexes of the protagonists.

But *The Sign is V* had a major competitor of its own in the year it was first released. While it dominated the adult schedules on TBS, the rival Fuji network hit back with *Attack Number One.* Also based on a manga, by Chikako Urano, *Attack Number One* featured an essentially identical volleyball plot, but this time in anime form, with special effects too expensive for 1960s live-action — freeze frames, crash zooms and split screens. *Attack Number One* lasted for 104 episodes, and many of its anime crew were reunited almost a decade later for another volleyball anime, *Attack on Tomorrow.*

The Sign is V was recently re-released on DVD to capitalize on the nostalgia market, but it's *Attack Number One* that may finally win TV gold. It has a full-blown live-action remake this year on TV Asahi, starring Aya Ueto, whose last Living Manga outing was in the similar sports tale *Aim for the Ace.* But unlike its original incarnation, the new *Attack Number One* will only have a dozen episodes to make its mark, fighting for survival against bigger, stronger network competition, not in the cartoon schedules, but slap-bang in the middle of primetime. It's an underdog story. Maybe someday someone will write a manga about it...

(*Newtype USA*, May 2005)

AN OSCAR WINNER?
Review: *The Rose of Versailles*

Not all Living Manga are TV shows. There are also movie versions of many popular titles, though they too often suffer the same fate as anime incarnations. Some are simply released as tie-ins to ongoing series, left with open endings designed to attract new readers to the original manga. This makes them hard to sell to foreign markets where the original manga remains untranslated. Others are simply designed to keep a title in the public eye, and excerpt iconic moments of plot and action from the middle of an ongoing story. This makes them equally impossible to push onto foreign viewers. But every so often, something comes along that can be viewed as a standalone title, because it has that rarest of tie-in qualities: a beginning, a middle *and* an end.

The Rose of Versailles was one of the manga successes of the 1970s. Riyoko Ikeda's tale of revolutionary France mixed historical details about the last days of Louis XVI with the completely fictional tale of Oscar Francois de Jarjayes, personal adjutant to Queen-Consort Marie-Antoinette. As implied by the story's alternate title, *Lady Oscar*, de Jarjayes is actually a woman. The daughter of a prominent nobleman without a male heir, she is reared as a boy and inherits her father's commission in the palace guard.

She becomes a friend and confidante to Marie-Antoinette, the historical figure who famously joked that starving peasants demanding bread should go away and eat some cake instead. Oscar must protect the Queen, but also cover for her, aiding and abetting in Marie-Antoinette's illicit affair with Swedish nobleman Hans Axel von Fersen. All the while, Oscar struggles with her feelings for her beloved André, the lowly stable boy who has been her companion since childhood. However, the couple are torn apart by events beyond their control, as news arrives of the American Revolution, and the disaffected poor of Paris begin to plot their own revolt.

The Rose of Versailles is over thirty years old, but it remains popular to this day. It has been kept in the public eye by constant revivals of the live-action musical version, performed by the all-girl Takarazuka Theater, and by the continued availability of the 1980 anime series, which told the whole sprawling story in twenty hours. The story also remains so well known because it, along with Osamu Tezuka's *Princess Knight*, sets the tone for a whole series of anime tomboys. Tough cross-dressing heroines with a soft romantic heart are a staple of many modern anime, and there is much of Oscar de Jarjayes to be seen in a modern uniformed duelist like *Utena*.

However, there is also a lesser-known incarnation — in 1979, the French director Jacques Demy made a two-hour live-action movie based on Ikeda's story. For extra exoticism, he made it in *English*. Called *Lady*

Oscar after the title of the French translation, it features former *Dempsey & Makepeace* guest star Catriona MacColl in the title role, amidst a veritable Europudding of continental stars. It even features a very young Patsy Kensit (of *Absolute Beginners* infamy) in the supporting cast.

With no expense spared, *Lady Oscar* was filmed on location at the Palace of Versailles itself, and almost entirely in English, making it the most accessible version of Ikeda's story for non-linguists. As one might expect from a movie based on a Japanese comic, directed by a Frenchman and intended solely for consumption in the Far East, the result is often unintentionally hilarious. Some of the dialogue is highly inappropriate, and so rude that I am not allowed to repeat it in this family magazine. The acting varies from the mystified to just plain bad, and the foreign accents of the multinational cast form a car-wreck Babel of biblical proportions. For reasons known only to Demy and his collaborator Patricia Louisiana Knopp, there are some pretty laughable songs in it, too.

However, Demy's film remains a true collector's item for the anime/manga completist, and contains most of Ikeda's original story for those fans who cannot read French or Japanese. Only a few minor subplots are trimmed, as is the ending itself — Demy stops short of Ikeda's original finale, perhaps to end on a more upbeat note, or possibly to allow viewers to discover the true ending for themselves, through the manga original or the anime series that was to follow.

Ikeda was also responsible for the Russian revolutionary epic *Window of Orpheus*, and the controversial Japanese girls' school drama *Brother Dearest*. This latter work was also turned into an anime and exported to France, where some rather frank depictions of nudity and same-sex relationships led to its sudden disappearance from French airwaves. As for the *Lady Oscar* movie, it remains unavailable in its 'native' France. The only version of this camp classic on sale is the English-language DVD released in Japan, with Japanese subtitles provided by Ikeda herself.

(*Newtype USA*, August 2003)

WILD AT HEART

Minetaro Mochizuki's *Shark-Skin Man & Peach-Hips Girl*

T oshiko Momojiri (Shie Kohinata) is bored with her life. An orphan forced to work in her uncle's fair-to-middling hotel, she feels on the shelf at twenty-one, and constantly dreams of escaping from her mediocre existence. But Toshiko gets more than she bargained for when a semi-naked man runs into the path of her car. Seeing that he's on the run from a nasty-looking creature not unlike her uncle, she offers him a lift, and is dragged into the underground life of tough guy Samehada (Tadanobu Asano).

And so begins a shotgun honeymoon to rival the best of Tarantino, as Toshiko finds herself in the role of gangster's moll. True romance blooms as the couple spend Samehada's stolen money with abandon. Toshiko surprises herself by throwing away her humdrum past in a flash. Samehada, a suave Errol Flynn used to working alone, falls for Toshiko's mixture of vulnerability and savvy, especially when she saves his life and proves she's more than attractive baggage. But they can't stay on the run forever. Their enemies are on their tail, the cash is running out, and Toshiko's jealous uncle is on the warpath.

Shark-Skin Man & Peach-Hips Girl (a literal translation of the protagonists' surnames) was first published in *Mister Magazine* in 1993. Writer-artist Minetaro Mochizuki is notable for his punchy, carefully organized and often circular stories, which, unlike many manga, never outlive their welcome by running for a trillion episodes. Despite rumors to the contrary, the Western market for manga translations still leeches off a very limited genre bracket, and Mochizuki's manga is explicitly aimed at an *adult* male audience with no interest in science fiction, school life or tentacles.

It's refreshing to find a manga artist who, while still keen on exploiting the nude female form, clearly prefers women who are old enough to vote over the jailbait fantasies of some of his contemporaries. The same novel approach applies to the violence — Mochizuki is more interested in the dramatic tension that leads to a fight scene than in the bangs and crashes of its resolution. But that's not to say he holds off on the heroic bloodshed, which is just what you'd expect from a man who names his lead character's dog John Woo.

Mochizuki's other works are equally tempting to film-makers. His *Room Service* is another one-volume tale, this time of a ghostly girl who appears out of nowhere and starts stalking an unsuspecting college kid. *Dragon Head* is much longer — apocalyptic science fiction featuring two Japanese children trapped underground by a disaster in Tokyo. They wander through the hellish world that was once the Tokyo subway system, encountering tribes of savage survivors, and searching all the while for a way out. *Swimming Upstream* is much gentler, a love story about a boy who joins the school swimming team to impress his would-be girlfriend, and vows to compete in the Olympics. But it's *Shark-Skin Man* that has gained him the most attention, particularly when adapted into a live-action movie in 1998 by *Party 7* director Katsuhito Ishii.

With a frustrated spinster lured into a life of crime, *Shark-Skin Man* shares plot elements with Ryoichi Ikegami's *Crying Freeman*, but Mochizuki junks Ikegami's quasi-realistic style in favor of a warts-and-all menagerie of strangeness. Ishii's movie, in turn, throws much of that away in favor of self-conscious cool, with quirky fashion-victim gangsters debating the meaning of life between shoot-outs, in a style that mixes *True Romance* with the runaway lovers of *Wild at Heart*.

As if Mochizuki's one-volume original didn't have enough weirdos, Ishii's movie throws in some new characters. Yamada (Tatsuya Gashuin) is a dorky, fey hitman in a tank-top, like Mr Bean with a sniper rifle. He is a funny, psychotic, original creation not found in the manga. Nor is Sawada (Susumu Terajima), the eternally-loyal best friend of Samehada, who chats to God about his role in the plot and strides around in the background like an oriental Christopher Walken looking for trouble. Director Ishii relished the chance to pit long-time Beat Takeshi co-star Terajima against Asano in their first movie together. Surviving the transition from the manga is the fetish-clad lead gangster Tanuki (TV drama stalwart and former pop star Ittoku Kishibe), who never leaves a fight without burying a series of fearsome throwing knives in his victims.

Mochizuki's manga exhibits a symmetry of plotting ideally suited to a Hollywood-style revenge tragedy. Both leads begin the story on the run from odious little men with dark secrets, each needs to be rescued and each is missing something that only the other can provide. Mochizuki's not afraid of burying twists in his story either: with Toshiko's uncle providing some harrowing surprises of his own, and an ambiguous ending that forces the reader to flip back in search of clues in the earlier chapters. The movie version takes a slightly different tack, lifting from *Pulp Fiction* with a pre-credit robbery, to which the action returns throughout the movie, progressively revealing just a little more of what actually happened before the film even started.

Since Tarantino himself helped popularize the term "manga-in-motion," it seems only fitting that a Living Manga should strive so hard to emulate him.

(*Newtype USA*, January 2004)

DEAD LIKE ME
Tsutomu Takahashi's *Sky High*

Murder victims have one last chance before they leave the world behind. If someone dies in suspicious circumstances, they end up at the Gate of Malice, a portal guarded by the mysterious Izuko (Yumiko Shaku). A pretty woman in a kimono made of rags, Izuko will give them one last choice: they can accept their fate and journey on into the afterlife and reincarnation, they can reject their fate and walk the Earth for a eternity as a ghost, or they can destroy their hopes of reincarnation but gain the chance to avenge themselves on those who wronged them.

Such is the premise of *Sky High*, a former *Young Jump* manga by Tsutomu Takahashi, which gained a new lease of life in Japan after the American success of *Six Feet Under*. Takahashi's story was swiftly optioned and put into production as a ten-part late-night series on TV Asahi in 2003, featuring numerous cult directors from the film world, including Ryuhei Kitamura (*Versus*) and Shun Takahara (*Consent*). Each corpse-of-the-week arrives at the Gate of Malice and is presented with their spooky choice — their decisions allowing each episode to steer in a number of different directions. In the first, a pregnant murder victim relives her early life with her husband, turning the episode into an office romance with a twist ending the audience already know to expect. The second begins with the battered corpse of a girl being dumped in the trunk of a car, and threatens to become a police procedural, with the added twist of a victim who can stand at the sidelines and comment. However, once the flashbacks begin, it becomes a tragicomic tale of a bad-girl's last days, like Ai Iijima's *Platonic Sex*, but without the happy ending. And so on.

It's not the first Japanese TV show of its kind — three similar concepts were broadcast in 1999. Its predecessors include *Heaven Cannot Wait*, in which a man is assigned good deeds by his guardian angel to keep the Grim Reaper at bay, *Heaven's Kiss*, in which a dead girl must convince her rock-star lover to get back on stage, and *I'll Be Back*, in which a man is forced to relive the late 1990s over and over again until he gets his life just right. But what singles out *Sky High* is the glorious nastiness of its premise. Where Hirokazu Koreeda's acclaimed movie *After Life* assembled dead people and asked them to focus on their happiest moment among the living, *Sky High* takes a very negative stance. All of Izuko's charges have met with sticky ends in the land of the living, and many relish the chance to grab revenge before they enter the land of the dead. There is plenty of scope for differing attitudes towards death — some victims simply refuse to believe that they are ghosts, while others relish the opportunity.

The disparate weekly guest stars are united by recurring characters, including the rag-and-bone man who scours the streets of Tokyo for the flotsam of the modern world, and also serves as an inadvertent bus service for the spirits. Similarly thrown on the scrapheap of society, the ghosts are able to hitch a lift on the back of his truck. His child assistant occasionally sees them, but who's going to believe a kid?

If anything lets down Takahashi's original vision from the manga, it's Yumiko Shaku's performance as Izuko. Considering Japanese horror's never-ending supply of creepy, spooky, and downright unhinged performers, one wonders why a role of such weight should have been given to someone whose last part was in the infidelity drama *Love Outside Marriage*. It's no fault of her own, but Shaku is clearly miscast as the unearthly Izuko. With a role most actresses would kill for, she is neither a creepy innocent nor a powerful goddess. Instead, she lurks uneasily around the Gate of Malice, delivering lines devoid of gravity or portent, and ultimately failing to convince. I don't know how the Gatekeeper of Malice is supposed to stand, talk, move or pose, but I'm pretty sure it shouldn't be like a beautician on her lunch break.

Sky High returned in 2003 as a Japanese movie with a spin on Quentin Tarantino's *Kill Bill* — a very different tale of a bride who is left for dead but returns to exact revenge. And just as proof that you can't keep a good franchise down, despite relatively low ratings of 8.96 percent, Yumiko Shaku returned as Izuko for a second season in January 2004. Right now it's sharing the airwaves with *Salaryman Kintaro*, *Fire Boys* and *Aim for the Ace* — all similarly based on manga, and proof that the idea of Living Manga won't find itself standing before the Gate of Malice any time soon.

(*Newtype USA*, February 2004)

PRACTICAL MAGIC
How *Bewitched* Bewitched Japan

Magical girls are a staple of Japanese animation and comics, but manga heroines like *Little Witch Sally* and *Comet-san* are the children of very American parents. Their inspiration arrived in 1966, when Japanese audiences turned on their televisions to see a bizarre opening sequence to a new TV series. Instead of photos of the cast, they got a plucky theme song and an animated short of a perky girl dressed in a pointy black hat sprinkling fairy dust over an American city. For those viewers unable to read the arcane English letters on the screen, the Japanese credits added a new title to explain the show's theme — 'My Wife is a Witch'. So began *Bewitched*, in which pretty young sorceress Samantha (Elizabeth Montgomery) promises her mortal husband Darrin (Dick York) that she will stop casting spells and causing mischief.

The cute-but-maternal, houseproud-but-ditzy Montgomery melted the hearts of the Japanese nation. She was even one of the first American stars to appear in Japanese commercials, endorsing Lotte's Mother Biscuits brand in the 1960s. In the Japanese-language dub of *Bewitched*, her voice was supplied by Haruko Kitahama, who can also be found in a number of anime from the period, from *Jungle Emperor* to *Little Goblin*. For her part, Kitahama is best known as the voice of the monstrous Silene in *Devilman*, and as Rafflesia in *Captain Harlock*. In the live-action world, she also dubbed Nurse Chapel in the second season of *Star Trek*.

As often occurred with Japanese translations in the 1950s and early 1960s, there were slight changes in emphasis. Unfamiliar with the strange name Darrin, the translators of the original turned it into a pun, with the Japanese Samantha lengthening the 'a' sound until hubby's name sounded more like "Daaaah-lin'". The sound of this foreign term of endearment became a watchword for incoming woman trouble, and the show stayed in re-runs for decades to come.

The world changed around it. At some point in the long process of buy-outs, shuffles and deals, the rights for the hit show ended up in the hands of Sony Pictures Television International — a Japanese company. And so in January 2004, forty years after the show first appeared in America, it returned in an all-new incarnation, as *Bewitched in Tokyo*, a Japanese remake. It is the first time that Sony has flexed its corporate muscle to combine two elements of its Japanese and American properties, but as we enter the global TV culture of the twenty-first century, it is unlikely to be the last.

So in the Japanese version we have Alisa (Ryoko Yonekura), who leaves her homeworld to explore the domain of humans, coming to Tokyo and falling in love with unassuming advertising executive Joji (Taizo Harada). *Bewitched in Tokyo* credits the American writer Gerald Sanoff as a "script supervisor", although the original scripts formed only a basic outline for the serial. Japanese TV rarely runs for longer than twelve episodes, and so the original *Bewitched*'s full running time of 254 episodes needs to be thinned down, at least for now. Actual credit for the scripts themselves goes to Japanese writer Noriko Sato.

The series was previewed in a sneaky way on TV Asahi, in a commercial that framed itself as a news item and showed Ryoko Yonekura announcing that she was looking forward to married life, only to then reveal that she was speaking in character as Alisa, and had not suddenly found Mr Right in real life. But as befits a modern Japanese drama, the action moves from the home-centered original to the office, as Joji is enmeshed in a series of business battles. The Japanese version throws in *Shall We Dance* star Naoto Takenaka as Joji's crazy boss, fighting to preserve a vital corporate client. In a Japan hit by recession and cost-cutting measures, it appears that only a miracle can save Joji's job. Luckily, Alisa could be just the person to provide one, even if it risks unmasking her as a modern-day witch.

But this isn't the first time that Japanese creators have acknowledged their love of *Bewitched*. Manga author Rumiko Takahashi drew heavily on the sit-com when she wrote her seminal 1978 manga *Urusei Yatsura*. She, too, focused on a hapless, mild-mannered Earth boy, tormented by a sorcerous wife. And just like the Japanese Samantha, the witchy wife would address her husband in a punning combination, calling out "Daaaah-lin'!" whenever she required his attention. Since *Urusei Yatsura* is the ancestor of all modern geek-gets-girl anime from *Tenchi Muyo* to *Love Hina*, the original *Bewitched* has a lot to answer for.

The Japanese version of *Bewitched* has just a few months to make it before it is likely to be swamped by the forthcoming Hollywood movie remake of the original, currently slated to star Nicole Kidman and Will Ferrell. But perhaps that is all part of Sony's masterplan, to whip up nostalgia in the older generations, and create new interest in the remake among fans of Japanese TV. Could *Bewitched in Tokyo* be the frontline of an attempt by Sony to bring Japanese drama to *American* TV? Stranger things have happened in Hollywood.

(*Newtype USA*, March 2004)

THE FIREMAN COMETH

Masahito Soda's *Firefighter Daigo*

Ever since he was rescued from a burning hotel at the age of nine, Daigo (Takayuki Yamada) has dreamed of becoming a fireman. Now, after six months of hard training, the twenty-two year-old youth finally gets his chance when he is assigned to Medaka-ga-Oka, his hometown.

But Daigo's fellow firefighters are not the heroic figures he was expecting. They regard him as a foolhardy newbie, whose desperate desire to prove himself only puts others' lives at risk, while he, in turn, soon becomes disenchanted with a life spent chiefly rushing to false alarms or rescuing cats from trees.

Of all the emergency services, firefighters are the *least* dramatized. Although no girl can resist the uniform, and despite endless tales of heroism, firefighters get a raw deal in the TV world because of the spectacular nature of their enemy. Cops chase criminals, doctors and nurses patch people up, but filming firemen means lighting up your production budget. In the Japanese TV business, which prefers to leave locations intact and re-use props, burning the sets down was never going to be a popular decision.

It takes Hollywood to get a really good blaze going, such as Ron Howard's 1991 movie *Backdraft*. The pyro-effects won an Oscar of their own, and *Backdraft* sparked a series of low-budget Japanese imitators, that culminated in our Living Manga of the month. *Backdraft* inspired a Japanese movie, *119*, starring screen idol Naoto Takenaka — although that's not saying much, it's difficult finding a Japanese movie that *doesn't* have Naoto Takenaka in it. But before long, *119*'s stint at the Tokyo box office inspired manga author Masahito Soda to create *Firefighter Daigo* for *Shonen Sunday* magazine. Soda's manga won a Cultural Affairs Media Arts award in 1998, and was adapted into a one-shot anime video in 2000, never making the jump to a full-fledged series, at least not in animated form. But this January on Fuji TV, *Firefighter Daigo* spared no expense to become the latest Living Manga, running for an entire season, with real-life actors, high-budget flames and all.

Anime was Daigo's perfect home — when all you're paying for is paint, animation allows for monstrous conflagrations at no extra cost. Animation also allows for every element to be under the director's control, with a powerful subtext of fire and water themes picked out in background details like sunsets and rain. The anime Daigo also took his cue from Hollywood heroes — he didn't play by the book, was ready to steal a fire-truck and ram it through the wall of a burning building to save lives, "and if they don't like it at City Hall, they can bill me!"

But when Daigo went live-action, the change in media brought a few concessions to Japan and Japanese TV, starting with a title change. The name *Fire Boys* played up the cast as a team ensemble, and reminded TV drama's large audience of young women that they could expect some male eye-candy. Conveniently, it implied a link between this drama and the earlier *Water Boys*, which also featured Takayuki Yamada in a starring role. Based on the movie of the same name, *Water Boys* was about a team of synchronized swimmers, so its connection to *Fire Boys* is tenuous at best.

The most obvious change in the format came in the focus on Daigo's early days. Whereas Akira Nishizawa's anime version showed him as a seasoned maverick risking disciplinary action to save lives, the live-action incarnation plumped for a different cliché — the rookie. The script for the series fell to Tomoko Yoshida, who also wrote the paramedic comedy *Shinjuku Punk Rescue Squad* and the love-among-veterinarians drama *Rocinante*. Yoshida's storyline plays it safe with a learning-hugging-bonding series of events that take our hero from school out into society at large.

We first see Daigo graduating from the firefighter academy and rushing to tell his would-be girlfriend Shizuka (Manami Konishi) that he's finally accomplished his dream. Shizuka is a school teacher, and has new romantic rivals in the form of fire-truck driver Mahiru (Rina Uchiyama) and paramedic Jun (Mimura). Since one of Daigo's fellow fire-school graduates is also in town and also chasing the girls, the set-up creates the traditional double love-triangle that no Japanese TV writer seems to be able to live without. *Fire Boys* also rolls out the TV drama staple of reluctant colleagues forced to pull together into a powerful team, as the bumbling rookies eventually transform into the very heroes they always wanted to be — just like in writer Yoshida's earlier *Beauty Seven*, in fact, except in that drama the cast were beauticians.

Fire Boys finished its run on Japanese television in March, but the manga has already made it to these shores, translated and published by Tokyo Pop. This makes this TV series one of the Living Manga that stand a much better chance of setting America on fire sometime soon.

(*Newtype USA*, April 2004)

ACES HIGH

Sumika Yamamoto's *Aim for the Ace*

New tennis club coach Jin Munakata (*Mrs Cinderella*'s Masaaki Uchino) puts his schoolgirl pupils to the ultimate test. Not one of them can return his serve adequately, not even the snooty prodigy Reika (Rio Matsumoto). But then Coach Munakata asks the shy, retiring Hiromi (Aya Ueto) to try. She's only a freshman, and she can't even hit the ball properly, but Coach sees something in her dedication that impresses him. Next time he has to choose a tennis team for a match against a rival school, the rookie Hiromi makes the cut, much to the annoyance of the other girls.

Tennis is Hiromi's religion. She blows her chances with boys, she loses friendships with girls, she sacrifices all her free time to train herself up, because she is determined to be the best tennis player in the world. One day, she tells her friend Saki she is going to play at the center of the tennis world — Wimbledon, England. And then, once she's made it to the top and proved to herself she can do it, only then will she get on with the rest of her life.

First appearing in *Margaret* weekly, Sumika Yamamoto's manga *Aim for the Ace* helped establish many of the traditions of girls' comics in Japan. It has the klutzy wallflower with hidden potential, the rich bitch who wants all the attention, and a handsome Coach with a tragic fate. But *Aim for the Ace* attracted viewers of both sexes when it became an anime series in 1973. When Osamu Dezaki's series premiered on what would later be known as TV Asahi, young schoolboy Shuzo Matsuoka was just six years old. The moment he got to high school in 1977, he signed up for the tennis club, and aspired to be just like Hiromi.

Tennis was his religion, too. Matsuoka was the first Japanese player to shine on the world stage, when in 1988 he played John McEnroe in the Japanese Open, propelling himself into the world's top 100. A higher media profile for the sport, and, more predictably the presence of a handsome star, led to the sudden revival of *Aim for the Ace*'s fortunes. The anime series was brought back as a movie and video anime, optimistically taking its heroine from Japan all the way to Wimbledon itself.

The same year, the anime fanboys at Gainax couldn't resist lampooning it all. They took the set-up and style of *Aim for the Ace* and turned it into a sci-fi parody about girls at a Japanese high school, developing a crush on Coach while learning how to pilot giant robots. Far more than the sum of its parts, *Gunbuster: Aim for the Top* remains the quintessential anime of the video era and is, without a doubt, my personal all-time anime favorite.

Shuzo Matsuoka's tennis career was stalled by an injury in 1989, and it took him a further six years to regain his full fitness and ranking — he made it to the Wimbledon quarter finals in 1995. During that time, he endorsed tennis shoes, gained a reputation as a TV sports pundit, and started coaching the next generation. But in 2004, the handsome sportsman was back in the limelight in an unexpected role — *Aim for the Ace* was being made into a live-action TV series, and the producers decided that just as martial arts shows had fight choreographers, *Aim for the Ace* needed a Tennis Director.

TV Asahi's producers cast Aya Ueto in the role of Hiromi, fresh from her high-profile performances in the controversial drama series *High School Teacher* and the ninja movie *Azumi*. The sometime-singer stars opposite a gaggle of seasoned drama favorites, including Yu Yoshizawa, last seen in the sci-fi series *Flowers for Algernon*, as her mild-mannered love interest Todo. As usual, it's the school bad girl who gets to have all the real fun, and Rio Matsumoto (whose last sports drama was the bowling romance *Golden Bowl*) has a straggly ugly-stepsister hair-do to match her bitchy role as 'Madame Butterfly' Reika, the school's most arrogant and proud tennis player, but one who lacks the true soul of a tennis princess. Remember, folks, curly hair means Evil in any Living Manga — just check out *Mask of Glass*.

Hiromi's live action adventures lasted for just nine episodes in the January-March season on Japanese TV. But *Aim for the Ace* ran as a manga for many years, and exists in anime form for five times as long. In theory, Hiromi's adventures can continue for as long as TV Asahi are prepared to keep up the funding, Masaaki Uchino plays Coach in front of the camera, and Shuzo Matsuoka plays Coach behind it.

But original creator Sumika Yamamoto stayed out of the limelight. She had quit the manga business back in the 1980s, leaving her follow-up *Seven Eldorados* unfinished, and going into the family business. Her father was the leader in one of Japan's "new religions", and Yamamoto left manga behind to become a priestess. Religion, it turned out, was *her* tennis.

(*Newtype USA*, May 2005)

PURE OF HEART
Keiko Tobe's *With the Light*

Sachiko (Ryoko Shinohara) has a problem child. Her son Hikaru (Ryusei Saito) never seems to pay attention. Whereas his kindergarten classmates can't stop talking, he sits in silence. He develops strange obsessions with drawers and closets, and delights in creating a mess. If she tries to stop him, he throws a tantrum, and when she scolds him, he stares idly into the distance, not even acknowledging her presence. Sachiko simply doesn't know where to turn...

NTV's Wednesday-night drama *With the Light: Living with Autism* might have seemed to be an unlikely choice for the 2004 schedules. It lacked both the tacky high-concept of TV Tokyo's *Vampire Gigolo*, or indeed the slavish fad-following of the spring season's two (count 'em!) unrelated firefighter dramas. But it was also the latest in a long line that stretched back almost twenty years to a distant Hollywood ancestor.

Barry Levinson's 1988 road movie *Rain Man* featured Tom Cruise as a car-trader who discovers that he has a long-lost relative, and Dustin Hoffman won an Oscar for his portrayal of Cruise's autistic brother. *Rain Man*'s plaudits helped usher in a new age of worthy disability-centered dramas in Japan, starting with a wheelchair-bound cast member in *Under One Roof*. Before long, the *Rain Man* element had been taken perhaps a little too literally, with the release of *From the Heart*, the tale of an autistic weather girl. From there it was a short while until 2000's *Pure*, the show by which all other subsequent disability dramas are judged. The tale of a down-at-heel photographer who falls for an autistic artist, *Pure* was such a success that it even lent its name to the genre. When producers say their next show is going to be "Pure", they mean that it will hinge on a handicap — blindness, deafness, personality disorder, you name it, it's been the subject of a drama series.

Considering the number of disability dramas on Japanese TV, *With the Light* requires considerable suspension of disbelief — has Sachiko *really* never heard of autism before? Unfamiliar with the term, Sachiko first assumes it is some form of disease of which her son can eventually be cured. When she is told this is not possible, she enters a state of desperate denial, trying to convince herself and others that Hikaru's behavior is completely normal. Her family are little help. True to Japanese TV tradition, her mother-in-law is a heartless harridan who blames Sachiko for Hikaru's condition. She turns to her husband for comfort, but eventually he admits that he, too, regards Hikaru's handicap as her fault. It's only when she meets a kindly therapist that she finds some solace… and hope.

Sachiko's ignorance, however, is a benign trait. It was designed from the very beginning to create a character who would ask questions on behalf of an audience, because *With the Light* began life as an educational manga.

Creator Keiko Tobe graduated in economics, and first found herself a job in public relations. She moved to Tokyo when she got married, and discovered that the capital city offered her opportunities to turn her manga hobby into a job. In 1985, after working as an art assistant in girls' comics, she enrolled in *Princess* magazine's annual Manga School program. A year later, *Princess Gold* published the result, the marathon runner story *Aki's Goal*. Tobe stayed in girls' comics through the late 1980s, following a contemporary fad by writing a story set in the world of women's wrestling. The same era that saw the *Dirty Pair* parodying lady wrestlers also saw Tobe's *Dream Warrior Shadow* appear in several installments in *Princess Special*.

Towards the end of the 1980s, Tobe began writing titles such as *Glass Staircase* and *Mystery Theater*, and her most prominent early work *Bakumatsu Sorcery*. Set at the end of the samurai era, it told the story of a surgeon trained in 'Dutch' (i.e. Western) medicine, who becomes involved in lifting curses from unlucky people. But she followed it with a very different form of affliction — she turned from girls' comics to women's comics, and picked a new way of haunting her lead character.

With the Light began running in *For Mrs* magazine, a title aimed at young mothers. The manga aimed to educate its readers with steely fervor, regularly running additional features on real-life mothers whose children suffer from autism, tracking their progress from birth, through school, and into the workplace. In Japan, of course, getting a day-job is a happy ending. The TV version, however, sticks resolutely to Hikaru's early years, as Sachiko fights to put her son into a normal school, deals with the prejudices of the people around her, and observes his separation from the everyday world. It doesn't take long before her son goes missing, and she is forced to deal with the worry of how a boy who can barely talk can somehow navigate his way back home. In regularly returning to the concerns of every parent, Tobe's story skillfully reminds viewers that Hikaru is not all that different from other children after all. It's an unusual addition to the world of Living Manga, but its motives are pure of heart.

(*Newtype USA*, August 2004)

CHINESE WHISPERS

Hana Yori Dango in Taiwan

Shy teenager Shancai (Barbie Hsu) unexpectedly wins a place at the prestigious Yingde Academy, where the pretty girl is soon scandalized by the behavior of some of her fellow students. The school is ruled by the infamous F4, a quartet of spoilt rich brats who even strike fear into the hearts of the teachers. Their word is law, but the plucky Shancai stands up to their bullying.

She earns the guarded respect of some of her classmates, and a mixed reaction from F4. The bullies' nominal leader Dao (Jerry Yen) finds himself falling for Shancai, but she has no interest in him at all. Instead, she discovers that she is developing feelings of her own for the withdrawn Hua (Vic Zhou), a quiet member of F4 who is too hung up on his childhood sweetheart Qing (Qian Weishan) to notice.

It may sound unfamiliar when read out in Mandarin, but the story should ring bells with any fans of Yoko Kamio's 1992 manga serial *Hana Yori Dango*. The names sound strange to Chinese ears, too, but they have the added exoticism of a Japanese pedigree: Shancai is the original's Makino Tsukushi, Dao is Tsukasa Domyoji, and Hua is Rui Hanazawa. *Yingde* is simply the Mandarin pronunciation for the Japanese *Eitoku* Academy — the 2001 Taiwanese TV series *Meteor Garden* is no more or less than *Hana Yori Dango* replayed with a Chinese accent.

Ever since the surprise success of *Love Generation* in Hong Kong, Japanese TV has been one of the cornerstones of programming right across Asia. On any night of the week, from Singapore to Taipei, local trendies can be found on their sofas in front of Japanese import TV, preferring the sight of Asian actors with Mandarin subtitles to the inscrutable Occidental entertainments of *E.R.* or *Dawson's Creek*.

At the beginning of the twenty-first century, Asian TV channels are awash with Japanese TV serials, creating a rush to duplicate their success with homegrown talent. Japanese producers themselves began to pander to their new-found foreign success by adding foreign stars to their cast lists — recent years have seen the Taiwanese Takeshi Kaneshiro appear in *Love 2000*, the Cantonese Faye Wong in *False Love*, the Taiwanese Vivian Hsu in *Lady of the Manor*, and the Korean Won Bin in the international co-production *Friends*. Producers across Asia also tried to discern what it was that made Japanese TV successful, leading some to hit on the source for many of the most popular shows — manga.

This, then, is why some manga have suddenly found themselves transformed into TV serials *outside* Japan. The popular romance *Asunaro Confessions* was remade as *Tomorrow* in Taiwan, alongside live-action local versions of *Marmalade Boy* and *Taro Yamada*. But the biggest of the remakes was the Taiwanese production of *Hana Yori Dango*, a.k.a. *Meteor Garden*.

If anything, Yoko Kamio's comedy of class and manners plays even better with a money-conscious Taiwanese audience. Barbie Hsu plays Shancai as an endearing Cinderella figure, eternally tormented by two tall, gold-digging ugly-sister types, and railing against the injustices visited upon her by F4. If there's any downside to the Taiwanese remake, it's the generally poor quality of acting from a cast that has clearly been hired for looks over talent, and shunted around each scene like shop dummies by a crew who expect nothing better from them. Needless to say, the boys of F4 and Barbie Hsu all have singing careers outside their acting projects, and all remain a popular fixture on Taiwanese youth TV.

When real actors arrive on the scene, the difference is palpable, such as when the show is regularly stolen by Huang Yet and Tong Che Chen as Shancai's social-climber parents, utterly shameless in their pursuit of their daughter's advancement. Endlessly complaining of their poverty (*"I had to sell my blood for you!"* Dad boasts), they would dearly love their daughter to get swiftly pregnant by one of the college rich kids, thereby allowing them to marry into a wealthy family and stop paying the college fees in one easy step. In an eye-opening difference to viewers used to the gentle innuendo of Japanese TV, the chaste, childish nature of the teenagers' flirting is regularly blown out of the water by the parents' earthy humor — *"The only thing stiff about you is your liver!"* Mom yells at her hubby on one memorable occasion.

Meteor Garden is already an underground hit with many anime fans, particularly since the release in Hong Kong of a legitimate DVD version of the entire series, complete with English subtitles. Surprisingly, this puts this Taiwanese remake several years ahead of any of its Japanese contemporaries — if a drama series does get subtitled, it tends to be solely for broadcast on US cable for Asian immigrants, and such shows have yet to make it to video in America. Could it be that the first Living Manga to achieve true success in America will have to come through the filter of a Chinese adaptation? Only time will tell.

(*Newtype USA*, December 2003)

QUITE FAST. QUITE FURIOUS.
Review: *Initial D*

Takumi's father, a washout and former car racer, does his son a massive favor when he makes him do early morning deliveries on Gunma prefecture's twisting mountain roads. By the time Takumi is legally old enough to drive a car, he has literally years of experience on the hazardous bends, and has developed a local reputation as the legendary Mountain God of Akina. The result is a martial arts movie with cars — as a series of surprisingly gentlemanly challengers arise to test their mettle against the reluctant hero.

Regardless of all the hype over *Infernal Affairs*, co-director Andrew Lau also has a superb track record in adapting comics for the screen, dating back to his peerless movie version of *Young and Dangerous* in 1996. It's hence no surprise that his *Initial D* is lovingly, box-tickingly faithful to Shuichi Shigeno's manga, flashing into moments of freeze-frames and split-screens, zooming through windscreens and into engine components. Nor does Lau trip up with his cast — pop idol Jay Chou is given a taciturn role as Takumi that does not force him to act beyond his limited range, Anne Suzuki is an unnerving doppelganger for the manga's tainted love-interest Natsuki, while Chapman To plays a geeky comic turn as spoilt bastard Itsuki.

As with Lau's earlier *Storm Riders*, faithful precision can backfire when the original is lacking — misogyny, violence, homophobia, bodily functions and alcoholism are all presented for comedic effect, and it can be difficult to care that much about the tribulations of a bunch of privileged boy-racers whose idea of suspense is chilling out while Daddy fine-tunes their ball-bearings. Moreover, despite recent controversies over *Memoirs of a Geisha*, nobody seems bothered about a largely Chinese cast acting in a Japanese story. Although much of *Initial D*'s international success has been with PS2 'racers' and overseas Chinese, it is also still a trifle weird seeing Chinese actors pretending to be Japanese — they stand, move and emote differently. But this is a minor consideration in a movie that manages that rarest of achievements, successfully translating manga into a new medium, warts and all.

(*NEO* #19, 2006)

MANGA
GOES TO
H O L L Y W O O D

THE LOST BOYS

Udoh Shinohara's *Interview with the Vampire*

"It seemed almost pointless to even start," says Udoh Shinohara. With large round glasses, sensible clothes and oversized, dangly earrings, she's the epitome of your favorite aunt, but Shinohara is a manga artist with a very peculiar specialty: occult-cute.

She is speaking of one of the most difficult jobs in her life, a break-neck schedule to adapt Anne Rice's *Interview with the Vampire* into manga form. "It was daunting," she smiles. "I'd actually read and enjoyed the novel before I was asked to adapt it. In Japanese, it was 500 pages long." But since the manga needed to be published in time for the film's Japanese release, Shinohara did not have the luxury of a normal high page count. Instead, she was restricted to just 182.

"I knew I couldn't adapt it page-for-page," she says, "and that many of my favorite episodes from the book would have to go; there was no other way." But in combining her love of the original and the need to adapt the film as faithfully as possible, Shinohara has created an intriguing appendix to Rice's *Vampire Chronicles*.

TALKING TO THE ANIMALS

Shinohara is best known in Japan for her the 1991 *Quart & Half*, which surprised critics by combining a love of horror and the occult with nice-looking young men and plenty of cute cats. In fact, critic Miya Takaragi even went so far as to say that Shinohara's love of animals surpassed that of other writers of girls' comics. The story was published in Asahi Sonorama's 'Sleepless Nights' series — though nobody is quite sure whether they were supposed to cause them or prevent them. It featured a beautiful, long-haired boy in the lead role, accompanied by his friendly cat. The boy, of course, isn't all that he seems. He's a necromancer and the cat is his familiar, but fate has played a cruel trick on him — the only souls he can raise from the dead are those of animals.

After the success of *Quart & Half*, Shinohara was approached by Tokuma Shoten in 1995 to create a manga to tie in with the Japanese release of the *Interview With the Vampire* movie. "It wasn't the kind of material I was used to working from," she admits, "an America-wide bestseller, adapted into a Hollywood movie — the thought of the project ahead left me simply stunned."

VAMPIRES OF THE DAWN

Using the Japanese title *Daybreak's Vampire*, the *Interview With the Vampire* manga is an excellent example of how editing can streamline a story. Shinohara retains the interview framing device in which the 400 year-old Louis de Pointe du Lac (Brad Pritt) is quizzed by reporter Daniel Molloy (Christian Slater) about his life. Only returning to the interview where it's going to save her space, Shinohara concentrates on the three acts of the film: Louis' induction into the vampire world by the senior vampire Lestat de Lioncourt (Tom Cruise); Lestat's attempt to keep Louis in thrall by creating Claudia (Kirsten Dunst), a surrogate 'daughter' for them to raise; and finally, the justice meted out by the Parisian vampires when they discover that Claudia has tried to murder her maker.

Shinohara specializes in the pretty young boys, or *bishonen*, of many a girls' manga, but the mixture of brooding gothic, eternal youth and narcissism that characterizes the *Vampire Chronicles* seems perfectly suited to Shinohara's style. The homoerotic overtones of the relationship between Louis and Lestat are also perfect for the *bishonen* genre, and would not be as controversial to a Japanese audience as they often were in the US.

During the long gestation period of the *Interview with the Vampire* film, the rights at one point resided with Lorimar, who convinced Rice that the project would be unfilmable with two male stars. Instead, Rice opted for another *bishonen* staple: cross-dressing. She rewrote her original to suggest that Louis was actually a woman, disguised as a man in order to retain control of her plantation. "To dress as a man means to be a totally different legal entity," she told Michael Riley in *Conversations with Anne Rice*. "I got enchanted with the idea. I also felt that Louis was me, and because of that the whole thing made better sense when it was a woman. I didn't see it as in any way betraying the material, but my readers let me know right away they didn't like it."

TEARS OF A CLOWN

The manga version is one of the few places to retain the vestiges of that idea, with typical androgynous *bishonen* characters who could conceivably be either gender. Shinohara also tries some other tricks from girls' manga, turning Louis into a dark-haired pasty-faced Pierrot on the book's cover, with the trickle of a single bloody tear.

As is common with many manga in the *bishonen* genre, the passive point-of-view character who is acted upon has 'normal' black hair, while the proactive senior partner has the blond locks of a brash foreigner. So it is with Rice's vampires — while the meek Louis has the sable hair of a Japanese national, the dark, handsome Lestat that gazes out from the covers of the English-language books is restored in the manga to the blond, blue-eyed, angel-faced creature of the text itself.

As the writer of the screenplay template, Anne Rice is credited as the manga's author, but Shinohara, with her love of the original, often turned to the novels for inspiration. There is, after all, no shame in stealing from the same author's earlier work, especially considering the public feud between Rice and the film-makers, which although eventually resolved to everyone's satisfaction, would have been widely reported at the time the comic was drawn.

In the film version, it is the death of Louis' wife in childbirth that sets him on the rocky road to ruin, but in Shinohara's manga she restores the original reason — the death of his beloved younger brother. Shinohara also returns the doll-like Claudia, the child who is turned into a vampire and hence never allowed to grow up, to her original five years of age. In the film version, Claudia was played by Kirsten Dunst, and consequently needed to be a little older than in the original.

THE RISING SUN

There is an understandable interest in Japan in the rising sun, in Rice's idea that a vampire would watch his final dawn with a new-found wonder, never to be repeated. It is exploited in the film when Louis goes to a cinema and sees (on celluloid) his first sunrise for centuries. The ending of the film, which rather pointlessly featured Lestat hiding out in Molloy's car, is replaced in the manga by a much more convincing monologue. Molloy the interviewer stares after Louis' retreating back, and watches as the sun comes up over San Francisco. As is Shinohara's wont on several occasions, departing vampires are represented by birds or bats in the sky, even though Rice's original did not include this stereotypical image. The interviewer looks at the birds, and remarks that this shall be the last sunrise he will ever be able to see.

As he continues to stare out of the window, his hand falls from his neck and we see the tell-tale marks of a vampire's fangs.

(*Manga Max* #14, 2000)

THE TANGLED WEB WE WEAVE
The Amazing Spider-Manga

In the early 1970s, Japanese media companies enjoyed a brief flirtation with inscrutable Occidental publishers. Only a few of the projects ever materialized, including the anime TV movies of *Dracula: Sovereign of the Damned* and *Frankenstein*, both based on properties from Marvel Comics. In the live-action team-show world, there was an abortive attempt to make a *Captain America* TV show, which was eventually de-Americanized and turned into the insane proto-Power Ranger entertainment of *Battlefever J.* Featuring a group of international crimefighters who defeated enemies with the power of dance, it was suitably ludicrous and bore little resemblance to the comic that supposedly inspired it.

And then there was *Spider-Man*, the 1978 TV show in which Japanese motorcyclist Takuya (Kosuke Kayama) is injected with alien spider venom at the site of a crashed spaceship and forced to take on an arachnid identity to fight off evil invader Doctor Monster (Mitsuo Ando) and his deadly assistant Amazoness (Yumie Kagawa). Although technically a remake of the Marvel comic, the Japanese *Spider-Man* owed a far more obvious debt to the alien-defender plot of *Ultraman*. Part of its alterations lay in the demands of Japanese network TV, but others had their origins in a previous attempt to bring the web-spinner to Japan.

Half translation, half original material, the 1970 Japanese *Spider-Man* manga was produced by a twenty-six year-old newcomer called Ryoichi Ikegami. Japanese schoolboy Yu Komori goes through a similar origin story to Peter Parker, and Spidey's early battles with Electro and the Lizard are repeated, but the Japan-centered action makes for strange reading. Japan has a long tradition of superheroes, but usually in teams. Spider-Man has few friends, few allies, and works alone.

The *Spider-Man* project began life as a straightforward 'versioning' of the Marvel original. Translator Kosei Ono took the American script and put it into Japanese for Ikegami's benefit, but the artist wasn't satisfied with redrawing Spidey for a Japanese audience. He baulked at drawing large tracts of New York, and hit on the idea of replacing Peter Parker with an all-round Japanese hero. It soon became plain that the Japanese setting was grating far too much with the American stories. The scenes in which Spider-Man is the subject of a newspaper smear campaign were particularly dangerous; the thought that a newspaper would lie was anathema to the seventies reading public. As Ikegami freely admitted "the cultural differences kinda did for us," and the complete run of the Japanese *Spider-Man* finished at volume five, by which time the original Marvel scripts had been dumped and wholly rewritten by *Harmageddon* creator Kazumasa Hirai. The changes made to the later TV incarnation of *Spider-Man* were largely based on the experience of publishing the manga edition.

But working with Hirai encouraged Ikegami to concentrate on art thereafter, and leave stories to someone else. In 1973, he hooked up with Kazuo Koike for the first of many popular collaborations. Ikegami and Koike went on to create *Crying Freeman* together, while Ikegami's work with Kazuya Kudo resulted in *Mai the Psychic Girl*. Most recently, Ikegami is enjoying even more fame thanks to *Sanctuary*, the anime version of his team-up with *Fist of the North Star* writer Sho Fumimura. Thanks to his later fame, his early work with Marvel is still a collector's item. In a final irony, it was re-imported back into the US with its translation as a thirty-one-issue comic in the late 1990s.

(*Newtype USA*, February 2005)

TURNING JAPANESE

David Hughes and Jonathan Clements investigate Hollywood's latest obsession.

To the untrained eye, *Crying Freeman* appears to be just another action film unleashed upon a weary and overcrowded market. Yet the film's premier this month may herald a new trend in motion pictures. It is the first live-action movie based on a Japanese comic (manga) to be judged worthy of a big cinema release, and has already proved successful in several territories.

With the likes of *Batman* and *Superman* providing lucrative franchises and major merchandising opportunities, Hollywood already has a vested interest in comics as source material. However, many directors are now turning to manga as an untapped area of ready-storyboarded scripts to bring to Western cinema audiences over the next five years.

Crying Freeman director Christophe Gans scripted his own adaptation of the manga by Kazuo Koike and Ryoichi Ikegami. Like Japan, but in sharp contrast to the Anglophone world, Gans' native France does not regard comics as a solely juvenile medium. Both countries have healthy adult comic markets, and it should come as no surprise that the first major live-action film based on a manga should have a French director. Japanese is a famously complex (and expensive) language to translate, but the visual component in manga has made it easier for the movie industry to appreciate the many great stories waiting for the film treatment.

Gans initially encountered *Crying Freeman* in Japanese, a language he does not read, and was struck by its simplicity and elegance. He immediately began pursuing the rights, seeking advice from Brian Yuzna, who had previously adapted the best-selling manga *Guyver* into a straight-to-video feature starring *Star Wars*' Mark Hamill. "The Japanese people were pretty convinced about my adaptation, but they were absolutely not convinced that I would direct it," says Gans of the project. "They proposed that I do a segment of a film called *Necronomicon*, inspired by H.P. Lovecraft, which basically became my exam. When the review came out in *Variety*, my segment was the only thing praised, so I passed!"

Crying Freeman, featuring martial arts star Mark Dacascos, was filmed for $8 million, with finance from Asia, Europe and America and pre-sales to a number of other territories making it profitable before a single frame was even shot. In France, it became the year's most successful action film, despite running against big names such as Kurt Russel and Steven Seagal in *Executive Decision*, and Jean-Claude Van Damme in *Sudden Death*. "We just crushed them," says Gans, "simply because it was a choice between [*Freeman*] and two post-*Die Hard* action films." This success has allowed him to fully finance his next feature, a $45 million adventure based on the early exploits of Jules Verne's Captain Nemo, following which he will adapt another best-selling manga, Masami Yuki's futuristic police drama *Patlabor*.

There is already a steady stream of manga-inspired projects from other interested parties. Gossip in the movie business has linked *Lethal Weapon* director Richard Donner with the movie adaptation of *Speed Racer*, and both Francis Ford Coppola and Tim Burton have tried to get the green light for film versions of Kazuo Koike's *Mai the Psychic Girl*, with Winona Ryder tipped to play the eponymous heroine. Terry Gilliam passed on a Hollywood *Godzilla* remake, before rumors linked the project to *Speed*'s Jan de Bont. The job now lies in the hands of Roland Emmerich, who obviously failed to do as much damage to the USA in *Independence Day* as he would have liked.

Japan's most vocal Western supporter is James Cameron, director of the *Terminator* films, whose enthusiasm for Masamune Shirow's animated feature *Ghost in the Shell* helped sell it in several cinema territories. Cameron describes Shirow's film as "a stunning work of speculative fiction, the first truly adult animation film to reach a level of literary and visual excellence. The poetry of its visuals," he continues, "and the depth of its themes set it apart amongst science fiction films… a new benchmark for animation and design." Cameron's enthusiasm for *Ghost in the Shell* fuelled suspicion that the director would remake it, rumors which Gans discovered to be untrue. "I found myself asking why James Cameron would want to," he says. "It's not very commercial; it's too complicated; Cameron has already written a 'cyberpunk film', *Strange Days*, which was the biggest flop of his career; and *Ghost in the Shell* is already perfect. What would you do, reproduce it frame for frame? So I asked the people who own the rights if Cameron has ever asked after them, and they said, 'No, do you want them?' I figure that people think he wanted to adapt the film because they saw his signature on the poster, but it's just an urban legend."

Cameron's interest in manga, however, did stretch beyond mere appreciation. Industry bible *The Hollywood Reporter* had already outed him as holder of the remake rights to the most famous manga in the West, Katsuhiro Otomo's *Akira*, but surprised its readers by revealing his purchase of an untranslated work, Hitoshi Iwaaki's *Parasyte*. This darkly humorous tale of a Japan invaded by vicious, bodysnatching aliens is less notable for its success in Japan than for the presence of doppelgangers that can turn their bodies into fluidic metallic weapons. It is thought that Cameron's optioning of *Parasyte* did not demonstrate an intent to adapt it for film, but rather a pre-emptive strike against litigation for any resemblance between the late-eighties manga and his 1991 blockbuster *Terminator 2*, which featured a similar shapeshifting assassin. Cameron had already endured a successful plagiarism suit from the writer Harlan Ellison over coincidences of plotting in the first *Terminator* film, and it seems that buying up even remotely similar works is a far cheaper option than risking another court case.

But what is it that attracts directors such as Cameron and Gans to manga as potential source material? For Gans, *Crying Freeman* was a classical tale far beyond the level of most American comics. "The setting is contemporary, but the story is a period piece," he explains. "The characters are not fighting for money or drugs; they are fighting for honor, pride and passion, just as you would imagine in the fifteenth century, in Japan or at the court of the Borgias." For Cameron, whose Digital Domain is a world leader in special effects, there are shots that can be achieved in animation as yet unimagined in what he describes as real-world photography. "As the ability to create these effects increases," he says, "it becomes more important to create a style, and I think digital artists in the US are looking to animation to see what kind of style can be imposed upon it."

Yet directors are not the only industry insiders with a growing interest in Japanese material. Disney's Buena Vista subsidiary is now the Western distributor for Hayao Miyazaki, a leading creator whose animated films consistently outperform Disney at the Japanese box office. An earlier deal between Miyazaki's Studio Ghibli and Buena Vista is said to have collapsed over Miyazaki's mistrust of the Hollywood giant's motives. The first release under the new, improved deal is Studio Ghibli's latest production, *Princess Mononoke*.

Disney are well advised to pursue the rights to such high-quality product. In Japan, the third largest box office territory in the world, video sales of *Toy Story* and *Pocahontas* were both eclipsed by the homegrown success of *Evangelion*, a fervently anti-Christian tale of invading angels from outer space. Ironically, Disney's *Lion King* was well received in Japan, amid Western allegations (vehemently denied by the company) that the film owed much to Osamu Tezuka's highly-regarded 1966 television series, *Jungle Emperor*, screened in the US as *Kimba the White Lion*.

The Japanese themselves are instigating much of the international interest in their material, actively seeking both foreign finance and talent. Marvin Gleicher, whose company Manga Entertainment brought the animated versions of *Ghost in the Shell* and *Patlabor* to the West, is currently co-financing a number of projects in Japan. "The projects that we are doing as joint ventures are based on the strength of the Japanese market and community, but we're attempting to make them a bit more Westernized, not with character designs, but maybe storyline and music." Pioneer's leading producer, Taro Maki, who invited composer Christopher Franke to score *Tenchi Muyo in Love*, and actors Keifer Sutherland and Elizabeth Berkeley to voice roles in *Armitage III*, is among those who value such participation. "Character designers and directors need to be Japanese for the sake of communication and style," he says, "but the Americans and the French have some great talent in other areas."

This may explain why, following the success of his live-action *Crying*

Freeman, Christophe Gans was approached by Japanese licensors with a selection of other properties. "They said, 'What do you want to do?' and gave me a list of comics: *Midnight Eye Goku* by Buichi Terasawa, Yukito Kishiro's *Battle Angel Alita*, and *Patlabor*, which I am going to do." Anyone interested in these titles can check out the appeal for themselves, years ahead of any live-action release, as all the animated versions are already available in UK video shops.

Gans is not the only French director negotiating to shoot a live-action feature based on a popular Japanese cartoon. He relates the tale of Mathieu Kassovitz, director of the Oscar-nominated *La Haine*, who when invited by Steven Spielberg to choose his next project, immediately suggested *Dragonball*, a phenomenally successful TV series in Kassovitz's native France, but unreleased in the UK.

Yet despite Hollywood's sudden interest in the phenomena, Manga Entertainment's Marvin Gleicher feels that the studios may come unstuck if they lose sight of what gave the material its initial appeal. "The fact that some of these live-action films are based on manga will increase the awareness of Japanese culture in a positive sense," he says. "But some of the studios will fail if they attempt to Westernize it too much."

(*The Guardian*, 14th April 1997. This article was printed with a new title, 'Manga Goes to Hollywood', and with some unwelcome editorializations. This version reprints the authors' original text, not the version that appeared in the newspaper. The intervening years saw many of the 'forthcoming' films mentioned above disappear into development hell, though a live action *Dragonball* film, directed by James Wong, finally went into production in 2008, and James Cameron now own the rights to *Battle Angel Alita*.)

TOP MEN

The genesis of *Spriggan*

At the end of *Raiders of the Lost Ark*, Indiana Jones was assured that his priceless, powerful archaeological find was being looked after by 'Top Men'. But as the credits began to roll, we saw it nailed into a crate, dumped in a giant warehouse full of similar boxes, forgotten and abandoned. The image was Lucas and Spielberg's homage to Orson Welles, a little piece of *Citizen Kane* recycled for a modern audience. But in Japan, Hiroshi Takashige didn't get the joke. Instead, he asked himself, what was in all those other crates? And more importantly, who were these Top Men?

In collusion with artist Ryoji Minagawa, he decided that they were a secret, self-sustaining unit within the Pentagon, tasked with nabbing any weird and wonderful artifacts that come to light, many of which had been left behind by an ancient, highly-advanced civilization. They began work on the comic project that would become *Spriggan*, only to find themselves influenced by real-world events.

They were writing at the time of the First Gulf War; a very difficult prospect for the Japanese. A nation supposedly sworn to avoid violence and military aggression was forced to sit on the sidelines and watch while the rest of the world got involved in a conflict about resources in the Middle East, the cradle of civilization, resources that Japan itself needed as desperately as everyone else. It resulted in such tales as the desert robot combat anime *Gasaraki*, and in an interest — partly fuelled by *The X-Files* — in presenting the Pentagon as the bad guy.

There is more than one agency searching for these artifacts. The Pentagon competes with the KGB, and both are in opposition to ARCAM, a global corporation that wants the artifacts for itself. Its crack, super-powered agents are spies-cum-archaeologists named after ancient Celtic temple guardians, the Spriggan.

Minagawa and Takashige initially wanted to feature an adult agent, but ended up selling their concept to an anthology magazine aimed at boys. Consequently, they moved their original lead into the background, and concentrated on his teenage nephew, Yu Ominae.

Rights for a movie adaptation were soon sold, and *Spriggan* went into production as an anime. The film-makers plumped for a script that emphasized the Indiana Jones parallels, chasing after a different Ark (Noah's, in this case) at Mount Ararat, with cyborg Pentagon agents roughing it up with the ARCAM Spriggans in an action-packed thriller.

As Ominae, producers cast Shotaro Morikubo, better known in Japan as the movie-dub voice of Johnny Depp. Originally intended to go straight to video, the budget received a massive injection of cash, sufficient for a movie, when Katsuhiro Otomo announced he would be "involved". *Akira* creator Otomo was supposed to be working on his own project, the long-delayed *Steam Boy*, but fancied *Spriggan* as a kind of busman's holiday. In fact, he is rumored to have been the director in all but name; his fingerprints are all over *Spriggan*, in the design of the space-faring Noah's Ark that the agents unearth, in the blue-skinned Pentagon child-telepath General MacDougall, and in the large amount of night-time shooting — an expensive luxury in animation that relies so heavily on light coming through the cels, but one that Otomo often enjoyed for the artistic hell of it. The credited director, Hirotsugu Kawasaki, has not had another movie to his name since, only emphasizing the impression that Otomo's more nebulous title of 'General Supervisor' was only adopted for contractual reasons. But for those in the know, there was no mistaking who the Top Man on the production really was.

(*Judge Dredd Megazine* #236, 2005)

TO LIVE AND DIE IN L.A.
Shadows of Spawn

L ife is tough in the City of Angels. The local kids call Ken Kurosawa the "karate monkey" for his prowess in martial arts, but they still give him a pretty wide berth. Ken had to learn to fight at an early age — with his parents gone, he has to do everything he can to make sure that his little sister Mariko is safe. She's cute, a nine-year-old girl with a funny outlook on life. She once burst into tears because the clock stopped while she was waiting to blow out the candles on her birthday cake. She thought that time had stopped with it, and that she'd never get any older.

But now there's a different reason for the tears. Ken has so much on his mind that he forgot all about her birthday. He promised he'd make it up to her... He's got her a nice gift, and he's not going to let anyone get in his way as he races home to wish her many happy returns.

Except Ken never reaches home — his gangland enemies see to that. After he crosses one hood too many, he's burned alive in a terrible car bombing. The last thing he sees is what's left of his own hand reaching out for the charred photograph of his beloved sister. When Ken wakes up, he's dead.

SPAWN: MUTATION

Worse fates have befallen manga characters, but a fat, blue-faced man turns up and starts talking to Ken as if they've been friends for years. "Over on the East Coast," he hisses conspiratorially, "they call me 'The Clown'."

This is no ordinary funny guy, it's the human form of Violator, henchman of pure evil. Violator knows his way around the newly-dead. He reminds Ken that there's nobody there to look after little Mariko now, and makes him an offer he can't refuse. He can become a Hellspawn, a general in the armies of Hades, and for service to the dark lord Malebolgia, he will be given magical powers and incredible strength. Out of fraternal duty to his beloved sister, Ken Kurosawa accepts, and a new Hellspawn joins the ever-increasing ranks of pandemonium.

So begins *Shadows of Spawn*, a genuine manga version of Todd McFarlane's famous character, published in Japan to tie in with the release of the *Spawn* animated series. 'Supervised' by McFarlane himself, *Shadows of Spawn* was created by the young artist Juzo Tokoro. Born in 1961 in Shizuoka, Tokoro published his first strip in 1985 in *Shonen Magazine* — the inspiringly-titled *Noble! West Rooting Group*, about a street-punk more interested in studying than cruising for fast women with his friends. Although he has also contributed to *G-Hard* and *Shougun*, Tokoro's other big manga was 1991's *Breaking up the Special Attack*, another story of gangsters, heavily influenced by Japanese crime movies and Quentin Tarantino. Tokoro treats *Spawn* in much the same way as Ryoichi Ikegami treated *Spider-Man* twenty years ago — taking the same essential story and squeezing it through a filter of manga-style stereotypes.

Whereas the original's Al Simmons had a life and a wife before he was turned into Spawn, the only girl in the world for the chaste Ken Kurosawa is his little sister. Of course, this doesn't stop Ken gaining a whole host of manga babes to almost chase after him and almost form a love interest. There's Beezlebub ("Just call me 'Bee'"), the diminutive fairy sent from Hell to help Ken get around. And not forgetting Michaela, the bad-girl freelance Spawn-hunter, who's supposed to be chasing after Ken, but seems to take a shine to him. Disguising herself as a hooker, she drags a hapless victim into the deserted chapel where Ken Kurosawa makes his home, only to discard her cover the moment she discovers that her quarry is indeed inside. But Michaela can't bring herself to finish Ken off, preferring instead to join forces with him and fellow Hellspawn Zombie.

SPAWN: PROTECTION

Shadows of Spawn is not merely a simple rewrite of the Spawn story with a few Japanese elements. It fits into Todd McFarlane's *Spawn* universe as a whole — hence the West Coast setting to keep Ken out of Al's way, and the presence of Chibiolator, a 'Mini-Me' version of Violator, grown from the original's own severed arm. Tokoro also introduces several characters created by McFarlane for the *Spawn* line of toys but unseen in the original comic, such as the Grave Digger, who shambles around the cemetery where Ken's mortal body is laid to rest. Similarly, Ken's combat suit is the one originally sold as the Battleclad Spawn toy.

Other parts integrate directly with the original story. A secret military project to create artificial Spawns with 'psychoplasm' runs off the rails when one of its experimental subjects, codenamed 'Tremor II', escapes in Los Angeles. Tremor II, who first appeared in episode 46 of the original comic, has had a manga makeover for his appearance in *Shadows of Spawn*, but firmly links Ken Kurosawa's West Coast milieu to that of Al Simmons in the East.

It's difficult to imagine the tough, gruff Simmons protecting an idol singer, but as the months turn into years, that's exactly what his opposite number Ken has to do. Mariko grows up to be a perky sixteen year-old, and seems to be on a fast track to that actress-singer career she's always wanted. Success in the media brings all kinds of hangers-on, and many of them are unsurprisingly in league with evil powers. Harold Carter, for example, is an Egyptologist who tries to convince Mariko to sign up for the role of Miss Cleopatra, without revealing that the small print involves her being tied to an altar and having her heart cut out in order to turn him into the living incarnation of Anubis.

As with the early *Spider-Man* comics admired by original creator McFarlane, Ken often gets the raw end of the deal. He saves Mariko's life from the evil Carter by killing him, but since Carter never had the chance to reveal his dark side, all Mariko sees is the 'friendly' Carter getting stabbed to death by a strange masked man in a prehensile cloak. Ken can never reveal to Mariko what he has become, and now he must contend with the knowledge that while she still dreams of her beloved brother Ken, it's Spawn who haunts her nightmares.

For once in his life, Violator may not have been too far from the truth. Mariko most certainly isn't out of danger, and nobody else but Ken is looking out for her.

When her kind-hearted agent introduces her to one of LA's most famous starlets, Ellis, Mariko is speechless with awe. But Ellis is speechless with rage, regarding the young Miss Kurosawa as just one more example of the increased competition she's facing with girls younger than herself. Once she's alone in her room, Ellis is approached by someone... or some*thing* that has a proposal for her. The clock can be stopped, it is possible to turn back the hands of time — Ellis can be young forever, but there will be a price to pay. Next day, Ellis presents Mariko with a gift box containing a snake. As Mariko tries to escape, the scales begin to fall from Ellis's skin, and she transforms into the soulless, snake-charming Medusa of her deal with the devil, and Ken must come to save his sister once more.

But will Mariko ever realize who Spawn really is? If so, will she be able to do what she couldn't do on her birthday — turn back time so she can be with her brother again? There's plenty of scope in the *Shadows of Spawn* manga, because it has clearly been designed to interact with the events of its US sister-title. Who's to say that we can't find out sooner rather than later, if someone picks up the translation rights and taps into the growing crossover markets of those who like manga, or *Spawn*, or both?

(*Manga Max* #15, 2000)

ABOVE & BEYOND HOLLYWOOD

The *Starship Troopers* Anime

It is a time of peace. The people of a united Earth are taking their first, halting steps out into the great unknown. On an insignificant ball of rock known only as Alpha III, a scout team finds a mysterious artifact. The routine mission is fated to go down in history as the first encounter of the Alien War…

None of this means much to the all-American hero Juan 'Johnnie' Rico, just finishing his senior year at Daniel High. But his life is about to change forever. He fumbles a throw in a football game, losing the match for his school and maybe ruining his chances with Carmencita Ivanez, the cheerleader he adores. In a rash attempt to make it up to her, he swears to follow her in whatever she does. Unluckily for him, Carmen decides to join up.

Tetsuro Amino's 1988 anime *Starship Troopers* was a six-part video series destined for historical obscurity until the release of the Hollywood movie. Robert Heinlein's 1959 book was a watershed moment in his career. At the time known primarily for children's fiction, he was forced to return to adult writing when his editor rejected *Starship Troopers* for being "too militaristic". Heinlein switched publishers, and rarely wrote for a juvenile audience again.

His books were translated into Japanese by Tetsu Yano, an accomplished science fiction author in his own right, and a living guarantee that Heinlein's work would not be mangled in translation. The Japanese publication of *Starship Troopers* would have far-ranging effects on the anime industry, starting in the 1970s when it inspired a young storyboard artist called Yoshiyuki Tomino.

Tomino began working for Tezuka Productions in 1963, where he produced, wrote and directed many episodes of Japan's first big robot show, *Astro Boy*. Work followed on many TV series, including *Princess Knight*, *Heidi* and *The Moomins* before Tomino hit on the idea that would make his fortune. He thought that Heinlein's 'powered suits' were an exploitable idea, and came up with the first concept for what would become one of Japan's biggest TV series ever, *Gundam*.

That's one story anyway, and one that Tomino told Fred Schodt for the book *Inside the Robot Kingdom*. Several years on in *Animerica*, he was to downplay the importance of Heinlein in favor of the *Star Wars* movies and the hypothetical space colonies proposed by the American scientist Gerard O'Neill. But it's partially thanks to Tomino that Heinlein's books have never gone out of fashion, and that the word 'mobile' (from *Starship Troopers*' 'mobile infantry') manages to sneak into so many show titles instead of the more usual Japanese word for 'robot', from *Mobile Infantry Gundam* (to give it a more literal translation) to *Mobile Police Patlabor*.

The powered suits were little more than window-dressing in the original *Starship Troopers* (and indeed, were regarded as unimportant enough to be discarded altogether in the Hollywood version), yet they caught the Japanese imagination in a unique way. The Japanese book cover of *Starship Troopers* was the first to show the soldiers' robot armor in anything approaching the way that Heinlein originally described it. It took the British publishers more than thirty years to realize there was more to the concept than spacesuits with jetpacks, but thanks to the success of *Gundam*, the *Starship Troopers* novel was assured of a place in Japanese bookshops.

Gundam's effect on anime was irreversible, and Tomino has had little time to do anything else for twenty years. It was only a matter of time before someone decided to animate the original inspiration, and the job fell to Tetsuro Amino.

Amino was only twenty-six years old when he landed a director's job on the *Goshogun: Time Étrangere* TV series. He also storyboarded several episodes of *Dirty Pair* before returning to direction with the chef show *Mr Ajikko* and the bikes-and-baseball tale *Batsu & Terry*. But *Starship Troopers* was Amino's entry into science fiction; following its release he spent several years making *Gundam* spin-off titles before hitting the big time with *Iria* and *Macross 7*.

Script adaptation started in the hands of Tsunehisa Ito, already known in Japan for another take on alien invasion, the 1987 *Zillion*. However, several episodes fell to veteran scribe Noboru (sometimes credited as 'Sho') Aikawa, one of the most prolific writers of anime screenplays, whose projects have included *Legend of the Overfiend*, *Angel Cop*, *The*

Hakkenden, *Yotoden* and *Vampire Princess Miyu*.

The series went into production at a time when Hollywood had rediscovered the war movie. After a decade in hibernation following the embarrassment of Vietnam, gung-ho movies were back in fashion, and a diet of *Tour of Duty*s and *Iron Eagle*s was filtering back to the Japanese audience.

Amino approached *Starship Troopers* as an antidote to the then-popular *Top Gun*, announcing that he was unhappy with Hollywood's trend for glamorizing warfare, and that he wanted to create a more 'documentary' feel. This he certainly managed, in a very different take on Heinlein's original.

Amino's version retains the scenes of training and combat, but also plays up the 'downtime' spent by men off the battlefield. His soldiers get into bar-room brawls with disgruntled civvies, bury one of their comrades and are then forced to attend his girlfriend's wedding before her bold lover is even cold.

The romance between Johnnie and Carmen becomes one of the central pieces in the anime, which ends with their tearful reunion in hospital, where they have both been evacuated with injuries. Carmen hardly appears at all in the bulk of the novel, but intermediate scenes were inserted in the anime to remind viewers what Johnnie is fighting for. In addition, each episode closes with Carmencita bouncing along a beach in a bikini, just to hammer the point home.

Johnnie's mother, Maria, also has a larger part to play in the anime version. In the book her role is to die when the aliens attack Buenos Aires, galvanizing Johnnie's pacifist father into enlisting. In the anime, it is she who opposes Johnnie's enlistment, slapping his face as he prepares to leave. Her death is also made far more immediate — Amino's version keeps the trainees closer to Earth, so that we see Johnnie and his platoon fighting fires at the fall of Buenos Aires, unaware that his mother is breathing her last nearby.

Heinlein's book contrasted Johnnie's real-life stay-at-home dad Emilio with the martial valor of Sergeant Zim, who becomes his 'spiritual' father from the moment he signs up. The book ends at the Battle of Klendathu, with Zim out of the picture and Emilio taking his rightful place as

Johnnie's sergeant and sire. Conversely, the anime ends after the battle of Klendathu, without the appearance of Emilio, but Amino still instructed his team to play up the contrast between the two very different fathers.

In fact, the anime actually takes the family aspect further, with Johnnie's mother paying the ultimate price for her pacifism, while Carmen fights for her country and is rewarded with the dubious honor of fussing around Johnnie in the final episode.

Despite Amino's attempts to de-fang Heinlein's militarist message with some home truths about the evils of war, he was still accused by some of over-Americanizing the anime. He defended himself by pointing out he was working from an American original, which was bound to influence the outcome, but nevertheless a few of the novel's international aspects were surprisingly dropped.

Only Johnnie's full name remains to remind of us of his Hispanic origins; in the novel he was from the Philippines, in the anime he's as blonde as they come. The only Japanese character in the original book, Private Shujumi, is not present in the anime. He is replaced by the jug-eared, happy-go-lucky Private Azuma, who has 'dead man' written all over him from day one.

Shujumi may have been dropped for a reason, as this martial artist with a Japanese general for a dad might have been too much of a stereotype for the home audience to cope with. An ex-naval officer, Heinlein harbored considerable resentment for the race that bombed Pearl Harbor. At the time of *Starship Troopers'* release, only one of Heinlein's adult novels remained untranslated into Japanese. Funnily enough, it was *Sixth Column*, in which evil Orientals, unfit to call themselves human beings, overrun the United States before being wiped out by an all-American biological weapon. One of Heinlein's tips of the hat to his military past did manage to survive untouched in the anime *Starship Troopers*; Johnnie's ship, the *Rodger Young* is named after a real-life Ohio private, posthumously decorated for single-handedly destroying a Japanese gun emplacement in 1943.

(*Manga Mania* #45, 1998)

ITCHY... TASTY...

Resident Evil and Game Adaptations

I once wasted a week playing the pant-wettingly scary game of *Resident Evil* on the PlayStation. My flatmate wouldn't play it on his own, so I babysat while he turned corners, hoping not to get savaged by a zombie devil dog or sentient shark. He'd hurt his back, so he slept like a baby every night dosed up on painkillers. I wasn't so lucky. I would lay in bed, trying to think of new places to look for flame rounds... mulling over a new route to the basement... wondering why the radiators creaked so loudly...

Sitting in the darkened cinema, it all came back to me. The long, agonizing expectation. The creamily lit rooms of the science facility. The eerie music. The strange euphony of the term "viral weaponry". I knew there would be devil dogs. I knew. And like the return of unwelcome zombie friends, a question came back to haunt me. Why wasn't there a *Resident Evil* anime?

Anime and the gaming industry have long enjoyed a close relationship. It started in 1978, with the Japanese release of the first arcade mah jong game, called (wait for it) *Mah Jong Game*. Some of its imitators attempted to up the ante by including a strip-poker variant — you could play against pretty girls who would slowly denude. But back in those days, memory wasn't cheap, and one way of packing more into the chip was by junking real photographs in favor of an anime-style look.

The distinctive look of anime characters — the big eyes, the one-piece hair, and so on — isn't just a reflection of the way they look in manga. In fact, if you look at the Japanese comics world, you'll soon see that there are myriad types of 'manga look'. The one that has become best known in the mainstream, however, is the one most often used in anime because it's easy to animate, it's easy to convey to in betweeners in Korea and China, and in the computing world it saves memory. Games started to look like anime, and as the power of the gaming companies increased, anime started to look like games.

There was a tie in the race to make the first game-based anime. The joint winners in 1986, released on the same day, were *Running Boy* and

Super Mario Bros, and after that, game-based anime grew exponentially. By the end of the 1990s, mainstream anime were reduced to tiny little broadcast-runs, while gaming money grabbed large chunks of the schedules. The Capcom company's *Power Stone* and *Street Fighter II* were two of the biggest anime on TV, simply because they had better staying power and more episodes.

When I translated Capcom's *Street Fighter II* manga, I was surprised at how easy they were to deal with. They made a point of saying what they liked, and of thanking me for my work. And when they didn't like something, they didn't just pout and make me do it again, they suggested alternatives. They were market led in the best sense of the phrase, discovering what the fans wanted, and then working out the best way to give it to them. When *Resident Evil* came out, there were certainly plans to turn it into an anime — there were even manga-style designs, which crept onto some of the spin-off products. But the anime never materialized, chiefly because Capcom saw the chance to avoid second best, and went for it.

Resident Evil was asking for it — 16 million units of the game sold worldwide, and a gross of $600 million was enough to get Hollywood's attention. Then it was only a matter of time. Original rumors speculated that the zombie shoot-'em-up would be helmed by George Romero, he of *Dawn of the Dead*. Eventually, the director who brought it in was *Mortal Kombat's* Paul Anderson, who spent five days in pre-production meetings with Capcom so that everybody knew they were on the same page. It's the perfect way to deal with them. He demonstrated that he knew the game backwards, that he understood the look, the feel, the things the fans would need to see. Once he'd done that, Capcom could relax, and a happy producer makes a happy production.

Make no mistake, the Japanese make anime because they can't afford to make 'real' films. Give them the chance to shoot with live actors and millions of dollars, and you won't see them for dust.

(SCI FI channel (UK) website, April 2002)

DIGITAL
A N I M A T I O N

DIGITAL ANIMATION

A speech given at Dundee Contemporary Arts, Projectorfest, 1st February 2008.

Before I kick off, I think it's a good idea if I show you how old fashioned animation is done. This is what we call a cel — it's a piece of cellulose, covered in acrylic paint, and it's the basic building block of traditional animation. This is our foreground, which is a man in a sailor's hat, and this is our background which is a load of men sitting on chairs, and to turn this into a scene from an anime, we slap down our background and our foreground on a flat surface, and take a picture. There we go, we have a single image. And we only have to do a dozen or so of those every second, and we've got an anime.

And I think you can see the advantages of cel animation already. If the background remains the same, we can leave our background image on the table, and simply replace the one in the foreground. If we're using a thing called a multi-plane camera, we can have up to five layers of cels, so there's scope for a lot of things to go on there. Your only real expense is paint and a camera, and it's a simple yet effective process that has worked in animation all over the world for the better part of a century.

Film as a medium is less than a hundred years old, and it remains a medium that thrives on spectacle. Movie audiences can get little stories at home on their TV — the popcorn rustlers want to see something impressive, and movie-makers are often searching for ways to do that with new gimmicks.

Film has always been a slave to new technologies. People will try any gimmick if they think it will put bums on seats. Vistavision, Technicolor, Panavision, Panascope, Supermarionation, Tohoscope, even 3-D. Sometimes, like color film, these are gimmicks that eventually take over the entire industry. Sometimes, like 3-D, they stay as gimmicks, because the technology does not really exist to apply them properly... yet.

When I talk about spectacle, what I really mean is 'showing off' and that's something that was done very well in 1982, in Steven Lisberger's movie *Tron*. For those of you who don't know it, it was a Disney movie, a cyber version of *Fantastic Voyage*, in which a man is shrunk down to pixel size and sent on an adventure through the innards of a computer. A lot of what people remember today about *Tron* is the strange recoloring of the images and the film's very distinctive look, but it also contained conspicuous computer graphics.

Another thing about it was *Tron*'s director, Steven Lisberger. He hasn't made that many movies in his time, but before *Tron*, in 1979, he had made a cartoon movie called *Animalympics*. So because of that, he was more likely to show up on the radar of people working in the Japanese animation industry. When *Tron* came out in 1982, it was seen by one of Lisberger's Japanese colleagues, a man called Osamu Dezaki, who was at the time working on an animated movie of his own. And because he rather liked the showy-offy bits in *Tron*, Dezaki decided that he would throw some computer graphics into his own movie.

Why? I don't know. Because *Golgo 13* wasn't a film about talking computer viruses fighting inside a machine, it was a modern James Bond-style fable about a contract killer. There was no actual need to have any computer graphics in it, and that was part of the problem. With early computer graphics, we're talking about severe limitations on how much time and money you can afford to put in. We're also talking about severe limitations on what you can show. Realistic human movement is still a decade away. Realistic human faces are twenty years away. All we can really trust 1980s computer graphics to handle are big, unwieldy solid objects. So Dezaki found a scene which would work, and he got his animators on the case.

When *Golgo 13* was released the following year, it featured a brief CG scene of helicopter gunships. With a sudden wrench, *Golgo 13* jumped from 'traditional' anime style to something that looked like an old Atari console. It was over in a flash, and it was the first computer-generated sequence in Japanese animation.

That jolt between cel and computer graphics is a constant problem in early digital animation. Some people were already suggesting that computers, as they fell in price and increased in numbers, could be put to better use in the animation industry... eventually. But we are talking about the early 1980s. The most affordable personal computer was a ZX Spectrum or a BBC Micro. They weren't really suitable for use on films. People weren't even using word processors in Japan at this point, many scripts remained hand-written for another ten years.

The kind of computers in use in the *movie* business were much bigger, more powerful and exclusive. I am talking about the Cray. Cray computers were used on *2010* to do some of the computer animation, and it struck another anime director, Yoshiaki Kawajiri, that it would be nice to buy some time on a Cray and put it to use. Notice the use of that phrase "buy some time." These days, if you want to use computer hardware in your movie, you can buy a big chunk of it in the high street. Back then, we are talking about renting space on some huge device, like a radio telescope, or a satellite.

But anyway, Kawajiri knew that using computers would get him noticed. At the time he was working on a TV series called *Lensman*. But he was not sure how to stretch his limited time to the best use. So he thought about things logically. If we are going to make a TV series, and we only have a limited budget for computer animation, where are we going to stick it? At this time, budgets for TV series in Japan were actually falling. The average TV episode of twenty-five minutes, costs about £80,000, but TV companies were only offering £75,000 in payment for each episode. You had to find a way to cut corners in order to meet your budgets. One way is to make sure that the opening and closing credits take as long as possible. Not because that's necessarily a good thing, but because with opening credits you only have to make them once, and you can use the same footage every week for as long as your series lasts.

So yes, Yoshiaki Kawajiri threw a massive amount of money into showing off with computer graphics on *Lensman*, but unlike *Golgo 13*, he was able to put that money and that investment to work for him every week. Every time somebody sat down to see *Lensman*, they would get to look at the graphics and say, "Wow, they've thrown some money at this!" It's a self-fulfilling prophecy in a way, but it still makes better use of the hardware involved.

Let's face it, these are just gimmicks. They are special effects used in their most conspicuous way, not to help us believe the story or concentrate our attention on the plot and milieu, but simply to show us how clever the special effects are.

An equation to bear in mind, as a rule of thumb, is that the power of computers doubles roughly every eighteen months. Any of you who have shelled out for a PC or a Mac will know the truism that the moment you've bought it, some sod will release one with better widgets and more RAM, and a DVD-ROM drive and coffee-making facilities. But just think for a moment how this impacts on a business.

Two directors in particular started to play with computers in a different way. Instead of using them purely to show off, they used them to make their animated films look more real. After all, what would require special effects in a live-action movie, is often actually quite easy to do in animation. If you want to draw a spaceship the size of a planet, you only have to use paint. This ability to have exploding worlds and robot armies and so on, has encouraged many big-budget anime productions to be science fiction stories. What interested directors like Katsuhiro Otomo and Mamoru Oshii was using computers to represent reality. So if we look at *Patlabor*, we will see computer graphics turning up on viewscreens, but we also have them used to do refraction patterns in water droplets, reflections on windscreens, and things like focus pulls and contra-zooms.

Now for those of you who don't know, a focus pull is where the camera's eye chooses to focus on one aspect of a scene. Let's say that I'm talking and that the focal length of the camera is set to me. In other words, I will be talking and in focus, and the background behind me will be out of focus. Then, you see a fuzzy figure walk in at the back... You don't know who it is for a moment. Then suddenly, you realize, oh my God, it's Nicole Kidman! Far more interesting than Jonathan Clements, and so therefore, to reflect that visually, suddenly we pull the focus, and

I go out of focus, and Nicole Kidman is suddenly in sharp view. That's easy to do with live-action film-making because it uses the equipment you already have with you... a camera, and a lens. But you can't do it so easily with animation.

Nor can you do a contra-zoom, which is where a camera dollies back while keeping the subject in focus, and zooming forward, so the subject stays seemingly in the same place, but the background seems to mutate behind him because the focal length of the lens is changing. Very costly and time-consuming with animation, but not too difficult once you have a computer.

Ghost in the Shell didn't just make use of computer graphics to look real, it also used them behind the scenes. It was one of the first anime to use online editing. In other words, they dumped all their traditional animation cels and all their computer graphics into a computer, and edited it there, instead of using a pair of scissors and some sticky-tape. If you watch the *Making of Ghost in the Shell* documentary, you will see them say in breathless, hushed tones, "We used this incredible new device called an... Avid Editing Suite." Which is laughable. It shows you how much times change, because in 1995 they were making a big deal about having an Avid. There are probably several hundred Avid suites in all sorts of offices in the middle of Soho today. They are commonplace, but back then, all of thirteen years ago, it was something so impressive that they spent five minutes showing off about it.

Avid and other online editing devices allow the combination of computer graphics and animation with relative ease. It allows the film-maker to have a CG background with a cel character in the front, or vice versa. It means that separate shots can be put together using the good points of both media.

This is all very well, but the need arises in such situations to find an excuse for this integration. So you get CG used in readouts or in cyberspatial situations, or, in the case *Macross Plus*, you get a computer-generated pop star. Of course she's going to look like she comes out of a machine. Also note that when they want to distort an image, or show it decomposing, they use digital animation.

But as computer graphics began to fall in price, and slowly took over the industry, we get a new problem… the atrophy of talent. Work was sent abroad to countries like Korea and Taiwan, where there was a cheaper labor pool. Which meant that you could save money, but also that an entire generation of people who should have been learning how to work with cels, weren't.

Let me give you an example from *Macross Plus*. There's a scene in *Macross Plus* where someone is plugged into a monitor that checks their heart rate or brain waves or something like that. And so the producers said to their staff, "We need some of those zig-zaggy lines." And the animators couldn't be bothered, but the computer guy, who was called Yoshinori Sayama, said, "Hey, I'll do it."

But he didn't draw it. He wasn't really an artist. Instead, he made the readout happen and recorded the data! He went down to a hospital, plugged himself into a heart-rate monitor, and recorded the results on his laptop. But he realized that he needed some variation in speed and height, so he had to work himself up into a sweat. He discovered — and this is a true story — he discovered that the only way he could get the right effect was to run around in circles waving his hands in the air.

But here's the thing, the business was filling up with people like Sayama. Not nutters, as such, but people who found it easier to work with computers than with traditional methods. An entire generation grew up in Japan without the skills to work properly on cel animation. It was getting hard to find colorists and in betweeners, and the price of foreign minions was going up… But the price of computer power had dropped, and Toei Studios had just bought a truck full of computers — initially more expensive than Chinese shift-workers, but you could run them all night. The 1997 series of *Doctor Slump* was colored in a computer, and people realized it was easy.

But by now, the gaming industry had started making its own animations, and its personnel were vastly more experienced. It pioneered motion-capture (vastly more cost-effective than the analog animation equivalent, rotoscoping), and perfected the art of recycling code. You could create a character at vast expense, but instead of redrawing it again and again, you could simply ask it to move *itself* around. The budget for sequels could be spent largely on improvements (or lunch). People apprenticed in games, and who'd grown up playing them, started to turn up in the anime world.

Suddenly, the price of computers has fallen to the point where it is possible to make something without cels at all. One of the earliest examples was this movie, *A.Li.Ce*, which was written by a guy whose previous work was on the story of a computer game called *Shen Mue*.

The funny thing was that if you really wanted to learn more about employing CG technology, traditional animation methods didn't give you your only precedent. Another one was puppet shows. When Gerry Anderson made *Supercar*, he'd already worked out that puppets were more convincing if you didn't have to see them walking, so he tried to keep them in their vehicles as often as possible. He'd worked out that faceless minions or robot enemies were easier to move around than humans, and this idea of playing to strengths instead of weaknesses gives us a lot of the look of something like *A.Li.Ce*.

I'm going to end by showing you clips which demonstrate where I think anime is going in the near future. The first is from a show called *Blue Submarine Number Six* — a mixture of *War of the Worlds* and *Stingray*. What we have is an Earth threatened by melting polar ice caps, and a mad scientist convinced that humanity has lost the right to live. So he genetically engineers a race of gilled mermaids, and prepares to wipe out the human race. Standing between humanity and destruction are a small number of United Nations supersubs, particularly *Blue Six*, which is the Japanese representative.

The reason I'm showing you a sequence from *Blue Six* isn't because of the subject matter — in fact, the original story for this dates from the 1960s. I'm showing you this because of the method of animation. Cel animation, using acetate sheets, is a dying art. Over the last couple of decades, more and more of the labor has been outsourced to companies in China and Korea, and the Japanese workforce have let their skills atrophy in that area. In the interim, computer graphics have become increasingly prevalent, chiefly because of all the investment dragged into the medium by computer games companies. *Blue Six* is one of an increasing number of modern anime that mixes old and new techniques.

Some of the animation is drawn by hand and colored by computer, while some of it is fully rendered computer graphics. One of the reasons that the film-makers chose this marine setting is that in underwater sequences a blue sheen over the action helps to hide some of the joins. It is my belief that, very shortly, most anime will look like this

A little bit more about playing to strengths. Computer power is advancing at a very swift rate, and the moment someone masters a new gadget or piece of software, it gets thrown up on the screen. Only a few months later, we get the next thing I'm going to show you — *Blue Remains*. Once again, this plays to the strengths of the animators. In particular I want you to notice the fact that a large part of this movie takes place underwater, where both human movement and depth perception are quite limited.

What we have here is the daughter of a group of terraformers, who has returned to a planet Earth that she believes to be deserted, only to find it inhabited by evil disembodied brains who want to wipe out all life. Which is nice.

Note also how our baddies look. If we know that humans are going to be a little bit boring, but we can have a laugh with disembodied brains, let's throw in the disembodied brains. They work on a single loop of animation and they don't have any lips that need synching — a great way to save money.

But I've been showing you some of the high end of Japanese animation — the stuff that was made with expensive bits of kit. In fact, there was some equally interesting stuff going on at the lower end.

The next clip I'm going to show you is from something called *M@lice Doll*. This was made in 2001 by a group of animators including Chiaki Konaka, the writer of *Armitage III*. However, it was fatally delayed for just a few weeks while they made a few last-minute changes, which meant that by the time it was ready for the Japanese market, the entire country was swamped with the hype for *Final Fantasy: The Spirits Within*. The original three-part *M@lice Doll* sank without a trace.

M@lice Doll (that "@" symbol is just for show, by the way, you're not supposed to pronounce it) is an intriguing movie because it shows a group of film-makers playing to their strengths.

Firstly, the film-makers know they aren't going to be able to compete with animation that represents reality, so they manufacture a plot that calls for surreal flights of fantasy. If you make your cast all 'dolls', then you know that they are not supposed to have complex expressions, then you're able to make it a virtue that their skin tones look unnatural, and if they move a little stiffly, then you can say, "Hey! They're dolls! They're supposed to move stiffly." Chiaki Konaka's script cunningly calls for a virtually expressionless cast, and the animators conceal the shortcomings of their work in copious shadows and montages.

Those of you who are fans of *Evangelion* will know that Japanese animators are not beyond putting a single image up on the screen, and simply leaving it standing very still. But how long can you hold that before people notice? Famously, in one scene in *Evangelion*, Gainax held a single still image for sixty seconds, but that was, frankly, taking the piss. Have any of you heard of a film called *La Jetee* by Chris Marker? Okay, *La Jetee* is almost nothing but still images, but audio and sound effects and cutting between several still images gives the illusion of movement. *Malice Doll* is very good at doing that, which helps it to stretch its budget further.

It also took a leaf from the rule book of Tsui Hark, a Hong Kong film-maker. He specializes in snipping out a millisecond of footage just before you're likely to see the join. *Malice Doll* does that, too, so it always cuts away from the action just a little bit too early.

The trouble, however, with *Malice Doll* is a problem that often troubles the animation world, which is that digital animation dates really fast. The stuff I'm showing you today was state of the art in the years that it was released, but it often already looks dated. You can all go home and fire up a PlayStation and see better animation. When *Malice Doll* was released in England it was given a misleading copyright date. The date said © 2003, in an attempt to make it sound more modern. Of course, this backfires, and what you get is a bunch of disappointed consumers who think that the Japanese are behind the times.

I get this a lot actually. When I was working on the final stages of the

Anime Encyclopedia, an anime company (that shall remain nameless) decided to play silly buggers with one of their titles. Let's call it *Schoolgirl Milky Crisis*. They said, "Oh no, that thing that you think came out in 1998, it didn't. It came out in 2000." And I said, "Well, I have to keep very careful records of my expenses, for tax. So I can tell you that I bought a ticket to see it at a cinema in November 1998. So that's when it came out." And they got very pissy about it, because there was obviously a company policy to make everything that began with a twentieth century release date suddenly sound as if it were released in the year 2000 or afterwards. So there are a lot of very unreliable company info sheets between around 1997 and 1999.

Anyway. The digital animation industry is one place where a date makes a big difference. If *Malice Doll* had come out when it was originally intended, it would have gained a lot of coverage. It could have won awards. A few months later, it was still the same film, and would look dated. But many digital works are very much of the moment. The thing that killed *Malice Doll*, that confined it forever to the dustbin of history, was *Final Fantasy: The Spirits Within*.

Now, technically, *Final Fantasy* is not anime. The producer was Japanese, the company that made it, Square, was Japanese. The production budget, all $50 million dollars of it, was Japanese. But the production was made in America. In Hawaii in fact. I remember there was a UK journalist who bragged to me that he was going to do a report on the set of *Final Fantasy* in Tokyo. And I said, "Good luck with that. They're shooting it in Honolulu. On someone's laptop!"

But I'm going to show you a clip from *Final Fantasy* just so you can get a handle again on what was feasible, if you had cash to spare, in 2001.

Now even the youngest among you probably remember when this film came out, and what a big deal was made about how much was spent. Millions of dollars. Millions were spent getting the lead character's hair right. And the movie bombed, incredibly, at the box office. Or did it? Because *Final Fantasy* is always written off as a failure because of the balance sheet, but I have a suspicious mind. I think that *Final Fantasy* could have always been intended as a failure. I think that a very, very cunning Japanese accountant found a way to do research and development on some incredible animation techniques, programs and processes, which were then written off as part of the costs of an American production. *Final Fantasy* wasn't dead. All that technology was immediately put to use, the code recycled on other games and videos.

However, the supposed box office failure of *Final Fantasy* did raise the issue of the Uncanny Valley. Ever since *Star Fleet* bombed in the Japanese TV ratings in the 1980s, Japanese producers have argued that puppets do not sell. And to their voices was added the prospect that there was something eerie and unpleasant about the look of the hyper-real animated creatures of *Final Fantasy*. So the perfection of digital animation, its use to recreate humans, went back underground. In the special effects world, it's less obvious of course. But in animation, producers turned to a process called Toon Shading, in which, instead of striving to make animated characters look more real, they strove to make motion captured characters, i.e. real people, look more animated. I'll show you an example right now from 2003, which is the exact opposite of *Final Fantasy*. That's because it is a very Japanese sequence, made in Japan, as part of a supposedly American movie.

In the last twenty years, Japanese animation has been "taking the world by storm", and various people have developed their own ideas of what Japanese animation should be, and many of those people have based their ideas of what Japanese animation should be on a bunch of crappy exploitationers full of sex and violence and guns and girls. And some of those people have money.

They have enough money to go back to the Japanese, hand over some cash, and get them to make anime as bad as they want it. Which means the dodgy dialogue and the extreme violence and the fetishized oriental women that were a feature of the 1990s, when anime was sold to teenage boys, are now being packaged and re-sold. My case in point, Quentin Tarantino, who gave the Japanese a ton of money to make this — the anime sequence from *Kill Bill*.

Since 1995, cel animation has effectively died out. Modern anime are not shot on rostrum cameras, but scanned into computers, and exist wholly digitally. That means that they can also incorporate digital effects. It's changed the way that anime get made, most importantly in the boundary line between live-action and animation. Just as scanning artwork made it possible to introduce digital effects, using digital animation made it possible to introduce motion capture.

For those who don't know, that means a high tech method of rotoscoping. Putting people into little suits and digitizing their images, and then creating the backgrounds and animation around them. However, such attempts at a quasi-real animation, at a representation of reality, have not been all that successful so far. The result is Toon Shading like this, where live-action footage is treated to look like a cartoon. I imagine that we'll be seeing a lot more films like this in the future, but I didn't want to end on a blockbuster note. I wanted to end with something that takes us all back to where we started.

There was a time when it looked as if the rise of the computer was going to make it impossible for anyone to make movies without massive amounts of capital for special effects. But the rise of the computer has made it a lot easier. Now, thanks to the falling price of computer power, editing, mixing and shooting has become something *affordable* to independent film-makers.

Although movies are largely regarded as the preserve of the big and the mighty, animation has always appealed to some because of how cheaply it can be done. Make no mistake, many of the people who work in Japan's animation business would far rather be working in live-action, but animation is cheaper. The advances in digital technology have changed the skills required in the anime business, but also condensed the roles of many hundreds of laborers into simple algorithms and programs. I have shown you several possible futures for the anime business, but before my big finish, I want to demonstrate the return of the geeks.

The penultimate clip I'm going to show you is from *Voices Of a Distant Star*. There are bits of it that look a little clumsy. But *Voices Of a Distant Star* impresses because it is chiefly the work of a single animator — the young Makoto Shinkai who assembled much of it solo, using software packages liberated from his day job at a computer games company, and conscripting his girlfriend to play the lead. It all goes to show just how much it is possible for a lone animator to achieve now without leaving his house!

Actually, by the time the anime was in the form I'm going to show you, Shinkai had had a little extra help, from the Mangazoo Corporation, which sunk in some extra money and provided some logistical help, but even so, what we're looking at here is essentially a homebrew anime, put together with a high-end home computer and a few bits of commercially available software.

Just one more, to show you where we are now. I was going to finish with a clip from *Appleseed*, but just as I was getting ready to come up here, I managed to get hold of a copy of something that has yet to be released in the UK. It's directed by Fumihiko Sori, who began as a live-action director and came to animation through motion capture. It's called *Vexille*, and I do commend it to you as a wonderful example of everything that is good, and bad, and interesting about modern Japanese digital animation.

It has some fantastic tricks to get around many of the problems I've discussed today. It occupies a very interesting area between Toon Shading and motion capture. You can tell that there's been motion capture, here. There's a lot of cloning, there's a lot of super-fast cutting, changes in perspective and camera position. There is snow to dampen your expectations for sound or distant high-resolution images. There are characters who show an outrageously cavalier regard for the laws of physics, like they're in *The Matrix*. There's also some cool slow-mo.

So there you have it. I've taken you through the development of Japanese animation in a digital world, from its first, faltering steps only twenty-six years ago. It's come a long way and it's fascinating to watch history being made around you.

Eighty years ago, people complained that the act of drawing cartoons directly onto film was pure animation, and that people using these new-fangled cels weren't "real" animators. I hear the same accusations leveled today at computer graphics. But as I said, film-makers use whatever they've got to hand, and they always follow the path of least resistance. Computer graphics are here to stay, whether you like it or not.

Thank you very much.

OBITS

&MEMORIES

A BOUQUET FOR KANUKA

Obituary: Yo Inoue

Her real name was Yumi Urushikawa and she wanted to be an actress. Born in 1946, she was only nineteen years old when she joined one of the best-known talent houses in the business. She took the stage-name Yo Inoue, and her unique talent lay in her voice. Yumi could go deeper than most other actresses — it meant that she could play certain male parts as well as female ones — she got to be Manabu in *Dartanius*, and the pretty-boy bad guy Gepelnich in *Macross 7*. And when she played a woman, she often snagged the bad girl parts. She played the slightly unhinged Ran in *Urusei Yatsura*, and for an entire generation of viewers she was Sayla Mass in *Gundam*. But Yumi was always a bridesmaid, never the bride — Japanese producers' eternal obsession with the timid, unthreatening, childish voices for a female lead meant that Yumi hardly ever got to do romance or appear in a long-running series. Instead, she embraced her fate, and became one of the toughest anime women around.

I first heard her voice in *Patlabor*, when she cut a swathe through the cast as Kanuka Clancy — a name that could be translated as 'Fragrant Heartfelt Flowers'. A relatively minor role in the original manga, Kanuka stayed for much of the anime remake, as she was too good a character to waste. An American-born Japanese with a strange accent and an imperious contempt of her co-workers, Kanuka knew she was good and wanted to make sure everyone else did, too. In a workplace drama that glorified teamwork and camaraderie, she railed against Japanese sentimentality and bureaucracy. They didn't like what she said, but what irked them most was that she was normally right. Kanuka was a mandatory inclusion in the first *Patlabor* movie, and audiences cheered when she was seen getting back off the plane from New York and standing impatiently in front of a Japanese customs officer.

"Business or pleasure?" he says.

"Combat," she replies.

I suppose it's one of those things that tells you anime is starting to take you over when you start recognizing individual voice-actors. When you find yourself saying, "My, isn't that Nozomu Sasaki I hear?" it's probably time you had a break. Either that, or make sure such observations are how you make your living, because people will just stare at you in a cinema otherwise. Despite advanced training that gives them the ability to alter their voices and maintain them over long recording sessions, they always resort to their natural setting for longer roles. They don't have any choice — you might think you can impersonate Excel or *Akira*'s General for a line or two, but do you think you could do it for two days... three... an entire series, of multiple takes, in the studio? And when you hear the actors playing themselves, it's like meeting an old friend.

The *Anime Encyclopedia* has neither the time nor space for actors — doing them justice would have required several hundred more pages simply to list them show by show. But there were a handful of voice actors who somehow still sneaked in — people who my co-author and I could not resist mentioning, people whose work we had come to know and love in the course of countless hours of anime viewing. Yumi Urushikawa, a.k.a. 'Yo Inoue', was one of them, not for her role in *Patlabor*, but for a miniscule bit-part in *Domain of Murder*, where she plays a bar girl past her prime. With only a few words, she conveyed a woman who knew the good days were behind her, a voice resonant with the comfort of whisky and cigarettes, but a mind sharp enough to sniff out a cop on her premises. Realizing that her latest customer is in search of information, her Japanese switches from friendly flirtation to icy politeness — the interview is over, and she has shown him the door without lifting a finger.

In anime and audio, an actress's voice is unquestionably her greatest asset — there is literally nothing else by which an audience can recognize her. Voices have to be preserved and cosseted, treated with care — one day of screaming in a studio can ruin a narration job the next morning. But in 2001, it was clear that Yumi was ill. She was hospitalized in 2002, but countermeasures were not successful. Even as the *Patlabor* series came back into the public eye with the release of the new movie *WXIII*, she was rushed back into hospital, with reports of serious difficulty breathing. Her condition was clearly worsening. She died this February, aged just fifty-six, of lung disease.

That's life. Time is short. It could happen to any of us tomorrow. But when it happened to Yumi Urushikawa, she left us with many mementoes of her career. Her friends and family said goodbye to her at a small Tokyo funeral, but for those who fell in love with her through her performing, if you seek her monument, you only have to listen.

(*Newtype USA*, June 2003)

THE MEASURE OF TAPE
The Lost World of VHS

It's amazing how much crap you collect. The mail comes in, it's press releases and review copies… you put it to one side. Something else gets put on top of it. You forget it's there. And then, one day, you move house.

I left the bed behind, I left my cutlery. The only stuff I ended up taking was work related. My desk, my computer, my books, and a few anime. I say a few, I mean a lot. I say a lot, I mean ten years of accumulated review copies, piles of unmarked tapes, box after box of ancient VHS tapes bearing the logos of long forgotten companies and the plaintive sticker: "Not for resale. Please return to [whoever] after use."

Back when I worked for the SCI FI channel, Debbie the cute brunette production assistant used to call them "bitsies," because they all had BITC stamped on the side. "Burned In Time Code" — that little black bar of spooling digits in the corner of the screen that shows this is still a work in progress. When they arrived from abroad, sometimes US anime companies would have to estimate their worth for customs purposes — "Tape. Value $1."

Actually, when I was young and stupid, I did once try to return some review copies. I turned up at Kiseki Films with a large bag of their tapes, and proudly handed them back, so they could send them out to other people. It was my little bit for the environment and the general health of the anime industry. The people stared at me aghast while I shoveled tape after tape onto the receptionist's desk.

"Oh great," she lied, "*Overfiend III.* I thought we'd lost that."

Back then, Kiseki were just down the street from Manga Entertainment, and so I went there afterwards to deliver some work. On my way home, I passed the Kiseki building again and I saw them throwing my tapes into their industrial-sized trash cans.

So I decided that was it. I was going to liberate VHS. I was going to hoard my review copies until my office burst at the seams, and one day a grateful university library would come along and open the Jonathan Clements Wing, packed to the rafters with PAL copies of obscure titles like *Ambassador Magma*, and errant NTSC dubs of *Fatal Fury*. Researchers would come from far and wide to leaf through my collection of ancient Japanese-language *Newtypes* and make notes for their dissertations. And once every few years, when I needed to check a scene in episode #8 of *Ushio and Tora*, I would pop back and visit my old tapes, just for the day. That was the plan.

Sometimes, admittedly, I culled a few things. My girlfriend took exception to having *Bondage Queen Kate* in the house. I figured I could live without it. I made what notes I needed for the *Anime Encyclopedia*, and then I got rid of it. But even then I couldn't bring myself to throw it away. Instead, I stashed it at the offices of Titan Magazines, along with a bunch of other Anime 18 titles, in a large box marked CARTOON PORN. It's still there, somewhere, along with the rest of the *Manga Max* archives, down in the basement along with the Ark of the Covenant and a crashed alien spaceship. I thought maybe I would come back one day and take it all off the company's hands. You know, turn up with a truck and liberate my old magazine archives, take them to a new home in the Jonathan Clements Wing where they could be filed in the way God intended, and used by a new generation of scholars. It would be the review copy equivalent of retiring to a family farm. With a dog, and trees and stuff.

What was I thinking? Nobody wants VHS. DVDs are cheaper to make, cheaper to mail, and don't have any moving parts that break. I saw what happens to a VHS of *Master Mosquiton* when dropped from a height onto a concrete floor. It ain't watchable after that. They get dusty. They seize up, they drop out. They only have one language track. And now we're all living in the twenty-first century, where we don't have food pills or trips to the moon, but we do have TiVos, harddrives and Internet downloads. Heck, there's even an anime *channel*. And *Newtype*'s available in English, I hear.

What am I supposed to do with a full set of BITC *Evangelion* dubs, when everyone already owns a boxed DVD set that takes up a fraction of the space and has two language tracks? I can't sell them. I *literally* can't give them away. But I can't bring myself to throw them out.

I can't put a Gainax product in a trash can. I would feel guilty. I'm going to have to hang onto it. Store it somewhere safe. Like the garage.

(*Newtype USA*, November 2003)

TACTICAL ROAR
The Man Who Gave Godzilla His Voice

"As for his roar," says Akira Ifukube, "that was... What's the word? Reptilian? Yes, reptilian."

He is an old man, already in his eighties, although he still has almost a decade to live. His hair has receded far from his forehead. He wears a light grey suit, and in a gesture of polite rebellion, a Texan-style bootlace tie.

He waits expectantly for a response. Eventually he realizes that nobody in the room is following him. They are a film crew from England making a documentary about *Godzilla*. As is traditional, most of them wish they were somewhere else, doing something associated with a subject they actually cared about. All, that is, but the two lowest-ranking members of the production team — two avowed fanboys who are breathless with excitement at being in the room with the man who gave the Big G his music. And, as it turns out, his original roar.

"But reptiles *don't* roar, do they?" says Ifukube. "So, we all went down to the zoo to look for ideas, but that was no use, there was no precedent in the natural world. We tried different bird noises, but none of that worked either. There's no animal around today that's as large as Godzilla. So how would we blow enough air to imitate his roar? I supposed I'd need something like a tuba, but I decided to use a double bass."

Ifukube planned on scraping the strings of a double bass and speeding up the sound, much as Doctor Who's TARDIS would later gain its wheezing noise from the slowed-down noise of a scraped piano wire. But Ifukube's troubles were only beginning — since double basses weren't so easy to find in 1954.

"Back then there were only a few of them in Japan," he remembers. "One at NHK, with the Broadcast Orchestra, and there was another one at the Fine Arts University." NHK was the better bet, but NHK was television, and television people *hated* the movies. The last thing they wanted to do was help.

"The people at NHK just wouldn't let me take theirs," says Ifukube, "so I 'borrowed' the one in the university, did the recording, and sneaked it back again."

There is something strangely impish about the look in Ifukube's eyes. Just for a moment, this frail old man sparkles.

He stares for a moment at his shoes.

"I saw him born," he says. "I was there when Godzilla came to life. From the time that we made the first *Godzilla*, because I was on the staff of the very first one. I'd been involved in so many of the films, but in the final one, *Godzilla versus Destroyah*, after forty years, Godzilla was going to be killed off. I mean, after all those life-threatening battles, he was going to finally go out for the count.

"Right at the end, when Godzilla died, everyone at the recording felt a very deep sense of sorrow. It welled up inside all of us, as if we were witnesses at our own execution. It was… it was…" his voice falters, "it was a very emotional moment."

R.I.P. Akira Ifukube, 1914-2006.

(*Newtype USA*, January 2007)

TETSU YANO (1923-2004)

Remembering a Translator and Author

Just old enough to qualify for the draft, Tetsu Yano found himself serving in the Imperial cavalry in World War Two. In a defeated Japan where people would take any job they could get, the youthful Yano ended up as a janitor on an Allied airbase. Amid the junk, he discovered garish American science fiction magazines. Yano the sci-fi fan became Yano the translator of over 300 foreign novels. Yano's interest lay in the works of the hard science fiction writers of the late golden age, particularly Robert Heinlein.

Heinlein was an unlikely case for Japanese adulation; his work often displays a deep mistrust of the race he fought, most infamously in *Sixth Column*, in which brave Americans steadfastly resist an Oriental invasion. Heinlein saw action in the Pacific, and named the *Rodger Young*, mothership of his *Starship Troopers*, after an American Marine killed in 1943. But Yano saw something in Heinlein's works that transcended modern antagonisms, particularly in the robotically enhanced 'mobile infantry', that would later inspire the Mobile Suits of *Gundam*, and a host of robot anime.

As well as translating science fiction, Yano became an author in his own right. One of his novels was adapted into the anime *Dagger of Kamui*, in which a ninja warrior travels to America in search of a mythical artifact, a journey to the inscrutable West that could be seen as an allegory of Yano's own life. His greatest work is also the only one available in English prose, the haunting *Legend Of the Paper Spaceship*, in which a researcher uncovers dark yet wonderful secrets knotted in the everyday folklore of a Japanese mountain village. Elements of Yano's style live on in modern Japanese horror, most obviously the nursery rhyme chills of *The Ring*. He helped create the world that made this magazine possible.

(*NEO* #2, 2005)

LAST ORDERS

A Farewell to the London Anime Club

The December 2008 meeting of the London Anime Club is, pending a last-minute reversal of fortune, the last. The announcement brings to an end almost fifteen years of monthly meet-ups, watchathons and drinking in a series of London pubs, and, in a brief and posh interregnum, at Daiwa House.

Some people regard it as a mournful day for anime. Clearly, however, not enough to actually take up the baton and keep it running. This is because the closure of the LAC has less to do with lack of interest, and more with changing times and changing modes of fan behaviour.

The London Anime Club first met on 12th April 1994, in the bad old days when Take That were at number one and Internet access was a series of pings, bouncy noises, and a long, long wait. The LAC's first screeners were contraband tapes shipped in from Canada. A *London* anime club was a necessity, not only to afford fans the opportunity to see new shows, but to ensure enough fans were available to meet the minimum room rental requirements — London's catchment area extending into plenty of accessible suburbs. Even then, numbers were not always high, and, wrote founder David Cotterill, "I wondered if it was all worth it."

We live in a different age. There is not one anime club, in That Fancy London, but dozens all over the country. Whereas it might once have been worth one's while to commute in once a month from, say, Reading, or Harlow, or Slough, to meet your mates, many now meet online, every day, in a continuous semi-literate babble in the corner of their computer monitors.

Moreover, anime fandom is younger, much younger. The generation that enthused over *Akira* in 1989 were, by legal stipulation, over 18 by the time that the London Anime Club was founded. Through the 1990s, they were students and twentysomethings (at the very least), devoting their efforts to a style of fandom that risked being left behind.

When fan numbers grew, the LAC welcomed anime traders, or rather, any anime traders that weren't at each others' throats. Members of the LAC moved into convention organising, and into travel, pioneering some of the first anime-themed tourist trips. But the LAC was run as a labor of love, by committed amateurs, who were sure to be wondering fifteen years on whether they were wasting their time sourcing films that people could already watch at home, finding obscurities that members could already buy in shops, or setting aside drinking space for a generation that did not show up, and even if they did, could not drink!

In pubs all round the country, in student halls, on sofas, there are thousands of anime fans who will mark the passing of the LAC with indifference. If it seems like an anachronism, or simply one club among many, that is a sign of our own times, but certainly not the fault of the LAC itself. On a day in 1994, there were but a dozen enthusiasts present, gathered excitedly around a video cassette of a show that was all but unknown in the UK outside that room. They were the people who talked of Miyazaki, *Evangelion* and *Pokémon* when many you were still a mere twinkle in someone's eye. They toiled for a decade to bring anime to others, and end their labors unthanked, but unforgotten.

(NEO #54, 2008)

BESTIMOST

Obituary: Steve Whitaker

Steve Whitaker's sole credit on Japanese comics was thirteen years ago, when he colored *Street Fighter II*. I only remember it because I was the translator, and quite boggled at the luscious flesh tones and crashing hues he introduced.

He made lovely chili con carne. I'd perch by his telly, a lager in one hand, translating *Escaflowne* live off Japanese tapes for a small audience of artists and anime fans. Steve literally wrote the book on comics; he was a teacher and a mentor to many in the UK graphic arts. For years he tinkered with his own comic, based on Greek epic, but he never quite got round to it. He'd sign letters with his own word, "bestimost". And that was pretty much all I knew about him.

Last month, he was rushed in a taxi to the doctor. Long story short, he died on the way. He was fifty-two, and his death took everyone by surprise, including him. I was amazed at the number of stories that came out of the woodwork. All were deeply loving and fond, although many had an undertone of melancholy — that Steve's fastidiousness had hobbled his own career, even as he taught so many others. I discovered that Steve had colored the original *V For Vendetta*. That he had just missed the gig on Neil Gaiman's *Sandman*, because he had been faffing too much with his samples. I wonder about the money that would have made him; maybe he wouldn't have ended up working in a call centre, but been able to make a career out of what he did best, drawing stuff.

Even as they remembered him, his friends lamented the perfectionism that left him never quite ready to sit down and write his magnum opus.

"I keep asking myself whenever something goes wrong," said one, "would Steve have remembered this when he was sitting in that taxi? Would it have bothered him on that last ride?"

If you've got something to say, say it now. Tomorrow might be too late. (*NEO* #45, 2008)

HISASHI NOZAWA'S LAST MYSTERY
The Strange Case of a Screenwriter's Suicide

Nagoya native Hisashi Nozawa was only twenty-three years old in 1983 when he won the Kido Award for aspiring scenarists. He first came to Western attention with his script for Takeshi Kitano's dark thriller *Violent Cop*, but was better known in Japan for his televisual work. Nozawa excelled at putting dark twists into his stories. His drama TV debut, *Dear Beloved*, featured a childless couple whose life falls apart when they solicit their ex-lovers' help in having a baby — spousal troubles soon became Nozawa's trademark. *Wonderful Life* focused on a woman who receives two marriage proposals, unfortunately coinciding with her discovery that she has breast cancer.

Nozawa also flirted with the manga and anime world, writing the *Boy Detective Conan* movie *Phantom of Baker Street*, and the 1996 TV adaptation of Satoru Makimura's manga *Delicious Liaisons*, starring Miho Nakayama as a bereaved girl who seeks to keep alive her father's memory by sponsoring the chef who made his favorite soup. But it was the following year's *Blue Bird* that truly made his name — the tale of a doomed train station attendant who runs away with a rich man's wife. Nozawa's later output centered on similar tales of twisted romance, vengeful lovers and unexpected surprises, most notably in *Sleeping Forest*, his story of an amnesiac woman (Nakayama again) who risks losing her life if she ever regains her forbidden memories.

Different ticking-bomb suspense awaited in *Limit*, in which a female police officer must cope with the abduction of her own child. Nozawa followed it in 2002 with *Sleepless Nights*, an intriguing, gripping combination of *Reservoir Dogs* and *The Firm*, in which the everyday inhabitants of a Tokyo street turn out to share a sinister past. He was also the author of three original novels, every one of which won a major literary prize. At forty-four years old, he was one of Japan's greatest writers, and a scenarist at the peak of his powers. In my list of top writers in the 2003 *Dorama Encyclopedia*, he took the pole position.

In late June this year, Nozawa's wife became concerned that her husband was not responding on the phone. She went over to his Tokyo office and knocked on the door, but there was no reply. Eventually, she forced her way in, and found him hanging in his study. Hisashi Nozawa had taken his own life, leaving her, their two children, and a partial script for what was to be his greatest work. Its name is *Clouds on the Hill*, and will be a 2009 drama series from NHK. Based on a novel by *Taboo* creator Ryotaro Shiba about the Russo-Japanese War of 1904, it is already being trailed as Japan's answer to *Band of Brothers*. In the wake of *The Last Samurai*, it is likely to attract considerably more attention abroad than earlier *taiga* series, particularly with Nozawa as its lead writer. If it is picked up by American broadcasters, it could finally introduce Nozawa to a foreign audience, but even if it does, such success comes too late for him. He left a suicide note, but the Japanese media have remained reticent about its contents. The question of why he took his own life at the height of his fame remains Hisashi Nozawa's last and most tragic mystery.

(*Newtype USA*, November 2004)

THE END OF THE WORLD. AGAIN.

For the inaugural issue of *PiQ* magazine in April 2008, instead of writing one of my usual columns, I contributed a thousand words to a discussion on the question: Is Anime Dead?

Japanese animation changes all the time. It's not the toast of Hollywood like it was in 2001, nor the child-corrupting evil that it supposedly was in 1997. Anime, or rather what we expect of it, dies every year. Anime died when Osamu Tezuka introduced sci-fi in *Astro Boy*. It died when the video player brought cartoons for adults. It died when *Akira* ran so far over budget that the Japanese needed foreign money to repeat the success. It died when Hayao Miyazaki won an Oscar.

The modern film world encourages its consumers to believe that they are participants. Fans want their voices to be heard, even if the 'voice' of fandom is a self-contradicting nightmare of mutually exclusive demands. Fans like to think that they steer a company into acquiring a product in the first place, that they are the reason that a particular voice-actor got a part. The trade-off is that those fans are expected to buy the crap they demand! Many US distributors have grown so reliant on the convention-going core of fandom, that when one company sneezes, everyone else gets a cold.

As many of you may know, after in-depth research lasting many months, a company called Geneon recently pulled out of the US market. The resulting damage was less about the temporary delay of particular serials, and more about the importance of advertising revenue, as the loss of Geneon's money hit dedicated anime magazines hard. Anime itself actually thrives in recessions. *Perfect Blue* only happened when the producers lost the funding for a 'real' film. Cartoons aren't going to suddenly cease to exist just because an American distributor shuts down. What worries many modern fans is that *their* anime is dying. Anime that patronizes and panders to them. The stuff they get 'free' from TV and the Intarwebnet.

But Geneon pulled out because it saw what was coming. Anime was popular enough to attract the big guns (Disney, Warners, etc), and that left nothing for the little companies but an ever-decreasing amount of self-referential product: fan service, anime about dressing up as anime characters, anime about liking anime, anime about making anime. Twenty years ago, such titles were curios for a small sector of the market. Today, they *are* the market.

The convention-going crowd is a goldmine of 'opinion-formers' — guys with websites, fair weather Facebook friends, bloggers who will big something up if they get a free sticker. But fandom thinks small. The big money is in Miyazaki, in *Batman*, in *Termination*, it is in *Dragonball* and *Pokémon*. It is not in *Schoolgirl Milky Crisis*. Convention-going fandom has been a fertile bed of interest and enthusiasm, but it is currently suffering, and will continue to suffer from a deadly blight.

Seven years ago, the median age of anime fans dropped below the point where it was legal to own a credit card. Online ordering and downloads, once hailed as the savior of niche anime programming, became closed to many of its likely consumers. What kind of teen rebel needs to ask mom if he can borrow her Visa card? Today, all we see of the new media is its piratic bad side, not its good potential.

Let's not argue today about fansubbing or the legality of downloads. We are standing in the middle of a huge change in the way that people get their entertainment. The very words we use to categorize — television, games, cinema — won't mean the same thing in 2018. Like all virgin territory, it's lawless turf. Someone, somewhere will make money out of it, but a lot of people are going to lose out.

Japan has mulled over this problem for a while, and has a couple of Band-Aid measures. It knows home taping takes place, so a government body takes a royalty from all blank tapes and discs sold, which is redistributed among creatives. Something similar happens in most civilized countries. Japan also loves the idea of 'added' value — exclusive boxes, collector's discs, free gifts and bonus things, all designed to make merely owning the anime itself seem like one is getting a raw deal.

But there aren't going to be any more discs.

Forget Blu-Ray. Forget HD. That fight is just a sideshow. The next format is No Format, and that's what's got the industry worried. No discs means no duplicators, no stores, nothing to pin the plushie on, the removal of entire echelons of the movie business. These issues face anime and every other part of the entertainment business today — you can even see it writ large over Hollywood.

The Writers Guild was first off the block, not because writers are smarter (although we are!), but because it was the first industry body with a contract up for renegotiation. The current strike concerns a deal that could last until 2028 — that's why people are thinking so far ahead, about issues that have yet to trouble the average consumer. By the time you read these words, the Screen Actors Guild will be gearing up for a similar fight. The groups involved in the debate have multiple points to discuss, but the big issue is *how to get paid*. If there are no solid objects in stores, no discs or tapes, then what do they get a royalty on? Who watches the servers that offer downloads? What proportion of the 10c, or $1, or whatever people end up paying for downloads, goes to the creatives who made them? I can't give you an answer for that, but I can tell you the question is going to hurt a lot of people.

This isn't going to kill anime. It's not even going to kill the niche interest shows. Ultimately, it makes them more likely because the cost of distribution will fall. Direct downloads are going to make more anime possible, more fan bait and niche programming, more big blockbusters, more of everything, because if there's an audience that will pay, soon it *can* pay. But anime, as you know it, is going to die, again, just before it is reborn... again.

Long live anime.

ACKNOWLEDGEMENTS

Thanks to Adam Newell, who was joking when he first suggested this book, and was soon wishing that he had never said anything. Also to Steve Kyte, whose artwork is always a joy to see, Jo Boylett, Martin Stiff, Rob Farmer, Natalie Clay and all at Titan.

Thanks to the editors, event organisers and producers who commissioned the original versions of these articles and speeches. At some point in their lives, they were all daft enough to hire me: John Ainsworth, Sarah Backhouse, Alan Barnes, Felicity Blastland, Robert Bricken, Paige Brown (née Record), Gemma Cox, Stephen Cremin, Erika Franklin, John Freeman, Doug Goldstein, John Gosling, Kimberly Guerre, Marcus Hearn, Leah Holmes, Bridgett Janota, Nick Freand Jones, Jerome Mazandarani, Helen McCarthy, Tom Mes, Nick North, Carol O'Sullivan, Keiichi Onodera, Andrew Osmond, Peter Preston, Cefn Ridout, Brian Robb, Louis Savy, Matt Smith, Gary Steinman, Stu Taylor, Leigh P. Williams, Susie Wilson.

Sadly, it is not possible to name most of the real stars of *Schoolgirl Milky Crisis*. I thank them all for sharing their lives with me, whether they wanted to or not. I would, however, like to offer my appreciation to those who have offered harmless, legal and entirely benevolent support, advice and anecdotes over the years: Laura Block, Lee Brimmicombe-Wood, Martin Capey, Lloyd Carter, Sasha Cipkalo, John Clute, Judith Clute, Sharon Colman, Stan Dahlin, Hugh David, Rhonda Eudaly, Jason Frank, Neil Gaiman, Peter Goll, Sharon Gosling, Gavin Graham, Matt Greenfield, Laurence Guinness, Ed Hooks, Jonathan Kopp, Huang Liming, David Hughes, Paul Jacques, AJ Johnson, Matt Johnson, Simon Jowett, Tony Kehoe, Biliana Labovic, John Ledford, Bruce Lewis, Mundee Lewis, Yuri Lowenthal, Carl Macek, Taro Maki, Garry Marshall, Leiji Matsumoto, Kaoru Mfaume, Cheryl Morgan, Kotono Mitsuishi, Emily Newton Dunn, Keiichi Onodera, Mamoru Oshii, Katsuhiro Otomo, Gichi Otsuka, Shelley Page, Sharon Papa, Bill Paris, Andrew Partridge, Simon Pegg, Jayne Pilling, Tara Platt, Bill Plympton, Lynn Robson, Ake Sasaki, Frederik L. Schodt, Julia Sertori, Apurva Shah, Rod Shaile, Toren Smith, Mark Staufer, Jim Swallow, Motoko Tamamuro, Mike Toole, Wang

Shaudi, Bob Whitehouse, Amy Howard Wilson, Dave Wilson III, Jasper Sharp, John C. Watson, Amos Wong, the guys at Anvil who let me play with their foley studio, Molinaire, Lips Inc., Toei, Manga Entertainment, ADV Films, NBC/Universal, Pioneer, Gonzo, East2West, Western Connection, Kiseki Films, Bloomsbury, Kodansha, Shueisha, Shogakukan, the girl who got me to sign her breasts in Dallas, the Sailor Scout who tried to pick me up in Atlanta, Simon the Hapless Boy, Mr Sato with the funny eyes, that weird guy from the Japanese embassy, whoever it was who tried to ban my industry report, Zorro, Biscuit Boy, the Whingeing Serpent, the *Manga Max* Minions, and the girls (and boys) from *Newtype USA*. I am sure there are many, many more I've left off. I'm sorry in advance if I've forgotten you. And even sorrier if I've thanked you and you'd rather be forgotten.

Two articles, typed up on office time at *Manga Mania* magazine, never made their way to my home hard-drive, and had to be scanned from archive issues found in an Australian garden shed by former editor Cefn Ridout. With typical irony, they were then dropped from this book due to lack of space. Sorry, Cefn, but it's the thought that counts! Maybe in *Schoolgirl Milky Crisis 2*...

Owing to the bizarre legalities of publishing and copyright, some articles still belong to Rebellion, publishers of the *Judge Dredd Megazine*, and are reprinted here with their kind permission. Contractually, anything I wrote for *Manga Max* magazine while I was its editor, such as the interview with Neil Gaiman, still belongs to Titan Magazines and appears here in this Titan Books publication with the cordial consent of the Big Giant Heads.

INDEX